PEAHEAD!

PEAHEAD!
THE LIFE AND TIMES OF A SOUTHERN-FRIED COACH

BY
TUCKER MITCHELL

First Edition
Second Printing

Copyright © 2016 by Tucker Mitchell

Cover designed by Katherine Barnette

ISBN: 978-1-61846-019-6

All rights reserved,
including the right of reproduction,
in whole or in part, in any form.

Produced and Distributed By:

Library Partners Press
ZSR Library
Wake Forest University
1834 Wake Forest Road
Winston-Salem, North Carolina 27106

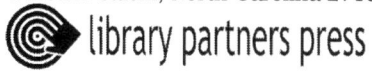

a digital publishing imprint
www.librarypartnerspress.org

Manufactured in the United States of America

ACKNOWLEDGMENTS

There are no laws requiring compliance in helping a writer dredge up material about a semi-obscure football coach from the 1920s, 30s, 40s and 50s, but at nearly every turn in my quest to know D.C. "Peahead" Walker folks were more than willing to lend a hand. Sure, some of them—many of them—were doing their jobs. Librarians, archivists, information officers and the like are supposed to assist in opening the doors to information about their institutions. But all I encountered were helpful. A few helped energize me by expressing real interest and curiosity about my subject. There is a long list of these archive gatekeepers. Here goes.

Many thanks to archivist Kate Nash at Elon University; to Clay Hassard and Megan Donald in Elon's Athletics Department; to Julie Bradford, Jesse Yates in Wake Forest University's archives; and to Steve Shutt, Wake's information director for football who made copies of ancient game film among other things. Thanks to J. Reid Morgan, counsel to the WFU trustees, and whoever helped him dredge up and review 60-year-old minutes from Board of Trustees meetings, and to Ed Morris of the Old Wake Forest Museum, a valuable repository for an (almost) 200-year-old tradition.

James Savage at the Oak Ridge Institute pulled together some obscure information for me without question, as did intern Carrie LeGree at the National Baseball Hall of Fame. Archivists Mary Beth Newbill and Elizabeth Wells of Samford University gave me run of the place for a day or so, and seemed happy to do it. A librarian in Roanoke, Ala., whose name I wrote down but then lost, called back twice with info on Peahead's early years. Truly unexpected. Thanks, whoever you were.

Another forgotten name of a helpful person belongs to a woman who was, apparently, the only bi-lingual librarian in the Montreal Public Library. I would have been *les miserable* without you. *Merci beaucoup.*

I noted at various points in the actual text of *Peahead!* the warm welcome I received from nearly all of Peahead's former players and associates. But let me say it again: they were great and if no book had come of all that, of all those hours on the phone and in person, well, it still would have been time well spent, time I'll always treasure.

Katherine Barnette, whose superb design is sure to make this volume leap off bookstore shelves and into online shopping carts, was a terrific asset. Bill Kane of Library Partners Press offered much encouragement and guidance. Both were needed.

Lastly, thanks to my wife Cindy who encouraged this crazy project from the first time I mentioned it, on an early spring walk in 2009, and who actually accompanied me on a number of research trips to garden spots of the world like Ensley, Ala., Kinston, N.C. and old Wake Forest. (And they say living with a writer isn't exciting.) Truth is, I've never done anything worthwhile without Cindy. This work is certainly no exception.

~ Tucker Mitchell, Fall 2016

Contact the author at tucker@peahead.com.

CONTENTS

A FEW TALES TO TELL, 1

A BOY NAMED PEAHEAD, 17

A BASEBALL MAN, 49

ELON: BIRTHPLACE OF A COACH, 79

A BIG FISH, 107

THE BAPTIST HOLLER BUILDER, 147

PEAHEAD AT WAR, 201

IN ALL HIS GLORY, 249

A STRANGE ENDING, 305

LA TETE DU POIS, 359

THE END OF A GOOD STORY, 423

INDEX, 445

IMAGES, 453

ABOUT THE AUTHOR, P 465

INTRODUCTION

A FEW TALES TO TELL

On a sunny morning in the spring of 1947, the southbound Silver Star pulled into the Seaboard Railroad Station in Raleigh, North Carolina and disgorged a load of passengers acquired from points all along the Atlantic coast. Among them was a strapping young man with an olive complexion and jet-black hair. Many would have called him handsome and none would have failed to notice. He was every inch of six-foot-four, possessed a graceful stride and, perhaps most of all, was draped in an ill-fitting suit—the coat too big, the pants too short. He had an excuse. It was the first suit he'd ever worn. But still, he stood out from the crowd.

Not far away, on a bench near the corner of the station building, a dumpy, silver-haired man watched the young man disembark. This man stood out, too.

He was wearing a trendy zoot suit, a black shirt, and an outrageous, hand-painted necktie featuring orange and red flamingos cavorting beneath a yellowish Miami moon. It was clear that it was a Miami moon. It said so right on the tie. A cigarette that was mostly ash clinging to a stub hung from his lip.

As a smile creased the man's lips, ash tumbled down to his belly, bounced off the moon, and fell to the ground.

The older man turned to his companion, a plain-looking man in a brown suit, and in a thick Southern drawl, said,

"Got-damn Greason, got-damn! Look at the size of that Wop. Got-damn! I think we got us something here."[1]

"Coach, I don't think he's a Wop," Greason said. "I think they're—his family—is from Armenia."

The older man shrugged, nonplussed. "Wal, I tell you what, Greason. You find out what we call the fucking Armean-yans and you let me know. Until then, he's a wop. . . . Now, let's go inter-duce ourselves. . . . And remember, be polite. Don't call him a wop to his face."

Greason, the man in the brown suit, nodded and shook his head. "Right, Coach," he said.

The baggy-suited duo sliced their way through the platform crowd to where the young man was standing, searching the crowd, a bewildered look on his chiseled face. Suddenly, the older man materialized in front of him, gripped his lower arm, and said, in a deep, gravelly voice, "Hey there boy. You George?"

"Um, yessssir. I'm Bill George," said the youth.

"Wal, Ah'm Peahead Walker, football coach at Wake Forest College, and this heah is my chief assistant, Murray Greason. Welcome to North Carolina, boy. Yo're gonna love it here."

"Yessir," George said.

"Greason," Coach Walker said, "grab the boy's bags. We got us some sights to see."

A few minutes later, accompanied by a sack of hot dogs and three bottles of cola from the station grill, the two coaches and their big recruit piled into Peahead Walker's massive Cadillac sedan. Walker wheeled out of the parking lot and onto the city street.

---

[1] The dialectal spelling of cuss words—and other words—spoken by Peahead Walker in this theoretical conversation, and others, is intended to convey some sense of his particular accent, which was noted by all who knew him. It is, of course, imagined, but adheres to typical Deep South speech patterns, sounds a bit like Walker in the lone audio recording of him uncovered while researching this book, and is exactly how the several Walker imitators interviewed for this book—all former players—portrayed his speech, especially the "gottdamn," which, if the imitators are any measure, was the single most common adjective/exclamation to pass Peahead Walker's lips.

As he drove he began a slow-but-steady banter on a variety of subjects: the prospects for Wake Forest's coming season, life in George's native western Pennsylvania hometown, the upcoming Big League baseball season, the many virtues of curvaceous women, and much more. George smiled and said "yessir" a lot. Greason, seated in the spacious backseat, managed the hot dog bag and kept his mouth shut.

The big green car rolled out of the city and through a wooded area sprinkled with dogwoods. Eventually, civilization appeared again in the form of a sprawling, heavily forested college campus. Walker's car weaved up and down the neat, car-lined streets, past sidewalks filled with smiling co-eds. George, who'd only been to one big city—the grimy steel town of Pittsburgh, and that only a couple of times—stared out the window. He had never seen anything like the tightly manicured lawns or the graceful stone buildings that towered over them. Everything was so neat and clean.

"There's the football stadium," Walker said, nodding to a parking lot and the stone wall beyond it.

The place was huge, thought George.

A few minutes later a site more majestic still hove into view. It was a gigantic square tower covered with intricate stonework and topped with majestic spires. Ivy was just beginning its ascent up the sides.

"Roll down yer window, boy," Walker said.

George cranked the handle. As the glass fell, music tumbled into the vehicle. Chimes pound out a catchy tune—it was "Faith of Our Fathers"—which sounded mildly familiar to George.

"Them chimes play six times a day," Walker said. "Lucky for you they jes happened to be playing right now. I would tell you we got 'em to play it jes for you but boy I ain't a gonna lie to you. You learn that right now, he-ah? Whatever I say, you can take it to the bank, boy. And there might be a couple t'other things I can give you that you can take to the bank,

too, if you get my drift." Walker looked over at George and winked.

George tried to digest that while chewing on another bite of hot dog. He wasn't really sure what coach Walker meant, but he nodded all the same.

"Yessir," George said.

They drove along some more streets, flanked by more students and more stone buildings. The campus seemed to go on forever. Eventually they made it back to a big road. They drove through some more countryside, and in a few minutes they were back in a city. Walker turned on a busy road—Fayetteville Street the sign read—and pulled in under an awning beside a substantial brick-and-stone building.

"Wal, here's the hotel where you'll be staying, boy," Walker said. "The Sir Walter Raleigh. Biggest, finest hotel in all of Raleigh, hell, all of North Carolina. Ah, know yo're probably tarred and all. Why don't you check in, get you a nap if you want, and we'll pick you up for dinner round about six o'clock? Maybe go get us some oysters over at the 42nd Street Oyster Bar. How's that sound? I'll bet you can eat a mess of oysters."

"Yessir," said George. "Oysters . . . six o'clock."

"Greason," Walker said, "why don't you help this here future All-American with his bags."

Greason escorted George into the hotel, returned a few minutes later, and piled into the car beside Walker.

"Wal, Murray, I think that went pretty well," Walker said.

Greason shook his head. "I dunno Coach."

"What, did he say something?" Walker asked.

"No," Greason said, "not a damn thing besides, 'yessir.' But I dunno. He may be a bit of a hick. But he ain't that dumb. We passed at least four signs that said Duke on them, and everything was painted blue and white, not black and gold. He'll figure it out."

Walker chuckled. "Hell, Greason. It ain't about being smart or dumb. It's about being dazzled. And that boy was dazzled. Did you see his eyes when them chimes kicked in? Good thing you called and checked about that schedule."

"Yeah, but Coach, he's got to see the Wake Forest campus sometime," Greason said.

Walker fired up a fresh cigarette, leaned back, and took a big puff. "You let me worry about that, Murray," he said. "I think we'll be jes' fine."

Walker was right. George was bamboozled by the old campus switcheroo and did enroll at Wake Forest, where he eventually became one of the Deacons' most celebrated players. But Greason was right, too. A day of reckoning did arrive.

A couple of months into George's freshman year the young man began to wonder about a few things related to his new school and coach. It was in this spirit that he approached Walker after practice one late October day and haltingly sought an explanation for what could only be described as a perplexing crisis of confidence.

"Uh, Coach," said George, "when I came down to visit and all there were these great big stone buildings, and a big tower that played music and . . . well, I was just wondering when I'd get to see those, you know, maybe have a class in one of them or something?"

Walker rolled his eyes and shook his head in abject disgust.

"You freshmen," he spat. "You jes have so much to learn. . . . Look here, boy. Them buildings and all you're talking about, they're on the West Campus. That's for upperclassmen. This here's the East Campus. This, boy—this right here—is where you belong."

And that's how Coach D.C. "Peahead" Walker brought Bill George, arguably the best player he ever coached, to Wake Forest College.

Or that's the oft-told story anyway.

Sounds implausible, but who knows? It *could* be true.

It doesn't really matter either way. When it comes to Peahead Walker the story is what matters.

In fact, it was Walker stories—the famous Bill George tale and many more—that launched this book. While covering Wake Forest football (among other things) for the *Winston-Salem Journal* in the 1980s, I kept bumping into Peahead stories. There were still a few people around the school back then who actually knew Walker, and there were plenty more who knew some of the stories. And so something would happen that reminded somebody of something that Peahead had said or done (it was an easy connection: he said and did a lot) and they'd launch into some story. It might be Bill George saga, by far the best-known Walker anecdote, the one about Walker ordering a team physician to revive an unconscious player, or something else.

The stories were entertaining and memorable, and the idea of uncovering the man who starred in them was back-of-the-brain idea that, after percolating for a number of years, eventually proved irresistible. How could there not be a book about a guy named Peahead, whose career apparently was just one humorous anecdote after another?

And so, here we are.

> *It was hot, and they'd just gotten the crap beat out of them again, so it was not surprising that the disgruntlement was building inside the Wilson Tobs' clubhouse. Mordecai "Stumpy" Bamberg, the Tobs' manager, could feel it. Hell, he could pretty nigh smell it.*
>
> *But what could he do about it? No, the players hadn't been paid in three weeks, but times were tough. Businesses of all kinds, and all over were struggling in what some of the big newspapers were calling the Great Depression. People were being put out of work left and right, and if Bamberg didn't hold back a little from what the Tobs' flinty owner gave him to run things, there might not be enough cash to pay the umps or pay the bus fare on the next road trip or . . . to make sure Bamberg himself had a little something in his own pocket.*
>
> *He finished taking off his uniform and then undid the wooden prosthesis from his left leg. The missing appendage was a souvenir from Uncle Sam's fight against Kaiser Bill*

back in 1918. Using the wall for balance, he hopped into the "training room" next door where a nice warm bath awaited. It was among the few perks afforded the manager of a ball team here in the deep, deep minors. Bamberg hoisted himself into the metal tub, cut on the radio, and laid his head back as the warm water lapped against his aching body.

A half an hour or so later, Bamberg went back out to his office to get dressed.

His leg was gone.

But it wasn't missing. Pinned to the bench where the leg had lain was a handwritten note, scrawled in a fairly neat hand. It read:

"Three weeks pay if you ever want to see your leg again. Leave it on home plate. You'll have the leg back by morning."

"Shit," said Bamberg. And then, after thinking about it a little more, "Peahead . . . Got-dam that Peahead."

Bamberg—or whatever the particular manager's name was—got his leg back and the players got paid. There are no details of how the "transaction" actually took place or of just where or when it took place. But all who told the tale were sure that it was Peahead Walker, the wily, worldly shortstop, who squeezed twelve seasons of professional baseball into his jam-packed career in athletics, who did the deed. While others grumbled Walker found some leverage, found a way. Which was Walker's way.

He'd been the leader on every team he played on since he was a schoolboy, and that didn't change when he became a grown man or when he turned the corner from player to coach. He got things done and he did them in a certain way, with a certain style, that set him apart. He enjoyed life, enjoyed a good laugh, and,. . . he loved to pull your leg, literally when applicable.

That's the sort of truth found in stories but not necessarily in facts. Biographers, from Suetonis to the modern day, have wrestled with this tension between man and myth. Which version is truest? The answer, of course, is that it is always a blend.

So uncovering a man who has been dead four-plus decades meant two distinct lines of inquiry, moving down parallel tracks. One passed through libraries, newspaper morgues, and an assortment of musty archives, where I pursued the "historical Peahead," the somewhat lifeless figure outlined by a fact-filled paper trail. The other meandered through the more entertaining twists and turns of oral history, the memories of about 60 men (and a few women), mostly former players, who knew the man. They all had their own stories to contribute to what might be called the Peahead canon, meaning, in this case, a collection of outrageous tales about an outrageous man.

Peahead!, I hope, ties them together, weaving legend with record, and vice versa, on the way to producing some biographical whole cloth. I have done this as diligently as I know how and with every intention of reporting the truth of the matter.

So long as it doesn't interfere with the stories.

> *The players eventually untangled themselves but one young man—he'd been the ball carrier and wound up at the bottom of the pile—lay motionless. A hush fell over the stadium. The officials motioned to the Wake Forest sideline. A man was down. Help was needed.*
>
> *The Deacons' team doctor was already rushing onto the field and in seconds began examining the player amidst a circle of concerned teammates. A few seconds later, Peahead Walker, coming at a fast waddle, joined him, kneeling on the other side of the stricken Deacon.*
>
> *The doctor, his eyes wide in near panic, looked up at Walker. "He's not breathing!" the M.D. exclaimed.*
>
> *Walker's eyes rolled back in his head, which he shook in disgust.*
>
> *"Well, hell," he said. "You're a doc. MAKE him breathe."*

Detailed research is the essence any good biography. Some of that is tedious, but it is work that must be done. So time was spent studying pages from the 1910 U.S. Census of Ensley, Alabama, Walker's birthplace, rifling through various archives, and perusing hundreds of pages from assorted old newspapers. That long slog helped build an accurate portrait of D.C. "Peahead" Walker, one of the best coaches, and, greatest characters of twentieth-century American athletics.

Those facts are interesting in their own way, but it is the stories that bring the man to life and that's where the most time was invested.

A few Peahead tales had been transcribed and were available in written form. Most I heard for the first time, or the first time in a long time. Some of those were delivered over the telephone by gracious men and women, willing (and in most cases eager) to recall days spent in the shadow of a very interesting man. When possible I went to hear the tales in person.

Walker's boys were getting old, of course. He coached his last college team in 1951 and his last pro squad in 1959. Most of the people who knew Walker well were in their late 70s and 80s when research for *Peahead!* began. Some I found just in time. Some—Sam Etcheverry, Walker's great Montreal quarterback, comes to mind—I just missed.

By and large this was a delightful pursuit that led to many hours that I will always remember fondly. Among the highlights: a chilly afternoon at Herb Appenzeller's house near Greensboro; a warm spring day with Dickie Davis who kindly showed me Peahead's stomping grounds around old Wake Forest; and an spiritual morning in a retirement home sitting room with the Reverend Dewey Hobbs, who was kind enough to bring his helmet and (neatly pressed) jersey to our talk, right before donating them to the Old Wake Forest Museum.

Some minds were sharper than others. Carl Haggerty's was working hard the day we met in a Durham restaurant. He had lots to say but worried about revealing details of recruiting inducements during his days at Wake Forest for fear the NCAA's statute of limitations might not have run out (they had, but I couldn't prove it to Carl). Dr. Jack Lewis recalled game plan minutiae and waxed philosophic about the nuances of Walker's sophisticated sense of humor—lost on most of his teammates most of the time, Lewis opined.

Dave Harris, one of Walker's best players and a successful coach in his own right, was in the throes of dementia when we met. An interview might have been a struggle—many would have simply declined—but his loving, and lovely, wife Mary Arden thought he might enjoy the experience and spent the morning before our early afternoon talk prepping Dave (and herself) for it. We sat in the living room of their Charlotte house and she patiently guided him through his answers, filling in blanks as best she could and adding her own commentary—she and Dave met at Wake Forest, so she had known Peahead, too. They were troopers and offered what they could, but some questions were just too taxing.

Or . . . maybe not.

I'd wanted to ask Harris about an incident related to me by Hobbs. It was about a fight, or near fight, between Harris and Clemson Coach Frank Howard, the day before a game against the Tigers. It was an interesting incident to say the least—what was Howard doing snooping around the visiting team's locker room the day before a game anyway, trash talking (according to Hobbs) the opposing players?—but try as I might, I just couldn't get through to Harris. Every time I'd rephrase the question about Howard, he'd listen and then shake his head in frustration. He became increasingly agitated as my attempts went on. Mary Arden was alarmed by her husband's building anger, or possibly by my insistence on asking a question he couldn't answer. Politely, she apologized. I did too. We moved on to something else.

Finally, as I was leaving I shook Harris's hand and thanked him for his time. He nodded. And then, as his still-strong grip faded away, he looked me in the eye with a searing intensity, then down at the floor, then off into space. "Howard . . . " he said, his head shaking vigorously again, the anger once more apparent, "that S.O.B."

Murray Greason, Peahead Walker's erstwhile assistant coach for the Wake Forest College football team, squinted into the sun and tried to make out details of the small knot of people disembarking from a sedan parked on the gravel drive on the far side of the field.

There were three, no, four men and one woman. All were neatly dressed—the men all had on suits and ties—but they weren't what he'd call, what Peahead Walker would call, well dressed. This was a button-downed, conservative crew. They even moved conservatively.

"*Baptists,*" *Greason thought to himself.*

He had known something was up when he saw his boss heading toward the practice field in those pants. Walker, a dapper dresser at games and on the town, was just the opposite when it came to practice attire. Except for one singular day when he'd showed up in brand-new coaching togs he'd just received from a sporting good rep—Greason's relentless ribbing about the outfit assured it would be a one-time event—Walker was prone to throw on any old thing for the practice field. But the particular pair of ancient baseball pants he wore this day were in a class by themselves. They were stained with grass and tobacco and God only knew what else, and the seat of the pants was ripped from stem to stern. They'd been hanging on a hook in the coach's locker room for a year or more, a kind of running lockeroom joke more than anything else. But here was Peahead with them on.

That was Greason's first tipoff that this was a special day. The second was when Walker sidled up to him and said, "Murrh, why donchu get 'em started. Ah think Ah'll just watch a little bit from over heah on the side."

Greason looked at Walker sideways. Peahead never delegated. Most of the time that was because he had so few assistants there was no one to delegate to, but even when better staffed he managed the details of most every workout.

But not today. Today was . . . special.

The Baptist were here to watch.

A visit from a Baptist group was not a rare phenomenon with Walker during his long stay at Wake Forest. Wake Forest was a Baptist-founded and -supported college, and the Southern Baptist Convention took a keen interest in its doings. Especially its moral doings. The activities of one Peahead Walker, a known smoker, drinker, and cusser who was also rumored to enjoy the company of women who were not his lawfully wedded wife, garnered him some special attention. That he was a successful and talented football coach there could be no doubt, but there was more to life in Southern Baptist minds (some of them anyway) than beating Duke and North Carolina. Walker's lax morality was a thorn in these Baptist sides, and there were some who thought it ought to be removed.

And so, periodically, Walker was the subject of an investigation or a fact-finding mission in which some upright Convention members would descend upon campus to interview coaches, players, faculty, administrators, and occasionally even Walker himself in hopes of getting to the bottom of things.

And so, today, another load of "Baptist spies."

Greason nodded to Walker, turned, blew his whistle, and set the players to their paces.

Soon the Baptists were in position beside the field. Immediately, Walker began to gyrate and gesticulate, to hold his head and gnash his teeth, apparently agonized beyond bearing at what was taking place on the field. Most of all he began to bend over . . . and over, and over . . . which, given the aforementioned state of his practice pants, gave the visitors a personal view of the Deacon coach unlike anything they might have expected.

The fact finding moved along swiftly. Indeed, in a few minutes the Baptists had, literally, seen enough of Peahead Walker. More than enough according to some accounts.

In his haste to get down the practice field before the guests arrived, Walker had neglected to put on his underwear.

Peahead Walker was not a saint. He was no more *unsaintly* than lots of men, then or now, but let's not mince words. He could be vulgar, he regularly indulged in a number of vices, and took ethical shortcuts right and left while building successful football teams. Were he coaching today he'd surely have an NCAA probation or two on his rap sheet.

Walker's darker side is displayed on these pages, if not in full then completely enough to make the point: he had his warts. Although a talented coach and a good man to many he was, he was not universally laudable. But that is who he was. It's part of the story.

Readers will also note that Walker lived in interesting times. That's a part of this story, too. The times offer context. Some of Walker's ethical woes, for instance, were quite specific to his day. For instance, there was serious debate throughout his collegiate coaching career as to the moral correctness of paying young men to play football and other college sports. That's still a debate today, of course, but the "pay" in question then was (for the most part) scholarships, which today are a given for teams at nearly every level of collegiate sports. Walker was all for "scholarshipping" (or for doing just about anything else that would help his team) his boys, but that was not a universally held view back then.

So to produce a background against which Walker can be correctly viewed, brief forays into the broader history of these times are required. Bits and pieces of football history are included, along with mini-biographies of some of Walker's closest friends (and enemies). The reader needs this larger story to make sense of all the rest.

And besides, they're some good stories in all that, too, which is what this is all about.

> *One pleasant fall afternoon, warmups were underway for an important Wake Forest football game. Out on the field Wake's punter's was lofting high, floating kicks into the October sun . . . and the Deacons' main punt returner kept fumbling them as they dropped into his hands. Deacon Coach Peahead Walker watched the display, his blood pressure rising. Muffed punts had been a problem all year long. He'd been devoting extra practice time to it and now . . . this.*
>
> *"Awwwww sheeee-it!" Walker said, flinging his fedora to the ground and marching over to the butter-fingered young man who had just managed to drop six of the seven kicks directed his way.*
>
> *"Whaaat the hay-ell is goin' on here?" Walker said. "I mean, got-damn boy, you done dropped everything that's come your way. Got-damn, boy. You couldn't catch a got . . . damn . . . cold . . . "*

To the surprise of Walker, and just about everyone else in earshot, the player interrupted the coach at this point. Few Deacons ever dared do that when Walker was in mid-tirade. But this player did. He was trying, it was just . . . too hard . . .

"I'm doing what you told me, Coach, putting my hand up and all, but that sun . . . it's always in my eyes," the fumbler moaned.

Walker screwed his face up, squatted to obtain some leverage, and planted his nose right under the player's chin.

"Hay-ell, son," said Walker, "whatchu want me to do? Call in a got-damn e-clipse?"

On and on the stories go. String them together, mix in a few facts, and an image begins to appear. Actually looking at old photographs may help. I know it did me. I gathered up as many Walker photographs as I could find and spent some time gazing into his face, looking for a clue. Who was he?

Words and ideas eventually appear. Funny, profane, tough, sarcastic, smart, likeable, unlikeable, mean, kind, and many more.

Walker was easy to root for, an eternal underdog who pulled off one upset after another—a man with a sense of fun, a sense of humor. He was a friend of sportswriters and, for the most part, his fellow coaches; a terror to his players; and a bane to the Baptist moral police. The general public, informed by the sporting press who Walker assiduously courted with strong camaraderie and even stronger drink, thought him a character and a clown, but one who could really coach. For many, this was reinforced in person on the banquet circuit, where Walker's spontaneous wit and self-deprecating cornpone persona was a long-running hit.

Some of it was just an act, of course. Long-time Florida State University Coach Bobby Bowden, who had some experience at playing the hick before a crowd, says Walker was "in truth a very sharp man, literate, quick, very funny."[2]

Likewise, the venom Walker spewed at players was neither deep-seated nor heartfelt. It did reflect Walker's competitive

---

2 Bobby Bowden, interview with author.

instincts but was also just part of most coaching repertoires in those days. Many of his players figured this out. They genuinely feared him and may have found his policies and/or his personal behavior unsavory. But as they got to know him—in some cases many years after the fact—the view softened.

Walker was fondly remembered—maybe even revered. He cared about his boys and wished them well on the football field and beyond. And, he was just an interesting guy to be around.

Most of Walker's players were proud to have been one of Peahead's boys. They wanted others to know that they played for him, that they had been a part. This came through in interviews and was evidenced in other cases by obituaries that almost always included a line that read, " . . . and played football for the unforgettable 'Peahead' Walker."

Of all the words that might be used to describe Peahead Walker, unforgettable is probably best. We know this is true because he spawned his own collection of oddball stories. They were told again and again, most often by Walker himself. They were his legacy and define him still.

And now a final word about truth.

As noted, the stories about Peahead Walker speak to a truth, even if they're not exactly true. But some of them, even the most preposterous, may actually *be* true.

That crazy Bill George East campus/West campus story, for instance. No logical person can hear this tale without lifting at least one quizzical eyebrow of disbelief. George visited one place but thought he was at another? Who could possibly have fallen for so ridiculous a ruse?

A fair question, but one that's not as simple it looks; so say those closest to the matter. You had to be there, had to know the people and the places. It was a different time and Peahead Walker was a different person—a gifted salesman who regularly talked college-aged boys into seeing things his way. Show a recruit one college, then bring them to another? That's not crazy, it's . . . creative, it's Peahead in a nutshell.

That is, more or less, the verdict of Biff George, Bill's son. Biff says that, crazy as it sounds, his dad always told the story as the truth:

That story was part of dad's banquet talk. It always drew a laugh, had them rolling in the aisles usually, but it never seemed to me that he was joking. I never specifically asked, but if I had to say, if you asked me to come down on it, I'd say it's true at least to a point. I say that and people say, 'c'mon.' But you have to remember that dad was seventeen then, very young and very country, not from what you'd call a sophisticated background. His parents were first-generation immigrants from Syria. His father died when he was nine, so he stayed with Mom who owned and operated a grocery store in Waynesburg, Pennsylvania. I'm sure they didn't have much money and he didn't travel much. So he was very un-worldly, if that's a word. I suppose he figured it out later, but by then he was already there at Wake.[3]

Others who heard Walker tell the tale agree. It sounded more like truth than spoof when Walker told it, too. Their proof? It was in what they didn't hear. Those who heard Walker speak regularly, knew his cadence, his inflection. The real whoppers he told, the outright fabrications, were told using particular techniques and inflection. The George story, which Walker told a lot, was delivered in a different way. It sounded like the truth.

Gene Hooks, a baseball player at Wake Forest at roughly the same time Walker was bringing George to school, says the story sounded right to him—except for one part. If Walker had pulled some kind of recruiting trick on George, said Hooks, "he [George] certainly wouldn't have called him on it. None of those guys would have. They were scared to death of him and didn't want to cross him."[4]

But as for the rest of it?

"Sounds like Peahead to me," said Hooks.

Yes, it does.

---

[3] Biff George, interview with author.
[4] Gene Hooks, interview with author.

CHAPTER 1

A BOY NAMED PEAHEAD

The nickname came early and maybe with good reason. His given first name was Daniah. Whether that was a mother's invention, an accident, or an old family name of some description is impossible to say. Daniah is the female form of the Hebrew name Daniel and is a familiar appellation among some Jewish families for their baby girls. That's probably not the origin in this case. D.C. Walker wasn't a girl, and his family religious affiliation, though somewhat tenuous, appears to have been Southern Baptist. "Daniah" was consistent with the family's early naming policies. He was the second child and his older brother, born two years before, had the equally improbable name of Frana (he went by his middle name, Earl, for most of his life). After Daniah and Frana, the names of the children sired by Zachary T. and Miriam Walker of Ensley, Alabama, defaulted to solid monikers typical of the time and place: Lester, Zachary, Erskine, Howard, Archie, Katherine, Ralph. No more is known. Family members don't possess any clues to the unusual names, and the records of the two families who combined to form the union were lost to a string of courthouse conflagrations in the county seat of their Carroll County, Georgia, home. The first blaze, of course, is attributed to General William Tecumseh Sherman, even though there's no record of "Uncle Billy" passing through that side of the state. The rest of the fires were from the "post-Yankee" period, although in some minds Mr. Sherman is still the most likely culprit.

The middle name was the more conventional Clyde. Like many adult males of the time, he would eventually go by his initials, D.C., and, less formally, by Doug or Douglas—the new first name he had begun to use before he was out of his teens. Whether he actually went to the trouble to have it legally changed at some point is unknown. It does appear on official documents, beginning with his draft registration card for World War I. He was 18 when he made his mark for Uncle Sam, who may or may not have cross-referenced draft cards with birth certificates back then.

So it was Doug later on. But as a boy growing up in the bustling Birmingham suburb of Ensley all he had was Daniah, or Clyde, or maybe D.C. That might have been why he ended up with Peahead and why it stuck. Nearly all of his adult friends called him Peahead, the notable exception being Herman "Half-Ton" Hickman, Yale football coach and radio/TV personality, who called him Clyde (possibly because it ticked him off). Walker's preference for Peahead suggests some distaste for the formal choices afforded him. Family members have a vague sense that this was the case.

So, from whence Peahead? Walker himself told at least three different stories to back up the name. All point to incidents in his youth. All were told years after the fact. The truth could be elsewhere, or it could be somewhere in between. Peahead did like a good story. It is not surprising that his nickname would produce more than one.

The origin tales are all plausible, the scenes painted easy to imagine.

The first dates back to Walker's boyhood. Picture a group of 10- and 11-year-olds right out of *Our Gang* or *Peck's Bad Boy*[1] at a favorite neighborhood haunt, figuring out what they're going to do next. Someone, maybe Walker himself, brings up the fact that none of them have nicknames. This ain't right. All the men in the neighborhood have one.

"We oughta have nicknames," he says.

"Yeah," says another.

"But where do we get 'em from?" says someone else.

---

[1] *Our Gang* is the title of a series of film shorts created by Hal Roach in the 1920s. The series chronicled the trials and tribulations of a loveable, but mischievous "gang" of kids in an unnamed American town. *Peck's Bad Boy* was a popular 1934 movie based on the newspaper columns of George Wilbur Peck, a Wisconsin newspaperman and governor (he was elected Mayor of Milwaukee and Governor of Wisconsin). The titular "bad boy" was an insatiable prankster. The two franchises merged, after a fashion, for the 1938 Peck's movie sequel. Spanky McFarland, one of the stars of *Our Gang*, co-starred in the Peck movie.

"Aw, don't be stupid," says Walker. "We'll just use the ones the adults have. . . . You'll be Shorty, and you can be Lefty, and you can be Big Pete and you can be Sparky."

"Who will you be?" someone asks.

"Well," Walker say, his eyes lighting up, "I guess I'll be Peahead."

It might have gone like that, or someone else might have done the assigning. That part isn't known, and the only authority for the origin tale is Peahead himself. The neighborhood boys all adopted nicknames used by the neighborhood adults, Walker said. He took on Peahead, the name assigned to a man Walker affectionately described as the neighborhood drunk. Walker offered the *Our Gang* version of his nicknaming to a student newspaperman at Wake Forest in 1937. It was published as fact. But Walker possessed a dry, devious wit and enjoyed a good prank. The student may have been yet another in a long line a victims. Or—hay-el boy, don't you know the truth when you hear it? — maybe that's what really happened.

Another possibility, related by Walker in 1949, also involves his boyhood. In this tale, the youthful Walker is taunting a neighborhood kid, a surly youth with a reputation as a big dumb bully with a bulbous body and a tiny head. Anytime Walker would see him he'd say, "Hey, look, there goes ol' Peahead . . . Hey, Peahead c'mere," and so on—until one day the kid finally snaps, blindsides Walker by surprise, locking him quickly and forcefully in a mean, suffocating chokehold.

"You'd better quit calling me names, son. I don't like it. And now that I'm thinking about it I'm gonna call you Peahead, *Peahead*."

And that's how it all went down.[2]

In a similar a vein is yet another tale that Peahead told several times in his later life for attribution when responding to the "where'd you get that name from?" question from sportswriters. In this version Walker's in high school and a star quarterback on the football team. After scoring the game-winning touchdown on a long run in a big game, a young, naive, enthusiastic newspaperman

---

2 *Dallas Morning News*, Sept. 24, 1949.

intercepts one of his teammates and good friends coming off the field.

"Who was that boy!" he shouts.

"That's Peahead, sir! Peahead Walker!"

The name sounded authentic to the reporter but was nothing more than a sophomoric inside joke. It's like this: A regular member of the neighborhood gang growing up was a younger boy with a small head who was naturally nicknamed Peahead. The boy wasn't Walker but for whatever reason took a liking to him and started following him around here and there like a pup. So when the reporter asked Walker's teammate for his name he thought it'd be funny to use the nickname of Walker's "shadow." Before Walker had a chance to protest the name it had already been recorded in the local papers, and hence, everywhere else.

"It came out in the paper like that [and] soon everybody forgot about my name being Douglas and started calling me Peahead," Walker told Neale Patrick of the *Gastonia Gazette* in a 1967 interview.

The two stories based on the common theme of what might be called the "pea-sized head premise" suggest a kernel (or perhaps a peapod) of truthful origin. Surely at some point Walker was a small-headed boy or man, right? If true, then all of the more complicated stories could have been set aside. But alas—the photographic record argues against this most obvious of explanations. The earliest photos of Walker, pictures of the man to be in his late teens and early twenties, show that he was a chiseled five foot seven, a handsome, well-proportioned man with a raffish haircut—dark locks always parted down the middle—and, if anything, a rather *large* head. In practically every photo from that time period—and these are all posed, athletic team photos—his wry and puckish eyes beam from out of the group of otherwise sullen mugs; his arms are usually folded across his chest or propped on his hips in a gesture that suggests both confidence and defiance. In one baseball team photo from his Howard College days, Walker is wearing a uniform that looks pristine and tailor-made. The fit is magnificent and is easy to note because everyone else's uniform looks like a big burlap sack of potatoes.

What does seem clear is that Peahead was Peahead for a long time. Birmingham newspaper accounts of his exploits as a 15-year-old high school shortstop and quarterback identify him only as Peahead. So do reports of his arrival at Howard College. No other name is used. Were he a lesser player we would not even have that. Journalistic convention at the time was to list most players by last name on all references. It was only when a player gained some notoriety that a first name would begin to appear. Folks who knew Walker exclusively as a grown man (with the emphasis on *grown*, especially, after age 45, around the midsection) often made the mistake of associating his nickname with his appearance at that time. The middle-aged Peahead was no different than the younger Peahead in that his head was not especially small—or pea-sized—but rather round and fleshy. Over time, however, as the rest of his torso continued to expand, his head finally did indeed seem small, so much so that later in life the nickname fit. Or maybe fit again.

There is one other potential source for the nickname. It is derived from inference and Walker family lore, although it too is a story passed on from Peahead himself. His mother, Miriam "Zoe" Maddox Walker, was a tiny woman. Zachary Taylor Walker III, the son of Peahead's younger brother Zachary Taylor Walker Jr., says his dad told him that even after he was a grown man he could still encompass his mom's waist between his outstretched hands.[3]

Miriam Walker was under five feet tall with a narrow frame and a waist of not much more than twenty inches. Small children were a necessity, but Daniah Clyde may have been smaller than most. Zac Walker III remembers his famous uncle telling a story about his mom carrying him around on a throw pillow when he was an infant. A baby small enough to fit on a throw pillow would have had to have had a small head—perhaps even a peahead.

***

The origin of the name may be impossible to know for sure, but what can be said is that Peahead was Peahead from an early age and was still Peahead when he died. Indeed, the nickname was so

---

[3] Zac Walker III, interview with author.

distinctive, so much a part of his unique persona, that it ended up spawning nicknames of its own. His college and professional players, none of whom would have dared call him Peahead to his face, quickly took to referring to him as "the Head" in their private conversations. The name no doubt stemmed from Walker's authoritative position and nature as head coach—"Hey Smith!" for example. "The Head wants to see you!" (And as at least one player noted, the fact that it was also slang for toilet made it even more appropriate.) Walker's second wife, Flonnie Hornthal Watts, despised the name Peahead, which she thought was ill-fitting for the classy, older man she married. So she called him "Petey," which was her shorthand for Peahead. It seemed like an improvement to her.[4]

There then is the name and here is the man: a colorful and unique individual whose public coaching career and associated sidelines produced enough funny stories to . . . well, to fill a book and to merit a distinctive nickname. But in all this, a chicken-and-egg questions remains: Was Peahead born to his suggestive nickname? Or did his nickname help turn him into the man he was? There is no simple answer, maybe no answer at all. Peahead Walker was a man with several distinct sides to his personality. He was both funny and stern, gruff and affable, goofy and practical.

Zac Walker III, whose mother wouldn't let his father take him to Uncle Peahead's football practices because of the language he used, said the Peahead Walker he knew was an affable man and a lot of fun to be around. Another nephew, Mickey Walker, said that most people didn't know the "nice" side of him and that away from football he was that person.

And a man who liked nicknames. Throughout his coaching career, if one of Walker's players didn't have a ready-made nickname, he'd come up with one. For some fortunate few, he devised two or three.

A handful of Walker's players—Wake Forest's William "Nub" Smith comes to mind—brought their informal handles with them to school, but most of his players received their nicknames directly

---

4 The adult Walker was a snazzy, sometimes even foppish dresser. In the 1960s, late in his life, he tooled around New York City in spats and a pinstripe suit while carrying an ornate cane.

from Walker. Many came directly from off-the-cuff invective spewed by Walker while chewing a player out at one his rugged practices. Most of that dealt with the mental shortcomings of his charges.

George Sniscak, a sometimes dense Wake Forest lineman from western Pennsylvania's coal country, was Anthracite Head. Deacon quarterback Dickie Davis said his difficulty remembering plays, coupled with his mediocre classroom work, earned him the sobriquet Amoeba Brain (sometimes shortened to just Amoeba). Davis was also known as Dynamite, a highly alliterative title (Dynamite Dickie Davis) that the school's publicists and some sports writers covering the team used in the context of Davis's explosive abilities as a runner and passer. That was the public story, but teammates remember the nickname as shorthand for a Walker one-liner—it wasn't original—regarding the relative impotence of Davis's cranial material: "Davis, if your brain was made of dynamite you still couldn't blow your nose." The Dynamite nickname was not applied uniquely to Davis. Walker also renamed one of his Montreal players Dynamite. A team manager at Wake also carried the name, and Wake Forest's first-ever sports publicist was known as Dynamite Holton thanks to a rechristening by Walker.

Along similar lines, Deacon Melvin Layton was forever known to teammates as Molly, which was not a feminization but the short version of molecule, which was part of another memorable Walker lambast: "Goddammit Layton, your brain must be the size of a molecule," Walker said, while sputtering over a mistake at practice one afternoon. "It's so small it's like a BB rattling around inside a boxcar." Future Tennessee Coach Johnny Majors recalls Walker using the term "celery seed" in a similar context. A brain power-challenged player had a brain so small it was like a celery seed rolling around in his head. How much smarter (or dumber) Amoeba Brain was than Molecule or Celery Seed or even Dynamite is not clear.

Other nicknames were less random—that is, they only applied to a single player—and hence were more biting. Hulking Wake Forest tackle Tom Palmer was known as Hogjaw for reasons obvious to anyone who saw him in profile. Davis recalled another played who went by Whalebone (or maybe Whale Butt, another anatomical reference). End Ed Butler, who as a collegian at Wake still had a noticeable scar from cleft palate surgery during childhood, drew the moniker Frankenstein from the ever-sensitive Walker. Mercifully, his teammates later renamed him Congo after a movie character. Walker liked that and picked it up as well.

Hard-hitting linebacker Jimmy Arakas was the Greek Water Boy, which he had, in fact, been at his father's restaurant back in Wilson, NC, where Walker often dined. Tough-as-nails Bob Gaona, a defensive star on some of Walker's later Deacon teams, was Mexican because his mother was Mexican.

All of Walker's ministerial students were tagged Preacher or Reverend. Carl Haggard, who was from Norfolk, VA, told Walker during a recruiting interview that he was plenty fast enough to play in the backfield, thus becoming the Norfolk Flash, and later, just Flash. Glen Rheinhard, a 280-pound tackle without an aggressive bone in his body, was Teddy Bear, and later, just Teddy. Spindly Deacon safety Terry Gwinn was Spider or, as some recall, Spider-Man.[5] Walker's war-era teams at Wake included both Rock Brinkley and Hard Rock Harris. Players whose last name ended in "ski" or "vich"—and there were several—were called Polack or Sausage[6] at some point. Walker usually avoided Wop for players of Italian ancestry but didn't shy away from addressing them as Spaghetti, Lasagna, or Meatball.

"He had something for everybody," said Pride Ratterree, a Walker favorite during the war years at Wake. "I can only remember two or three who didn't and I was one of those. I already had a funny name."

So prolific was Walker's nicknaming (or name calling) that some players were confused. Tom Donahue, who played at Wake near the end of Walker's tenure, remembered asking guard Leonard Paletta one day what his real name was. He had heard his teammate called so many things on the practice field that he was no longer sure of the reality.

"I'd heard one coach call him Joe and another Lennie, and I think there was a guy from his hometown (New Kensington, PA) on the team who called him Skeets," said Donahue. "So I wasn't

---

5 It could have been either, but the comic book character didn't appear until 1962.
6 Sausage was apparently a condensed form of Polish sausage.

sure. I said to him one time, 'Hey, tell me your real name.' And he said, 'Well, Coach Cochran thinks it's Jesus Christ because every time he says anything to me it's Jesus Christ Paletta, and as best I can tell, the Head thinks it's Goddammit. To be honest, I'm not sure anymore myself."[7]

As Walker grew to adulthood, the various aspects of his adult personality grew with him. As a boy and a teenager he was a live wire, an imp, a rounder, and eventually something of a family outcast, although that probably had more to do with geography than anything else. The Walkers' restless son left home at an early age and never returned. Almost everyone else in the family stayed behind.

He was the second of Zachary and Miriam Walker's nine kids. The couple was from western Georgia but moved to Cullman, AL soon after they married and then on to the Birmingham/Ensley area in 1899 when D.C. was born. They were part of a wave of newcomers who descended upon Ensley just as the steel boom was just beginning.

In hindsight, it's obvious why mighty industrial works were situated somewhere around Ensley on Birmingham's west side. A fluke of nature had deposited all the natural elements required for steel making within a 50-mile area. Red Mountain, which splits modern Birmingham in two (the imposing ridgeline is the current site of the city's famous Vulcan statue), was filled with a particularly rich iron ore as well as limestone, another element necessary to the process. The famed Black Warrior Basin coalfield was just west and south of Ensley. It was the vision of Memphis native Colonel Enoch Ensley that made it all happen for the town that would eventually bear his name. An executive with the Tennessee Coal and Iron Railroad, Ensley saw the possible economies of scale if large factories could be built in the area. Birmingham was already a manufacturing hub for iron and steel, but the consolidation of small factories into large ones was just beginning. Among the missing elements was a large workforce. Most of Alabama consisted at that time of tiny towns and family farms. Ensley sought to rectify that by building a brand-new town

---

7 Tom Donahue, interview with author.

around a group of steel mills that the Tennessee Coal and Iron Railroad was building to take advantage of the new Bessemer process for making cheap steel. Ensley and other Birmingham-area industrialists engaged Englishman Henry Bessemer himself to redesign his famed, Bessemer steel converters to work with the peculiar Alabama ores. The first "Alabama-style" steel ingots were tapped near Ensley on Thanksgiving in 1899. The rush began soon after.

Ensley led an investment group that bought up 4,000 acres of land for what he envisioned would become "the great industrial city of the nation."[8] He imagined it would quickly outpace Birmingham, which would have been no small achievement. Although just founded in 1871, Birmingham's population topped 100,000 shortly after the turn of the century. But Ensley's 4,000-acre plot, with its well-designed street grid and endless array of worker's housing, might have done the trick if his luck had been a little better. As it was, he overextended himself just as an economic downturn hit. He was forced to sell most of the land at a steep discount—just $15,000 for most of the holdings in total. As a result the town never developed quite the way he imagined.

Although Ensley's timing was off, the town that bore his name still popped up out of the ground like magic in the early 1900s. By 1910, when Ensley merged with Birmingham (town officials held a funeral procession to mark the event), there were a dozen or so large manufacturing concerns in the town, one bona fide skyscraper was in the works (the McCormack-Ramsey building), and according to a report 20 years later by Ensley businessman J.A. Smith, twenty-seven saloons were up and running.[9] It was a good way to attract a large workforce.

Ensley was a lively workingman's town where women and children knew to clear the streets by 4:55 PM or face death by trampling. Even though the town was designed with (for the time) wide boulevards and well-organized street grid (Avenues A through T ran as parallels the length of town), when the quitting time whistle blew and some 5,000 workers spilled out of the mills they

---

8 *History of Ensley*. p. 17. Pamphlet, Ensley Historical Collection, Birmingham Public Library, with some original material dating to 1907.
9 *Birmingham News*, June 5, 1926.

would literally fill the streets. The daily stampede did not last long, however. The throngs split up and rushed down the side streets that led to other side streets, and so on, until everyone had found his home . . . or perhaps stopped in at one of the twenty-seven bars to hoist a few drinks with good ol' Peahead—meaning, in this case, the original.

Ensley's hard-working and hard-living population quickly created its own culture and nightlife. The famed Glenn Miller hit "Tuxedo Junction" (written by Ensley native Erskine Hawkins) celebrated the nightclub district where streetcar lines crossed at the intersection of Ensley Avenue and Bush Boulevard. At the junction there was a tuxedo shop with a prominent showcase window, hence the nickname.

Growing up in a place like that, the wonder is not that one young, impressionable member of the Walker family would develop a lifelong love of high times and fast lanes, but that all of them didn't. Although D.C. wasn't the only family member who moved away from the Ensley/Birmingham area, he was the leader of the pack. Indeed, he was the direct cause of most of the family's migration. Two brothers left Alabama to play football for Peahead at Elon College near Burlington, NC. Both wound up staying in the area, either directly or eventually. Another brother, Erskine (who went by the nickname Bub, which in turn was short for Bubba), was the family's best athlete. He starred on the great University of Alabama football teams of the mid-1930s and then spent a couple decades coaching in the Southeast. Again, it was Peahead who first led him astray. Not long after Bub left college, Peahead hired him as a coach at Wake Forest College. He later coached at Peahead's alma mater, Howard College in Birmingham, and did wind up living back home.

D.C. Walker III, Peahead's grandson by his oldest son D.C. Jr., grew up in Birmingham with his dad, his grandmother, and the rest of the family. His recollection of Grandpa Peahead, whom he didn't meet until he was four because he simply didn't come around that often, was that he was on the outside because he left. Although Walker doubtless had more regular contact with his family through his college years, he didn't live regularly at home past the age of sixteen, except possibly in 1918 when he became so ill he had to drop out of college (perhaps a victim of the great flu pandemic of 1918 perhaps). When Peahead left, his youngest siblings were still just toddlers. The oldest still at home, Lester and Zac Jr., were in their teens.

"I always got the sense that he just wanted out of there as fast as he could," said D.C. Walker III. "No one else in the family really did that, not until later. But [Peahead] wanted to get away. He went to Howard, which was all the way in Eastlake, a suburb on the other side of Birmingham from Ensley. So he went there and he did get away and there always seemed some separation because of that."[10]

That assessment also fits Zac Walker III's admittedly limited view of Walker family life. He recalls his father driving him into Ensley from their home in nearby Miner Heights, AL, every morning so he could attend Bush Elementary School, which was right next door to Ensley High. Zac Walker III says the family left in the 1940s for a business opportunity in the South Boston, VA, area. "And we didn't go back much," Zac Walker III said. "I wouldn't say the family, as a whole, was very close."[11]

Five of the children made their homes in and around Birmingham for their entire lives, and Erskine "Bub" Walker lived there part of the time. Peahead Walker's first wife (a Birmingham girl) and his oldest son also returned after Peahead's marriage broke up during World War II. At least some of the Walker kids lived at home after they finished school. The 1930 census, taken the same year that Zachary Walker Sr. died, lists Lester Walker as a resident and mill foreman, and 19-year-old Howard Walker as a resident and shoe store clerk. Howard suffered from polio as a child and was the only Walker who didn't play sports. The 1930 census also lists Zachary Walker Sr.'s mother, Kate Walker (i.e., Peahead's fraternal grandmother), as a member of the household.

The Walkers who stayed behind worked in less glamorous fields than did the coaching wing of the family. Howard (after his shoe clerking days) and Earl both ran movie projectors at local theaters. Ralph serviced vending machines.

---

10 D.C. Walker III, interview with author.
11 Zachary Walker III, interview with author.

As noted, the family did move a bit around Ensley. But it seems to have fared well enough. One of the family addresses listed, on Avenue E, is still occupied by the original structure. It's dilapidated now, like much of modern-day Ensley, but appears to have been a fairly substantial home for the time. Census data list a string of middle-class occupations for the Walkers' neighbors: pipe fitters, machinists, electricians, carpenters, bookkeepers, time clerks, barkeepers, washerwomen. That Zachary Walker made a decent living as a "collector," presumably a rent collector, for a local real estate company (his listed occupation in both 1910 and 1930), is further supported by the fact that so many of the children in the family went to college. That was hardly common at that time. Of course, athletics played a big role in that. At least four of the boys, including Peahead, appeared to have some or all of their schooling paid for by athletic scholarship or some similar device.

Somewhat after Peahead's trailblazing path, sports did become a big deal in the Walker household. Miriam Walker was selected as the "Football Mother of the Year" by the *Birmingham News* in the early 1930s, when five of her sons were playing or coaching high school or college football.

Peahead was long gone by then. Before he went away, however, he was educated in Ensley's new public school system. He graduated in the Ensley High class of 1916 along with 32 other students. The school had just come under the jurisdiction of the Birmingham school system (part of the 1910 merger) but remained a source of civic pride in Ensley, in large part because of its sparkling new two-story building. The general courses of study were mathematics, English, history, and Latin. Modern foreign languages and the sciences were added in 1913, although it is not clear whether students in the 1916 graduating class received the benefit of that addition. The school was growing in size. It would expand to house more than 2,000 students in the 1920s, Peahead Walker's class being one of the last of the small classes to graduate.

Walker was a Big Man on Campus (BMOC), albeit on a small "c." Most of that had to with athletics. He was quarterback and captain for the 1915 football team, a basketball regular, and a star shortstop of the 1916 baseball team. When previewing the 1916 football contest between Ensley and local power Birmingham

Central, the game the year after Walker left, the *Birmingham News* noted that "[Central] is not worrying over its first game as Ensley is in deep water. An entire backfield has got to be built before the Steel City lads [i.e., Ensley] will loom up as dangerous. 'Red' Brown, Lewis and Walker of last year's team are no more."[12]

Central did not seem especially worried the year before when it mopped the field with Ensley 27–0. The Walker-directed offense managed just one first down against a Central team that was a physical overmatch for Ensley. Two Ensley players had to be hospitalized on account of injuries suffered in the game. It was not an unexpected result, at least not to the newspaper correspondents/sports handicappers of the day. Central was an established athletic power that regularly vied for state crowns and a massive school. Ensley was a tiny upstart.

That made Ensley's success on the baseball diamond in the spring of 1916 all the more astonishing. The Birmingham papers covered every game Central played. Schools such as Ensley, although in the same city, usually weren't covered unless they were playing Central.

Previewing the first of two spring baseball games between the schools, an unnamed *Birmingham News* correspondent did some reporting on Ensley's prospects. It is impossible to say whether or not he actually saw Ensley play, but he did pick up some "dope" (sports writer jargon of the day, referring to good information) on the squad somewhere.

"The [Ensley] students are boasting of their infield this year," the *Birmingham News* reporter wrote, "and it is ranked next to Connie Mack's $100,000 combination."[13] The newspaper's scouting report of Ensley infield included this assessment of its gritty shortstop:

Captain Walker, at short, is the mainstay of the infield, and is covering a world of territory. Walker knows baseball from the beginning and is the most scientific player that has ever played ball on the high school teams. Besides being able to make some

---

12 *Birmingham News*, Sept. 19, 1916.
13 Connie Mack was manager of the Philadelphia Athletics from 1901 to 1950; his famous "$100,000 Infield" started to break up in 1916.

wonderful stops, he is one of the best little field generals in the game, and knows how to get results out of his men.[14]

The effect of Walker's field generalship during Ensley's first meeting with Central is debatable, unless his dugout razzing helped rattle the Central fielders. Central committed a whopping ten errors in the contest, which Ensley converted into a 7-5 victory. Despite Central's errors the game remained in doubt until "Bull" Durham drove in Walker and another player with a sixth-inning double. Durham's big hit apparently was a squeaker down the line that didn't miss being foul by much—if at all. The *Birmingham Age-Herald* reported that "there was (sic) some questions as whether (Durham's game winner) was fair or foul. But the umpire failed to see the ball hit the ground and consequently it went as a fair ball."

Central won a rematch with Ensley 6-5 a few weeks later after establishing a 5-0 lead early and then holding on late. Walker, batting second, collected two hits in that contest, including a double. He also had a stolen base, two assists, and an error. The defeat did not slow Ensley's march to the Institutional League title, however. In the school's next game, the "pitching of Sherdock" and "Walker's all-around play" led Ensley to a 9-4 victory over Owenton. The *Age-Herald* reported that the victory gave Ensley a two-game lead in the league race, which Ensley eventually won. The other members of the Institutional League were not noted. Central may or may not have been a member.

After high school, Walker enrolled at Birmingham College, which was on the edge of the Ensley community and operated as both a college and a high school at the time. School records do not offer details of Walker's work. He stayed just a year, and it may have served as a kind of prep school.[15]

Walker arrived at Howard in East Lake, AL in the fall of 1917. Football Coach Dr. J.B. Longwell may have sought Walker's

---

14 *Birmingham News*, Apr. 16, 1916.

15 In 1918, just after Walker was there, Birmingham College merged with Southern Methodist College in Greensboro, AL. Birmingham College was also a Methodist school. The new school was known as Birmingham Southern College and moved to the existing Birmingham campus, near Ensley. Birmingham Southern was Howard College's biggest rivals during Walker's time at Howard.

services or Walker may just have showed up—a true walk-on in today's parlance. There is no doubt that players from the greater Birmingham area were being recruited by Howard College (and other schools) when Walker came through. Football, and the general tradition of highly competitive collegiate athletics, was already approaching entrenchment in the early 1900s. As a lengthy feature article in the September 19, 1915 edition of the *Birmingham News* reported, "From Florence to Mobile, and from Livingston on the west to Opelika in the east, alums of every alumni association have worked with all the skill, diligence and the gumshoe tactics of a Sherlock Holmes in landing football materials for his dear old alma mater." The article went on to say that while "no one will swear on it in a court of law, the *News* has been told that players have received offers ranging from free books and tuition, to out and out pay for those who are last in line when it comes to coin in pocket and may not appreciate the fulsomeness that an education can afford."

That is, agents of various schools were offering what would today be called scholarships, and if that didn't work they were giving them cash. The more things change . . .

That Longwell might have been up to something like this would not have been a shock. An alleged Pennsylvania grad and licensed dentist (a useful skill for a football coach in the facemask- and sometimes helmet-free era of football), Longwell was the author of Howard's greatest football glory. Arriving at the school in 1909, he led the team to a 5–2–1 record that included a near upset of Auburn, the regional powerhouse of the day. Longwell's secret? He brought two "ringers" to Howard with him. The players, probably Otto Wickham and J.L. McAteer, were alleged to have been ex-Penn stars, although that school's roster of all-time lettermen does not list either. They may well have been "tramp" players, migrant footballers who moved around the country and played for whichever school was willing to hire them. In a 1969 interview with Howard athletic history chronicler Avalee Willoughby, Dr. I.F. Simmons, a Howard student in 1909, said the general impression on campus was that they were paid to play and didn't attend classes. The pay was likely from alumni or what would today be called boosters—not from the school itself.[16]

Famous Birmingham sportswriter Zip Newman counted the Howard College transplants as part of the "Year of the Ringer (1909)" in Alabama sports, and alumni and locals joked about the way they stuck out. Howard alum Ed Berry said the two Pennsylvanians were really just "good ol' Eastlake boys with an Eastern Brogue." A Howard legend contends that brogue was so thick that the school had to hire a translator for the two men so that they could accomplish small life feats like buying groceries and going to the post office.[17]

Longwell, who also played for Howard in 1909 and 1911, was every bit as itinerant as his players. He coached at Howard in 1909, at Wittenburg College in 1910, and back at Howard in 1911. He left again in 1912. The savior of Howard football was lured back to the tiny school in 1916 with the promise of a greater commitment to athletics by the school. No information is available on Longwell's salary, but the school did up the athletic ante considerably in other ways. The administration and student government approved a new student athletic fee of $5 per student for the 1916–1917 school year. The amount seems trivial, especially considering that Howard's enrollment was under 400. But the money obviously had a much different weight then. The $5 fee, on top of a $10 student activity fee, was part of a total tuition/room/board package that cost most students less than $200 a year. The $2,000 or so raised by the fee, combined with gate receipt money and alumni contributions, produced a good cash reserve for athletics. It was enough, at any rate, for the school to construct a brand-new athletic field that was 415-feet long, 375-feet wide, and covered with 2 inches of "screened dirt" (that is, with most of the rocks removed) on top as a playing surface.

Like many schools at the time, Howard was attempting to join the athletic elite. As was the case at most schools in the early 20th century, the issue was a matter of much debate. But Howard's

---

16 *History and Philosophical Foundations of Health, Physical Education, Recreation and Athletics at Samford University*, 1900–1970, Avalee Willoughby, University of Alabama, 1972. Pages 45–46.
17 Ibid. Page 45.

stance was pretty clear. In one form or another the school had been playing football since 1892, and the popularity of the game made it unstoppable. The *Christian Advocate* newspaper, which covered the goings-on of Alabama Baptists (Howard College was founded by the Alabama Baptist Association in the 1840s), noted in a 1894 edition that "Football seems to gaining favor daily and has begun its report of broken ribs, jaw bones and legs. We don't know of an institution of any note that has not a team. Even our Howard is represented."

Although the Bulldogs had been playing football since the 1890s, the school officially fielded its first serious, organized team in 1902 when it brought in J.S. Counselman, a former Virginia Tech player and Coach at Michigan under the legendary Fielding Yost, to direct the program. Counselman went on to become Assistant Coach to John Heisman at Georgia Tech. A few years later, Longwell arrived for his first stint. By then, Dr. Simmons recalled, there was no doubt that football was at Howard to stay and that it was something the college took very seriously. "It seemed that winning was the main thing," he said in his interview with Willoughby. "At least this was the impression that the regular student had."[18]

Longwell's third stint at Howard was not an immediate success, but it wasn't from a lack of effort. Ed Berry and others recall him as a tough, hard-working coach who "came on the practice field with his football suit on . . . and showed you how to do it."[19] His first team managed a very respectable 6-4 record, although the football credentials of some of the victims (Alabama Presbyterian, Blountsville, Hamilton) might have been less than top drawer. The Bulldogs lost to Auburn 25-0 and dropped a late-season game to Birmingham College, who used a back named Walker in the contest. No first name is given, so whether it was D.C. "Peahead" Walker is not clear.

Longwell's second team took on a more ambitious schedule and had more skill-position talent. That included quarterback Peahead Walker and halfback Claude Carr. The Bulldogs beat Blountsville to open the season and then surprised regional

---

18 *History and Philosophical Foundations* . . . Willoughby, page 46.
19 Ibid, page 45.

observers by battling the Mountain Tigers of Sewanee College, a serious player in the college football game at that time, to a 6–6 tie.

"The Mountain Tiger was still a very much dazed beast of the football jungles this morning, having yet to recuperate from the terrific battle the Howard Baptists put up in holding the Sewanee Eleven to a 6–6 tie. Howard outplayed the Purple Tiger in every department of the game and deserved a 6–0 victory."[20]

Longwell was proud of the team but knew sterner tests awaited. He had scheduled games with both Auburn and Vanderbilt, two of the top teams in the Southeast, and his squad still lacked both quality and quantity. He thought he could work through the quality part if only he had a few more men. Alas, it was not to be. Mike Donohue's Auburn crew blasted Howard 53–0, and Vanderbilt followed up that humiliation up with a 69–0 Bulldog beat down a few weeks later.

In between, Howard met Marion Institute, a foe that was more its own speed. There was an edge to the game because Howard College had relocated from Marion to East Lake in 1887. It was a controversial move, tinged with both racial tension and bitterness on the part of the Marionites who, correctly, felt snubbed. Howard leaders believed that Marion, a small town in Alabama's "wild west," was stagnant. The bright lights and supposedly bright future of Greater Birmingham beckoned, so they left. All did not go as planned. Howard struggled for many years in its new home, and newly created Marion Military Institute blossomed in the old Howard College buildings (and still exists there today).

In the early 1900s, some of the animosity had faded, but the contest was still a rivalry. The 1917 game produced controversy all its own, centered on a play involving Peahead Walker. Trailing 7–6 late in the fourth quarter, Howard and its new quarterback mounted a drive. With Walker directing the Bulldogs' T-style offense, Howard drove to the Marion five-yard line. Three straight dive plays netted next to nothing. On the fourth-down snap, Walker called his own number and plunged over for the score. But the ball popped loose just as he crossed the goal line—or maybe just before.

---

20 *The Crimson.* Oct. 11, 1917

Which was it? Touchdown or fumble? Long before the days of instant replay there was nothing to do but argue and fight, which players from both sides did. In the end, all had to abide by the referee's decision: touchdown Howard and a 12–7 Bulldog victory.

On November 8, shortly after the massacre at Vanderbilt, Longwell resigned. Official word was that he was returning to Pennsylvania and his dental practice, but the abruptness of the move suggested something more. Longwell's successor, Bill Streit, recalled many years later that Longwell "had a disagreement with someone at Howard and left almost overnight."[21] The nature of the disagreement is unknown, but the departure left Howard's football team in disarray. Still licking its wounds from the Vanderbilt shellacking, it now faced life without a coach. Rumors surfaced that the rest of the football schedule would be cancelled and as historian James Sulzby noted, "gloom covered the [entire] athletic department."[22]"

The administration moved quickly to salvage what it could. Streit, a friend of Howard booster Ed Berry, was contacted about stepping into the void. A former all-South player at Alabama Polytechnical (Auburn), Streit readily agreed, provided he could get some time off from his job with the cement company. Howard officials gladly acquiesced, and the season was saved. Indeed, the campus rallied around the wounded team. When Professor T.R. Eagles, the faculty manager for athletics, put out a call for football players, more than twenty-five showed up (including the existing team members). That more than doubled the size of the roster and gave Streit something with which to work, even if much of it was raw and untested. In his memoir letter to James E. Sharman, Streit recalls that he had some "fine men" to work with and recalled in particular that "Peahead Walker was a quarterback on the team and did a fine job.[23]"

The team played just three more games that season, two of which may have been more like scrimmages against an industrial

---

21 *History and Philosophical Foundations of Health, Physical Education, Recreation and Athletics at Samford University, 1900-1970*, Avalee Willoughby, University of Alabama, 1972. p. 47.
22 Sulzby, *Toward History of Samford Univerity*, Vol. II p. 390.
23 Bill Streit personal letter to James Shaman, Samford University archives.

team from the American Cast Iron Pipe Co. Howard won both of these, one of which is recognized as an official victory in the school's record books. The team closed with a narrow loss to Spring Hill School to finish 3–3-1 (or maybe 2–3-1, or maybe even 4–3-1 depending upon how one feels about beating up on the local pipe company). There's no indication that any games were cancelled, but Sulzby notes some campus-wide disappointment that the Bulldogs didn't have a turn with Birmingham Southern, its crosstown rival.[24]

Professor J.A. Hendricks hosted a postseason banquet for the bedraggled gridders. Eleven men were given letters for wearing the Blue and Crimson. One of them was freshman Peahead Walker, about whom the student paper the *Crimson* gushed, "[He] has starred in practically every game the Howard team has been in. . . . He has proven to be an excellent field general, as well as one of the best men at advancing the ball (i.e., a good runner)."[25]

Walker's athletic career continued in the spring—though just barely. Longwell's resignation had department-wide repercussions for the athletics department. In the wake of his departure, athletics in its entirety was reconsidered, which, combined with the onset of baseball season soon after the start of the second semester, called Howard's diamond venture into question. With an eye toward reducing the importance of intercollegiate athletics, the school's "football authorities" had suggested or recommended that Howard take up an informal "club" version of the sport in the spring. Given the relative shortage of manpower at a coeducational school with an enrollment of less than 400, the club football system would replace baseball as the spring activity. But at a meeting convened by Professor Eagles and attended by a group of prospective players that included Walker, it was decided to move ahead with baseball. It was managed by three senior players and did pretty well. The Bulldogs dropped a three-game series to the University of Alabama but lost just one or two other contests and finished either 10–4 or 10–5 (records differ). Peahead Walker, whom *The Crimson* reported had been Birmingham College's star shortstop the year before, quickly

---

24 Sulzby, p. 391.
25 Ibid.

earned a starting role. He played shortstop, pitched some, and batted third or fourth.

Athletics during the 1918–1919 school year at Howard were curtailed for several reasons. The most obvious were America's entry into World War I and the onset of the great flu pandemic of 1918, which hit the Birmingham area just as it did most major metropolitan areas in the country. Peahead registered for the draft but wasn't called. Whether he was "enlisted" by the flu is unknown, but he did miss the entire first semester as a result of his illness.[26]

It was just as well. The football season was an abortive, two-game affair that included a 101–0 defeat at the hands of Marion, a military college whose team was stacked with soldiers obtaining last-minute training before being deployed.

By spring the war was over, and operations moved closer to normalcy, although the baseball team was still coached by players. Walker was part of a team that tackled a strenuous twenty-three-game (but informal) schedule. It included several games against YMCA teams and the like. Howard went 12–11.

Streit served as Football Coach and overall Director of Athletics for almost two years, and although his service was appreciated, it obviously left something to be desired. He was an unpaid volunteer because "at that time (1917–19) the Howard athletic department was very low on finance."[27]

The school got what it (or the cement company) paid for. Streit did his best with what he had, presided over limited schedules, did little or no recruiting, and found whomever he could to coach the school's other sports teams. As noted, students led the baseball team. The director of the Birmingham YMCA coached Howard's 1918–1919 basketball squad.

Although Howard College was still struggling—the school was in debt and had been without a full-time President since J.M.

---

26 *The Crimson*, Feb. 4, 1919.
27 Streit letter to Sharman. The letter was written in 1965, as Sharman gathered information for a scholarly work.

Shelburne left for active military duty in 1917—the faculty committee did not give up on athletics.[28]

After a year and a half of Streit's volunteerism, the school hired Charles C. Dillon, a recent graduate of the University of Illinois (class of 1913), where he was a three-year football letterman and an all-Big Nine[29] halfback in 1911. Dillon arrived with no time to bring in new men. Somebody lined up a killer schedule for him, and he threw what he had into the fray. It wasn't pretty. Howard's opening games were against Auburn and on the road at Sewanee, Alabama, and Mississippi A&M (now Mississippi State). The Bulldogs were pelted by a combined score of 124–6 but actually felt pretty good about that, especially the Auburn game.

In the opener, played at Birmingham's all-purpose Rickwood Field, the Bulldogs held their own for much of the game and then surprised the Plainsmen with a second-half touchdown pass. Walker, his nose broken earlier in the contest, threw it. The thirty-yard heave was caught by end Lee Head (so the passing combo was Peahead to Head, or, using the later vernacular for Walker, Head to Head) in stride at the goal line. Unsure of where he was, Head roared full speed through the end zone and into the bleachers behind it. The touchdown was the first Howard had scored against Auburn since the series began in 1903.

Although Auburn won the contest, the *Birmingham Age-Herald* sung the praises of the hometown boys in its review of the

---

28 Dean John Dawson was appointed to serve as acting President in Shelburne's place, but he too was soon off to fight in the war. The aforementioned Professor Theophilus R. Eagles served as acting President—or maybe it was acting-acting President—until Dr. Charles Williams was appointed at the start of the 1919–1920 school year.

29 The conference now known as the Big 10—even though it now has more than ten members—was formed as the Western Conference in 1895. Being at numerical odds with its name is nothing new. The league included seven members at the time, including Illinois, Iowa, and Indiana (who joined in 1899). The league was commonly, though not officially, referred to as the Big Nine beginning at that point. Michigan pulled out of the conference from 1908 to 1917, dropping the number of league members to eight, but Ohio State joined in 1912, making it nine again. When Michigan returned, the league was up to 10 again, although that only lasted until 1946 when the University of Chicago deemphasized athletics and dropped out. Michigan State became the new tenth member in 1949.

contest: "The outstanding feature of the game was the work of the Bulldog quarter, captain Walker, and the stone wall defense of the Bulldog line."[30]

The Bulldogs followed the Auburn loss with a road trip to Sewanee, where they fell 18-0 on a rain-filled fall afternoon. Harden Field on the Sewanee campus was described as "a lake." Howard faithful believed the conditions favored Sewanee because the wetness curtailed Howard's "powerful overhead game," meaning its passing attack.[31]

No excuses were in order the next two weeks as Howard was pummeled by Alabama and Mississippi A&M, but Howard finally managed to break through for a victory over Morgan School, an academy in Lewisburg, TN, then tied the Hamilton Aggies, another prep school-like institution. That left the Bulldogs at 1-4-1 heading into the game against Birmingham Southern.

In short order, that contest had turned into a real rivalry, complete with all the trappings. Patrons of both schools filed into downtown Birmingham for rallies and dinners the night before that featured speechifying, singing, and organized cheers. At a Howard rally, a correspondent for *The Crimson* counted 31 speeches. He considered them all great but apparently being a listener of great stamina, was disappointed that several expected speakers did not orate as planned. The next morning parades led the faithful out to Rickwood Field in the eastern outskirts of Birmingham (near Ensley) before the 2 PM start. The crowds were estimated to be more than 6,000, massive by the standards of either of the combatants. A $1 tax was charged to see the contest. Newspaper accounts note that it (the tax) was not popular.

Birmingham Southern, which had fared better than Howard up until that point in the season, was rated the favorite by the local newspaper even though the Panthers had not played as difficult a schedule. Howard's Coach Dillon agreed with that sentiment and cooked up some special stuff for the contest. Howard had adopted the tight, single-wing-style offense under Dillon's reign and played a "straight" game—the term used for basic running plays—with very little passing. Against Southern, which

---

30 *Birmingham Age-Herald*, Oct. 5, 1919.
31 *The Crimson*, Oct. 17, 1919.

had a bigger line, Dillon employed "an unusual spread formation."[32] The newspapers likened the Howard spread to the "western style of play," although it is hardly certain that any Birmingham newspapermen of the day had ever seen a team from the West (meaning West Coast) at work.

The emphasis of the spread in Howard's upset victory suggests a great offensive explosion. In fact, Howard won the game 2–0, pinning Southern in its own end for several minutes before finally blocking a punt for a safety. The game ended with Southern trying a series of drop-kick field goals. Rules at the time did not cause the ball to change hands if a drop kick was missed, and it was not fourth down. So Southern attempted three of them—none of them close enough for three points, however, thus preserving Howard's triumph.

Dillon's first team wound up with a 3-5-2 record. The other victory was an 82–0 drubbing of Hamilton, the same team that Howard tied several weeks before. No explanations were offered in the press as to the sudden difference. The Bulldogs finished the season by tying Spring Hill Prep.

Walker earned postseason kudos by the bushel. The school yearbook records that he was "one of the finest quarterbacks in the South." Sulzby noted that he "never failed to distinguish himself and in every game Howard played, Walker was considered the best man on the field."[33]

Walker's skill set was considerable. He was a capable passer and ran the ball with speed, purpose, and strength. Most important, according to the vast majority of accounts, was his leadership and intelligence. When Howard pounded Central High in a preseason scrimmage, *The Crimson* noted that Walker "showed

---

[32] Willoughby dissertation. p. 70. The information comes from Willoughby's interview with Chester Dillon.
[33] Sulzby, *Towards a History of Samford University*. p. 427.

wonderful headwork and proved his worthiness as a field general."[34]

Walker's brilliance on the football field was well established, and he set about making a name in every other sport he could find for the rest of the year. He joined the Bulldog basketball team and quickly became a regular (if not always a starter) at guard. His buzzer-beating shot from the corner upended Mississippi A&M by a point in a game during that 1920 season. That spring, Walker was once again a key cog on the baseball field, playing short and hitting in the middle of the order, usually third. Walker was also the team's student manager, having nipped teammate Rupert Lindsey in a 33–28 vote by the student body (voter turnout for this vital post was not high). Dillon coached the team, so Walker's role wasn't as big as it had been in the recent past, when student captains ruled the roost. Still, it was here that he assumed some official coaching duties for the first time.

Howard went 14–8, taking three of four from Mississippi A&M and splitting a doubleheader with Illinois. Walker had a key hit in the 14th inning that led to an extra-inning triumph over Southern. Among the star players on the team was a pitcher named

---

[34] Positional terminology, and the correspondent's alleged knowledge of the same, is a regular stumbling block to researching games and players from long ago. The fact that Walker played during a time of transition can lead to even greater confusion. During Walker's first season, and possibly his second as well, he played quarterback in a T-formation offense that featured a direct snap handoff from the center, much like that used in modern football. Walker noted this himself when he switched his 1948 Wake Forest College team to the 'T.' Under Dillon, in Walker's third season, Howard went to the single wing, which, under most circumstances, uses a short center pass—much like the modern shotgun formation—to start the play. The blocking back position, about a yard behind the line, was often called the quarterback position by outsiders. The confusion is not surprising. The blocking back often called the signals because his position was closer to the line, thus affording the frontliners a better a chance of hearing him. But many teams, especially small colleges, couldn't afford the luxury of placing a skilled player at the blocking position. The player at that spot might play that role on certain plays, but for the most part the players who could run, throw, and kick, all the while running the offense, usually played the position that came to be known as the single-wing tailback. It seems likely that Walker played that position, although again, he is often referred to as "Howard's quarter" in the press of the day, even during his last two years.

King, who went by at least three different nicknames: Rat, Bud, and Big Boy. How many of these were bestowed by Walker is unknown.

Records of Walker's academic progress at Howard disappeared during war, transition (the school moved from East Lake to a less bucolic setting in southern Birmingham in 1957) and a campus fire in the 1930s that destroyed a number of records. Later events—Walker needed three or four years of part-time school at Elon before he could obtain a degree—suggest he was not an honor scholar, or perhaps even a regular student, during his Howard years. Of course, he missed at least half his second year at the school while sick, and he does not appear to have continued his education at the school after the first semester of his fourth year the 1920–1921.

Or at least he didn't continue it at Howard.

After the 1919–1920 school year, Walker embarked on what can only be described as a "tramp" career in which he played football for three different schools over the span of two seasons. Between the 1920–1921 football seasons, Walker also began his professional baseball career, joining the Wilson, NC, entry of the Virginia League for a full season in the spring/summer of 1921. The record is sketchy, but he likely played summer-league baseball, possibly for some pay, in a semiprofessional league a year or two before that.

Walker's football journey after 1920 began in Atlanta, although not as a hireling for any school based there. He showed up instead as the starting quarterback for a Wake Forest College team in town to face a powerful Georgia Tech club. The Tech team was still quite good even though it was the first bunch of Engineers (or Golden Tornadoes as they were then known) in more than a decade not coached by John Heisman.[35]

Even without Heisman at the helm, Tech was still a formidable foe and a big-time program with the numbers to prove it. On a blisteringly hot Atlanta afternoon, the Golden Tornadoes

---

35 Heisman, the future trophy's namesake, left Tech in 1919 after divorcing his wife. Because she chose to stay behind in Atlanta, Heisman, ever the gentlemen, decided to leave to save her from constant embarrassment. That's the legend anyway.

used four different elevens, subbed in and out at regular intervals, and ground the Baptists into a sweaty, heat-baked pulp. Wake, which played only fifteen players that day, held Tech scoreless for a quarter but then succumbed to the onslaught of fresh meat 44–0. Postgame reviews in several papers credit Walker with strong play despite the final score and Wake's obvious lack of offensive punch. He wasn't given a lot of help. Wake Forest College was not much of a club. The lone star was three-time Captain Harry Rabenhorst, a fine player whose primary claim to fame was the sensational, 98-yard punt he launched against NC State in a 1918 game.[36]

Perhaps because of the beating received, Walker's Wake career turned out to be a one-game affair. There is no record that he ever enrolled at the school or, for that matter, set foot upon the campus until years later. Because the one game played was in Atlanta, not far from Walker's Birmingham home, the intent may never have been to play more than that.

The week after the Wake-Tech game, Walker showed up at Howard again. School had already been in session for a week or so, but he was welcomed back with open arms—and more. Charles B. Williams, the school's newly appointed President, thought the news of Walker's second (or third) coming so significant that he announced it to faculty and the student body during the school's mandatory Friday chapel event. According to *The Crimson*, the announcement "caused quite an ovation and resulted in many cheers for Walker."[37] The spontaneous celebration over the reenrollment of a student of dubious scholastic intent and not entirely certain loyalties speaks to Walker's popularity as a person and to Howard's acute athletic desperation.

Under new Coach R.C. Marshall—Dillon had flown the coop after one year to coach at Oshkosh State Teacher's College—Howard had opened with a less-than-inspiring scoreless tie against the Morgan School. Auburn was up next, just two days after

---

36 A State player actually fumbled the kick at the end of the play, and Wake recovered it for a touchdown, making it one of the strangest plays in football history. Rabenhorst, a Louisiana native, later went on to some fame as the coach at Louisiana State University.

37 *The Crimson,* Sept. 1920.

Walker's arrival. Given that, the return of the one of the finest quarterbacks in school history seemed auspicious.

But not auspicious enough. Howard was humiliated in the first two games after Walker's return. Auburn blasted the Bulldogs 88–0. A week later, Centre College (in Kentucky) handed Howard the worst defeat in school history: 120–0. Centre was a national power at the time and on its way to an unbeaten season (see chapter 4), but still, that is quite a whipping. It is not clear whether Walker participated in either of those contests. Local coverage of the shellackings was non-existent.

Remarkably, Howard returned from the Centre debacle and beat Mercer College 33–13 the next week on a typically hot and humid day in Macon, GA. The following account of the game carried in several newspapers related that the main cause of Mercer's defeat was Walker's play: "The plucky little quarterback of the visitors handled the Alabama eleven in approved style, was ever on the alert, cool under fire and when carrying the ball not once did he fail to gain." Walker was injured in third quarter but returned to the field shortly thereafter. He ran for one Howard touchdown and passed for another.

The Bulldogs went 2–3 the rest of the way and finished 3–5–1. Football is a team game, but observers thought Howard's misfortunes were in spite of Walker's best efforts, not because of them. He scored two touchdowns in a win over Marion and passed for the lone score in a 21–7 loss to Mississippi College. In explaining Howard's narrow, 14–7 loss to archrival Birmingham Southern, *The Crimson* exonerated Walker with glowing prose:

> "In spite of the brilliant and untiring efforts of 'Peahead' Walker, one of Dixie's best little quarterbacks, Howard College went down to defeat before Birmingham Southern here last Saturday afternoon, 14–7. Walker gained ground, ran the team with superb generalship, played a great defensive game and scored Howard's lone touchdown, yet all his efforts were in vain. He could not direct the course of forward passes which fell in eager, waiting Panther

arms, and these passes scored both of Birmingham Southern's touchdowns, barely enough to win the game."[38]

Walker's excellent play had been anticipated. Previewing the contest in a position-by-position matchup, the *Birmingham Age-Herald* noted that Southern's three possible quarterbacks were promising but added that "they are incomparable to the great Walker."[39]

When the football season ended so did Walker's career at Howard. He was not on the basketball or baseball teams, a report on the prospects for the later noting the severe impact of his departure.

The end of his Howard experience may not have been the end of Walker's collegiate athletic career, however. Although his next athletic stop was professional baseball (see chapter 2), Walker was apparently engaged in some fashion as a member of the 1921, and maybe the 1922, Vanderbilt football team(s). Walker always claimed some Vanderbilt ties throughout his career and told would-be biographers that he played at Vanderbilt for the legendary Dan McGugin, although he readily admitted that his Commodore career was a "quickie bit."[40] Some Vanderbilt players and coaches, men who would be a part of Walker's career for years to come, allude to his participation as well. Future Duke Coach Wallace Wade was McGugin's crack defensive assistant. And future Clemson Coach Jess Neely was a star player there at the time.

Walker is not listed in Vanderbilt's official football records as a letterman in 1921 or 1922 (or any other year), but it would have been relatively easy for a player to get lost on the Commodore juggernauts of that day. Vanderbilt went 14–0-2 in those two years while barnstorming across the South and beyond. McGugin built a powerful program that at the time would have meant dozens of players arrayed into first-, second-, third-, fourth-, and maybe even fifth-strings that could be deployed in succession to wear out opponents. That was a big part of football at that time. Recall the tactics Auburn attempted to use on Howard during the Longwell

---

38 *The Crimson*, Nov. 25, 1920.
39 *Birmingham Age-Herald*, Nov. 18, 1920.
40 *Atlanta Constitution*, Jan. 4, 1969.

administration and what Georgia Tech did in fact do to Walker and Wake Forest in 1920. A coach directing a program like that scoured the landscape for all the players he could find, and players, looking for opportunities, gravitated to the big boys. Could one of the "best little quarterbacks in Dixie" have slipped onto the Vanderbilt roster for a game or two in either or both of those years? Perhaps.

If he did, he would have seen (and been part of) some of the best college football games of the time. In addition to all of the Southeastern powers of the day, Vanderbilt played two games at Texas and hosted one of Fielding Yost's great Michigan teams at Dudley Field in Nashville.[41] To prep his Southern-bred players for the 1922 matchup with Michigan, McGugin allegedly invoked some of the most stirring pregame rhetoric in the annals of college football history. Understanding that the Civil War's bitter end still lingered in the hearts of Southerners, McGugin pointed to a military cemetery across the road from Dudley Field and said, "Men, in that cemetery sleep your grandfathers." Then he turned and pointed toward the Michigan locker room. "And men, over there are the grandsons of the Damn Yankees who put them there."[42]

Great words to inspire a football team.

Or maybe to enlighten an aspiring young coach.

---

[41] McGugin was able to arrange the Michigan contest, which was a first at Dudley Field, in part because Yost was his brother-in-law.

[42] McGugin's speech is a well known part of Vanderbilt football lore. Less known: how many of McGugin's players knew the coach's relatives were officers in the Union Army during the Great Unpleasantness, 1861–65.

CHAPTER 2

A BASEBALL MAN

Peahead Walker's career in professional athletics, a long and fascinating march to fame (but not much fortune) in college and professional football, did not begin on the gridiron. It started instead on a baseball field in Wilson, NC. Walker, fresh out of college, which is not to say freshly *graduated* from college, signed on to play for the Wilson Bugs of the Class B Virginia League for the 1921 season.[1]

Exactly how Walker found his way to Wilson is unknown. The Bugs, like most minor league teams of the day, were not directly affiliated with a Major League club and depended upon the contacts of its managers and owners to scrape up talent. Those contacts could be diverse and the scraping widespread. It is not hard to imagine word of Walker's outstanding play at Howard College reaching Wilson's ears or him making his case by phone, telegram, or at a tryout. And it may be that Walker had already established some nonscholastic baseball bona fides even before arriving in Wilson. Long-time friend and coaching pal Herman Hickman suggests in *The Herman Hickman Reader*, a compendium of humorous tales and possibly true anecdotes, that Walker played summer baseball in West Virginia while still a collegian.[2]

---

[1] Professional baseball used a letter-based ranking system for its leagues from the 1920s in an effort to reduce the amount of interleague raiding that went on. The higher the letter, the bigger the league and the better paid the players (generally speaking). The official classification extended from Class AA (and later AAA) to Class F, although in point of fact hardly any leagues and teams ever played under the E or F classifications. The formal minor league hierarchy in place today, controlled by the managing Major League teams that own or pay some expenses for affiliates in their farm system, was unknown until the 1930s and was in a formative stage until long after World War II.

[2] Hickman, H., *The Herman Hickman Reader*. 1953, Simon & Schuster, New York, p. 11.

Placing Walker in West Virginia may just have been a literary device to place him in the clutches of a gun-toting mountaineer (one of the stories in the *Reader* involves that exact situation), or it may actually have been true. Hickman was not one to let facts get in the way of a good story. If he did play there, then it was likely for a semipro club of some description during one of the summers while he was enrolled at Howard. If Walker ventured as far afield as West Virginia for summer ball, it's hardly a stretch to imagine him in Wilson. It's all a guess until his Wilson days—either that or a Herman Hickman anecdote. Records of professional baseball were spotty during Walker's career; semipro rosters and statistics are all but nonexistent. Given that, what has to be said is that there is no obvious connection between Birmingham or Howard and Wilson or North Carolina other than the fact that Walker and Howard College teammate Lee Head (also from Birmingham) both showed up on the team at the same time. Whatever the reason, package or no, connected or otherwise, Peahead Walker saw a door opening in Wilson and, ball glove in hand, was more than happy to step through.

There's no written record of Walker's intentions as he began his professional baseball career, but in retrospect, all seems perfectly clear. He was embarking on a career as a professional ballplayer and all that professional ball entailed and required. It was not an easy life. The schedule was grueling, the travel rugged, and the potential rewards in no way certain. Major League Baseball was heading toward its Golden Age when Babe Ruth and others would create the first model for big-time, high-salaried professional athletes. But the game wasn't there yet, and even when it arrived the gilt often turned out to be meager. A few stars made out extremely well and some did okay, but most fell somewhere (and oftentimes far) short of that.

And that was in the Majors. The road to getting there, a labyrinth that passed through small leagues and small towns was an arduous path. Teams bought, sold, and jettisoned players like worn-out shoes. Player pay was usually better than the wages of common laborers, but it was nothing special—the prospects for employment eternally uncertain. If a player's performance diminished even slightly he could be gone. If a team's play and, hence, its attendance, declined, the payroll could be delayed, devalued, or disappear altogether. It was not uncommon for struggling teams to fold in midseason, leaving players high and dry.

Whether Peahead Walker (or most 22-year-olds for that matter) knew all this when he began his career is unknown, but he doubtless came to know it soon thereafter. As noted earlier, he is credited with leading a successful team revolt at a stop somewhere in his minor league career, stealing a manager's prosthesis and holding it hostage until salaries were paid..[3]

On another occasion, while playing for yet another awful squad, Walker's shenanigans didn't work out as well—as related in Hickman's book. With the team unpaid for a stretch of a month or so, Walker was allegedly forced to steal just to eat. Having made off with a couple of fat chickens from a nearby farm, Walker was confronted back at his base camp by a mountaineer with a squirrel rifle. With the "cold steel right at my forehead," Peahead related years later, the mountaineer asked him where he got the chickens. Peahead smiled beatifically but said nothing. The mountaineer, gun still at the ready, ordered Walker to eat the chickens right on the spot, feathers and all, leaving Walker purportedly to remark that "chicken don't taste very good that way."[4]

Minor league teams of the day were mostly independent operations that existed on the edge of fiscal survival. In small towns, there was often a civic component—buy a ticket, boost the town—that helped a bit. Some professional and semiprofessional teams even had booster clubs with regular dues and benefits (discount tickets, priority seating, etc.). In the town of New Bern, NC, the local volunteer fire department once "adopted" the team for a brief period of time, raising money at chicken dinners and the like and hosting players for firehouse meals on a regular basis. A counterweight to the benefits derived from the civic component was the fact that ownership tended to be in the hands of small local businessmen whose dreams were usually deeper than their

---

[3] This story was related in several interviews conducted by the author and is included in several interviews given by Walker during his coaching career. The story may or may not have been true, but what is most certainly true is that he never tired of telling it.

[4] Hickman, *Hickman Reader*, p. 12.

pockets. Period newspaper accounts of minor league start-ups are filled with pleas for help, notices of bake sales and barbecues, and assurances that new investors would soon be located. The strategy of actually "passing the hat"—taking up a collection during a game—was not unheard of. Indeed, it was the forerunner of actual admission.

The sums in play were meager of course—or at least meager to modern sensibilities. Tickets sold for twenty-five cents and less, and the price of a ticket was an important, much-debated item by both fans and league officials. Most of a team's income came from ticket sales. Concessions, investment/fundraising, and outright donations (the civic aspect again) provided the rest. In the lower minors, income from Major League affiliations provided big boosts, but that system did not come into widespread use until the mid-1930s. Teams in the Coastal Plain League (CPL), for example, where Walker managed from 1934–1939, received sums of $1,500 to $2,000 per season from Major League clubs in the late 1930s, when the league turned fully professional. The cash—enough to meet a team payroll for a month—guaranteed the Major League club first dibs on any talent uncovered.[5]

The sale of player contracts was another minor league money maker, the chief means of support for most clubs in the high minors.[6] Such talent sales, although occasionally available, were less lucrative in the lower minors. Walker himself appears to have been "assigned" by Wilson to Rochester of the AA—contract language for the sale of a player in that era—early in his career. He may have "sold" on other occasions as well. Later, while managing CPL teams, Walker sold off a few players himself, including one

---

[5] Gaunt, R.I., We Would Have Played Forever: A History of the Coastal Plain Baseball League. 1997. Durham, NC: Baseball America. p. 43.

[6] As an example, the Baltimore Orioles, who were then a minor league team, sold the rights to a promising young pitcher named George Herman Ruth (plus three other players) to the Boston Red Sox in 1914 for a large amount of cash. The exact amount is still disputed by historians today—bookkeeping and financial records were not a strength of most organizations at that time—but was said to be enough, by itself, to keep owner Jack Dunn in the black for at least three years.

reported transaction involving a hard-hitting catcher who was exchanged for a good hound dog and an assortment of groceries.[7]

Despite the creation of a classification system and the establishment of a governing body for minor league baseball, it was still possible for a larger team to just snatch up a good player, the offer of a much fatter contract trumping any feelings of loyalty or contracts, written or otherwise, in place with the lower-level teams. That was one of just several disasters that could wreck a team's season. Natural calamities, such as the rainout of a holiday doubleheader or the outbreak of a typhoid epidemic such as the one that forced the Rocky Mount, NC franchise to abandon a season in the early 1900s, could ruin a team. So could extended poor play, which would drive the fans away, killing both the gate and the donation business.

Myriad fiscal woes could inflict both collective and individual pain. Teams could fold, entire payrolls could be delayed, or players could be dropped individually as a cost-cutting measure. The player's lot was not a happy one when that happened. The young base baller could be put out of work miles from home with no immediate means of support. If he had saved some money he might be all right, but that was not the typical ball player's modus operandi—at least not by reputation. The professional ball player before World War II was viewed as a rough and ready man with proclivities toward an assortment of vices, not the least of which was heavy drinking and the expenditure of all available cash on that endeavor and various other "recreational activities" related to it. Ball players were not welcome in the nicer parts of town, and because of that, the nicer parts of town often didn't feel welcome at the ballpark. The issue reached a head in Tarboro, NC one year when young women working in the downtown area reported ball players "loitering" in the streets, trying to initiate conversations with them. Town leaders sought to undo some of this unseemliness by organizing a baseball dance where players could loiter and flirt with chaperones present.

The leaders of a Wilson team after Peahead's playing days worked hard to recruit a ball-playing preacher to the team, the

---

7 Kinston Free Press, July 28, 1937, p. 12, but probably not original to that source.

better to "attract women and children" to the games. The first part of the equation was successful. A preacher/player was found. Just how much the team's attendance improved was not recorded.[8]

Like most eastern North Carolina towns, Wilson already possessed a prominent baseball legacy when Walker's career began. Organized baseball had been played there since at least the 1890s on an assortment of increasingly formal fields and was quite popular. When Walker signed on with the Bugs in 1921, games were played at a field in north Wilson near the current Dick's Hot Dog stand, a local landmark that opened the year Walker arrived and when the team was peaking (and as of this writing still serves up the best hot dogs around—some 90 years later). Dick's was one of Peahead's favorite hangouts from his baseball days in Wilson and throughout his career at Wake Forest.

The Bugs were coming off a pennant-winning season. They nearly duplicated that feat in Walker's first year but lost the championship series to Richmond. Walker played a critical role in determining the outcome: his throwing error in the fourteenth inning in one of the games in that series allowed Richmond to score the winning run and go home with a victory in a marathon game that local baseball fans talked about for years. The play was not atypical for Walker in Wilson. An offensive-minded player throughout his career, he was, statistically at least, an unimpressive fielder. In back-to-back seasons as the Wilson's regular shortstop in 1922–1923, Walker made 97 errors, high even by the standards of that day and time, when equipment and field conditions made defensive precision more difficult than it is today.

Walker played more shortstop than anything during his minor league career. Fielding deficiencies aside—and Walker had several good years with the glove later in his career outside of Wilson—shortstop was a fitting post for a player noted for his intelligence and leadership. Shortstop was the standard station for a defensive captain and leader. Walker fit that bill but was valued as an effective man with the bat as well. During twelve-plus minor league seasons, he hit just under .300 and during the peak of his career hit in the top third of the order. He didn't have great power—

---

8 Utley, R.G., The Independent Carolina Baseball League, 1936–1930.

only four homers in five different seasons—but he was good for twenty-five to thirty extra base hits every year and rarely struck out. His speed and anticipation also made him a tough out on the bases.

These skills extended Walker's career, but life in the minors is the life of a nomad. During his thirteen-year professional career, Walker played baseball in twelve different cities in seven different leagues and in five different states stretching from North Carolina to New York to Illinois. Wanderlust was typical for a veteran minor leaguer—and an almost certain sign of an incurable dreamer and/or lover of the game.

Sad to say, Walker never made it to the Bigs. But Major League glory did come into view a time or two. After three solid seasons in Wilson, Walker was acquired by Rochester of the AA International League, the highest level outside of the majors at that time. In Rochester, Walker was surrounded by guys who had been major leaguers and some who would become one. Opponents included future big league pitching stars Lefty Grove and George Earnshaw. Teammates included Walter Beal, a pitcher on his way up to the Bigs and veteran Fred "Bonehead" Merkle, a former New York Giants' regular on his way down.[9]

The Rochester experience was invaluable and doubtless helped shape Walker's managerial, coaching, and scouting careers, but his play in AA was not inspiring. He hit just .224 in ninety-eight plate appearances while playing second base. The Tribe (Rochester would not acquire its famous Redwing nickname until

---

9 Merkle and his nickname hold a storied place in baseball lore. He earned the unfortunate moniker in a 1908 game against the Cubs when his baserunning error cost the Giants a midseason victory and, ultimately, the pennant. The mistake was bizarre to say the least. Merkle was on first when a teammate singled home the game-winning run in the bottom of the ninth with two outs. Believing the game was over, Merkle trotted into the Giants' dugout without touching second base. An alert Cubs' player—accounts vary as to which member of the fabled Tinkers-Evers-Chance infield did the job—saw what had happened, retrieved the ball, and touched second. Merkle was ruled out and the run disallowed. The game was called because of darkness. Months later, when the Giants and Cubs finished in a tie for first, the outcome of the suspended game became important. A playoff game was held in its stead, and the Cubs won it and went on to win the World Series.

1928) sent or sold him to Norfolk of the Virginia League, the same circuit from whence he came. He hit .311 for the Tars, but at the age of twenty-five, his career had peaked.

***

The next four years, as Walker was entering his late twenties and beginning his collegiate coaching career, were his best, even if he was too old to earn a big league look. He hit .328 with thirty doubles and fourteen stolen bases for Norfolk in 1925, .349 during a brief stint with the Parksley (Virginia) Spuds of the obscure Eastern Shore League in 1926, and then .326 back in Wilson later that same year. The 1925–1926 seasons may have been a turning point in Walker's career. His professional baseball contract card shows he (or his contract) with Norfolk was suspended at the start of the 1925 (the consequences of stealing a managerial prosthesis?) and then reinstated. In 1926, Norfolk sold him to Buffalo of the top-rung International League, a hopeful development until Buffalo sent him back to Norfolk (he never appeared in a game for Buffalo). He was then assigned under some unknown arrangement to Class D Parksley on the Chesapeake Bay and from there eventually reacquired by Wilson.

Walker slumped to .283 with the 1927 Wilson club, now called the Tobacconists, perhaps struggling as he made the move from coaching Atlantic Christian College to coaching Elon.[10] He rebounded with spectacular seasons in 1928 and 1929 with the

---

[10] Wilson's name changed in 1923 to the Tobacconists, or Tobs, in a tip of the hat to the king of local agriculture and industry—and a common minor league baseball name. Both the Danville, VA team and the team in nearby Greenville, NC were, at one time or another, named the Tobs.

York (Pennsylvania) White Roses[11] in the New York-Penn League where pitchers, perhaps, didn't know him as well.

Walker was a star and a thorn in the side of the Roses' opponents. He hit .338, a full-season career high, in 1928 and .329 in 1929 while playing short. Walker may have been acquired by York on the recommendation of Dave Robertson, a former NC State athlete who was player-manager for Norfolk in 1925 during Walker's excellent season there. Robertson, a two-time National League homerun champ (he hit twelve in both 1916 and 1917), was one of six former or future major leaguers on the York roster in 1928.

Walker turned thirty in 1929—too old for any serious Major League looks for a player still in Class B ball but too young to end a career for a man who loved the baseball life. So, Walker ground on, moving where he had to move, finding baseball work where he could. In 1930, he hit .274 for Bloomington and Decatur (both towns in Illinois) in the Three-I League. If the performance was mediocre, the experience at least gave Walker some useful material to draw upon later in life. Gerry Hogan, who played football for Walker in Montreal during Walker's Canadian Football League years (1951–1959), recalled the following memories about a pregame speech Walker made before taking his team to play an archrival in Hamilton, an industrial city just across Niagara Falls from Buffalo, NY:

---

11 Although the record is muddy, the York nickname almost certainly was derived from the War of the Roses, a dynastic struggle between rival families contending for the throne of England in the fifteenth century. The symbol of the House of York, one of the two principal contenders, was the white rose. The symbol for its rival, the House of Lancaster, was the red rose. A second War of the Roses erupted in 1908 when the baseball franchise in nearby Lancaster, PA changed its name from the Maroons to the Red Roses. The maneuver left York leaders incensed and led to a heated rivalry of several years that ended when the Lancaster franchise moved to New Jersey just before World War I. Just to add an exclamation point to the confusion, the York franchise moved to Lancaster in 1914 and changed its name from the White Roses to the Red Roses. The contretemps suggests there was greater familiarity with fifteenth century English history then than there is now. Source: *Lancaster History Society: The York-Lancaster Rivalry.*

> *He [Walker] always wanted us up for Hamilton—because they were always pretty good I guess—and it also seemed to piss him off that here we were in beautiful Montreal and there they were in Hamilton, a city kind of like Pittsburgh only not nearly as pretty, and he'd say things to try to fire us up like "I thought Bloomfield, Illinois as the armpit of the earth, but that was before I went to Hamilton. Come on boys we can't go up there and lose in place like that."*[12]

In 1931, after a year in the armpit, Walker split time with three clubs closer to home, starting the season with the Binghamton (New York) Triplets and finishing it with the Winston-Salem Twins. In Winston-Salem, Walker was reunited with Charles Bunn "Bunny" Hearn,[13] a teammate and manager during his first stint in Wilson. The older of the two, Charles Bunn was a Chapel Hill, NC native and a savvy baseball man who played, managed, and owned professional baseball teams during a career that lasted twenty-seven years. Overlapping that work were two stints as baseball coach at the University of North Carolina in his hometown. The second of those lasted from 1932 to 1946 and generally coincided with Walker's college coaching career. Hearn likely helped advance Walker's college work. Whether Walker could be described as a protégé isn't clear, but the two shared a sense of humorous irreverence as well as a flair for the dramatic. During his coaching days, as a memorable example, Hearn routinely bestowed

---

12 Gerry Hogan, interview with author.

13 In an astonishing coincidence, there were actually two pitchers named Bunny Hearn playing minor league (and, briefly in both cases, Major League) baseball during the 1920s and 30s. Walker's pal, Charles Bunny Hearn, aka Old Stuff, was thirteen years older than Elmer Lafayette "Bunny" Hearn. The two crossed paths in 1937 while the Bunn from Carolina was managing Tarboro in the CPL and the Bunn from Brooklyn was finishing up his playing career with the Goldsboro, NC team of that same league.

upon his players a "bouquet" of stinkweed[14] as they rounded third after jacking one out of the park.

For all intents and purposes Walker's playing career ended in 1932 with the Wilmington (North Carolina) Pirates of the Class B Piedmont League. He hit .248 in twenty-eight games. Among his teammates that year was Charles "Lefty" Briggs, the star of the first three baseball and basketball teams Walker coached at Elon. Walker made still briefer appearances as a player in both 1934 and 1935 while managing Snow Hill (North Carolina) of the newly formed Coastal Plain League. Walker was the team's designated professional as well as the field manager. In the early years of the league each team was allowed only one true pro. Teams split on bringing in an actual player or hiring a professional manager such as Walker or his old pal Hearn, who coached Kinston's 1934 team and later in Tarboro.

The CPL was formed between 1933 and 1934 from the ashes of the Virginia League. Civic boosters in several east-central North Carolina towns desired a more formal baseball league than what had sprung to life when the Virginia League died in 1928. Some towns had fielded teams in 1932 and 1933, playing a haphazard "exhibition" schedule. A loose organization of four town teams was formed in 1933. Additional structure was added during meetings in the winter of 1933–1934, and the league was expanded to six clubs: Kinston, Ayden, Tarboro, Greenville, New Bern, and Snow Hill (all in close proximity in eastern North Carolina). At its inception, the league was designed and designated as a semipro loop. The players were mostly collegians who received a small part-time stipend and possibly room and board to play summer ball. Each team was required to post a $250 bond against league expenses (mostly for umpires). Teams played five games a week. League-wide admission was set at thirty-five cents for reserved seating for men, twenty-five cents for women, and fifteen cents for

---

14 The term "stinkweed" can refer to any of several hardy field weeds but is mostly commonly associated with Pennycress, a noxious-smelling weed that grows wild throughout Eastern North America. That Hearn could find it so easily does not speak well for the quality of turf management in North Carolina during the 1930s. Hearn reputedly also pitched for a US all-star team that toured England and performed before sellout crowds that included the royal family.

children aged fifteen and under. Women were allowed into the grandstands, if they existed, for free. Blacks could get into the general admission part of the park (which meant standing up at many of the league's fields) for twenty-five cents. All other grandstand patrons had to cough up only 10 cents.[15]

As noted, each team was allowed one professional, and teams used their pro exemption strategically (and sometimes illegally, sneaking in extra pros under assumed names). Because of the nature of the league—the roster was made up of local boys (or pros in disguise) and whatever collegians a team could recruit—coaches with collegiate contacts and an understanding of the current "amateur" athletic pay system, men like Peahead Walker for instance, were quite valuable. Walker's pinch-hitting work and spot starts at third were of far less importance to the amusingly named Snow Hill Billies than his ability to lure talented collegians to the middle of nowhere for the summer. Walker's teams were heavily populated by Elon stars. Horace Mewborn, Paul Cheek, Paul Roy, Hal Tuck, and, later in Walker's career, Mike Briggs (brother of the aforementioned Lefty Briggs), all spent time in Billie Land. Not surprisingly, Hearn's Kinston team included six of his Tar Heel players as well as two University of Maryland players. The system—the very idea of a college-based league—was designed to reduce costs and entice fans by presenting well-known college stars from nearby on local fields. The marketing angle was logical—college baseball was a big deal at the time, and many of its best players were also college football stars—but the system was problematic right from the start, in large part because the "semiprofessional" aspect of the league was mostly fiction. Teams busted the budget right and left, paying extra to land top college stars. When the league switched to an all-professional format in 1937, several franchise owners breathed a sigh of relief, thinking (correctly as it turned out) that they'd save money with an all-professional team.[16]

The college-based league created other problems. During several Coastal seasons, the postseason playoffs barely came off at all because players drifted away to return to college duties, which

---

15 Kinston Free Press, May 11, 1934.
16 Gaunt, We Could Have Played Forever.

often included fall football practice. The same sort of scheduling problems also plagued clubs at the start of the season as spring terms were ending. Hearn brought in one UNC battery to open the season in 1934, all the while warning them they couldn't stay.[17]

The regulars showed up a few days later after their exams were over. A year later, Hearn had to scramble to find a catcher after the player he thought was coming, one "Love of Maryland," telegraphed that he'd received a summer employment offer in Washington, DC. He'd been invited to work at the Department of Agriculture . . . and to play on the Department's baseball team.[18]

The collegiate coach's ability to lure players to their Coastal teams had some reciprocal benefits of course. The players picked up the invaluable experience of a sixty-one, and later as many as ninety-game schedule, plus some handy pocket cash. And the coach became an authority on talent in the area. It was during Walker's CPL coaching years that he became loosely affiliated with the New York Yankees' organization as a low-level scout, sometimes called a "bird dog" because the primary role was "pointing" higher-level scouts to prospects. After the Carolina League turned professional in 1937, Snow Hill fell under the Yankees' official umbrella and received some players from the organization as Major League clubs began the building of the modern farm system. During his Wake Forest years, Walker served a dual role, derived from his Snow Hill days, scouting baseball players for both the Yankees and Wake Forest. Wake Forest, like most successful college programs of that time, had an unofficial (and clandestine) working arrangement with the Yankees, who placed a few players on the Deacon roster and may have paid for their scholarships. Gene Hooks, a star third baseman for the Deacons during the late 1940s and later the college's Director of Athletics, said he was recruited by Walker for the baseball team after returning to his hometown of Rocky Mount after the war. Some other players Walker scouted wound up signing professional contracts with the Yankees. "He got me a scholarship, which was good since that was about the only offer I had," said Hooks. "But I don't know if that

---

17 Kinston Free Press, May 24, 1934.
18 Kinston Free Press, May 21, 1935.

meant [Walker] thought more or less of me [since he also could have signed Hooks to a pro contract]."[19]

The age of professional connections and farm systems was a few years away when the CPL kicked off its 1934 season with all-American fanfare. Teams held parades and picnics. The opening day celebration in Kinston, which was celebrating the opening of Grainger Field behind the new high school, included music by the 113th Field Artillery Band and a first-pitch ceremony featuring Mayor Dal Wooten. Wooten broke with the tradition of the day, which called for the first-pitch dignitary flip one from his front-row seat to the home team's catcher, and moved out to the mound for a regular toss. The ball landed wide and 10 to 12 feet short, the 71-year-old Wooten having lost a little something since his days as a town team pitcher during the 1880s. Wooten took some ribbing for it too. When quizzed on the matter by a Kinston newspaperman, he replied with a tale from his heroic days a youthful pitcher. He'd once walked 12 miles to nearby LaGrange to pitch a game, and then walked 12 miles back. "Did I win the game?" replied the Mayor to an obvious question. "Certainly I won. Imagine anything like that in this day and time."

When the warm feelings and nostalgia-evoking events subsided, reality set in and the 1934 CPL season quickly ran amok. The Tarboro entry was clearly inferior to the rest, winning just two of its first twenty-three games. Gate receipts in that town dried up faster than the region's sandy soil during drought season. The team was on the brink of folding.

Tarboro leaders pushed for a change in the league's format. They wanted to move to a split season, with the first-half winner taking on the second-half champ. The proposed format would have wiped the slates clean in mid-July, theoretically rekindling some interest in Tarboro's chances over the last six weeks of the season. The rules in place at the beginning of the season gave Tarboro no hope. They called for the first- and second-place teams to engage in a best-of-five series for the title at season's end. Officials of the other five teams, especially the top three (Kinston, Ayden, and Snow Hill), were understandably reluctant to give up advantages

---

19 Gene Hooks, interview with author.

already gained. On the other hand, losing a franchise in the middle of the year would not be a positive step, especially for a fledgling league. So a compromise was reached. Beginning on July 11, Tarboro's record was "adjusted" to 11-15, the same as fifth-place New Bern. The Tars would have a chance—or more importantly appear to have a chance—at a playoff spot.

That bit of fiction was overshadowed a few weeks later when Greenville Manager Milton Harrington lodged a protest with league officials. Harrington's beef: Kinston had used a professional pitcher named Gus Fletcher in several games. The charge, if true, violated two rules: Kinston would have had two pros on its rosters, Fletcher and the aforementioned Charles Hearn, and Kinston would have been using a pro to pitch. The league rules stipulated that the pros could be field players only—not pitchers. The critical issue was whether Fletcher, one of Hearn's UNC imports, was actually a professional. At a heated league meeting, Greenville presented evidence that Fletcher had signed a contract and pitched in two games with the all-professional Winston-Salem Pirates in 1933. Kinston's Hearn countered a telegram from a former Winston-Salem manager claiming that although Fletcher had worked out with Winston-Salem he hadn't signed a contract. League officials found the evidence weighted against Kinston's case and ruled Fletcher ineligible. Kinston officials pleaded for mercy: not only was the offense trivial, if it existed at all, but bringing it to light would ruin Fletcher as a collegian. With regard to the latter concern, some may have been thinking of a similar tragedy some years before when Olympian Jim Thorpe's amateur status was spoiled by his dalliance with summer league baseball in North Carolina.[20]

Fletcher, who despite all the hoopla surrounding his eligibility, wasn't that good a pitcher, did see his college career end following the revelation of his professional status. There is no

---

20 Thorpe, who went to college at Carlisle Indian Academy in Pennsylvania, played baseball for Rocky Mount (some historians believe part of his career was spent in Winston-Salem, the same town that brought Fletcher down) in the summers of 1909 and 1910. Like collegians in the CPL three decades later, Thorpe was paid. Estimates of his fees ranged from $2 to $35 per game, according to the *New York Times* and other sources. Thorpe's real mistake, however, was not playing under an assumed name as most collegians at that time did.

record that he ever played professional baseball, so the scandal—or perhaps just a lack of talent—apparently ended any potential pro career as well.

More important than Fletcher's personal tragedy—or at least more important at that moment—was the fact that the league ruling called on Kinston to forfeit eight games in which Fletcher had appeared and the Eagles had won, four each against Greenville and New Bern. The Kinston club, in first place at the time, plummeted to fifth. Other teams shifted upward in the upheaval.

Kinston's feathers were ruffled, but the Eagles bucked up and vowed to reclaim their rightful position. Hearn immediately "resigned" to take the presidency of the club, the president's office cynically moving to the dugout for the rest of the season. A real playing pro, second baseman Virgil Weathers, took his place as the team's pro. Weathers was summoned from Asheville of the Piedmont League and lent a strong bat to the Kinston lineup. In his first game, Weathers slugged a double, a triple, and a sacrifice and drove in all the runs as Kinston beat Walker's Snow Hill squad 3–2.

In a fit of provincial pique, the Kinston newspaper began running two sets of CPL standings, one showing the "games actually played," the other the "official" standings. With Weathers blasting the ball and Hearn relaying signs and signals from the president's office, Kinston went on a tear, moving further atop the games actually played ledger and gaining ground on the leaders in the official book. Snow Hill, which gained nothing from the Fletcher fiasco because it didn't play Kinston until after he was banished, took the brunt of the Eagles' wrath. The unbalanced CPL schedule didn't pit Kinston against its tiny neighbor to the northeast until the first half of the season was over. In the second half, Kinston and Snow Hill played regularly, and Kinston got the best of it. Pitcher Orlin "Lefty" Rogers, who was 16–2 for Kinston in 1934 before getting a brief trial with the Washington Senators the following season, was especially tough on the Billies. Kinston managed to regain a playoff spot, overcoming the forfeits to regain first place by season's end. A bitter playoff series against Greenville didn't go the Eagles way, however.

As for Walker, his Snow Hill team, decimated by the Kinston steamroller, finished fifth. His second Snow Hill team, still laden with Elon stars, opened play in a brand-new ballpark nestled on a flat plain along a bend of the Contentnea Creek, which flows through the middle of town. The little ballpark's setting was unique and was remembered as being quite pleasant (it no longer exists; the site is apparently now a creekside pine glen), although it was something less than perfect in terms of functionality. The positioning next to a large creek made flooding a regular problem—Snow Hill couldn't play home games for almost two weeks at the start of the 1938 season—and access was difficult even when dry. In one anecdotal tale, the Greenville team arrived at the park after a powerful summer thunderstorm to find it so far underwater that the young boys of the town were using it as a swimming pool. "We got us a town pool and all," one of the boys reportedly told the Greenville players, "but this here is deeper." Parking was separated from the park by the creek, which could be surmounted only by a footbridge. At least one set of visiting team's equipment was soaked when a player carrying the team's gear fell into the creek. The fences at the field were also closer than normal, making the fly-ball homerun a Snow Hill specialty—and helping hitters such as Harry Soufas and Joe Bistroff place among the league's homerun leaders on a regular basis. A more neutral flaw was a noticeable ridge running from behind second base well out into right field. It was finally regraded prior to the 1940 season. Walker's second team made the playoffs but lost to Kinston in a first-round series.[21]

The new Williamston, NC franchise hired Walker away from Snow Hill for the 1936 season. The Martins (named for the town's home county, not the bird) dominated the regular season but lost to Kinston in the playoffs, the key game a 13–12 loss marred by arguments and ejections. Such melees were relatively common occurrences. The umpiring was at least as bad as the baseball—probably worse. When the 1936 CPL season began, the league had a five-man umpiring staff. With the league having grown to eight teams, that meant that three of the four games each night were staffed by one umpire, and in case of illness or injury, all four

---

21 Gaunt, We Could Have Played Forever.

would be. This arrangement had the distinct advantage of being cheap, but almost everyone considered it unsatisfactory. Additional umpires were hired before the end of the season, but given their lack of training, that was not especially satisfactory either.

Umpires were the butt of jokes in the CPL, as elsewhere, but because of familiarity they were sometimes the target of slander and innuendo as well. At a mid-1930s game in Kinston, a fan reportedly hollered at umpire Jim Putnam after a disputed call, "Hey, Jim: Is that the way they call 'em at Dix Hill?" The reference was to the Dorothea Dix Institute for the Mentally Ill, which was situated atop a hilly piece of land in Raleigh and may have sounded to many like a generic taunt. An umpire from Dix Hill? That's a good one. But in Putnam's case it was also the truth. The ump had been a patient there on several occasions, although never for long and not because he was crazy but simply as a necessity. As he explained in an interview with the *Kinston Free Press*, "There is nothing wrong with my head. I went to Dix Hill three, or four, or maybe five times because North Carolina is dry and I had to drink the bad liquor one gets in the state or go without liquor. One time I went (to Dix Hill) only after drinking beer."[22] The fact that umpire Putnam was merely an alcoholic who was occasionally poisoned by moonshine must have been very reassuring to Coastal Plains baseball fans.

There is some circumstantial evidence that Walker may have used umpiring incompetence as a marketing tool. In three different seasons Walker was ejected from games on July 4th. Usually doubleheaders, these games were well-attended affairs. The chance to spice them up a bit would have appealed to Walker, who early on his career grasped that what he was doing was, at its soul, entertainment. One of Walker's best remembered pregame football speeches at Wake Forest—he wasn't big on that tactic—implored his players to go out and put on a good show, and during his professional coaching days in Canada, his tactical choices were at least partly based on what the fans would like. That the fans would have liked a good manager-umpire argument would have been obvious to Walker. Showmanship or real live kookiness,

---

22 Kinston Free Press, July 5, 1935.

Walker was revered in the league as a character. He was selected three straight years to manage one of the squads in the league's annual all-star game. Twice, the managers were picked by a vote of the fans. The third time, Walker seems to have landed the job by acclamation.

Facing increased financial pressure, the CPL moved to an all-professional format in 1937. Ironically, paying pros turned out to be cheaper than paying collegians and—although it never quite shed its seat-of-the-pants style of operations—the league prospered. In its defense, minor league baseball rules of the day were complex and confusing. The CPL, like most leagues, used a player rating system that divided players into categories based on their professional baseball service time. There were "class men" (players with three-plus pro seasons), "limited service" players (1 to 3 years in pro ball), and "rookies" (players new to pro ball). Teams could play as many rookies as they wanted, but the number of class men and limited service players was limited. The idea was to balance play and pay by requiring each team to use a mix, but the system ran afoul of the lax recordkeeping of the time. The service time of a particular player could be very hard to track, and figuring out his true identity wasn't much easier. That was important because playing under an assumed name was a long-standing baseball tradition. It had allowed players to dodge an assortment of rules and other predicaments almost since the game's nineteenth-century beginnings and was still going strong into the late 1930s.

Two-thirds the way through the 1938 CPL season, charges and countercharges of roster abuse nearly caused the league to collapse. Although the initial charges were leveled against Williamston, fingers were eventually pointed in almost every direction. Threatened with mass forfeits (as many as forty games in the case of Williamston), several teams threatened to pull out. A compromise, similar to the one that rescued the 1934 season, was eventually accepted. The standings were once again adjusted, with four teams being dropped into a tie for fifth but all teams retaining (or in some cases gaining) a winning record. The result encompassed both penalties for alleged cheaters and a tip of the hat toward the retention of pennant interest in all the league's towns.

Walker, who had returned to Snow Hill in 1937, was not heavily implicated in the roster scandal. The Billies actually gained a game in the standings adjustment, a sign that they had received a (relatively) clean bill of health. Whether that suggests that Walker ran a clean program or was simply better at coming up with assumed names and unknown "rookies" is impossible to say. There is no doubt that he already had considerable skill and experience as a recruiter of athletic talent and all that came along with that talent. His Snow Hill teams were dotted with former collegiate stars, cast-offs from other pro leagues, and players obtained from the Yankees in Snow Hill's new farm system connection. His college football connections helped him corral at least two important players. Infielder Harry Soufas of Wilson had gone to UNC to play football, but his mother forced him to quit after he received a disfiguring facial injury during his freshman season. Walker, who knew about Soufas from Soufas's days as a high school star in Wilson, contacted and persuaded him to hitchhike 30 miles to Snow Hill for a tryout. He made the team and was a key cog in Snow Hill's 1937 championship run. Walker's football connections also landed hard-hitting catcher "Big" Jim Tatum. Tatum was a football player at UNC from 1933 to 1935, at which point he joined the staff of former UNC Coach Carl Snavely at Cornell. Walker and Snavely were long-time acquaintances, possibly even friends, and he kept up with Tatum through that connection as well as through his contacts with Bunn Hearn, Tatum's baseball coach at UNC. Tatum had been an excellent baseball player in college and high school. There is no record of his playing professionally until Walker brought him to the CPL in 1937. Tatum, later the football coach at UNC, Maryland, and Oklahoma, played well for the Billies until he was traded to the Serpents[23] in mid-July.

---

23 The Tarboro franchise changed nicknames almost as frequently as socks. The club was known as the Tars, the Tartars, the Combs, the Goobers, the Bunnies, and finally, by 1937, the Serpents. The last two names were coined largely because of the team's managers at the time: Bunn Hearn led the team in 1936, hence the Bunnies, and the following season he was replaced by Fred "Snake" Henry, hence the Serpents.

Tarboro received a hard-hitting catcher for the stretch run. The other side of the transaction is foggy. According to one of Walker's ever-changing banquet-circuit stories, the Billies received an odd combination of goods that may have included Confederate money, sore-armed pitchers, chickens, mules, hunting dogs, and possibly a sack of peanuts in exchange for Tatum. All seem plausible, but peanuts—because there is evidence that Walker was already trading in that commodity—seem especially so. They were, and are, a staple crop of the area, and in a July 1936 letter to Walker, Elon President L.E. Smith thanked him for the bag of peanuts he had sent him.[24]

Whatever the price of the trade, Tatum was back in Billie colors the following year either because the CPL was short on long-term contracts or because peanuts/mules/chickens had been found wanting. Walker clearly had an affinity for Tatum, perhaps because of their connections and perhaps because he thought he knew how to get a little more out of him. Tatum, like many free-swinging sluggers, had a weakness for the curve ball. In fact, according to Walker's after-the-fact stories, he could barely hit the curve at all. The savvy Walker could, however, steal most team's signs, so with Walker managing, Tatum wouldn't get fooled as often. In theory this would mean more hits for Tatum. Statistics don't bear out the alleged fruits of the Walker-Tatum pairing (he hit about as well for Walker as he did in Tarboro), but CPL stats are obscure, and the sign-stealing tale is certainly the better story.

It's likely that Walker found the CPL's informality quite comfortable. The absence of hard-and-fast rules would have magnified his abilities with regard to player recruitment, and the lack of structure would have allowed him to come and go as he pleased—an important consideration for any manager trying to work in some baseball (playing and coaching) around a collegiate coaching schedule. Although the CPL started ever earlier as it marched to full-fledged professionalism, it never began before May 1 while Walker was involved. And unless a team went deep into the playoffs, the season was over by September. This fit Walker's schedule—though just barely. There were years when the overlap

---

24 L.E. Smith Papers, Elon College Archive.

was too much. In 1937, as Snow Hill was prepping for the title series, Walker felt compelled to go to Wake Forest, about an hour's drive away, to begin supervising his first football team there. Outfielder Dwight Wall took over the managing duties, although Walker kept a hand in. He returned to watch at least one game of the championship series against Tarboro (which was without Tatum, who left to join Carl Snavely's football staff at Cornell). The contest, held in Snow Hill, was a legendary affair, attended by nearly 3,000 fans—more than three times the town's total population at that time. Extra bleachers were constructed to accommodate the throng. Walker's enthusiasm for managing in the bush leagues suggests a clear love for the game. It's doubtful he was well paid for his trouble, although CPL crowds were known, on occasion, to take up special collections for much-beloved managers.

Snow Hill's 1937 playoff run helped the team meet all its 1937 obligations as well as finish paying some holdover bills from years past. But finances were an issue at every CPL stop. In 1935, the owners of the franchise in Kinston, among the largest CPL towns, implored fans through stories in the local newspaper to attend the playoffs so the club could retire $1,500 in back salaries owed to the manager and players.

One funding ploy created more trouble than it was worth—at least initially. A drive to open the door to Sunday games spurred controversy in CPL country, just as it had elsewhere in North Carolina and throughout the South. Bible Belters thought such an enterprise was wrong, especially where professional players were involved, and a North Carolina law written in the early 1900s banned baseball games on Sunday. Civil disobedience broke out in some places, most notably in Greensboro, NC, where the police chief handed out citations—but nothing—to players and team officials of the Greensboro Patriots for a violation in the late 1920s. Because of the need to draw fans, the weekend games, played when other work was halted, were important. Many towns observed a Wednesday afternoon holiday to give locals an opportunity to attend that day's game, a majority of the fields not being lit at that time. The number of lighted fields increased in the second half of the 1930s—the CPL didn't play any lighted games until 1938—but pressure for more weekend play, driven by financial necessity, continued to increase.

During his first years out of Howard, the Walkers were constantly on the move. Peahead spent three summers in Wilson with the baseball team there, but because the Bugs/Tobs played in the Virginia League, a fair amount of time was spent on the road in the commonwealth. Records show that the Walkers' first son, Douglas Clyde Jr., was actually born in Virginia.[25]

It would be surprising, to say the least, for Walker's bride to have followed him on the road, especially in the latter stages of pregnancy. No other known circumstance explains the Virginia birth, however. Family members could shed no light on the matter.

The Walkers' second son, Walter Hill, was born three years later in Alabama, in the winter. As noted earlier, Walker may have enrolled/played football in Nashville, TN (and other points) in the fall and winter of 1921 and 1922. In the baseball offseasons from 1922 through 1926 he apparently coached and taught at high schools in Georgia, Alabama, and possibly Florida. In an interview near the end of his life, Walker confirmed coaching stops at West Point, GA and Roanoke, AL. A would-be biographer, relating a story about Walker's early teaching, also placed him in De Funiak Springs, FL, an old panhandle town northeast of Pensacola. In that brief account of his early coaching and teaching career, a skeptical friend of Walker's who Walker had been being hired to coach—and to teach chemistry and physics—asked what he knew about chemistry and physics. Walker's reply: "Just a little more than them high school boys do. And really I don't have to know nothing. I got the book and they don't."[26]

Walker apparently taught at West Point, GA, on the Alabama border, from 1923 to 1924. School system records show he taught at Handley High School in Roanoke, AL, about an hour north and west of West Point, from 1924 through 1926. Minutes from the Roanoke school board show that Walker was approved as a coach and teacher at a salary (for nine months) for the 1925–

---

[25] The particular record in question is the 1930 census form, which is based on information supplied by Walker or his wife. It records D.C. as having been born in Virginia in 1922 but does not stipulate exactly where.

[26] *Old Gold & Black*, March 12, 1951.

1926 school year. Walter Hill Walker may have been born in Roanoke. As with his older brother, the records are not specific.

The effect of Walker's early wandering—especially unusual for that day and age—on his family is unknown, although his first marriage did end in divorce. Walker and his first wife Carolyne, a Birmingham gal five years his junior, married in 1921.

With regard to his career, Walker's athletic-based "worldliness" was an essential part of his later success. He knew his way around half the country, built up contacts left and right, and was, in the sporting world, a known commodity. Although the exact connections are not certain, there's little doubt that Walker's exploits as a professional baseball player in Wilson and in the Virginia League led to his first collegiate coaching appointment in 1926 at Wilson's tiny Atlantic Christian College (ACC). The school, founded by the Disciples of Christ denomination out of the leftovers of a defunct Christian academy, was still very much in its formative years when Walker got the nod as its new athletics man. The school was especially new when it came to intercollegiate sports. ACC did not form an athletic association or a faculty athletic committee until 1922. The first athletics director, Wake Forest grad E.M. Pearce, was hired in 1923 after school officials tacked an extra $5 per year onto student fees for the purposes of creating a program. Football, or something akin to it, began in 1920. ACC's first team beat Wilson High School and some other prep teams. When the "Little Christians" went to play the "Big Christians" of Elon College, however, the result was different. Elon won a Thanksgiving Day game by a score of 88–0. The teams of 1921–1924, writes ACC historian William Jerry McLean, "followed the pattern" established by that team, not willingly it is hoped.[27]

The 1921 team won three games but lost four. The next three teams lost all their games, or all but one, many by extravagant margins. Coach John Barclay reversed the course in 1925 when he built a rugged defense that a *Raleigh News & Observer* writer (who probably had not seen ACC play) thought "the equal of any small college team in the state." The Little Christians

---

27 McLean, W.J., *Barton College, Our Century*. 2002. Wilson, NC: Barton College.

won four out of seven games and beat Elon and the brand-new Catawba College in Salisbury, N.C.

So the cupboard was not bare when Walker arrived, but it wasn't overflowing either. Following a pattern he was to repeat on three other occasions, Walker turned things around by quickly injecting new talent into his lineup. "The announcement of Coach Walker's hiring in August reportedly caused a large number of promising athletes to register at ACC in September," wrote ACC historian W.J. McLean. That several of them were from Walker's home state of Alabama, including a three-sport regular named Jones, suggests this was not entirely a spontaneous reaction.

Walker was late reporting to ACC for the start of football practice, probably because he was obligated to finish his D League season at Parksley. It's possible he was also on the recruiting trail. Whatever the case, holdovers John Barclay and George Blauvelt held down the coaching fort until Walker showed back up about 10 days into practice—the team already rounding into shape.

ACC was sharp right out of the box. Halfback C.D. (or in some listings C.B.) Riggan ran a punt back fifty yards for the game's only touchdown as ACC topped its old tormentor Elon 6-0. The team beat Blackstone Academy 50-0, nipped Guilford 6-0, beat a couple of military unit teams, and defeated Catawba. ACC suffered its only defeat in midseason, falling to Jack Boylin's tough High Point College club 7-0.[28] A player named Mulligan, described in newspaper accounts of the day as "midget fullback," scored the game's only touchdown. The loss was disappointing but the 6-1 record was a school best by a long shot and it was enough to gain for ACC the unofficial Little Six football championship.[29]

Walker's first collegiate football season showed his penchant for both organization and innovation. The Christians were much improved because they had better players. But they were also on the cutting edge tactically. In a swamping of a Fort Bragg team late in the season, Walker's team completed 17 of 23 passes—an almost unheard of rate and quantity for that day and age—and gained 290 yards in the process.

---

[28] See chapter 3 for more on Boylin and his work at High Point.
[29] The Little Six refers to an informal group of smaller colleges in North Carolina. It is discussed more thoroughly in chapter 3.

As was expected of any small college athletics man of that era, Walker moved directly from the gridiron to the hardwood. His basketball experience was more limited, but with a heaping dose of crossover talent—five of the six basketball regulars were also football starters—Walker proceeded to win his second Little Six championship in as many tries. He very nearly made it a sweep in baseball season, but the Christians faded late in the year. Walker's top pitcher on his lone ACC baseball team was Roma Boykin. Five years later, Boykin and Walker were reunited as minor league teammates in Winston-Salem.

Walker's work at ACC is more remarkable when considered in context. The tiny school—the total enrollment in the mid-1920s just slid past 200—had next to no athletic tradition before Walker arrived. And it had only a poor tradition afterward, which, as fate would have it, turned out to be the following year.

Buoyed by recommendations from some of his baseball buddies, Walker resigned the ACC post in the summer of 1927 to take a (slightly) bigger and better job at Elon. ACC hired Edward Tweddale, the coach at Eureka (Kansas) College, to replace Walker. Alas, Tweddale's arrival "proved that dedication and hard work could not replace experience and talent in assuring success on the gridiron."[30]

Tweddale was replaced after one season by Mark Anthony, an ex-Georgia star. The ACC team was renamed the Bulldogs because of Anthony's connections to the University of Georgia. No matter what they were called, Anthony's teams were terrible, the squad seemingly having fallen "under a jinx."[31] From 1928 to 1930, ACC went 4–18 in football. In 1931, the school elected to drop the sport altogether. Perhaps the post-Walker demise is a testament to his abilities. Perhaps not.

Walker's work at ACC put him on his eventual career track as a collegiate football coach. But during—and for a long time after—his ACC days, the idea of a baseball career did not fade. Walker was still dreaming of the diamond well into his Wake Forest coaching days. When Casey Stengel landed the New York Yankees' managing job in 1949 and then received a raise in 1950 for winning

---

30 MacLean, W.J., *Barton: Our Century*. 2002. p. 53
31 Ibid.

a World Series, *Winston-Salem Journal* sportswriter Frank Spencer said that the news could be tough for Walker because he knew firsthand that Walker had always wanted the job.[32]

Of course, Walker might have been joking when he told Spencer of his dreams of managing the Yanks.

Then again, maybe not.

---

[32] Winston-Salem Journal, Oct. 7, 1949.

CHAPTER 3

ELON: BIRTHPLACE OF A COACH

September 1927 was a hectic time for Peahead Walker. He left the Wilson baseball club at the end of August, just as the season was ending, packed up his wife Carolyne and two young sons, and installed them in a house on East College Avenue in downtown Elon sometime around September 4. Then, as fast as he could, he set about assembling some football hopefuls for his very first Elon team.

It was a daunting task. There was little time before the opening game and much uncertainty with regard to the roster he'd be inheriting. Would any veterans from Elon's awful 1926 team return? Did Walker even want them back? Even if some players had deliberately tanked it during the 1926 season, as was commonly thought, protesting the school's decision to move away from professional coaching, it was still clear that the Elon talent pool was not overflowing.

Walker had some inkling of what he was (or was not) inheriting because his Atlantic Christian team played (and defeated) Elon the year before. But since being hired in May he'd spent most of his time on assorted minor league baseball fields in the Coastal Plain League, which made both keeping in touch with veteran players and rounding up new ones, difficult. In the prime of his baseball career, Walker played a full 120-game season with Wilson in 1927. There is no sign he took any significant time off to recruit athletes for his new school.

But he did what he could, reaching out to friends and family to fill key positions.

Sometime after his hiring was approved, Walker contacted his younger brother Zachary Taylor Walker Jr., a whiz of a quarterback and a pretty good baseball outfielder, and persuaded him to come play for him at Elon. Little brother Zac was a little long in the tooth as college students go. In the fall of 1927, he was 24, had already attended North Georgia College for a semester or so, and was back home in Ensley working. But he was willing and, in those laxer days, plenty eligible—i.e., he was breathing and of approximate college age. That and the fact that he was a pretty fair ball player was good enough for his older brother. And thus Zac Walker became Peahead's first Elon recruit. Better still, he brought some friends with him too.

At Peahead's urgent, perhaps even desperate, request, Zac gathered four or five football-playing pals to make the journey with him. Zachary T. Walker III, Zac's son and Peahead's nephew, says his father managed to get his hands on a used automobile and then enlisted the aid of his future teammates in preparing it for the trip. The prospective Elonites rounded up every spare tire they could get their hands on and lashed them to the sides of the car. The combination of the poor roads and even poorer tires of that day meant they'd need all the rubber they could get their hands on for the roughly 500-mile trip from Ensley to Elon. "They stopped overnight three or four times," said Zac Walker III. "They all slept in the car, or under it. It's hard to imagine anyone doing that today."[1]

The intrepid Alabamans wound up as the core of Walker's first couple of football teams at Elon, and the start of an Alabama talent pipeline that was never really turned off during Walker's career. Zac Walker, all 5'7" and 130 pounds of him, wasn't any bigger than his older brother the coach. But he had inherited the family speed and some of Peahead's sports savvy. By all accounts, he was the team's fastest runner and was quickly made its quarterback. Other 'Bama boys filled the critical positions on Walker's early team. Paul "Hans" Waggoner started one game at tackle for Elon before moving to end and then fullback as Coach Walker shifted his newfound pawns on the fly. Birmingham native Louie Ziegler started at end and quickly became one of Zac Walker's regular passing targets. He and Waggoner handled the flanking position's critical defensive responsibilities, lending some stability

---

[1] Zac Walker III, interview with author.

to Walker's first few squads.[2] Two other Alabama refugees, Robert Hardy and Roland "Smitty" Smith, started on the line for the 1927 club and went on to be elected captains for the 1928 and 1929 seasons, respectively. Waggoner, Ziegler, Hardy, and Smith probably came up with Zac Walker in the car, piled in amongst all the spare tires. Another Deep South recruit, Joseph "Shorty" Cook from Roanoke, AL, arrived a few weeks into the season and soon nailed down a spot at halfback. Peahead Walker coached high school ball in Roanoke for a year early in his career, and may have still had some ties there.

So much for the first recruiting class. Walker did inherit a little material. H.H. "Hard-Boiled" Branner was, as his nickname suggests, a rugged end from New Jersey. E.W. "Mac" McAuley was a useful linemen who had played every quarter of the 1926 season, a feat of hardiness unusual in those days. Building around those players, Walker began the work of cobbling together a team, the first step in a decade-long project to rebuild the program.

The athletic history of Elon College probably began with a 1900 baseball game against Guilford, a school in nearby Greensboro that was destined to become an archrival. The two schools played twice that year. Guilford, which had fielded a team for several years, took advantage of the fledging Christians, winning the two games by a combined score of 70–6.

Undaunted, the Christian program grew. Tennis was added soon afterward and was followed by track and basketball. Intercollegiate football began in 1909, but football as an informal, intramural sport began even before the first baseball game, probably in 1895 with a game between the residents of a dorm and the denizens of a nearby boarding house (apparently an intense rivalry). A local seamstress was engaged to create some uniforms. Handbills recruiting players to school teams of that period called for able-bodied young men with at least six inches of hair. This was no fashion statement but a feeble stab at safety. A robust head of hair provided some padding for heads, both on the receiving and

---

[2] Ends in this age of football were often the best players on the team. They played key roles as blockers on the flank on offense and were essential in limiting end runs on defense.

the giving end of cranial blows. It was a useful possession in the days before the invention of the football helmet.[3]

Whether from the thrill of near-mortal (and on occasion indeed mortal) combat or just the buzz (pun intended) surrounding a new sport, football did generate excitement at Elon, as it already had across the country. And, just like everywhere else, with the excitement came debate.

Opinion of the day was split on the subject of football. Many just found it entertaining, of course. But among those who gave it a little thought, there was a division: some considering it to be sophomoric and others profound. The Elon community was of two minds as well, but interest in the game grew rapidly and became a part of the social fabric, as could be noted by the fact that an unknown college author (probably a student) found football a suitable topic for parody as far back as the 1890s. The "Football Commandments," modeled on the more famous set brought down from Sinai, was published for campus consumption: "Thou shalt have no other game before thee," it began. "Thou shalt show mercy unto all of those who are knocked senseless," it continued, "six days shalt thou practice and get thyself in readiness, for ye know not when ye will be tested upon other grounds . . . " and so on.[4]

Negative attention to the game and the violence and corruption that accompanied it set a national tide in motion. School after school gave into pressure and banned the game. Elon followed the trend, banning football in 1910, or one year after the school's first-ever intercollegiate team swung into action. Coached and led on the field by "Reddi" Rowe, who is described in the journals of the time as a professional baseball player, Elon's first football team won four of the five games it played against an odd lot of opponents (a seminary, two high schools, a military academy, and a YMCA team). That success was marred by the fact that Rowe, who also served as the team's quarterback, twice sent his charges into action after being forbidden to do so by the administration.

---

[3] Stokes, D.T., *Elon College: Its History and Traditions*. 1982. Elon, NC: Elon College Alumni Association. p. 65. The long hair story comes from an interview Stokes conducted with 1895 grad S.M. Smith.

[4] This verse is cited by James Waggoner in his 1989 book *The Fighting Christians* (Elon, NC: Elon College Athletic Department).

The wily Rowe performed an end run around the administrative prohibition, having the players show up to play at the appointed time and place by "coincidence." They were just there to play football—not represent Elon.

Rowe was canned for insubordination, and, presaging a later migration, next showed up as a coach at Wake Forest. The point was made, however: at Elon, football would *not* become the dog-wagging tail. At least not yet.

The ban lasted until 1919. When football did return it was on a more formal and institutional basis. Games and practices were held on a new multipurpose field complete with a wooden grandstand and on land on the southwest corner of campus. It was named Comer Field, after "Uncle Pinkie" Comer, a long-time custodian/servant to college leaders. Among his various tasks over the years was taking care of the athletic fields.

The school also school hired a University of Pittsburgh footballer named Frank Corboy, its first "professional" coach by most measures. Corboy enjoyed modest success during his tenure (1920–1925), including a 20–0 victory over Guilford in 1922 that drove supporters of the Maroon and Gold into a frenzy. Their wild postgame celebration included torching the ancient municipal jail in downtown Elon.[5]

In his seminal Elon College history *Elon College: Its History and Traditions*, Durwood T. Stokes reports that student enthusiasm "remained high" during Corboy's coaching reign. But such progress as the school made wasn't sufficient to keep Corboy's attention. He resigned in 1925 to enter private business.

The timing of Corboy's departure was unfortunate. The college was just cranking up a massive building campaign designed to rebuild and expand the campus in the wake of the 1923 fire that very nearly decimated everything. Spending on capital projects made cost cutting elsewhere a must, so school leaders chose not to replace Corboy. Instead, philosophy Professor A.R. Van Cleave was assigned to coach the football team, and English Professor William M. Jay was handed the basketball and baseball reins. The

---

5 By the time the students got around to burning it down, the jail was long out of use. Elon police used the jail in nearby Gibsonville on the rare occasion the constables there actually needed to incarcerate someone.

savings—something less than $2,000 a year because the school had to hire a part-time athletic director at $400 a year to handle scheduling and the like—proved to be no bargain. Van Cleave, who had some prior experience as a football coach at Union Christian College, slogged through what remains one of the most dismal seasons in Elon's long athletic history. The Elon gridders went 0–10 and scored just two touchdowns all season. James Waggoner's history of Elon athletics attributes the hideous season to injuries and a tough schedule (which included Wake, State, Davidson, Duke, and Georgetown).[6] Stokes's history, meanwhile, suggests Elon's rather veteran squad—Van Cleave inherited fourteen lettermen from the 1925 team—stumbled along on purpose, a passive-aggressive protest against the hiring of second-rate coach.

"This [hiring Van Cleave] was an unpopular move with the athletes, especially the football players," wrote Stokes.[7]

Van Cleave's abilities, or lack thereof, probably played a role. He looked the part of a philosophy professor—photographs from the time show a very dour, serious-looking man—and seemed intent on being one whether he was in the classroom or on the field. When the team stumbled out of the gate, losing its first four games by a combined count of 79-0, Van Cleave assembled the squad and all interested students and made an impassioned plea for the players to try harder, including practicing more dutifully and diligently—on their own. It was deplorable, Van Cleave said, his rhetoric soaring, that an Elon coach apparently had to be a "mule driver." His policy, Van Cleave affirmed, was to simply to oversee the mules as they drove themselves. He'd truck no other role.[8]

Suitably inspired the week of Van Cleave's stirring oratory, Elon went out and scored its first touchdown of the season in a 13-6 loss at Georgetown. The momentum didn't last, however. As noted, the season ended at 0-10 with just thirteen points recorded. When summing up the dismal season, Stokes wrote that, "whether intentionally or not, after the change was made [the hiring of Van Cleave], Elon lost every one of its games."[9]

---

6 Waggoner, The Fighting Christians. p. 47.
7 Stokes, *Elon College*. p. 233.
8 *Associated Press*, Oct. 19, 1926.
9 Stokes, Elon College.

Except for baseball, the rest of Elon's athletic work wasn't much better. So although the 1926 season was difficult, it did put Elon back in the business of using professional coaches. At the Trustees' meeting in May 1927, President William Allen Harper reported to the Board of Trustees that he had recommended Walker, a professional ball player, to coach the three major sports at Elon and that the alumni and faculty were pleased with the recommendation. The *Maroon & Gold*, the Elon student newspaper, confirmed the view.

Walker's job description included a light teaching load, some administrative work in the area of admissions and recruitment, and, theoretically at least, responsibility for campus recreation. Student recreation and fitness were, after all, the point, philosophically speaking, of intercollegiate athletics. The whole man (or woman—Elon was a co-ed school) must be sound of body as well as mind. Elon addressed this need in fits and starts. In the 1890s, the third floor of the administration building was fitted out in crude fashion with some gymnastic equipment. Students in charge of the project persuaded a local blacksmith to make some gymnastic implements, which a local upholsterer covered with a protective leather coat. A climbing pole was attached to a wall and a cannon ball—an essential for any workout—was dutifully procured. A new gym, or rather an actual gym, was erected in 1913. College officials believed it to be among the finest in the state at that time.

Walker's new job included many facets, but those that did not involve coaching an intercollegiate team may have received short shrift. A regular feature of the graduate manager of athletics' report to the Board of Trustees during the first few years of Walker's career at Elon was his concern over the lack of attention paid to the gymnasium program, meaning exercise, etc., for regular students.

Regardless of how hard he worked in the gym or classroom, there can be no doubt that Walker was a busy man at Elon. He taught physical education, coached three sports, managed athletics (including setting up schedules, etc.), continued to peruse his professional baseball dream . . . and was a student again.

Walker spent the better part of five years at college or postsecondary school after his graduation from Ensley High but did not receive a degree from Howard College or any of the other colleges he may or may not have attended while plying the semi-amateur football/baseball trade. So soon after he was hired at Elon as coach and teacher, he also enrolled as a student. Full records of Walker's scholastic career at Elon no longer exist. It does appear that he was what would now be considered a part-time student, and it is clear that he did graduate in the class of 1931 with a Bachelor of Arts in Education. His grade point average was eighty-five percent. A musty grade book inside the Elon archives shows a grade of ninety percent for Walker in an Old Testament class in 1929.

It's unclear whether Walker's schooling was a job perk. His $2,400 per year starting salary, however, was on par with all but the most senior professors and instructors at the school. His predecessors in the pure coaching field at Elon worked for much smaller amounts. Elon was certainly expecting plenty of work for the money. And in the critical sport of football, at least, there was much to do.

Although accounts of the early practices strike an optimistic tone, the first game of the season, and of Walker's Elon career, was the disaster that might have been expected. NC State overwhelmed Elon 39–0. The Wolfpack—or Red Terrors as they were sometimes known back then—outweighed Walker's men by twenty to thirty pounds per dude. Elon stayed reasonably close for three quarters, but the size advantage was just too much. State ran away with the contest in fourth quarter.

Elon came home battered and bruised. Lacerations to the head of Garnett Bock, the starting right halfback, knocked him out for most of the season and prevented him from earning a letter. Branner may have been hard-boiled as his nickname suggested, but he wasn't tough enough to play the next couple games after suffering an unspecified leg injury against State. At least two other first-game starters were knocked out as well, meaning Walker had to shuffle a lineup he'd thrown together just as Elon lined up against what appeared to be its toughest foe of the season: Wake Forest.

The Baptists—or the Deacons as they were just beginning to be called—were closing in on their football apex to that point. They were coming off four straight winning seasons, the first three under Hank Gerrity, the school's all-time winningest coach (by percentage), and had bludgeoned Elon in the last two meetings between the schools. The 1926 game against the folding Christians was a 53–0 Wake rout. The year before when presumably Elon tried a bit harder, Wake had won 65–0. A speedy halfback named Murray Greason was the Deacons' star in that rout.

The 1927 game didn't look like much of a match, but Elon, playing with unexpected fire, battled the Deacons to a 0–0 tie. Wake Forest supporters found the game boring—for Elon it was anything but. The team was greeted by a full-blown pep rally upon its return from Wake Forest replete with bonfire and several rounds of enthusiastic oratory. A euphoria reigned among the players as well. Halfback Daronce Daniels was said to have slurped up an entire bowl of gravy at the postgame meal before realizing that it wasn't the traditional first-course soup, and Branner was so excited by the result that he borrowed a professor's car to drive to Elon to make a phone call home to let his folks know about the team's success (this despite the fact that he had been out with an injury). Branner, his leg apparently feeling much better, then dashed back to campus on foot to rejoin his celebrating teammates as fast as possible. Not long after, he ran back to town to retrieve the borrowed car.[10]

Wake's Baldwin gave Walker full credit for the rather astonishing turnaround. "The teams which play the fighting Christians this season may expect to find a different team from that which has represented Elon in the past," said the Wake Forest coach. Walker, he said, had imbued "a fighting sprit" in the Christians that had not been apparent in past Elon clubs (especially not in 1926).[11]

One week after playing Wake to a tie, Elon was drubbed by Davidson 27–0. The following week Walker notched his first Elon victory when his team stopped budding archrival Guilford College 31–13. Despite still missing several starters, the Christians got an

---

10 *Maroon & Gold*, Oct. 9, 1927.
11 Ibid.

early jump on the outmanned Quakers and never let up. Elon scored in the first quarter after the teams exchanged fumbles. Then Hans Waggoner's long interception return set up another touchdown early in the second. The rout was on.

A big and surprisingly rugged High Point Panther team beat Elon the following week 6–0. The Christians followed that by beating tiny Lynchburg (Virginia) College on Armistice Day in Lynchburg by a 19–0 count. It was a pyrrhic victory: Zac Walker suffered a knee injury late in the game that ended his season.

Playing without Walker, Zeigler, McCauley, Bock, and several others, Elon dropped a 13–7 heartbreaker to unbeaten Emory and Henry in November and then closed its first season with a dramatic 7–6 victory over Lenoir-Rhyne. So a 3-5-1 finish. Nothing brilliant of course, but the team was competitive and vastly improved compared to recent editions.

A few weeks later, the team was feted at the home of the Reverend and Mrs. Foster with a postseason oyster dinner, the three courses of which consisted of "new" oysters, fried oysters, and oyster stew. A few days after that it was on to a lettermen's banquet at the YWCA Hall near campus. The buffet supper at the latter was catered by Elon's Domestic Science Department. The event included a smattering of guests in addition to the players receiving their letters or monograms (there was a distinction between the two: letters were more prestigious).

It's possible that it was at this ceremony that Zac Walker received a handsome maroon sweater onto which was stitched a golden E. The garment's existence was unknown until 2008 when an Elon grad named Mary Stevenson contacted school officials with an odd request: could they help her find the descendants of Zac Walker, class of 1930? She had a sweater she wanted to give them.

Stevenson, as it turned out, had been Zac's girlfriend at some point during his Elon career. He "won" the sweater for a daring deed on the field—Stevenson recalled that it was for scoring the first touchdown in a homecoming game—but had it made in Stevenson's size, not his. The romance didn't last, but the sweater did. Seventy-plus years after the fact Stevenson donated the memento to Zac's son, who in turn, donated it to the school's archives.[12]

Most of the guests at the season-ending banquet were faculty with official roles to play, but two were not: W.G. Stoner, a member of the Alumni Athletic Committee, and W.E. Lowe, who was noted simply as a local Elon fan. Their presence, at what otherwise sounds like a rather quaint event, suggests intercollegiate athletics was already something more than just good physical exercise for the student body at dear old Elon. Although Elon had no formal booster club at this time, it's clear that throughout his tenure there, Walker had the backing, spiritual and otherwise, of alumni and similar types who wanted to see the school's sports teams prosper. Among those alumni friends were faculty members such as L.E. Smith, Elon's President from 1931–1957. Smith played football during the infancy of the sport at Elon and viewed athletics as critical to the school's marketing efforts and to its general well-being.

The names of other helping alumni hands (or those belonging to the "fans" category such as the aforementioned Lowe) are lost to the mists of time, but evidence of their work still exists. As early as 1929, the Faculty Athletic Committee launched a special investigation into money "donated for the alleged support of Athletics at Elon by a few friends of the college."[13] The Committee was certain that the money was specifically going towards the "hiring" of athletes—meaning scholarship in today's terms—and did not think it was a good idea because it would reflect poorly on the college and likely lead to player jealousy. The Committee perceived the idea as antithetical to the Elon way.

The Committee had no doubt that Peahead Walker was involved in the unsavory practice. The money was being donated to someone at the college, but the Faculty Athletic Committee, which monitored the athletic budget down to the penny, was in the dark. "We have no knowledge of (the donations)," the report read. And, it noted, there really could be only one person on campus who did.

"We believe coach Walker has knowledge of some of these transactions," the Committee wrote in its May 1929 report to the

---

12 Zac Walker III, interview with author.
13 Elon College Faculty Athletic Committee Minutes, August 1929, Elon Archives.

Trustees, "and failed to tell the (faculty athletic) committee all that he knew."[14]

The Committee demanded a full report of the Alumni Athletic Council's activities for the past two years and asked that Coach Walker's "election" to his teaching/coaching post be tabled until he provided a satisfactory explanation as to just what was going on.[15]

Walker played all the angles while building a talent pipeline for Elon athletics. He used some alumni/friend money to pay players directly, and he also wrote some "promissory" checks under the assumption that they could be easily cashed. Most were. But not all. At the end of Walker's first season, Business Manager T.C. Amick, who was also a Math Professor at the school, complained in an official report to the President and Trustees in May 1928 about problems in collecting room, board, and tuition from some athletes:

> *During the later part of the fall Semester, when the Business Manager was trying to collect some bills, he was informed by certain students that they had been promised by certain persons connected with the college that there would be no bills for them to pay, that they were to have all expenses paid because they were athletes. The Business Manager promptly notified these same students that he would hold them responsible for their bills, that no person or persons had been authorized by the college to make an offer to 'athletes' and that the college did not recognize any such agreement.*[16]

He went on to note the following:

---

14 Ibid.
15 The teaching faculty of the college was elected, or reelected, on an annual basis by an oversight board, usually the Trustees. Few positions included real tenure, and long-term contracts were rare. Among the draws when Walker left Elon for Wake Forest College in 1937 was the fact that he was, for the first time in his life, offered a multiyear contract. He worked his entire Elon career on a year-to-year basis.
16 "Report of the Business Manager to the Administratrive Committee of the Board of Trustees of Elon College," May 1928. Elon College Archives.

> *Some of these bills are yet unpaid and probably never will be paid. The Business Manager is reliably informed that the board bills for these men at the Young Men's club have not been paid (either). The Business Manager has in his possession letters from the fall semester students implicating certain persons connected with the college in this work (i.e., the practice of promising to cover expenses for athletes). For the protection of the college and for the good name of the college, and for the financial good of the college, the Business Manager asks {the Board of Trustees} to stamp out this practice and put athletics on a high order and give coaches and all concerned to understand that Elon College maintains athletics for the sole purpose of the physical training and the sport of her students and that she does not provide a coach to train a lot of hired athletes who are of little or no credit to the college or themselves.*[17]

Professor Amick's tirade doesn't name Walker directly—he was either too polite for that or thought the covert hints made the situation sound more dire—but there can be little doubt as to who the "certain person(s)" were. Elon was, at this point, a school with a one-man athletic staff.

Nonetheless, Walker's reelection as coach was never actually held up, and there's no record (other than a rather lukewarm endorsement by the Faculty Athletic Committee in 1929) that suggests he was ever sanctioned in any way. The practice of awarding athletic scholarships—which is, in essence, precisely what Amick was talking about—does seem to have disappeared for a few years and probably led to some rather tough years on the field for Elon. Those were bumps in the road, but it all fell Walker's way in the end. Walker (with the assistance of President Smith) presided over Elon's full-fledged jump into the athletic scholarship waters.

Basketball was the diminutive Walker's weakest sport as a player, but he was still charged with coaching Elon's team. So he jumped into that venture with his usual verve. His first team was led by a gifted player named Dan Long Newman. Newman, who was nicknamed "Hawkeye" because of his sharp shooting—the left-

---

17 Ibid.

handed hook was his specialty—was well known around Elon even before his basketball success because of his famous family's long ties to the school.

John Urquhart Newman, Dan Long Newman's father, was one of the original faculty members at Elon and taught Greek, Latin, Hebrew, and Bible studies at the school for fifty years—from the college's inception until 1940. His wife, Patty Beal Long, was also a teacher—they met while both were at Antioch College in Ohio—but enjoyed a far more remarkable career as a homemaker. The Newmans had five children, the first four of whom were born deaf. Patty Newman taught them all to speak and read lips so they would "look, act and talk like any normal child." Why, she asked in a feature article on her life, published in the January 1946 issue of *Coronet* magazine, "should her children's affliction be made obvious?"[18]

Controversial and unorthodox today, Patty Newman's homeschooling met with great success—at least by her standards. All her children sailed along. Her oldest daughter enjoyed a brief career as a teacher before marrying and settling down with an Alabama lawyer; the Newmans' second daughter, Lila, was a superb painter and art scholar who directed Elon's art department for nearly forty years; and the two boys, John Urquhart Jr. (aka J.U.) and Joseph, both had successful professional careers as well: the former was a journalist and publisher, the latter a dentist.

All four children attended Elon ahead of Dan Long, J.U. preceding the baby of the family as a sports star. A 1914 graduate, J.U. was known by his somewhat insensitive classmates as "Dummy" Newman. Dummy was captain and leading scorer on Elon's 1914 state basketball champion. He also was a useful third baseman on the three Elon baseball teams. Dan Long Newman trailed his siblings by several years and was not deaf. And he could shoot the hook.

In addition to Newman, who also played a little football at Elon, Walker's first hoopsters included Thomas Hamrick of Leaksville, NC; Zac Walker; baseballers "Lefty" Briggs and his brother Howard, Paul Caddell, and Earl Sims; and a lone senior,

---

18 Coronet, January 1946 edition. p. 94-98.

C.J. "Tobe" Crutchfield. Those seven received postseason letters. The relatively low number of lettermen was connected to the playing rules of the day, which limited substitutions. Players could reenter a game just once (twice after 1934), and some leagues limited the number of subs allowed, further reducing possible rotations. Walker's first team finished 9–12, the first of four straight sub-.500 basketball teams he coached.

A cold and mediocre winter gave way to a warm and promising spring, brightened by the superb talent Walker had inherited on the baseball field. In addition to Lefty Briggs, a fine pitcher already under contract with the Greensboro Patriots, a local minor league club (rules regarding professional contracts and college eligibility were obviously different in those days), Elon had another excellent pitcher in Vernon "Daddy" Fowler and a host of fine hitters. The best was third baseman Red Smith, a new addition who led the team with a .441 average. But Carroll Clark, Earl "Squire" Sims, and Howard Briggs, Lefty's brother, could stroke it too. The defense was ruled by catcher Dave Shepherd, who's nickname, "Old Reliable," speaks to his chief attributes. A fine student, Shepherd was elected president of the college's student senate for the 1928–1929 school year. He later went on to become a preacher and a high official in the United Church of Christ. He was the first of many men of the cloth who would enjoy, or perhaps endure, Walker's oft-profane coaching vocabulary.

Elon ran roughshod over the opposition, giving up just three runs a game while averaging 11. Only once all season did Elon score less than six in a game, but once was enough to ruin an otherwise perfect season.

On April 7 at Wake Forest, Deacon lefthander Tom Lanning limited the hard-hitting Christians to just five hits and let only one runner get as far as second base. It was just barely enough. With Fowler pitching just as well for Elon, Wake managed only three hits and pushed just two runners to second. One of them made it home. Wake's E.B. Lassiter drew a one-out walk in the fourth and then scored ahead of Joe Clayton's double, the game's only extra base hit.

The outcome didn't seem especially momentous at the time but certainly did by the end of the season. It was the only blemish on a 17–1 record. The Christians would come that close to baseball perfection just one other time—in 1939—when Horace "Horse" Hendrickson's team went 20–1.

A footnote to Elon's near-perfect season: the Christians almost began the campaign with a defeat, although it might not have counted in the official records. To get his charges a little early competition, Walker lined up a game against the Greensboro Patriots, the team that had his ace pitcher Lefty Briggs under contract and which was coached by Charlie Carroll, Elon's baseball coach the year before.

The Patriots were part of the old Piedmont League, a class C league. Although the team became a part of the St. Louis Cardinals' mammoth farm system a few years later, it was apparently not affiliated directly with any major league team in 1928. Those arrangements were much less formal than today's major-minor connections. The Tigers owned some of the players on the team, but most were local fill-ins who played for fun or perhaps in the hopes of attracting some higher-level professional attention.

In the exhibition game at Greensboro's Cone Park, a field owned by a local mill, Carroll's boys lit into the collegians early. They jumped to a 3–0 lead after just two innings and looked like they had increased it a few frames later when a Patriot outfielder slugged one over the centerfield fence with two out and two aboard. But Walker noticed that a runner had missed second while rounding the bases, and, despite the fact that it was just an exhibition, appealed the play. The umps upheld his appeal, keeping the lead at 3–0.

That might have been enough, but Carroll pulled his regulars soon thereafter—it was a practice game after all—so he could see some of his new guys in action. Elon and Walker, meanwhile, were playing for keeps. The Christians rallied against the subs, scoring five in the ninth to win 13–8.

Modern readers may wonder how Walker's first baseball team fared in the postseason. The answer is not at all. There was no postseason for the Christians then or at the end of any other season Walker coached at Elon (nor for any other team as far that goes). When a season ended it ended—no matter the record. That was actually good news for Walker in this case. It was April and he had some baseball to play.

***

As Walker's second season of football began, hope sprang eternal, but his team suffered from the same lack of talent and depth as his first team. Gone were several valuable holdovers that Walker had inherited—Branner, Red Jones, and E.H. McAuley among them—and several members of the Alabama brigade were gone as well, most notably "Hans" Waggoner, who was a no-show when the semester started. Indeed, only five regulars from the 1927 squad were on hand the first week of practice. The Christians were inexperienced and small. Walker decried having to play "a midget backfield," which was led by the 135-pound Zac Walker.[19]

The relative merits of midgetry in the game of football was soon demonstrated. NC State blasted the Christians 57–0 in the season opener. A week later Davidson won 52–0.

Elon's next match was against the newly minted squad from Catawba College and offered more possibilities for success. Catawba was just three years removed from its historic physical relocation from Newton, NC to Salisbury, and although an athletic association was formed less than forty-eight hours after the move officially took place in 1925—Catawba students had, like students everywhere, caught the football bug—the school's soon-to-be-formidable athletic tradition was still in its infancy in 1928. Everything at Catawba was in its infancy. Football games took place in a setting that can only be called quaint. The space where the games were played was surrounded by a pasture on the edge of campus. David Faust, who served for more than two decades as the school's faculty athletic representative, collected an entrance fee (between $1 and $2) from those on hand in exchange for a ribbon that paying patrons pinned to their lapels. Faust wasn't ensconced in a booth or at a gate—there wasn't one because there was no wall or fence. Instead, he milled about on the sidelines,

---

[19] The Maroon and Gold. Sept. 29, 1928.

looking for folks without ribbons. By game's end he had several hundred dollars worth of "gate receipts" in his pocket.

Green and amateurish as the operation may have been, Catawba's football team was still more than Walker's men could handle on that particular afternoon. Catawba jumped out to an early lead, surrendered Elon's first points of the season, and held on for a 13–12 victory that ended with Elon holding the ball just two yards short of the end zone. Walker's club was now 0–3.

The season appeared to be slipping away. The players clearly were. Kenzie Dofflemeyer, a second-year back who lettered with the 1927 team, and "Brownie" Boyd, a backfield starter in the opener, both withdrew from school. Boyd never returned. Others left. The roster melted away.

Short on bodies, Walker issued a call for volunteers. Several new recruits reported to practice, led by some familiar faces, including baseball players Lefty Briggs, Earl Sims, and Fred Caddell. H.T. Effird, a 1927 regular and letterman, was approached about a return but couldn't get out of his academic requirements, a euphemism, perhaps, for academic ineligibility.

Effird eventually made an actual game appearance. The hijacked baseball players never did. Briggs, who was perhaps the finest baseball player ever to play for Walker at Elon, didn't even make it past the first week of practice. His daughter Charlesana Briggs Burea said that when her father told the story of his football career in later years, it was a tale of ceaseless woe. Walker all but twisted Brigg's arm (presumably not his left one) to get him to come out, he claimed, and then gave him a pair of ill-fitting cleats that brutalized his feet. The first couple days of football work were so awful that Briggs didn't return for a third.

"They had to carry him off the field one day," said Briggs Burea. "He said he felt like he'd been hit by a train."

When Walker asked where Briggs was on day three, a teammate joked that he'd gone to Greensboro to see about buying some life insurance. Walker countered that he was a lightweight and had no guts. Briggs heard about this and sent a letter to

Walker that according to his daughter said the following: "What guts I *do* have are sore!"[20]

The influx of new recruits stimulated some renewed hope and interest in the team. But to no immediate avail. Richmond pounded the Christians 34–0 in the next tilt, which was played at Greensboro's fancy new War Memorial Stadium. Elon made a big deal out of it. The college chartered a special train from Elon to the station near the stadium to carry students and other interested parties safely and conveniently to the new park.

None of Elon's new players got into the fray, and as subsequent events would reveal, it probably wouldn't have made any difference if they had. The special train, which had helped swell attendance to close to 2,000, chugged back to Elon carrying a disconsolate bunch of passengers.

The following week, Elon dropped a 7–0 decision to Guilford, the eventual conference champs. A loss to High Point followed that dropped the Christians to 0–6, but a glimmer of hope emerged from the game. The Christians fell behind 13–0, but with freshman fullback Pete Williams running ball with power and finesse, Elon began to move the ball a bit, demonstrating some promise for the future.

The sixth straight defeat was an all-time record for Walker but ended the following week in what could probably best be described as a bizarre contest, if only because it found Elon trading in its team bus and North Carolina road map for a train trip to south Florida to play the University of Miami. The long road trip marked the first time Elon had traveled beyond South Carolina or Virginia to play a football game. How it came to be scheduled is unknown, although some educated speculation is possible. First, Miami was brand new. The college was founded in 1925 in the midst of the great south Florida real estate boom. It added intercollegiate football in 1926, and its early schedules were a crazy patchwork of teams from all compass points—including, even, some to the south, no easy feat for a team based in Miami.[21] Second, Walker was never averse to scheduling a few games in exotic locales, Miami being a special favorite. Wake Forest

---

20 Charles Briggs Burea, interview with author.
21 Miami opened the 1928 season by pounding the University of Havana 62–0.

continued to visit Miami under Walker's reign, and on occasion he vacationed there.

No matter how much Walker may have enjoyed the trip, the main point was to play—and hopefully win—a football game. To the surprise of almost all involved, Elon did just that, upending the Bucklets—Miami's nickname at the time—22–18.[22] The Christians fell behind 12–0 early but used a pass play out of their punting alignment to power a scoring drive that cut the lead to 12–7. When Miami scored in the third quarter, however, "with all their first-string men putting out not all they had" into the contest, things looked bleak.[23] Time was running out, and apparently Miami was good enough to win even if part of the starting team just went through the motions. But trailing 18–7 in the fourth quarter, Elon rallied without benefit of its still moribund offense. First, Zeigler intercepted a pass and ran it back some 40 yards for a touchdown. Minutes later, the newly activated Effird came crashing through the line to block a kick—diving quickly on the ball for the winning score.

Elon finished the season on the rise as Williams began to assert himself. Although the Christians were blasted by Emory & Henry 37–0 the week after returning from Miami but closed the season with a 26–6 pasting of Lenoir-Rhyne on Thanksgiving Day at Elon. The offense, so inept for most of the season (shut out six times with just 59 total points), sprung to life in the finale. Zeigler hauled in a half dozen passes from both Walker and Williams, part of an Elon aerial attack that hit on nine of twelve tries and rolled up 163 yards. Moreover, Williams accomplished a rare feat by running for a touchdown, passing for a touchdown, and catching a touchdown pass all in the same game.

---

22 The nickname was derived from the last name of Miami's first coach, Howard Buck, and is a sportswriter/sports publicist contrivance. Peahead Walker's Wake Forest teams were sometimes referred to as the "Walkermen," and Wallace Wade's Duke teams were referred to as the "Wademen" or "Wadesters." Official nicknames often develop slowly. Miami's Hurricane nickname was in use early on, perhaps immediately after a hurricane ripped through the area in September 1926, delaying the school's first football season by a month. But accounts from that time refer to the team as the Bucklets as often as the Hurricanes.

23 Greensboro Daily News, Nov. 11, 1928.

Williams, an alum of West Point High School in Georgia, the school where Walker coached in 1924, was a revelation. And by season's end Walker was beginning to find ways to use him. The 190-pounder was one of those rugged sorts who just excelled at football. He was a solid passer, fast, and certainly didn't mind the contact, the last of which is evident from both first-hand accounts and Williams's appearance in photos taken from that time: powerful legs and thighs, broad shoulders, an air of calm determination in his eyes, prominent ears, neatly slicked back hair. And a tough son of gun, the kind of player whose mere presence often dominated play on both sides of the ball. When he first arrived at Elon, Williams battled with Walker over helmets. Williams didn't want to wear one and pointed out, correctly, that the rules did not require it (helmets weren't mandatory until 1937). Walker thought a helmet a good precaution, however, so Williams acquiesced—most of the time at least. Some Elonites recall him sneaking through parts of practice with his dark hair flapping in the afternoon breeze. Helmeted or otherwise, the emergence of Williams, one Elon's all-time best players, boded well for the coming years.

Prospects were bright—well, brighter—for Elon's gridders in the fall of 1929 thanks largely to the presence of Williams for an entire campaign. But the team started slowly and wound up losing a game it needed to win against Guilford. However, Elon put itself in position later in the season to win Walker's first conference championship by upending the defending champs from High Point College. High Point offered a good example of how a knowledgeable coach, especially one operating without ethical constraints, could lift a college team's fortunes in the wild and woolly days of small college football before the Great Depression.

High Point was a brand-new school opened by the Methodist church in 1924. The college itself ran on the sort of shoestring budget typical for that type of school in that day and age. The campus for the first year consisted of two completed buildings (only one of which was fully heated) and the shell of a third, which was intended to be the men's dorm. It wasn't complete when classes began in September, so the men were placed in the homes of neighborhood families willing to take them in.

It was a raw and rough-hewn place, but that didn't stop president J.W. Andrews from diving headfirst into competitive athletics. In 1925 he brought Jack Boylin, a coach at nearby High Point High School and former professional athlete, to take charge of the athletics program. Boylin was given control of everything—physical education classes, sports, the ticket booth—in exchange for his promise to present intercollegiate teams in at least three sports and be good in at least two of them. Although not explicitly stated, it was obvious to all concerned that football needed to be one of the good ones. Boylin, like Walker, understood that his success in that realm mostly depended upon what kind of talent he could round up. Boylin had carte blanche to do what was needed. He bagged players from nearly a dozen states, including two from faraway Minnesota, and demonstrated pluck, wit, and a healthy budget in doing so. When he got a line on a couple of big linemen from Duluth, Boylin rode the train there in the summer of 1926 to scout them. The boys were big, tough, and willing to get out of the cold for some college work—if Boylin could get them out of there in the first place. As it turns out he could. He bought a used Dodge in Duluth—it's not clear whether he spent his own money or the college recruiting budget (if there were any difference between the two)—and drove the hulking recruits back to High Point. College historian William Locke noted in his 1975 history of the school *No Easy Task: The First 50 Years of High Point College* that the return trip in the new car was not only novel as a recruitment strategy but also just plain novel all the way around. It marked the first time Boylin had ever been behind the wheel of an automobile.

Boylin's merry band was a rough and tough bunch that ran roughshod over most of the opposition from 1926 to 1928. Traveling from game-to-game in their oft-wrecked bus called the Hesperus, they owned the Little Six during those years—Elon included.

That changed on a chilly afternoon in High Point in 1929. With Williams in high gear, both on offense from the fullback slot and on defense where he backed the line, Elon ground out a 14–7 victory against what proved to be Boylin's last High Point team. The Christians jumped ahead early, scoring on their opening drive.

Williams got both the touchdown and the extra point. A forty-nine-yard pass from Walker to Roy "Country" Rollins brought Elon to the High Point one-yard line midway through the third quarter. Williams punched it in from there and again booted the conversion for a 14–0 lead, which proved to be enough.

The victory ran Elon's record to 3–0 against Little Six teams and set up the showdown with rival Guilford. That it was Guilford standing in Elon's way was an interesting turn of events. Although the Quakers regularly provided good competition in basketball, baseball, and some other sports, most years football just wasn't their thing. Perhaps it was a byproduct of the founding denomination's pacifist underpinnings, but in the thirteen seasons from 1913 to 1927—the years after the reinstatement of football at the school that followed the lifting of a decade-long ban—the Quakers won just fourteen games, just slightly more than one win per year. Robert Doak, the former Elon coach, absorbed most of that punishment before resigning in 1927 to launch a long and laudable career as the postmaster at the Guilford College Station.

The Quakers' football fate changed suddenly in 1929 under coach John "Pretty Boy" Anderson, a man who enjoyed a successful nine-year run coaching all three of the "major" sports (the same arrangement Walker labored under at Elon) at Guilford. The Quakers entered the showdown against Elon unbeaten in Little Six play and scratched out a 13–6 victory over the Christians. Guilford ganged up on Williams and kept the big bruiser under wraps. Williams's longest gain on the day went for fifteen yards, and he was thrown for losses on several plays. With Zac Walker unavailable—he was out with a rib injury—to hurl a few passes against the bunched-up Quaker defense, keying on Williams was a foolproof strategy. The victory sealed a Little Six title for Guilford. Elon finished the season 5–3, a respectable mark and one that signaled Walker was making progress.

That set the stage for a most unconventional title run in 1930, although as the season began there was nothing far-fetched about Walker's boys winning a crown. The superb Williams, elected captain by his teammates, was back along with a dozen or so lettermen, which was a lot in the days when letters weren't handed out much beyond the starting lineup. Just as importantly, the competition in the old North State League (it would be reborn the North State Conference by the end of the year) appeared to be flagging. Boylin was gone from High Point, ousted when too many questions arose about his long-distance recruiting work, and Guilford's fortunes were on the wane too. Because Elon had never had much trouble with Lenoir-Rhyne or Atlantic Christian, the coast looked pretty clear, unless someone cooked up a surprise.

In Salisbury someone did.

Dismayed by a mediocre 1929 season, alumni and friends of the newly minted Salisbury-based version of Catawba College proposed a complete revamping of the football program. The 1929 Indians, the fifth football team fielded by Catawba since moving to Salisbury from Newton, finished 3–5-1. Included in that record were losses to Guilford, Lenoir-Rhyne, and Erskine. This was disappointing to many in the Indians' camp, so when a group led by college Trustee L.F. Abernethy made an unusual proposal—the group would foot the cost of upgrading the program if the school would give the group a free hand in operating it for five years. The administration was receptive. Details of the proposed outsourcing of Catawba athletics included turning over college equipment and facilities to coaches chosen by Abernethy and company, handing over twenty percent of student athletic fees (about $5 a head at the time) and all the gate receipts to Abernethy's consortium, and letting Abernethy hire all necessary athletic personnel. Most importantly, the school had to approve a five-year contract for one Charles Moran as head football coach and George M. Chinn as his assistant.

Moran is on the tip of few tongues today, but in 1930 his name would have been easily recognizable to college football fans and to sports fans in general. "Unk" Moran (the nickname was short for Uncle Charlie) was a well-known National League baseball umpire and legendary football coach. A Tennessean, Moran began his coaching career as an assistant to the legendary Glenn "Pop" Warner at the Carlisle Indian School (alma mater of Jim Thorpe, among others). His first head coaching job was at Texas A&M, where he went 38–8-4 in six seasons. Not bad, but not nearly as good as Moran's work at tiny Centre (Kentucky) College from 1919 to 1923. Centre had fewer than 250 students when Moran arrived at the school. He'd come not to coach but to watch his brother Tom play football. The Colonels weren't well coached, however, and Moran wound up helping the squad ready itself for a couple of games. School officials were so impressed they offered the elder Moran the head job. Moran accepted and promptly turned Centre into a national power, greatly aided by an influx of talent from Fort Worth, TX, where a Centre alumnus was the high school football coach. The best of the Texans was quarterback Alvin "Bo" McMillin, a future member of the College Football Hall of Fame, but Centre's success was more about ensemble work than individual stardom. The tight-knit club—Centre was nicknamed the Praying Colonels because of the team's oft-emotional pregame prayers—quickly developed into a powerhouse. The Centre boys ripped through the normal fodder on Centre's schedule (recall Centre's 120-0 shellacking of Howard in 1920) and soon began hunting bigger game. With promotional help from Eastern sportswriters, Centre obtained games with Harvard in 1920 and 1921 and shocked the college football world by beating the Crimson 6-0 in the 1921 contest. The upset was one of the biggest in college football history and is now bathed in all kinds of gridiron lore.[24]

Moran's Centre teams posted a 42-6-1 mark, giving Moran an absurd 80-14-5 mark as head coach (.810 winning percentage) prior to moving to Bucknell College in 1924. Despite a stumble with Bucknell, it is no surprise that Catawba officials thought Moran could do great things for the Indians. What is surprising is that they thought they could land him. As it turns out they could.

Abernethy and company contacted Moran and made him an offer before taking their plan to the Catawba Trustees and administration. It wasn't quite a fait accompli—there were a few administrative objections and the usual sort of faculty hand-wringing about overemphasized athletics—but the plan was indeed eventually approved. Moran was signed to a five-year contract for $3,000 per year just for coaching football—and not even a full season of football at that. Moran, it turned out, wasn't available

---

[24] Perhaps the best tale involves McMillin, a notorious gambler as well as a cracker jack quarterback. He reportedly won so much money betting on Centre in the Harvard game that the pile of cash filled his berth on the train headed back to Kentucky.

until the end of September when his Major League umpiring duties were done. For most of his Catawba tenure (which didn't wind up lasting five years), he missed the Indians' first game or two. No matter. "Colonel" Chinn, a star lineman under Moran at Centre, knew the Moran "system," which was based on fancy offensive plays, rigorous conditioning, and iron discipline. At Centre, Moran sometimes whipped recalcitrant players with his belt. At Catawba he allegedly just stared, his reputation providing all the intimidation necessary.

Moran was no phoney. He knew how to build college football teams. He brought in new players from all over (including, in an encore of his Centre work, a shifty back from Texas named Joe Black) and blended them nicely with some holdovers in his new system. The Indians dusted Atlantic Christian 24–0 in the opener (before Unk arrived) and rolled rather easily through a mostly small-time schedule. Among the victims was Elon, which was baffled and beaten badly under the newly installed lights on a crisp autumn evening 32–0.

Catawba polished off the rest of its opponents and finished 8–0–1. The only blemish was a 13–13 tie against Appalachian State Teachers College in a brutal game that ended in a brawl. The thirteen points surrendered to the Mountaineers were the last Moran's men gave up. Overall they outscored opponents 287–19.

Despite those successes, the Indians' season did not end on a happy note. Just before Catawba squared off against Guilford on November 15 in its next-to-last game of the season, Guilford officials informed Catawba's leaders that they had evidence that one of the Indians' players—the high-scoring George Zaengle—was ineligible. Zaengle's alleged crime was playing for another college (and hence using up his eligibility) before coming to Catawba. Specifically, they said he had starred for the State Normal College in West Chester, PA (now West Chester University) for several seasons before 1930. Guilford officials stumbled onto the alleged perfidy when one of the school's coaches received the annual Spalding sporting goods catalog. Flipping through the pages, which included team photos from around the country, the coach spotted a familiar face: Zaengle.

Catawba officials denied the charges at first—they had Zaengle's sworn affidavit that stated he had not played at any other college—and, photographic evidence aside, professed complete innocence. The Guilford game went on. The score? Catawba 18. Guilford 0.

Not to be denied, Guilford pressed its case afterward, and given the rather damning evidence—there was no doubt it was Zaengle in the photo—Catawba officials finally investigated the matter on their own. In the end, Zaengle came clean about playing for West Chester. Still, he didn't think it counted as "real" college, a belief fostered by the fact that Zaengle didn't receive any college credits while at West Chester. It was a plausible defense, but conference officials were skeptical. Thus, a three-man committee appointed by Catawba's Trustees reached a similar conclusion. Four days after beating Guilford and apparently clinching the Little Six title, the Catawba committee ruled that Zaengle was indeed ineligible and that his story of misunderstanding just what constituted a college was a bald-faced lie. He was, in fact, a key player on at least two West Chester teams, including a very good 1928 squad that went 8–0. And there was little doubt that West Chester, founded in 1871, was a bona fide college. It had 1,000-plus students (more than most of the Little Six), full accreditation, and clearly offered a collegiate-style curriculum. Zaengle, said the commission, had deliberately supplied Catawba with a transcript that showed only his high school courses of study.

The report laid the blame squarely on Zaengle, absolving both the coaches who lured him southward and the faculty who farmed out their athletic program to a private contractor. David Faust, Catawba's long-time faculty representative to the (then future) North State Conference, wrote, some time after the fact, that Catawba had "innocently played an ineligible man in all nine games."[25]

Moran's reputation, coupled with common sense, led the conference committee investigating the matter to a different view of the Indians' purity. It recommended Catawba relinquish any claims

---

25 *A College of Our Own*, Donald C. Dearborn, Raymond Jenkins, Alvin Robert Keppel, J. Fred Corriher, David E. Setzer, Martha K. West, Copyright Catawba College. p. 101.

to the North State—or Little Six—title and that school President E.R. Hoke write letters of apology to the eight opponents Catawba had mauled up to that point in the season. However, the committee did not specifically recommend that Catawba forfeit the games, leaving the matter in a rather strange limbo. How could the school relinquish the title but not forfeit the games? There was little formal precedent—the "books" on these matters were rather thin at this point, but the logic still seemed warped.

The result of all this was that when the 1930 season ended the Little Six was left without a definitive, officially recognized champion. The obvious champion had been ordered to relinquish its title. And the North Carolina Intercollegiate Athletic Conference, which didn't formally recognize the Little Six in any event, didn't have provisions in place for determining conference champs in cases of irregularities. The issue was never resolved, and to this day the record books reflect the muddle.

Catawba still officially recognizes the 8-0-1 record and counts it as part of Moran's overall mark of 22-14-5 (had the games been counted as forfeits he would have ended up with a 15-21-5 mark). Catawba did beat High Point in the finale without Zaengle, a result that left the Indians with either a 1-4-1 record against Little Six foes, a 1-4 record (Appalachian, against whom Catawba battled to a tie, was sort of an unofficial first-year member of the conference), or maybe a 5-0 or 5-0-1 record but with an asterisk asserting that the school did not lay claim to a championship. The only point that was, and is, clear is that Catawba did not/would not/could not claim a conference championship. But if not Catawba, then who? Elon? Elon's dreadful performance against Moran's boys aside, Walker's boys enjoyed a good season. The club did start 2-3, taking to the road four times in the first five weeks of the season (despite Governor O. Max Gardner's plea for North Carolina's college sports teams to stay close to home because of the Great Depression).

The pivotal game in Elon's season—and to its unexpected title run—came the week after the Catawba fiasco in the annual match with Guilford. An especially chilly Halloween day at Comer Field helped produce a low-key defensive struggle. The Quakers blocked an Elon punt out of the end zone for a 2-0 lead early in the second quarter. Then, after a favorable exchange of punts, Guilford scored on a short drive. The extra point attempt was foiled, but Elon was called for slugging on the play. The penalty for this particularly flagrant violation included awarding the point to the Quakers and letting Guilford kickoff from the Elon 40-yard line. The latter didn't matter much because the score came at the end of the half. But on a bitter day when offense was difficult to come by, the single point was useful.

Guilford led 9–0 early in the second half, and it looked like that score might stand. The gang-tackling Quakers kept Williams under check, and Walker was reluctant to unleash a passing attack, which wasn't as potent as it had been back in the days when his brother Zac was the quarterback.

Finally, near the end of the third quarter, Williams got going, ripping off consecutive gains of twenty, eight, and fifteen yards. Then he hit Roland Smith, who split time at quarterback and halfback, with a long pass that carried Elon to the Guilford seven. Williams scored in two plays from there to make it 9–6 early in the final period.

Elon held after the kickoff and took over on its own forty-five. Hugh Caddell, a tackle under most circumstances but a baseball player with a strong arm, fired a pass to Williams that was good for forty yards to the Guilford fifteen. Elon ground out another first down to the five. Guilford stiffened here, giving little ground on three plays. But a determined Williams cracked over on fourth down from the two for the game winner. His extra point made the final 13–9.

Elon made relatively short work of its last two league opponents High Point and Lenior-Rhyne, meaning the Christians beat everybody in the league except Catawba and Appalachian. With Catawba relinquishing claim and Appalachian in membership limbo, Elon seemed a logical champion.

At the end of the season the *Maroon & Gold* certainly thought so, although reporting that news required some contorted English: "The victory [over Lenoir-Rhyne] places Elon on top of all the eligible teams in the North State Conference and gives the

Christians the title."[26] Catawba's bookkeepers had a different view, but in Elon's record books, the Christians are the champs.

That was something to cherish, especially with dark times on the doorsteps.

The Depression had arrived and Pete Williams's football days were nearly done. More football success for Peahead Walker—indeed success of any kind—was several years away.

---

26 *Maroon & Gold*, Dec. 5, 1930.

CHAPTER 4

A BIG FISH

The enduring modern impression is that the Great Depression struck one day like a lightning bolt and that it was immediately obvious that bad times had arrived for good when the stock market dropped so precipitously that fateful October Day in 1929. The newsreel footage of ruined investors jumping off the side of Wall Street towers (some of which may have been filmed several years later, when the crash finally engulfed the market) suggests a sudden plunge into the nation's longest stretch of economic woe.

In fact, no one—not economists, not bankers, not soon-to-be-embattled President Herbert Hoover—knew exactly what it all meant on that first of many "Black Fridays." And if the folks in the eye of the storm were baffled, then people in the hinterlands were completely clueless.

In tiny Elon, NC, the events of October 1929 passed without excessive comment or commotion. For college officials everywhere, the rocking of the financial markets caused eyebrows to raise since most colleges had some money invested in securities as part of their burgeoning endowments (Elon's was close to half a million dollars at the time, a nice sum for so small a school). But a double-digit drop in the leading indexes didn't seem like too big a pill to swallow. It had happened before. America's volatile economy in the late nineteenth and early twentieth century was full of depressions—or "panics" as they were know back then. So Elon officials did not begin to consider budget cuts until after the fall term in 1929 and didn't make any until 1931. And even as late as the spring of that year President W.A. Harper was still pushing a campaign to raise an additional $1 million for the endowment. In his report to the Trustees at that time, he included some $6 million in proposed new expenses. Much of that was new construction, to be paid out of anticipated capital funds. One notable item on the wish list was a modern football stadium—to be built at an estimated cost of $250,000.

At the same meeting, however, Harper laid out the rather dim view of the immediate future. Elon's operating income—mostly derived from tuition and other student fees—was falling at an alarming rate. Projections for the 1931-1932 school year showed income at $67,000 versus expenses of $159,293. The school did have some cash on hand—a reserve of $34,000—but the operations would clearly have to be "financed" to avoid depleting all the reserve funds or tapping into the principal of the endowment.[1]

A note was signed for $53,000. Other emergency measures were taken. Several teaching posts were eliminated, and the college sold a farm it owned. The faculty endured the first of what would turn out to be a regular series of salary payment deferrals or outright losses. That was bad news, but in the years ahead they would come to realize it could be worse: at least they were still at work in the relatively comfortable confines of a private college.

In many regards, Elon was no worse off than most American colleges, nearly all of which suffered through economic deprivations during the Depression. It was better off in some ways than many of its small college brethren, a number of which teetered on the brink of oblivion. Indeed, Elon actually benefitted from one closing. Atlantic University (not to be confused with Atlantic Christian) in Norfolk, VA, a sister college of Elon founded by the same Southern Christian Convention church group, folded in 1932. Nearly three dozen Atlantic students migrated to Elon, the next-closest Christian church-backed school, to complete their education. Tens of thousands of tuition and boarding dollars moved south to North Carolina, a significant windfall during bleak financial days. Elon also retained some financial support from the Christian church (although at reduced levels), and the industries for which it prepped the most students (clergy, teaching) did not suffer the utter devastation of some fields. As the hard times of the 1930s rolled on, people still wanted education, still *needed* salvation.

---

1 Elon Board of Trustees Minutes, Feb. 1931. Elon University Archives.

In one very specific way, however, Elon was in a bind when the economy went south. A fire had ravaged the campus in January 1923. Although quick work by students, faculty, and local volunteer fire departments had limited the damage to just one building, it was quite a building. The four-story main building housed everything from administrative offices to classrooms to science labs (a leaking gas jet in a lab was the suspected cause of the blaze). The flames destroyed almost all of the 129 × 57-foot structure. In the smoking ruins not much was salvageable beyond burnt bricks and the school bell, which added to the destruction in the early morning hours when its moorings burned through and it crashed through all four stories of the stately octagon tower in the building's center.

The school worked its way through the interim—honor-bound students were asked to fill out new information forms that included a list classes they had passed with approximate grades—and then launched a massive building campaign that not only restored the facilities in the incinerated building but expanded the campus as well. The plan proposed by Harper called for building a new administrative building, a new science building, a new auditorium, a new library, and, later, after a big donor specifically requested it, a new Christian education building.

The original estimate for the construction was $600,000. The figure quickly grew once the work actually started, eventually topping out at close to $820,000. A few big hitters stepped up to foot part of the bill, including Burlington industrialist Robert L. Holt, owner of the Glencoe mill and mill village; J.B. and Benjamin Duke, long-time Elon benefactors in the Carlton family; Colonel J.M. Darden; and College Trustee Michael Orban Jr. But even with sizeable private contributions, the school debt skyrocketed as the building campaign progressed. Elon borrowed $300,000 in 1925, then $350,000 in 1926, and then another $150,000 a few years later. As donations came in, portions were paid off. Still, when President Harper made his annual presentation to the Board of Trustees in February 1931, the debt was just more than $487,000.[2]

---

[2] Elon Board of Trustees Minutes. Feb. 1931, Elon University Archives.

The shiny new campus, completed in 1928, was impressive and seemed to be a smart, progressive response to the closing years of the Roaring 20s, even with much of the cost carried as long-term debt. But when the effects of the Depression began to take hold during the 1930–1931 school year, and more precipitously from 1931 to 1932, the burden was more than any school could bear. Enrollment at Elon dropped by 100 students—roughly 25 percent—to just more than 300 in 1931. The Southern Christian Convention (SCC) couldn't meet pledges made to pay the interest on much of the debt, and donations outside the SCC structure, as well as the school's endowment income, both dried up.

Stress was evident across the campus. Among the casualties was President Harper, who resigned in the fall of 1931 at just 51 years old. The move was abrupt—even close friends were surprised—but in retrospect the writing was on the wall. Harper never came right out and said he was quitting because of the pressure produced by the economic situation, but both he and the Board—and for that matter the SCC—had drawn criticism for both their slow response to the growing crisis and their role it creating it: how foolish to have engaged in a costly building campaign just before the outbreak of a depression. A particular symbol of their fiscal recklessness was the brand-new brick wall that bordered the newly constructed campus. It had been built for the princely sum of $2,000 and was an impossible-to-miss symbol of Harper's folly. After all, some critics noted, it was little more than an aesthetic luxury

The inability of Harper et al. to foretell the future cannot be counted as much of a crime, and the fact is they adopted many prudent measures. The "frivolous" brick wall, which still surrounds the older part of the campus, was made in part from bricks salvaged from the fire that destroyed the old main building back in 1923. Not much was salvageable from that conflagration, so complete was its effect. But many of the bricks survived, albeit in a blackened state, thanks to the work of local boy scouts. As part of an ongoing good turn, the scouts scraped the carbon deposits off the clay blocks for years, preparing them for reuse.

Whether Harper resigned or was ousted, whether his departure was merited or not, the college powers moved quickly to plant L.E. Smith, the current SCC head and an Elon alum, in the president's chair soon after Harper's abrupt spring departure. He was elected to the post, on an interim basis, at an SCC conference in Burlington in November 1931. At the same event, the Christians created a $50,000 emergency fund to aid the school. If fully funded, that was just enough to cover the reported slides in endowment income (down $23,000), donations (down $13,000), and contributions from the SCC itself (down $17,000). It was not fully funded, but as time wore on, that was among the least of the college's fiscal woes.

***

None of this was good news for any part of the college, especially not for extracurricular programs such as athletics. But Smith's ascension to the presidency was a countervailing boon for athletics. Harper may have been an athletic supporter, but Smith was an unabashed jock—a football alumnus from the hair-as-helmets days who could be counted on as a real friend of the athletic program.

Coach Peahead Walker, whose record—especially in baseball—was already commendable, took a small salary hit as the Depression ravaged the budget. His pay, which had peaked at $2,600 in 1929, was cut to $2,500 a year later. The next year, his salary remained at that same figure, even though many of the college's best-paid professors (the top salary was $3,000 a year) saw cuts of $200 to $300 per annum. Minutes of Trustee meetings during that time show that many of the old faculty hands also made donations to the college by accepting an additional $200 reduction. The report singles out several of them but does not mention Walker. However, in letters to President Smith several years later (while Walker was trying to collect back pay after leaving to go to Wake Forest), the Coach notes both the pay he didn't receive simply because the school didn't have it (more than $3,000 over the years, according to Walker) and the money (he says $200 per year) that he donated to the cause.[3]

Significantly, the athletic budget—essentially the money fronted to the department and used to pay expenses in excess of what was taken in at the gate—suffered only a small cut during the Depression. In Smith's emergency reorganization of the college for the 1932–1933 school year, the athletic deficit budget was cut from $2,000 to $1,500. That's a big slice in terms of percentage, but Walker wasn't used to dealing with a lot of money. Donations from friends and alumni undoubtedly continued to help. And the Coach, like most people from that era, was an expert at making do. Peahead Walker knew how to stretch dollars—Elon's baseball team often found itself playing with equipment that somehow made its way west from the Coastal Plain League, where Walker coached during the summer—and expected others to do the same.

For instance, after a 1935 football game played in a driving rain, Walker gave student manager William Maness a pile of hopelessly muddy uniforms and $5 and told him to get them clean. The resourceful Maness, who was from Snow Hill, NC, one of Walker's summer baseball hangouts, improvised. Locking himself into the North Dormitory showers late one night, he laid the muddy football suits on the floor, sprinkled them with powdered soap, and fired up the showers. Then he spent the next several hours stomping across the uniforms, grinding out the grit. The dirt finally came out, but it was slow work. In an interview with Elon chronicler Durwood Stokes, Maness reported that cleaning the uniforms was the toughest $5 he ever earned.

Through innovation and perseverance, athletics survived at Elon, and, as some normalcy returned to American life, the departmental budget stabilized. By the mid-1930s, it actually began to grow. By the time Walker left, the athletic budget had almost quadrupled from its pre-Depression levels.

That precipitous leap resulted mostly from one big change—the formal adoption of an athletic scholarship program at Elon. As noted earlier, the idea of awarding a young man an expense-free

---

[3] Minutes, Elon College Board of Trustees, Feb. 1933, May 1933, Feb. 1936; and personal letter D.C. Walker to LE. Smith, Sept. 30, 1937, L.E. Smith Papers. Both from the Elon University Archives.

ride through college just because he could run with a football or throw a baseball was hotly debated through the first half of the twentieth century. Most schools that played anything like serious intercollegiate athletics engaged in the practice to some extent. But the work was often done in the dark. The scholarships were "off-the-book" expenses funded by direct cash payments to the athletes or paid as salaries and earned by athletes in real, or sometimes makeshift, jobs.[4] The job program was particularly popular in the Northeast, which was still the center of the college football and athletic universe. It was (at least until the Depression) easy to find jobs for footballers in the big cities. In the more rural South and in the Midwest, this was not always the case. As a result, there was some chafing at Southern colleges when the Yankees began "moralizing" on the issue of "subsidies," that is scholarships. Of course the big city colleges would be against. They could find lucrative work for all their charges.

The Southerners, with a history of rebellion on their side, took the first overt step in 1935 when the Southeastern Conference (SEC) announced its member schools would give athletic scholarships openly. The Yanks were appalled, and some knees jerked in the upper South as well. A few years after the SEC move, the Southern Conference, which at that time consisted mostly of schools in the Carolinas and Virginia, voted in the Graham Plan, so named for University of North Carolina president Frank Porter Graham, a member of North Carolina's reform movement and, briefly, a US Senator.[5] The Graham Plan, which prohibited scholarships and other "proselytizing," was unpopular and did not last for long. Most schools saw far more benefit than bane from the presence of powerful athletic teams.

Elon was not affected by the Graham Plan initially, but the college community debated the matter, especially after football fortunes at the school took a downturn in the early 1930s.

---

4 Some schools were even more creative. Yale, for example, "paid" a gifted footballer in the pre-World War I era by sending him on a postseason vacation to Havana.

5 Graham was the brother of one Archibald "Moonlight" Graham, a real-life professional baseball player whose unusual Major League career—he appeared in just one inning of one game and did not get to bat—was popularized in the book *Shoeless Joe* and the movie it inspired *Field of Dreams*.

Although he was able to bring a second brother on board in 1931 (Arch, who went on to great success as a high school football coach in nearby Mebane, NC), Peahead Walker's recruiting work took a decided turn for the worse after 1930. The original Alabama brigade was all gone by 1930, and the stalwart Williams completed four brilliant years (33 rushing touchdowns, 16 passing TDs, 225 points scored) in 1931. Dofflemeyer and Rollins, two solid players, also went out with Williams. Walker managed to bring in a few skillful backs such as Charlie Roberts and Webb Newsome but struggled to find enough linemen, or other backs, to complement their play. As a result, the 1931 and 1932 seasons were not successful.

Walker's 1931 team, the last with Williams in harness, had to rally to finish 3–5. Williams threw for three touchdowns (and ran for another) in a 30–0 thrashing of the fading High Point College team in the next-to-last game of the season and then threw for two and ran for one in a 19–6 win over Guilford before 3,500 at Greensboro's Memorial Stadium.

That was the end of the Williams's era, although the true impact of the hard-hitting fullback would not be noted until the following year. Without him, the Christians suffered through a 2–7 season in 1932, defeating only a couple of amalgamations from military bases. A 6–0 home loss to High Point featured some especially dispiriting circumstances. The Panthers' hadn't scored all season and to observers, Elon was clearly the better team. But the Christians were intercepted three times and, at the end of the first half, missed a scoring opportunity when the clock expired. Newsome completed a pass to Arch Walker inside the one-yard line on the half's last play, but Elon couldn't get another snap off before the referee's whistle blew. The players, the *Greensboro Daily News* reported, were still in the huddle "doing the preliminary head work for putting the ball across"—that is, they were calling, or possibly drawing up, the next play—when the half ended. Stadium clocks and sophisticated scoreboards were not common at the time—Elon didn't have a functional clock until 1938—so the half ended with Elon's players calmly in the huddle, the ball inches from the goal line.

The season ended with either a 24–6 or 26–7 (records and accounts differ) drubbing by Guilford on Thanksgiving Day. The Quakers ran wild and spiced up the proceedings with a bit of razzle dazzle that was indicative of the haphazardly creative style of play then in vogue. None of the Quaker backs were particularly good passers. Quarterback Jimmie Bunn was a small, quick back, and halfback Bob Jamieson, the team's best player, was tall and fast. But neither possessed strong arms, so long passes were not part of the Quaker attack—at least not usually. What Coach John Anderson did have, however, was a player who could throw the ball long and with accuracy, but he was a lineman, guard Gordon Wilkie. So Anderson, who had a reputation for gridiron trickery, put in a special play for Wilkie for the Elon game that was designed to turn Quaker's weakness into a strength. Anderson moved Wilkie into the backfield as the last man of four backs arranged in a sort of a Z pattern. The fleet-footed Jamieson moved to end, giving Guilford the requisite seventh man on the line of scrimmage. The ball was centered to the back closest to the line. The back then lateraled the ball to the next back who lateraled to the next who, finally, lateraled to Wilkie, the guard turned passer. All those laterals gave Jamieson time to dash at, and then past, a startled Arch Walker, Elon's safety. Relating the story to Guilford Athletic Director and chronicler Herb Appenzeller many years later, Jamieson said Walker hollered "Where the hell are you going?" as Jamieson sped past. He quickly found out. Wilkie hoisted a long pass that the speeding Jamieson caught and carried into the end zone. The play reputedly covered seventy yards, fifty in the air—in those days an extraordinary feat.

Jamieson, a legendary high school coach at Greensboro (later Grimsley) High School from his Guilford graduation into the 1970s, recalled the play coming in a losing effort.[6] But he didn't score any other touchdowns on passes against Elon during his career, and newspaper accounts of the 1932 game does describe the play in terms similar to those Jamieson described (and diagrammed) it for Appenzeller.

---

6 Pride in the Past, Guilford College Athletics 1837–1987, Herb Appenzeller, Guilford College, 1987.

It wasn't the intent, but the dismal record in Walker's sixth football season had a salutary effect in the long run. After the season, Walker and President Smith met to discuss the overall situation, both of college athletics and the college in general. Smith was anxious for athletic success to boost pride (and hopefully fundraising) and to provide a distraction from ongoing bad press. Elon lost its school accreditation in September 1932, and there was a steady stream of news—all bad—regarding Elon's unending financial woes.[7]

Smith, writes Elon chronicler Stokes, had confidence in Walker, who was continuing to churn out successful teams in baseball and, to a lesser extent, basketball, even while football suffered. And so when the Coach told him that the main problem in football was obtaining good players, Smith listened and agreed, on the spot, to the establishment of a scholarship system at Elon. The resulting system was rather haphazard (and not completely transparent). It proved to be a work in progress that required constant monitoring, and no small amount of dickering, between president, coach, and assorted financial administrators in the years that followed. The gist of the Elon plan was to "let the boys [meaning athletically inclined boys] come to school" for $100.[8] That was a substantial discount from the school's mid-1930s tuition and board fee of between $400 and $500 (the differences depended upon lodging assignment and course of study). In addition, some sixty school jobs were also reserved for athletes. They were expected to work for the remainder of their fees, the idea being that their almost free labor would offset the loss of revenue. In fact, many of the jobs were makeshift work and not really of much value to the school. That explains Smith's irritation with Walker, expressed in a 1936 letter regarding alleged recruiting promises made by Ellis Fysal, Walker's new assistant coach.

"I'm afraid Ellis has gone too far in this case [the recruitment of a player named Wicker from Gulf, NC]," Smith wrote to Walker in the summer of 1936. "As you know, we cannot offer

---

[7] In a tip of the hat to the well-respected Smith, the accrediting organization, the Southern Association of Colleges, placed Elon on a list of "nonmembers" as opposed to the more defamatory "dropped schools" list.
[8] Stokes, *Elon College*, p. 259.

work amounting to $300." Walker responded by saying not to sweat it and that Coach Fysal wasn't overpromising but merely, you know, recruiting:

> *I told Ellis that the approximate amount of expenses for going to school at Elon was $400 and that he could tell Wicker the job would amount to $300 [the difference between the $400 fee and the $100 tuition an athlete still had to pay]. This does not make a great deal of difference, except to make the boy think he is getting a great deal for his work. However, the amount [Wicker] will pay will be $100 just the same.*[9]

The problem Walker faced was out-recruiting rival schools in bigger, or at least different places (he cited Washington and Lee as an example) where prospective athletes might be promised more lucrative jobs than what they'd get at Elon. A little creative math made the Elon job seem more worthwhile and helped counter opposition recruiting talk. That seemed fair to Walker—or certainly no more deceitful than deliberately showing a recruit both the East and West campuses.

There were other complications as well. The athletes were receiving a kind of a package deal—room, board, tuition, books, and fees all in one—and the assumption some held was that there was some actual breakdown of costs. In other words, a few athletes believed, or pretended to believe, that of their $100, $20 went to books, $32.50 to rooms, etc. Upon arriving at Elon, they discovered that there was private housing available for less than what their classmates who were not on scholarships were paying for dorm space. So they wanted to haggle. If they could rent a room for less, shouldn't the dollars saved come back to them?

"You see, after they get here they can figure around and scheme for cheaper accommodations and claim the amount of the scholarship offered," wrote Smith.[10] None of that mattered to the president or the institution, of course. They needed the $100, desperately, and certainly didn't intend to refund any of it to a

---

9 L.E. Smith Papers, Elon University Archive.
10 Ibid.

clever or frugal athlete. Those "boys" had already gotten a good deal.

Additional problems stemmed from Walker's inclination to cut further deals, if it meant closing a sale. He wanted a few athletes in for less than $100—tackle Jimmy Hauselt was one of several who came to school without an out-of-pocket expense—but was also happy to let some lesser prospects pay $200 instead of $100. Walker worked some of this out on the side, gathering funds from alumni and boosters to pay the $100 for some athletes, and some he just kind of left to chance. It appears that a standard Walker tactic was to tell the player they could come for nothing and then hope things could be smoothed over with the school when the bills came due. This contributed to the long-standing problem of athletes who thought, either because of the sweet nothings whispered by Walker or what they heard about such doings at other schools, that they shouldn't have to pay at all. Whatever the case, collecting the athlete's $100 fee, due in three installments over the course of the year, was a long-running campus headache.

Like coaches anywhere before and since, Walker also struggled with players who made poor grades, didn't go to class (Elon had a strict policy against "overcutting"), and, as noted, didn't pay their bills. He also had to make decisions based on a player's potential to actually help the school's intercollegiate teams. Recruiting in that age was even less of a science than it is today, and many players were brought in, sight unseen, for what amounted to a one-year tryout. If they didn't pan out, they couldn't come back the following year—at least not for $100.

Walker's response to a summer letter from Smith asking Walker to check a list of athletes receiving "special consideration" from the previous year and to "ascertain as quickly as possible the [players] who are eligible to play next fall and whom you wish on your team," illuminates how the process worked. Walker replied to Smith with a typed list that included handwritten notes beside each player's name: "withdrawn from school," "OK," and, in seven cases, "no good." The later appellation seems to have been an athletic evaluation, not a moral one.[11]

---

11 Ibid.

On another occasion, Walker responded to Smith with a letter that included the following:

> *The following names are boys we do not want to help (with a scholarship) next year that have proven to be failures as athletes: Hugo Minette, Ben Lilien, the Dow boys and Cannady. . . . If these boys should happen to write you, you can tell them that I told you we could not give them any further aid at the college because they had not come up to my expectations of their ability.*[12]

Strangely administered though they might have been, the sixty athletic scholarships were nothing to sneeze at, especially not when many of Elon's rivals were looking down their noses at such practices—or simply turning their back on it because of the cost. Guilford never cottoned to the scholarship idea, holding to a policy of "nondiscrimination" with regard to student aid—that is, no special aid exceptions for athletes—and preferring to build teams from athletes arriving at school "in the natural course of events."[13] High Point, in the wake of its brief dance with "professionalism," was struggling just to keep its doors open, forget about keeping sports teams going, and Catawba's enthusiasm for the big-time endeavor, post-Moran, began to wear thin, too. Amidst all this gloom and uncertainty, Elon pushed ahead. The scholarship program was put into effect, an assistant coach was hired, and new athletic facilities were planned—all as Walker continued to grow as a coach and recruiter. The effects of all of these changes were gradual but considerable. In 1938, the year after Walker's final season at Elon, the athletic budget finally began to reflect the cost of the scholarships. The department budget that year hit five figures, in large part because of a $7,520 line item for athletic scholarships.

The scholarship program was a prime element in the reversal of Elon's football fortunes. In Walker's last four seasons (1933–1936), the Christians were unbeaten in North State Conference play (11–0–2) and won three titles (a fourth was

---

12 Ibid.
13 Stoeson, A.R., *Guilford College: On the Strength of 150 Years*. 1987. Guilford, NC: Guilford College. p. 48.

disputed because of still more eligibility issues). President Smith's hoped-for blast of positive publicity did, in fact, materialize.

Walker's steel and skill was responsible for much of the success. Although the effect of a more organized and robust scholarship program cannot be denied, it was neither automatic nor instantaneous. Someone—for the most part Walker—still had to find the players. And even as the talent pool improved, the importance of an industrious and skilled coach never diminished.

Walker coached a team with only a handful of new faces to modest success in 1933 and then overcame a significant quantitative loss to produce an excellent result in 1934. That season began with only twenty-one players at practice—not enough for a full-scale scrimmage unless a coach or manager filled a space.

For the 1933 team Walker dipped back into Alabama and landed one key player, Ralph Neal, a fullback cut along Pete Williams's lines. Another freshman that year was Jack Stallings, a speedy back from Reidsville, NC. With Webb Newsome already on hand, and Archie Walker available as a multipositional reserve, Elon was poised to become a much more potent offensive team.

Playing a less-than-challenging schedule, Elon managed a 4–3 mark entering the last two games of the season and had a shot at the North State title.

First, Elon beat Lenoir-Rhyne 7–0. That victory set up the season ender against Guilford. At 2–0 in the league, the Christians could win the North State title if they beat the Quakers. Guilford was in the throes of another pretty miserable season but was 1–1 in the league and could throw the race into turmoil by winning. The contest was, as it turned out, a thriller—one of the best in the school's budding rivalry. Elon stopped Guilford drives deep in its territory twice in the first half and followed those up with long touchdown drives of its own. Neal did most of the offensive work. On one first-half drive he threw a pair of 30-yard passes and then completed the work later with a 24-yard scoring toss to Stallings. Guilford stopped Elon on downs inside the one on the Christians' next march, but after a Quaker quick kick out to the 31, Elon rolled in for a second score, Neal passing to Arch Walker for the touchdown.

That made it 13–0 at the half, and when Elon marched steadily downfield on its first possession after intermission, the Quakers appeared to be doomed. But Elon's drive stalled at the Guilford 10, and the Quakers were soon on the move in the other direction. J.T. Turner scored on a short run on the first play of the final quarter to cut the lead to 13–6. After a kickoff and an exchange of punts that went Guilford's way, the Quakers gained possession at the Elon 44. On the first play from there, Turner heaved a long pass to Danny Newman, who went the distance. That brought Guilford within one. Fullback Jordan Norman tied the contest when he charged through the Elon line for the extra point. Elon came close to scoring the game winner, but two Newsome passes at the end were batted down in the end zone. The contest ended in a tie.

That wasn't what Elon had hoped for, especially not when the game appeared to be so firmly in control at the start of the second half. But it did the job. All the other North State contenders finished with at least one loss.

If Walker's first season with the new recruiting tools in tow was a struggle, the second was less so, although as noted the team took awhile to come up to strength. Official graduation losses were not heavy—just four seniors played significant roles on the 1933 squad—but apparently defections of various types were.[14] In any event, practice started with just more than twenty. And when Elon traveled to Roanoke for their season opener in early September, the bus wasn't full.

It was just as well. A Shenandoah Valley gulley washer—four inches of rain fell on the field the afternoon before the scheduled night game—forced the contest to be cancelled. That sent Elon to another opener where a different deluge fell. This one consisted of Christian errors and the Davidson College points they produced. Elon fumbled on its first possession to set up one

---

14 It should hardly be surprising to note that, during the first half of the twentieth century, and especially during the Great Depression, it was not unusual for a young man to attend a year or two of college and then drop out to attend to family business, to start a career, or simply because they didn't have the money to continue. Acquiring even part of a college education was viewed as a benefit and as such increased one's opportunities for employment.

Wildcat score, had a pass intercepted on its second to set up another, and fumbled a punt into the end zone near to create one more. In between the Christians struggled to stop a pretty fair Davidson passing attack led by Johnny Mackorrell, the hard-hitting Wildcat captain, whose play was often likened to Pete Williams's and vice versa. The result was a 33–6 shellacking.

Among the promising developments that day for Elon, however, was the unveiling of a new star: all-purpose backfield man James "Jack Rabbit" Abbitt. Abbitt entered the game as a sub for Neal and scored the Christians' only touchdown in the closing minutes. Walker's ability to pull this particular rabbit out of his recruiting hat would pay off down the road.

Two weeks after the Davidson game, Elon returned to rain-soaked Virginia for its annual match with the difficult Wasps from Emory & Henry.[15] Slipping feet and slippery balls turned the contest into a defensive duel featuring a lot of punting (nearly forty punts between the teams). Late in the second quarter, Emory & Henry punted Elon into a corner. Newsome tried to escape it with a long quick kick, but the Wasps' Ray Marshall corralled Newsome's punt and ran it back thirty-four yards to the Elon sixteen. Helped by a penalty on Elon, Emory & Henry managed to gouge it in from there. It proved to the game's only score. The loss was Elon's second straight—and, as it turned out, its last of the season.

Walker's men beat Langley 7–0 to snap the skid. Unbeaten Catawba, now under the direction of Elon grad Gordon Kirkland, came to town the next week. The teams were apparently evenly matched. Both defenses made goal line stands. Elon had the ball inside the Catawba three times without scoring. Catawba ran a fourth-down pass out of a faked field goal at the Elon ten in the fourth quarter, but the Indians' "Captain" Pearson caught the ball "three inches" shy of the goal line according to the Catawba student newspaper.[16] Neither offense could do much. The game wound up a 0–0 tie.

---

15 Roughly ten inches of rain fell in western Virginia/Piedmont North Carolina in September 1934, making it one of the wettest Septembers in recorded weather history.
16 *The Pioneer*, Oct. 20, 1934.

The Christians won their last four games to close the season at 6–2–1 and claim another North State title. They beat Guilford 14–0 in Greensboro in the season finale, played, fittingly, given all the rain problems during the season, on "a veritable lake . . . covered with slippery mud from one goal post to the other."[17]

Buoyed by scholarships, and doubtless enhanced by Walker's growing experience, Elon's athletic program was on a roll. Beginning with the 1933 baseball team, teams that Walker coached won seven straight league titles in the three big sports (the figure is eight if the disputed 1935 football championship is included). Elon swept all three major sports titles in 1933 and 1934 and 1934 and 1935 and was just a win or two from winning everything in Walker's last four seasons. The steady parade of victories actually became monotonous to some. An unknown *Maroon & Gold* editorialist even went so far as to say that "the matter of winning championships has become so common that no thrill is connected with the announcement."[18]

Elon's success across sporting seasons was no mystery. Walker was a clever and determined coach who applied similar principles—intense recruiting, extensive preparation, solid tactics, an iron will—to all the sports he coached. Player cross-pollination of the sports helped as well. Only a handful of Walker's athletes at Elon played for him in just one sport. Most played two and a number played three (and in a few cases, even—there were a handful of other sports at Elon during the period that Walker didn't coach), and it wasn't uncommon for the same players to star in more than one sport. Zac Walker was useful in three sports early on, although his best work was in football. Lefty Briggs excelled at baseball and basketball (as noted, his football experience wasn't as good), and Pete Williams was good enough to hit .333 his junior year. During the halcyon closing years of Walker's reign, top multisport players included Paul Roye, a brilliant basketball guard and sturdy baseball catcher; Webb "Bull" Newsome, a gifted football back and baseball pitcher who was also undefeated as a collegiate boxer; aforementioned footballer James "Jack Rabbit" Abbitt, who also excelled at basketball; basketball/baseball players

---

17 *Greensboro Daily News*, Nov. 11, 1934.
18 *Maroon & Gold*, May 27, 1936.

Paul "Lefty" Cheek and Howard "Hoke" Smith; football lineman Norman "Muddy" Waters and Walter "Firpo" Latham, who both pitched for the baseball team; and Hal Bradley, an all-conference end in football and star center in basketball.

***

It should come as no surprise that Walker's coaching skills seemed most advanced in baseball, the sport in which he excelled as a player and as both a professional and college coach. He was able to build on some tradition at Elon in baseball but undoubtedly did a lot of the building himself.

Walker's baseball teams often piled up gaudy offensive statistics, but his intent always seemed to be aimed at developing pitching and defense first. His clubs were never without an ace on the mound and often had two excellent pitchers. Almost without exception, one of the Christians' top hurlers was a lefty. Some coaches might leave that last detail to chance, but a real baseball man would consider the ability to attack the opposition lineup from both sides as fundamental. Of course, Walker was blessed to have inherited a young Lefty Briggs on his first team. He made sure that process was repeated by recruiting several more southpaws, including Lefty's younger brother Mike, who won twenty-three games for Walker from 1933 to 1936, just four fewer wins than his brother.

Although Walker's team could, and did, score a lot of runs, they were also adept at what today would be called small ball. Twice his teams squeezed out victories over North Carolina with meager offensive production. The 1933 team beat the Tar Heels when Ike Lindley and Paul "Lefty" Cheek executed a double steal in the second inning. Four years later, Walker's last baseball team managed only two hits against the Tar Heels, but both brought runners home to score in a 2–1 victory. Freshman Andrew "Dopey" Fuller pitched a three-hitter for Elon to secure the win.

Elon wasn't a runaway baseball power, however. Even while winning four straight North State titles (1932–1935), the Christians seldom were able to distance themselves the likes of Catawba,

Guilford, and Lenoir-Rhyne. The Christians needed a late rally to beat Lenoir-Rhyne 6–4 in the clinching tilt in 1933. They managed a 9–2 conference record and wound up winning the league by a full two games that year. But the race was closer than that until the very end. Likewise, in 1935, Elon squeezed out a critical, 1–0 victory over Catawba despite a five-hit, sixteen-strikeout performance by Indian ace "Smiling Bob" Hampton. That helped the Christians preserve a 10–2 conference mark, one better than Catawba in the loss column.

The 1935 team may have been the best team recruited entirely by Walker. His first club, with holdovers Lefty and Howard Briggs leading a group of seven future professionals (some might be better characterized as "semiprofessionals" who played for small amounts of money or gained jobs because of their ability to boost the company baseball team), would be the only possible match during his entire tenure. The 1935 team was essentially a repeat of the very good 1934 team. Only pitcher N.B. "Muddy" Waters and hard-hitting outfielder Lawrence Tuck (.449 batting average) were missing from the 1934 squad that went 16–5 overall. The 1935 team finished 13–5. Mike Briggs and Webb Newsome handled pitching. Tal Jobe hit .429, which helped replace the loss of Tuck, and the other regulars back from the year before—catcher Paul Roye, first baseman Lefty Cheek, outfielder Sally Newman, and shortstop Howard Smith, among others—were solid again. The 1936 club should have made it five in a row but dropped a season-ending doubleheader at Lenoir-Rhyne and finished one game behind Catawba.

Walker's 1937 baseball team, his last at Elon, needed some retooling. He had to find two new pitchers to replace Newsome and the last of the Briggs's boys; he also needed a replacement for Cheek and shortstop Smith. Walker, in typical fashion, managed to round up some arms. Tommy "Grandma" Williams transferred from Campbell and joined freshmen Jimmie Edwards and the aforementioned Fuller on the mound. But Elon struggled in league play, finishing 7–5, well out of running.

Even so, Walker's baseball work was exemplary. He finished with a record of 124–61, including a dominating 52–19 mark and six titles in North State play. And he regularly beat the Big Five clubs, achieving a dream on the diamond that he never attained on the football field. At least not at Elon.

Basketball was a different matter. Walker clearly had less experience in this realm than in the rest—recall that he played just a year of college ball at Howard—but it probably mattered far less than it might have in football of baseball. Basketball was less than forty years old when Walker began coaching college teams. Experts were in short supply, techniques were rudimentary, and the rules were in flux. While Walker was coaching at Elon, the ten-second backcourt rule (1933) and the three-seconds-in-the-lane rule (1936) were both introduced. The repeating center jump, held after every made field goal, didn't disappear until the 1937–1938 season, by which time Walker was out of the basketball business. Players were disqualified after four fouls, substitutions were limited, and, as was the case with football, sideline coaching was forbidden or frowned upon. This anachronistic concept was based on the premise that no small part of a player's skill was his ability to discern proper strategy and tactics. Coaches could impart this knowledge at practice and before games, as they trained their charges to become complete players, but once the game began it was up to the player to do the right thing. To have a coach intrude with suggested maneuvers—setting up specific plays, changing defenses, etc.—was considered unsportsmanlike. Would it be fair for the coach to come onto the court and take a shot for the players?

Whether prepping in practice or not coaching in a game, Walker the basketball coach toiled in a different time. Although newspaper accounts constantly refer to "fast" or "snappy" games, the pace of play was undoubtedly far slower than today. That was due in no small measure to the aforementioned unending string of jump balls. These pace-killing set pieces—there could be upward of fifty jump balls in a single contest, counting field goals and held balls—helped hold down scoring. They also put a premium on tall players and the coordination of jump ball plays.

Walker's early teams came up—quite literally—a little short. He was halfway into his Elon tenure before he began to land giants like 6'5" (and, in some accounts, 6'7") Ryland "Obie" Johnson or

6'4" Hal Bradley. Coincidentally or not, Elon got better when taller guys started showing up for Christian games.

Walker had two losing basketball seasons at Elon, his first and his fourth. The latter marked the end of the first wave of talent through the program, and, as was the case with football, when that wave washed by Walker's cupboard was pretty bare. As the athletic recruiting pipeline began filling up again, however, Walker found himself on a roll in basketball as well as everything else. An important addition to his hardcourt arsenal was Roye, a basketball whiz from Chattanooga. Walker was probably more interested in Roye as a baseball catcher, but the hard-nosed Roye was better at basketball and was rather easily the finest hoopster in Walker's tenure. Roye averaged 12.6 points per game for his career, an astounding figure in an age when scores were typically in the thirties. His scoring average is nearly double the second best Elon player (Rollins) in the school's first three decades of basketball.

Roye served notice early on that he was a force. When Elon played in the Charlotte Jaycee's Tri-State Holiday Tournament, Roye poured in twenty-three points in Elon's 51–27 thrashing of Lynchburg College in the title game. He hit thirteen straight free throws in the contest. That particular statistic suggests that he could not only shoot but was difficult to defend as well. That he had an edge about him there can be no doubt. The Reverend James Waggoner, Elon's industrious (and self-appointed) sports historian, recalls meeting Roye at the check-in desk for an old-timers baseball game. When Roye told him who he was, Waggoner, who had researched Roye's many athletic exploits, said good naturedly, "Oh, Paul Roye, I know all about *you*."

Roye glared. "You don't know anything about me," he said.

When Waggoner demonstrated that "knowing all about" Roye meant he could recite his career statistics in both sports, the tension eased a bit. But it was clear Roye wasn't someone to trifle with. That attitude, whatever one may think of it, served him well as an athlete and later as a baseball umpire.[19]

Roye was not a one-man army at Elon either. Paul Cheek, the standout first baseman, was good enough as a basketball

---

19 James Waggoner, interview with author.

player in 1935 (his second year on the team) to win first-team all-conference honors along with Roye. Forward Howard Smith, also of baseball fame, was a second-team pick, as was center Hal Bradley, a 6'4" freshman from Kipling, NC, a tiny town between Raleigh and Fayetteville. Bradley was destined for football glory as an end, although no one knew it just yet. In the winter of 1934–1935, he mostly looked like a basketball player. Tuck, the second-leading scorer from the year before, was now the fifth man on a very good team that went 18-6 and 10-1 in the North State.

Walker and the athletic department—the two were practically synonymous—survived the hard years of the Great Depression because of perseverance and the support of a great friend in President L.E. Smith. Smith, described by school chronicler Stokes (who knew him well) as "tall, muscular, of commanding presence . . . almost stern,"[20] did what had to be done to keep Elon afloat. That included a number of innovative, possibly illegal, strategies that speak to the desperation of the times.

In January 1932, the mostly cash funds collected for spring semester registration were, on Smith's orders, "deposited" at the home of the school's treasurer, just in case a creditor, or some agent acting on their behalf, was lurking about and tried to get their hands on it. For similar reasons, Smith once deposited school funds in a local bank in an account with his name on it. Some of those funds were lost when the bank went under.

In perhaps his boldest act, Smith gave some $30,000 in school bonds—the actual promissory notes—to a secretary and told her to place them in a safety deposit box of her choosing somewhere nearby. "Don't tell me where you put them until I ask you tell me," Smith told the woman. His reasoning? If he didn't actually know where they were, he couldn't produce them and wouldn't have to lie about the matter. This stratagem came in handy not long after it was concocted. A sheriff's deputy showed up a Smith's office with a court order giving him authority to seize the bonds and attach Elon debts to them. Smith told the officer he didn't know where they were and then opened his office (and the

---

20 Stokes, *Elon College*, p. 247.

school vault next door) to a search that he was fairly certain would be unfruitful. It was. The bonds were saved for another day.[21]

Hiding the school money under rocks and trees was an innovation that makes for a good anecdote. More important, if less colorful, was Smith's ability to secure a two-year moratorium on school debt from its major creditors in 1933, followed by a broad renegotiation of what the school owed in 1935. The agreed-upon terms were appalling—from the creditor's point of view—but typical of the kind of pennies-on-the-dollar settlement folks were willing to accept at that time. The major debt was consolidated into a single $190,000 loan with Virginia Trust. That figure was knocked down to $160,000 a year later when long-time college friend D.J. Carlton passed away and left the school a handsome bequest. The big loan was a 10-year note. Elon paid it off in 1943 with two days to spare, Smith himself driving to Virginia to deliver the last payment.[22]

President Smith's snappy budget work improved the college's position in 1935 and 1936, and the athletic machine he helped create was in full swing by then. Scholarship-enticed recruits were rolling in and Walker actually had a staff. Ralph Neal, the star fullback from 1933 to 1934, was originally scheduled to assume an assistant coaching position. But he never actually made it into the school's employ. Instead, Walker hired former North Carolina star Ellis Fysal to help him in football. Fysal also began coaching the school's fledgling wrestling team and oversaw most of the spring work in football, which trimmed Walker's load down to one sport during that busy time of year.

As for Walker himself, he was also rounding into form. He was the master of the North State Conference and, with the worst of the Depression fading from view, his Elon domain. It is around this time that the Peahead stories that would entertain Elon alumni for decades to come were created, brought into circulation, or both. Secluded spots where Walker allegedly seduced one female employee of the college or another were noted, impersonators capable of cursing in an Alabama drawl popped up, and tall tales were recorded in print. One Walker told about himself involved his travails while coaching a color-blind quarterback/tailback. The

---

21 Ibid., pp. 248–260; also L.E. Smith Papers.
22 Ibid. p. 302.

young man was a whiz passing the ball in practice, where Elon's players wore a mix of light and dark jerseys. But in games, where both teams typically wore their school colors, he was constantly throwing interceptions.[23] Walker cursed the player up and down, but without effect. Finally, Walker said, "Boy, just throw the ball to the players wearing our colors." "But Coach," said the color-blind player, "they're all wearing our colors."[24]

Less apocryphal and more demonstrative of Walker's quick wit is a story told by the late Jake Thomas, a distant relative of the famed Briggs's family. Thomas lived in California, but frequently traveled to North Carolina, where he went to visit his relatives, among other things. He got to know Peahead Walker through the Briggs's brothers and eventually made Elon one of his regular stops. He drove by there the campus one autumn afternoon, saw the Christians practicing, and got out and walked through the gate to the field. A student manager met him and said, "Mister you can't come in here. Practice is closed. Coach Walker's rules." "Oh, it's all right son," said Thomas. "I know Peahead. I just stopped to say hello. I'm sure he'll want to see me. Take him my card."

The kid took the card and ran to other end of field where Peahead was managing a particularly lackluster practice. Peahead took the card, looked at it, and then blew his whistle and called players together. After a brief talk, the team exploded from its huddle and went to back to drills and plays with an unbridled enthusiasm. Thomas was amazed. He'd never seen such energy and passion for a mere practice, especially not given what he'd viewed during the first part of practice. This outbreak of Christian enthusiasm went on for half an hour or so; then practice came to an end. After Peahead walked over toward him and they greeted one another, Thomas said, "Coach, that was pretty amazing. I don't think I've ever seen a practice quite like that before."

"Wall," said Peahead, "I'll tell ya. That was one of the worst practices we'd ever had until you got here."

"Really?" said Thomas. "What happened?"

---

[23] The current arrangement, where one team wears its colored jerseys while the other wears white, is a modern convention. In the 1930s, teams typically had just one color jersey and wore it every game.
[24] Rev. James Waggoner, interview with author.

"Wall, I called them boys in and showed them your card, which had Hollywood, California written on it. I said, 'Boys, you see this card? That belongs to that fellow over there. He's a big movie producer from Hollywood and he's making a movie about football. If any of you want to be in it, you'd better show him something.' And that was the best we've practiced all year."[25]

Walker's X-rated vocabulary was already well developed by this point. And as would be the case during his next stop at Wake Forest, the torrents of profanity he could produce were legendary to players and adoring alumni—and a concern to the leaders of a faith-based college. President Smith visited practice one afternoon to address the issue with the coach. In a conversation after the workout was over, Smith told Walker that were some concerns about the language he had been using during practices and games. Although agitated, Walker apologized profusely and said that he'd get on the boys and made sure they cleaned up their act.

"Well," said the President, "there's also the matter of the coaches."

Walker issued even more apologies and swore he'd clamp down on his staff and their potty mouths right away.

"Well," said President Smith, "the truth is Coach, that most of the complaints are about you."

"Oh," said Walker. Then, after a lengthy pause, "I'm not sure I can do much about that."[26]

Inspired no doubt by his growing confidence, relentlessness, and pride, Walker's last two football teams were among his best and appeared to be on a trajectory toward bigger and better things. The 1935 team played Davidson to a virtual standstill in its September 21 opener, losing 7–0. At the start of the 1936 season, Elon and NC State battled toe to toe on a humid day in Raleigh. The larger (both in terms of quantity and individual tonnage) Wolfpack squad finally won 12–0, but many observers thought Elon the more organized and better-connected club. That theory gained more credence as the season wore on. Elon got better and better and State fell apart. Wolfpack players and coaches pointed fingers and generally sniped at each other all season long.

---

25 Charlesanna Briggs Burea, interview with author.
26 Various interviews.

Some players got the boot, and Coach Heartley "Hunk" Anderson resigned at season's end to take an assistant's job at powerful Michigan. The following spring, with the Wolfpack program still in turmoil pending the arrival of new coach Doc Newton from Davidson, Elon won a spring scrimmage by something like four touchdowns to two (the contest was a scrimmage, and elements of the game were truncated).

Walker's last two gridiron teams were loaded. The 1935 team returned four very solid backfield starters in Webb Newsome, speedy Jack Stallings, Joe Caruso, and, of course, "Jack Rabbit" Abbitt, now a sophomore. The line included end John Troppoli, who would become Elon's first All-American selection; rugged end-center Rudy Walser; and promising newcomers Jimmy Hauselt and Al Mastrobattisto. One more new face who would eventually work his way into a prominent role was Hal Bradley, the basketball center. The 6'4" Bradley came to Elon to play basketball and had never played a down of football when he arrived. But the spring after his freshman season he either asked Walker if he could try out or vice versa (accounts differ). Although something of a rounder who struggled at times with his academic duties (in an exchange of letters in 1936, both Walker and L.E. Smith signaled their concerns regarding Bradley's attitude and influence that another player with questionable study habits had over him), Bradley was an exceptional athlete.[27] He quickly got the hang of football and eventually turned out to be even better on the gridiron than he was on the hardwood. Bradley, Abbitt, and Mastrobattisto all signed with the Washington Redskins after graduation and played briefly in that organization and with its farm clubs.

The 1935 team lost a couple of close ones early then closed with a rush. The Christians pounded Lenoir-Rhyne 20–0 and Catawba 32–0 before blasting hapless Guilford 65–0 to cap a 7–3 season. The latter result, easily the worst drubbing to date in the seventeen-year rivalry, was almost embarrassing. Elon scored every time it had the ball in the first half, outgained Guilford 491 yards to 47, and kept scoring even after intermission when Walker put in what subs he had.

---

[27] Letter from L.E. Smith to D.C. Walker, July 14, 1936 and letter from D.C. Walker to L.E. Smith, July 15, 1936. L.E. Smith Papers, Elon University Archives.

That seemed to wrap up another North State title, but before it was made official a scandal brewed up. Not surprisingly, it arose in Salisbury, home of Catawba, and a school well acquainted with the athletic taint. A few days after Elon had dragged his team around Shuford Field, Catawba coach Gordon Kirkland drove to Hickory to present North State Conference President F.J. Marion of Lenoir-Rhyne with evidence showing Elon had used five or six ineligible players in the Catawba game. The gist of the charges was that the players were not full-time students or had been admitted, or readmitted, to the school less than a year before the start of the current (fall) season. The North State Conference, like many leagues at that time, had "anti-tramp" rules requiring a full year's student residency before a player was eligible for intercollegiate athletics. It was supposed to keep migrant athletes and other riff-raff off the collegiate playing fields.

Marion agreed to look into the matter and drove to Elon sometime before the Christians' finale against Guilford to confer with officials there. What he found was a gray area surrounding one player, tackle Alfred "Jimmy" Hauselt, a burgeoning star on the Christian line (and, readers will recall, the recipient of a special scholarship). The burly Hauselt (in some account's Hausfelt, but official Elon records list Hauselt) was enrolled at Elon in the fall of 1934 and started most of the football games that same fall. He withdrew from classes after the 1934 football season—personal reasons were cited—and didn't take exams. But he returned to school in the spring and, according to Elon officials, made up the exams and other work missed after his fall semester withdrawal. As far as Elon was concerned, Hauselt's enrollment was continuous, although technically speaking not so much.

Marion thought the technicality mattered and sent a telegram to Kirkland on November 27 in which he stated that his ruling was that Elon had indeed played one ineligible man.[28] Marion did not find evidence to support Kirkland's contention, however, that more Elonites were beyond the eligibility pale—but no matter. One was enough to gum up the works. Because Hauselt had played against Catawba (and, for that matter, against Lenoir-

---

28 *Salisbury Post,* Dec. 15, 1935.

Rhyne and Guilford), Elon's conference record was certainly in jeopardy, and the conference title picture was up for grabs. Both the Elon and the Catawba school papers published stories in early December celebrating the conference titles won by their teams. ("North State Champs!" read the caption under a Catawba team photo in the *Pioneer*, "Coach Walker's Eleven Win Third Loop Title," trumpeted the *Maroon & Gold*).

Neither was correct—not then. And not ever as it turned out. The fate of the North State's football championship trophy would be decided at the conference's annual winter meeting in December. Like many collegiate leagues of the day, the North State did not issue awards until representatives from all the schools involved could get together for a discussion. The disparity in schedules—not everyone played the same number of games and certainly not the same teams—and other potential anomalies made this a wise course, although by the time the actual meeting was held the voting on championships, etc., was usually perfunctory.

Not on this occasion. Marion presented his case, his research, his conclusion. Elon Professor J.W. Barney, Head of the Athletic Committee, explained Elon's technical rebuttal—Catawba had not filed its protest prior to the contest as North Carolina Intercollegiate Athletic Association rules prescribed. In addition, Hauselt wasn't, in Elon's view, ineligible—and he told the assembled representatives that Elon would not give up the championship, no matter that it hadn't actually been awarded it. A vote was taken on Hauselt's eligibility. Not surprisingly, given the whupping Elon had been laying on conference members in recent years, the tally was 6–1 against Elon and in favor of an ineligible ruling. That was the simple part. Trickier was what that all meant. There were no clear rules to act upon, the precedent skimpy. Recall that the earlier eligibility controversy involving Catawba's Zaengle was not, technically, a North State affair, because the league wasn't officially formed until after that case was decided. What's more, in that case it was the school, not the conference, that meted out the punishment; Catawba self-imposed the forfeiture of games and titles as a fitting penalty.

There was one other case. In the spring of 1931, Lenoir-Rhyne was awarded the North State baseball title after Appalachian

State was found to have used an ineligible player. That protest was also filed after the fact, and the conference commissioner at the time had ordered the games between the two schools forfeited to Lenoir-Rhyne. But that was precedent and not law. Marion told the delegates during the 1935 meeting that he didn't believe he had the authority to order games forfeited. Never mind said the delegates. Again they voted 6–1 to order a forfeit of the games in which Hauselt played. They also amended their rules to make it clearer what the league president could and could not do with regard to forfeits. And they instructed the league secretary to write a formal letter to Elon officially informing the school's leaders of what they had done and, oh, by the way, reminding the Elonites that the North State Conference had never *officially* adopted the North Carolina Intercollegiate Athletic Association rule on eligibility protests before the fact.

That seemed to be that, but then Catawba, which had started the whole mess, decided to take the high road, mucking things up again. The school's representative at the meeting took the floor and stated that Catawba didn't want the title since it hadn't actually won it *on* the field. Kirkland then moved that Elon be awarded the title. "We are not interested in having the championship forfeited," the Catawba coach said afterwards. "We are just interested in fair play."[29]

It is impossible to determine how authentic this bit of chivalry really was. But no matter. It died for lack of a second (Elon, which could have seconded the motion, apparently didn't want to gain a title in that manner). The situation was now a real puzzle. Elon, which had won the title on the field, had been ordered to vacate it, but Catawba, which had won the title off the field, wouldn't take it. With no other eligible or willing candidate available, the conference voted to simply leave the title vacant for the year, which officially ended the controversy.

That was not really the end of it, of course. The victors get to write the history and with two victors, two histories were written. Both Elon and Catawba count the 1935 game as a victory in their official records. The forfeit win over Elon is part of a 9–1 season for

---

29 *Salisbury Post*, Dec. 15, 1935.

the Indians that year. Hauselt, who admittedly was not known for his scholastic work, wasn't left out either.[30] Along with Newsome, Abbitt, Caruso, Mastrobattisto, Walser, and end Don Schlitter, he was one of seven Christians elected to the North State All-Conference team.

The success of the 1935 team lent a nice luster to the possibilities of the 1936 edition. Peahead Walker was apparently feeling a little flush himself and loaded the squad down with an imposing schedule. The Christians would start with five straight road games, none of them against slouches. The result was five straight losses. NC State was first, winning a by a narrow 12–0 margin. Then Washington and Lee beat the Christians 27–0. George Washington followed with a 39–0 pummeling, and West Chester State whipped them for the second straight year, this time by a 25–0 count. The next week the Christians traveled to Philadelphia for their one-and-only meeting with LaSalle. And, after three quarters, the result was the same as it had been all season. Elon's opponent had a bunch of points and Elon had none. But in the last four minutes of the last quarter against the Explorers, down 36–0, Elon suddenly found the end zone. Two quick scores put twelve points on the board, and although that was well short of LaSalle's total, the brief rally did reenergize the team and launched them on a winning streak that lasted two months.

To start the streak off, a banged-up bunch of Christians punished the Duke B team 51–0. W.C. "Alabama" Moran, a sub from the deeper reaches of the bench, surprised everyone by scoring three touchdowns against what was clearly more like a C or D squad from Duke. This may have been the contest in which manager Maness, he of the shower room uniform cleaning, got a taste of real glory. Maness said, years after the fact, that there was a blowout home game in which friends in the crowd began chanting, "We want Maness! We want Maness!" Contrary to his policy on such popular requests in later years, Walker supposedly let Maness suit up and go into the tilt. His teammates carried the lark a bit further, setting up a play in which Maness actually

---

30 A *Maroon & Gold* columnist, perhaps writing with tongue in check, once praised Hauselt as being without peer at the college for his uncanny ability to sleep—almost 'round the clock.'

carried the ball. It became a subject of much amusement when the starry-eyed manager grabbed the pigskin and took off . . . in the wrong direction. Teammates were forced to tackle him before he ruined the shutout.[31]

More serious work followed. Elon beat Naval Apprentice 6–0 the next week and then opened its defense of the North State title it may or may not have actually won by pounding Lenoir-Rhyne 39–0 in a homecoming game played at Greensboro's War Memorial Stadium. Elon followed the victory over Lenoir-Rhyne with a decisive 25–6 victory over Emory & Henry's always difficult Wasps. For a change, this one wasn't close. Emory & Henry scored on a kickoff return after Elon's first touchdown but was seldom able to move the ball. The red-hot Abbitt, his "swivel hips moving relentlessly," scored two more long touchdowns and had a sixty-one-yard gallop nullified by a penalty.[32] The next week the Christians hammered Guilford 39–0, exploding for twenty-six points in the second quarter. Amos Shelton, a quarterback from Greensboro, ran for two scores and passed to Rudy Walser for two more. (That was a bit unusual because Walser made the All-Conference teams as a center. But he was at end that day filling in for an injured teammate.)

That set up a late-season showdown with Catawba. The Indians were 2–1 in conference play but could lay legitimate claim to the crown if they could beat the Christians. For the second year in a row it wasn't close. Abbitt ran for three scores, Humphries got two, and Catawba couldn't keep up. The final, 33–13, was closer than it sounded.

So there, after a miserable start, was a 6–5 season and a third conference title in four years.

Or fourth in four by some counts.

***

In the spring of 1937, even as Walker's Elon football program was reaching its apex—achieving continuous domination of the North State Conference and even defeating Big Five member NC State in

---

31 Stokes, *Elon College: Its History and Traditions* pp. 261–62.
32 *Greensboro Daily News*, Nov. 8, 1936.

a spring game—plans were afoot that would end the coach's ultra-successful tenure at Elon. Those plans were being made at Wake Forest College, another small, denominationally based college, just an hour or so east of Elon near Raleigh.

Rumors linking Walker to an athletic rejuvenation plan at Wake Forest were already rampant in the spring of 1937. Sportswriters covering the Southern Conference basketball tournament that spring knew something was up. Wake Forest officials wandered around the tournament with I-know-something-you-don't-know grins and hinted at big news to come. Most of the sports writing community had heard that Wake was contemplating a move to kick Coach Jim Weaver upstairs to a newly created athletic director's post.

James H. "Jim" Weaver had been hired to coach football and basketball and to oversee athletics at Wake in 1933. Viewed through modern lenses, it was an odd hire because Weaver came to Wake directly from Oak Ridge Military Academy near Greensboro. The 6'3", 220-pounder was a superb (and for the time quite large) collegiate player at both Emory & Henry in Virginia and at Louisiana's Centenary College—and that was often credential enough for that time and place. But his experience in the coaching world was limited. Weaver stayed at Centenary for a year after graduation, coaching the freshman team; he then spent two years coaching in Texas high schools. In 1928 he moved to Oak Ridge, a military school that played a schedule somewhat like that of a modern junior college. The Cadets' regular foes included prep schools of various description and collegiate freshmen and junior varsity teams.[33] Because of the post-high school status of at least some of Oak Ridge's players, Weaver's job included a recruiting aspect. For reasons not completely clear, the school was also

---

33 In fact, the schedule was more collegiate than prep. In the 1930 and 1931 seasons, for example, Oak Ridge's football schedule included these foes: Hargrave Military Academy, the Davidson freshmen, the NC State freshmen, the UNC reserves, the Duke freshmen, the Wake Forest freshmen, Boiling Springs Junior College, Mars Hill College, the Langley Air Corps, the Parris Island Marines, the Virginia Tech freshmen, Weaver College of Asheville, the University of South Carolina freshmen, the Greensboro All-Stars, and the "High School" All-Stars.

allowed to compete for North Carolina high school championships on certain occasions. Not surprisingly, given the presence of exceptional seniors on the club, Oak Ridge won several titles while Weaver was in charge, and his clubs always dominated. For instance, in Weaver's first season, when he was part of a physically imposing staff that also included ex-UNC star "Ox" Shuford, Oak Ridge outscored the opposition 314–0.

Weaver's prep record, and his various personal attributes, were impressive enough to land him the Wake job in June 1933. The fact that Walton Kitchin, the son of Wake Forest College President Thurman D. Kitchin, starred in football under Weaver at Oak Ridge, probably didn't hurt either.

Weaver arrived in the middle of the Depression, a time of tremendous pessimism with regard to future plans. Even so, Wake Foresters were thinking positive, or at least bigger, thoughts with regard to athletics. An expansion of Gore Field was in the works, and it was a student-led rebellion against what was considered to be inferior football that had created the gridiron coaching opening at Wake in the first place. Students, including some football players, agitated for the ouster of F.S. "Pat" Miller in the winter of 1932–1933 despite the fact that he'd gone 18–15–4 in four seasons and had seventeen lettermen returning for 1933. Miller's teams weren't as successful as some Deacon teams of the recent past, however (Hank Garrity's 1923–1925 teams went 19–7–1 with a solid 6–2–1 against the Big Five), and . . . they were boring. What's more, Miller was a crusty sort who didn't win friends easily. Nonetheless, his sloppy dismissal—it was announced in March 1933 that his resignation had been accepted but that he might still coach that fall if the Trustees didn't approve a new hire at their June meeting—caused some internal rifts. A half-dozen lettermen, including the team's elected captain and co-captain, didn't return.

That may have contributed to the slow start by Weaver and his new assistant, Murray Greason, a star halfback under Garrity. Inexperienced coaching may have contributed more. Although Weaver was eager and earnest his first few teams weren't much.[34]

---

34 At the end of August, just as his first season was about to start, Weaver told a reporter from the *News & Observer* that he was the like the "little rabbit" being chased by the hound. Just as its legs were about to give out, a powerful

The 1933 team was shut out its first five games despite his switch to the newfangled "short punt" formation and only scored two touchdowns all season.[35] His first three teams were a combined 5–19–1—much worse than Miller's supposedly inferior teams. But in 1936, Weaver managed to put together a winner. Helped by a softer schedule and maturing players, the Deacons finished 5–4.

That was progress, but maintaining that sort of work, or, better yet, improving upon it, was a daunting task. Duke, with Wallace Wade in harness, was clearly headed for bigger and better things. UNC was a regional power with national aspirations, and NC State appeared capable, if not necessarily immediately ready, of ratcheting up its football as well.

Weaver, an affable and intelligent man with a penchant for administration, found this both daunting and frustrating. There was no way he could run an athletic department, coach a football team, and develop (that is, recruit) new players. He needed help. So he put together a plan under which he'd become the school's full-time athletic director while someone else, a new man, took over actually coaching the football team. That would solve the basic manpower issue, which was certainly important. But it's also possible that Weaver understood his own limitations. Especially with regard to recruiting for the big-time arena, he appeared to be in over his head.

After the fact, and in public, Weaver downplayed his own dissatisfaction with the situation. But in a 1937 letter from his wife, Kathrine Dunn Weaver, to her parents, the pressures were all too evident:

> *Jim knew it was the best thing because it has been such a strain trying to coach the boys, chaperone them on trips, to be responsible for their conduct and scholastic achievements on campus, and to*

---

jackrabbit caught up to him and asked him if he thought he could make it. "Man, I've got to make it!" the little rabbit declared. "I'm just like the little rabbit," said Weaver. Source: *News & Observer*, Aug. 31, 1933.

35 The "short punt" was, as the name suggests, a formation similar to the standard punt formation, but with the deep back not as far back as in the normal punt formation. The deep back would have been 5–6 yards behind the line, with two or three backs, mostly used for blocking, between him and the line.

play ball for them. People think coaches can do everything. . . . However, he was a little sad, I think, at giving it up. He will make the same salary in his new capacity, I think and it will be a nine month job instead of three—don't mention all that; it may have been told to us in confidence.[36]

Weaver found some mitigation for his sadness in coaching the Wake Forest freshmen in the years before World War II. He supported his new coach with other hands-on work as well. He and Walker became great friends and often went recruiting together. They also collaborated fully on scheduling, program administration, and even some finer coaching points. Jennie Brewer, who grew up in Wake Forest and worked in the athletic office as an intern while she was in high school, recalled that "the two of them [Weaver and Walker] just seemed to have the best time" and that "they really got along with each other."[37]

The strapping Weaver wasn't quite the character that Walker was, but he was loquacious, loved a good story, and didn't mind whiling away the hours swapping tales. Shortly after assuming the Deacon football post in 1933, he spent more than a hour talking to a Raleigh newspaperman just about his defensive philosophy. By the time Walker came on as coach, Weaver's status as a raconteur and friend of the press was well-established. In the fall of 1937, Jake Wade of the *Charlotte Observer* wrote this of the new Deacon athletic tandem: "Certainly a visitor to Wake Forest this fall will be subjected to some droll stories. Jim [Weaver] always could tell them and Peahead [Walker] is a past master. . . . This is going to be a good business team that will get results."[38]

Duke's Wade wrote a letter of endorsement for Walker to the powers that be at Wake, an interesting twist for two men who would soon become bitter rivals. Wade, of course, knew Walker, both from Elon and (possibly) from Walker's days at Vanderbilt (where Wade coached the defense).

President Kitchin appears to be have been on board with Weaver's plan since the winter, or early spring, when Weaver

---

36 Letter from Kate Dunn Weaver to parents, July 1937. Wake Forest Archives.
37 Jennie Brewer, interview with author.
38 *Charlotte Observer*, Sept. 7, 1937.

approached him with the idea. It was a bold move. The school, with right around a thousand students, was struggling to fight its way out of the economic gloom, and adding a new, well-paid position to athletics (plus boosting Weaver's pay to a more full-time basis) could not have been easy. But Weaver's plan was built not just on spending more money. He figured that better teams would bring in more as well. Lights had been added at old Gore Field during Weaver's first four years, and the Deacons were embarking on more ambitious schedules. Kitchin did not address the expected return on investment in writing but did note in one report to the Trustees that if it's worth having a football team at all, the school might as well have a good one.

The logic is unassailable, if not always executable.

The plan took shape during the spring but wasn't approved until the Trustees met at a Raleigh hotel in early July. After short debate, the plan was approved. When the meeting was done, Trustee Chair J. Melville Broughton of Raleigh stepped into the lobby and announced the hiring of Peahead Walker as the school's new football coach (the press had, presumably, been alerted in advance and were waiting outside to hear). Walker received a three-year contract starting at $4,000 a year—a sixty-seven percent raise from his for-the-record salary at Elon, which, as noted, was often not paid in full. What's more, he would be responsible for just the football team and would have not one but two assistant coaches. Walker, who by now had two children in tow and was doubtless in need of some extra cash, said publicly that the deal wasn't about the money. It was about the opportunity.

"I've been at Elon 10 years and believe I've gone as far there as possible," he told reporters the day the move was announced. "The change does not mean that I'm making a larger salary. I believe we can do a little better at a larger school with more material."[39]

The timing of the announcement was awkward for Walker. Both Elon and Wake were out of school, and he was in Snow Hill where he was well on his way to managing the Billies to a Coastal Plain League title. His current boss—that is, his current college's

---

39 *Raleigh News & Observer*, Sept. 27, 1937.

boss, Elon's President Smith—heard about the move from a newspaper reporter, a circumstance that created some bad blood between the two.

Not surprisingly, the feud wound up being mostly about money, although the row started when Walker and Assistant Coach Ellis Fysal, who moved to Wake along with Walker, returned to Elon one weekend night ten or so days after the news was out and "broke into" their office and removed their personal belongings. At least that's how Smith put it in a July 21 letter to Walker.

Walker had a different opinion and aired it fully in a long letter (written on Wake Forest College Department of Athletics stationery, which he had somehow acquired in Snow Hill) to Smith dated July 22:

> *If it was your intention to imply that I broke into North Dormitory or that I took things which did not belong to me, I hasten to say that I am neither a thief nor a robber. I did not have much time to be at Elon Sunday morning for I had to return for a baseball game at Snow Hill during the afternoon. That is the reason I did not take the time nor did I think it was necessary for me to have an escort on the campus. . . . Very Truthfully Yours, DC Walker.*[40]

Smith responded that he was disappointed Walker didn't at least leave him a note and then got to what was probably the real meat: the awkward aspect of his departure and his lack of communication with Smith while the Wake Forest deal was being done.

"I wonder you would have felt if last year you had picked up the morning paper and read that Elon College had elected another coach and you had not been conferred with in any way?" wrote Smith. "I believe in this matter of human relations that we should always do unto others as we would have them do unto us."[41]

Walker apologized for not leaving a note or informing Smith, although in regard to the latter, the matter was really out of his hands. Wake's Trustees made his election as the Deacons' new coach official and released that news to the press on the same day,

---

40 L.E. Smith Papers.
41 Ibid.

almost simultaneously, he told Smith. As to Smith's hypothetical, shoe-on-the-other-foot question, Walker said it wasn't a good analogy. A coach had to receive more notification from an institution than an institution did from a coach, because while an institution could always find another coach, a coach who resigned a job before it was certain he had a new one might find himself out of a job altogether. "I should think a football coach ought to be notified by Thanksgiving if he is to be retained the following year if he does not have a contract for more than one year," wrote Walker.[42]

There were plenty of other issues to resolve. Smith wanted to make sure that Walker didn't try to take any Elon recruits with him to Wake Forest (it appears that he didn't or was unsuccessful if he did), and he needed Walker's help in sorting through the murk of scholarship commitments to players still in the program.

Those matters were handled amicably. Settling up on Walker's salary was a different matter. It turned out to be a rather complicated issue because in large part to the informality of how it was secured in the first place. The key point was what the school owed Walker for July 1937. His employment with the school for the 1936–1937 school year ended in June. He had been re-elected for 1937–1938, implying employment (and hence, compensation) for that school year beginning in July. But of course that was the same month Walker (eventually) told the school he was leaving for Wake Forest. Would the school, in light of all Walker had done for its athletics, pay up?

It would, but when Smith mailed an exhaustive accounting of the matter (Elon's version, of course) to Walker along with a check for $57.63, Walker mailed it back. Among the issues in question were whether or not Walker should have to pay tuition and room bills still owed by his brother Archie.

"I have never at anytime in writing or in conversation with you agreed to assume the obligations of my brother," Walker wrote in reply. "I don't know how you ever got the impression that I was assuming Archie's obligations to the college. His affairs and mine with the college have no connection whatever."[43]

---

42 Ibid.
43 Ibid.

Smith sent Walker a new check, this one for $140, which represented the balance on the 1936–1937 salary (minus a $60 expense), and promised to pay the 1935–1936 back salary as soon as more money was collected from an ongoing fundraising campaign. As for the Archie mess, well, shame on you, Peahead . . . or words to that effect:

> *Because of the interest that I had in you and Zack [sic] and Archie, I persuaded [Archie] to return to school, and promised him that the School would cooperate by allowing him his tuition, which we did. I am glad that we did it, but of course if you and Zack, his brothers, are not interested in him and are not willing to trust him, I see no reason why Elon College should go further with him . . . the college is under no obligations to him. I regret to see him relegated to the ordinary mill worker's position through life.*[44]

As it turned out, Archie Walker eventually got his degree and was not doomed to life in the mill. He became, as noted, a very successful high school coach and teacher in and around Elon and Alamance County.

There is no record as to who paid for the rest of his schooling, and Elon did pay Archie's older brother the rest of his back salary.

But not a penny more.

Peahead Walker's Elon days were over.

He was a Deacon now.

---

44 Ibid.

CHAPTER 5

THE BAPTIST HOLLER BUILDER

The Wake Forest College (WFC) community greeted its new football coach with open arms in the fall of 1937. The Peahead Walker family—dad, mom, and two growing sons—moved into a nice house on US Highway 1, the main street running through the middle of the little college town, and the coach quickly got down to the business of putting together a team for the coming season—a necessary but not altogether exciting prospect for Walker and his small staff, which included Deacon holdover Murray Greason and Ellis Fysal, Walker's chief and only assistant from Elon. Walker came to Wake to build a program that would lead the Deacon football team to new heights, and that was an exciting prospect. But that would take time. Until then he had to make do with what he had.

Which wasn't much.

Although Jim Weaver had cobbled together a respectable 5-4 record in 1936, including a victory over Clemson that marked the competitive high-water mark of Weaver's coaching tenure, the guts of that team disappeared at the school's May 1937 commencement exercises. That included team captain Ed Rodgers along with the entire backfield: Dal Morris, Walt Kitchin (son of the school's president), Bob Warren, and the inimitable "Hobo" Daniel. Daniel, the first Wake player chosen All-Southern Conference (the 1936 season was Wake's first in the Southern), was a superb all-around talent who led Wake in scoring and rushing. Despite the implied itinerancy of his unusual nickname, he was a tried-and-true Deacon. His father, Raleigh Daniel, played on Wake Forest's very first football teams in the late 1880s and early 1890s.[1]

---

[1] The elder Daniel died in October of 1937 while driving to Wake Forest for the annual homecoming football game. Spectators at the contest observed a moment of silence to commemorate his passing.

Many others were missing, too. Walker welcomed back just three lettermen from the 1936 team plus four reserves who didn't see enough action to earn the varsity W. Just four sophomores were up from a miserable freshman team that went 0–4 and scored just two touchdowns.

None of this filled the coach with optimism, and before the Deacons' opener in 1937, a reporter for the *Old Gold & Black*, Wake Forest's student newspaper, pointedly asked Walker which games he thought his team might win during the coming campaign. Just as pointedly, Walker told the young man that "we are pointing towards [the season-ending game against] Davidson. I hope that the team will be able to win the Wofford and Erskine games [as well]. It might be that it won't win any of them, but these are the games that we have our eye on mostly." Elaborating on the overall position of the program, Walker added, "The schedule is not too hard for a school of this size and I see no reason to make it any different in the future. But this year our team is not up to normal and it will be hard to win."[2] In an interview near season's end with *Charlotte Observer* sportswriter Jake Wade, Walker was both more specific and blunt in his assessment of the team's rebuilt backfield. "Our backfield has been weak," he said, "and our secondary defense just hasn't had it."[3]

Walker's preseason prediction was on target. His first team had no offensive punch whatsoever. The Deacons were shutout five times and had almost no ability to move the ball against quality teams. The squad did manage to win the three games their coach said they might win, but hey didn't come close in any of the rest.

In time, Walker would become great friends with Jim Weaver. They became a great professional tandem and were close enough away from the field and court that as the two men battled terminal illnesses in the summer of 1970, their wives (meaning, in this case, Walker's second wife) turned to each other for solace.

But in the fall of 1937, Walker may have chafed at the mess Weaver left him. The paucity of talent that greeted Walker was a glaring indictment of Weaver's abilities as a recruiter. Although Weaver, future leader of the still-to-be-created Atlantic Coast

---

2 *Old Gold & Black*, Sept. 29, 1937.
3 *Charlotte Observer*, Nov. 27, 1937.

Conference, was an able administrator and by all measures a knowledgeable coach, he fell short in this vital area. The end result of four years' worth of recruiting by Weaver—that is, Walker's first varsity roster—was a group that was sorely lacking. There were doubtless many reasons for this, but the bottom line was that Weaver just wasn't very good at this part of the job. Among other problems, he was either disinclined, or unable, to expand the Deacons' recruiting reach. Weaver's boys were almost entirely a homegrown bunch. He recruited North Carolina, especially eastern North Carolina, but not much else. That might have been all right if Wake Forest were the only suitor for the cream of the Tar Heel state, but, then as now, that was hardly the case. The Deacons were no better than the third or fourth choice for in-state boys at that time. Powerful Duke, in particular, had positioned itself as the place to play and took pride in the fact that it was on its football field where the flower of North Carolina youth was molded into national football championship contenders. That situation is reversed today—Duke's athletic teams are mostly "foreign" born and bred—but the position as home state champion, which essentially began when Wallace Wade arrived as the school's coach in 1931, was maintained into the 1950s. Serious in-state rivals naturally looked elsewhere, a circumstance that led Duke apologist Harry Beaudouin to whine about the high percentage of "Yankees" on the rosters at Wake Forest, UNC, and NC State (all forty-one percent or higher versus a mere twenty-five percent at Duke) in a 1948 newspaper column.[4]

So it was later in the Walker era after Peahead worked his recruiting magic. His first squad, made up entirely of Weaver holdovers, was nearly an all-North Carolina bunch. Of the eighteen or so regulars, all but three were Tar Heel natives. The Deacons were never so geographically homogenous again. Walker recruited some talented North Carolina boys, including stars like Nick and Bo Sacrinty, Red O'Quinn, and Dickie Davis, but most of his best players came from afar.

By contrast, Weaver's best recruiting work as Wake's head coach came during his first season when he coaxed tailback Walton

---

4 *Charlotte News,* Oct. 17, 1948.

Kitchin, plus four others players, to come with him from Oak Ridge Academy, where'd he coached before coming to Wake. He also reached back to his coaching roots in Texas and Louisiana to corral a couple more players. None of this can be considered a major feat, with the signing of Kitchin, the star of the class, being a particular gimme. As noted, Kitchin's father Thurman was Wake Forest's president and was already a fan of Weaver for the work he'd done with his son at Oak Ridge. All those wells dried up soon thereafter, however—President Kitchin was out of sons—and Weaver didn't have the time or the knowhow, perhaps, to find more good players some place else.

Walker, by comparison, had already proved himself an able assessor and collector of talent long before he arrived in "Baptist Hollow." An extensive network of contacts, developed while recruiting for Elon, while playing and managing baseball, and, in all likelihood, through some his "social" activities, was already in place and ready to be utilized. As subsequent events would prove, he had a knack for that part of job.

Those skills would be sorely tested, not only by Wake's rivals but by the world of collegiate athletics itself, which was in a decided state of flux as Walker began his Wake Forest tenure. The turn-of-the-century debates about the propriety of scholarships (or aid of any type) for athletes were stirring back to life as the country and its colleges hacked their way out of the Great Depression. There were still significant voices who thought collegiate athletics in general had been grossly overemphasized and who continued to pressure the three-decade-old but still toothless NCAA to take a stand. The NCAA responded by repeatedly passing what it called anti-professionalism and anti-subsidy (i.e., scholarships) resolutions. But with no enforcement other than what member organizations were willing to do themselves, there was no chance for effective national reform.[5] And there probably wasn't majority support for big changes regardless. Nationwide, so many athletic traditions had been established, such a commercial force unleashed, that any serious unwinding was unthinkable. Big-time

---

5 The NCAA's main enforcement tool at this time was an annual questionnaire sent to member schools. It asked if they were in compliance with NCAA rules. Not surprisingly, most said they were.

collegiate sports, with all their moneymaking and morale-raising power, were here to stay.

Against this background, the three-year-old Southeastern Conference (SEC) announced in 1935 that it would allow its members to offer above-board scholarships for athletes.[6] This news caused gasps and some teeth-gnashing in other parts of the country. The Deep South was already reviled/admired for its aggressive recruiting tactics. The decision to award athletic scholarships, right out in the open where everyone could see, was viewed as an escalation of that problematic behavior. Some Western and Midwestern teams pondered blacklisting SEC teams by refusing to play them.[7]

Officially, the Southern Conference's leaders decided to head in the other direction. The same year as the SEC announcement, Southern Conference presidents announced the adoption of the Graham Plan, which banned recruiting and athletic subsidies of any kind. In hindsight, it is difficult to imagine what the presidents were thinking. The plan's namesake, Frank Porter Graham, was UNC president. Graham was a noted and liberal-minded idealist who was later investigated by the notorious House Un-American Activities Committee and buried by smear tactics in a famously racist US Senate campaign.[8] It's quite possible then that he had real hopes for reform. But since the school he ran was, at that time, among the conference's worst recruiting/subsidy offenders, the campaign was likely doomed from the start. It did have some effect, however. Graham apparently signaled enough serious intent to cause the Tar Heels' successful coach, Carl Snavely, to bolt for Cornell.[9]

---

[6] The Southeastern Conference was formed in 1932 when the thirteen western-most members of the twenty-five-team Southern Conference left to form a new league.

[7] Waterson, J.S., *College Football: History, Spectacle, Controversy.* 2002. Baltimore, MD: Johns Hopkins University Press, pp. 184–185.

[8] Graham lost in the 1950 Democratic Party primary in a runoff election after dominating the initial primary. His opponent, Willis Smith, covertly played the race card, raising fears of increased integration, and Graham's out-of-step intellectualism against him.

[9] Snavely would return to UNC 11 years later when the alumni decided it was time to get serious about football again.

The Graham Plan passed its initial conference muster by just one vote. But that was for show. In truth, the measure received only lip service, outside of Charlottesville, VA, home of the University of Virginia (UVA). UVA was the only league school at that time that wasn't giving subsidies (and the Wahoos were paying for it, in competitive terms, both on the field and on the court). Slightly more than a year later, just as Wake entered the league and Walker began his tenure there, the conference rescinded its earlier vote. Heavy lobbying from Duke's Wade played a prominent role in the reversal, although he was hardly alone in his dislike of the Graham Plan.[10] The brief rule of the Graham Plan did nothing beyond causing two significant departures: Snavely, as noted, bolted from Carolina, and UVA, disgusted with the unrepentant (and blatantly hypocritical) actions of its league brethren, pulled out of the Southern Conference.[11]

Depression or no, by the mid- to late-1930s big-time dollars were flowing into the business of college football, and, in particular, football recruiting. At Oklahoma, for instance, the Sooners were gearing up for their run at national prominence with help from boosters like E.C. "Big Boy" Johnson, who bankrolled recruiting trips, helped hide players from rival schools, and made sure that funds were available as needed.[12] Johnson reputedly was the leading contributor to the Lindell Pearson Ransom Fund, a pool of money said to have reached $100,000 that was put together to lure

---

10 The stiff-necked Wade, as was his wont, took what might be called a high-road tack when criticizing a plan intended to clean up college athletics. His stated reasoning: if Duke couldn't offer scholarships to athletes, then only boys of affluent families could play football and other sports for the school, which wasn't fair to the non-affluent. Wade's spirit of egalitarianism sounded laudable. It was left for others to point out that a subsidy ban actually would have made recruiting far more difficult for Duke. Who knew? Some excellent (non-affluent) players might migrate to cheaper schools nearby. *Wallace Wade*, 2005. Lewis Bolling, Carolina Academic Press. p. 207.
11 UVA was admitted to the new Atlantic Coast Conference, which featured many 1937 Southern Conference teams, shortly after the creation of the ACC in 1953. The ACC's seven charter members—Clemson, Duke, Maryland, UNC, NC State, South Carolina, and Wake Forest—were all former Southern Conference members.
12 Dent, J., *The Undefeated: The Oklahoma Sooners and the Greatest Winning Streak in College Football*. 2002. New York: St. Martin's Press. pp. 98–100.

a prized recruit (that would be Lindell Pearson) back from Arkansas, which had "kidnapped" the speedy runner after coercing him to renege on a previous commitment to play at Oklahoma.

These sort of antics were widespread and left some incensed. Sports writing legend Grantland Rice wrote the following in a 1940 *Sport Magazine* column: "More than a few players got paid—up to $10,000 a year. I have been reading lately statements by many college presidents that 'as far as they know' their alumni have given no financial aid . . . in too many cases, 'as far as I know ' is about as far as a midget can throw an elephant."

The corruption was spread far and wide. It even reached the rural backwoods of North Carolina and the Mills Home Baptist Orphanage near Thomasville, where a powerful and speedy tackle named Pat Preston was the subject of an intense recruiting battle in the spring of 1939. The offers poured in, and the dirt-poor orphan was dazed by it all. In a reminiscence taped by his son in 1994, Preston recalled the following:

> *A lot of coaches come by and talked to me, offered me a full scholarship. I guess I had at least fifteen or so offers. They'd say, 'Come on down to our school and play football; it won't cost you anything.' Room, board, tuition, fees, and $10 a month. But one of the schools, without mentioning any names, they really were after me. One [of the coaches] offered me a full scholarship, [and] they also offered me a checking account. . . . I didn't know what the hell that was. They said, 'Well, if you need anything, a shirt, a tie, instead of asking for that you just write a check.' I didn't understand that. I was dumb. . . . Now that same school was [also] going to give me a car. Now this was 1939. They said, 'Now it won't be a new car. It will be a '38.' I said, 'My Lord! Give me a car!? A '38!?' Over here at the orphanage I didn't even own a bicycle. I had to pick blackberries at ten cents a pint to get the town boy to let me ride his bicycle [in exchange for either the money or the blackberries, Pearson didn't say which]. We had one pair of skates for the whole dormitory [where Preston lived]. You skated around*

on one skate [so two could do it at one time]. I said, 'They must be lying if they're going to give me a car.'[13]

Puzzled by the lucrative offer, Preston consulted with Lamar Greer, the headmaster at the orphanage. Greer, a Baptist minister, reminded Preston of the almost lifelong support he had received from the Baptists and suggested he consider a school with ties to that denomination. A school like . . . Wake Forest College. Greer arranged a meeting with Coach Walker and others. As Preston recounted:

The coaches were sitting around [with Preston and Greer] and said, 'We want to give Pat a full scholarship, tuition, fees, $10 [for laundry—the Southern Conference and NCAA limit at the time]. Dr. Greer said, 'He [meaning Preston] don't have any way to buy any shoes, or clothes, or whatever.' Coach Walker said, 'I've got two sons, Dr. Greer. They live with me. When they need shoes I get them shoes. If they need shirts I get them a shirt. Any kind of need, I get that. What I'll do is I'll take him [Preston] in just like a son.' That made sense to me. I was 17. If it means that much to a school to pay a guy to play football . . . well, this is one way I can repay the Baptists who have taken care me of all through school.[14]

Walker told a slightly different tale regarding Preston's recruiting, which will be recounted later and includes a sort of kidnapping or player hiding event, like the Lindell Pearson affair. But the inducements mentioned—basically Walker promised to buy his new tackle what he needed when he needed it—were standard procedure for Wake gridders throughout the Peahead Walker era. In reality, the system was not quite as lucrative as it sounded. Although Walker clearly had access to some recruiting funds (most likely from boosters), his funding was not unlimited. He did pay for all kinds of player expenses—everything from clothes

---

13 Andy Preston says his dad told him that the school offering the car and checking account was UNC, coached at that time by Ray "the Bear" Wolf, Snavely's successor. So much for Graham's reforms. Source: Recording of Pat Preston, Aug. 1994. Courtesy of Andy Preston.
14 Ibid.

to dental work to date money and fraternity dues—but the payments were not uniform. Star players got more than the rest. Some didn't even get all that was promised. That may have been not-so-subtle motivation on Walker's part, or it may have been the result of an honest-to-goodness budget crunch.

Ken Bridges, who played for Walker near the end of the coach's Wake tenure, says he only got his promised $15-per-month laundry stipend (the rate went up after World War II) a couple times a year. "I'd go to beg him for it and he'd say, 'Well, that's real tough Bridges, but I just ain't got it right now.'"[15]

Walker didn't say no to recruits, however, not when they were still in the midst of the courting process, and he had enough cash to back up his yeses. That plus Walker's captivating personality and his readymade set of contacts up and down the East Coast transformed Wake's talent pool in just a few short years. The Deacons got better and they grew more diverse, at least in geographic terms. His first class of Deacon recruits included players from West Virginia, Pennsylvania, Alabama (his hometown of Ensley to be precise), Maryland, and Massachusetts. His second class added New Yorkers, Virginians, and one kid from New Jersey to the fold.

Walker's work in landing useful players from afar for the 1937 freshman class was remarkable because of his late start on the recruiting trail. He was not officially Wake's coach until July, and even after his appointment he was encamped for the summer with his baseball team in Snow Hill, NC. It is hard to imagine Walker landing players from Maryland, Pennsylvania, West Virginia, and Alabama in less than two months while traveling the Coastal Plain baseball circuit unless he had a head start. Was he recruiting for Wake while still being paid at Elon? As noted, Walker was cautioned by L.E. Smith, Elon's president, not to poach any boys already signed or recruited for Elon, and there's no evidence that he did. But in truth, Walker and Fysal were the only ones who really knew what was going on in that regard. Some NC State fans thought Walker took advantage of turmoil in the Wolfpack program at that time (State also changed coaches before the 1937 season—

---

15 Ken Bridges, interview with author.

Walker was mentioned as a candidate for that job, too) to lure some would-be Wolfpacker to Wake.[16] No player names were made public, so the allegation is impossible to consider in detail. But it was clear that Peahead Walker already possessed a reputation as a slick recruiter long before he reached Baptist Hollow.

Although Weaver worked the new recruits on the freshman team, varsity work continued apace for Wake's opener with the formidable Tennessee Volunteers. The late-September match up in Knoxville was not Wake's first game with Tennessee. The Vols beat Wake Forest 10–6 in 1892, and then Wake crushed Tennessee 64–0 in 1893 during a three-games-in-four-days road trip. Much had changed in the interim. Under Major Robert Neyland, Tennessee's coach since 1926, the Volunteers had become a regional and national power.[17] In the decade preceding the 1937 season, Neyland had turned out five unbeaten teams and compiled an overall 78-8-7 record.

Tennessee's 1937 squad was not one of Neyland's best, but it was many notches above what Wake could put on the field at that time. In a scrimmage just prior to the contest, Wake's first team could make little or no headway running against its second unit. The Deacons did better passing the ball, but that wasn't all that promising a development either since the Deacons' primary hurler was Dave Fuller, a letterman who'd spent the 1936 season on the other side of the pass-catch connection as an end.

The Deacons took a private train car to Knoxville, the Black Phantom Special the *Old Gold & Black* called it, arriving early the morning of Peahead Walker's first game at the Deacon's head

---

16 *Greensboro Daily News*, Oct. 19, 1939.
17 Neyland, who is better known as General Neyland, or just the General, was a bona fide US Army officer. In 1937, however, he was still just a major. He was promoted, eventually receiving his general officer's star, after he returned to active service in World War II. He retired from the military for a third time in 1946 with the rank of brigadier general.

coach.[18] An overnight on a train couldn't have done Walker's boys much good, but travel can hardly be blamed for the thrashing that followed. Tennessee scored twice in its first ten plays, twice more in the second quarter when Neyland played his second and third string, and rolled to an easy 32–0 victory.

The rest of the season brought more of the same. Walker goaded his team into better play overall, but the Deacons struggled to score and were pummeled by the better teams on the schedule. George Washington, a regional power in that day, whipped Wake 34–6, helped in large part by two blocked punts that led to touchdowns.[19]

Walker recorded his first Deacon victory the following Friday night when Wake beat visiting Erskine College 19–0 before a crowd of about 4,000 at Gore Field. But the good times didn't last long. Ray Wolf's Tar Heels overwhelmed and outnumbered the Deacons 28–0 as a crowd of 10,000-plus looked on at Gore Field. The Deacons managed just two first downs and punted fourteen times. One of those was blocked (of course), setting up a UNC score. A 20–0 loss to NC State was followed by a 32–0 loss to Clemson. That was tough, but tougher was coming. The Deacons headed to Durham the following weekend for a matchup with another Wallace Wade-coached powerhouse at Duke. The Blue Devils were coming off a 9–1 season in 1936 and were 6–0-1 entering the Wake game, the tie coming against Tennessee. Two weeks before the game,

---

18 Wake Forest's nickname, like many school nicknames, varied during its early years. The Deacon appellation, with its obvious tie to Wake's Baptist underpinnings, was in use by World War I but was not official until sometime later. A campus contest in the 1920s produced the nickname Tigers, but that handle never really caught on. Student scribes and others penned various nicknames on the team from time to time, including the Black Phantoms. Phantoms and creatures of similar ilk were apparently all the rage for colleges in the area at that time. UNC's teams were called the White Phantoms for years. NC State's boys were the Red Terrors.

19 Game film from the 1930s and 1940s show the punter standing perhaps ten yards behind the line of scrimmage (as opposed to twelve to fourteen yards today) but with the linemen aligned the same as on normal plays. Defensive players can be seen breaking through on most kicking plays, and the only wonder is that more punts and placements weren't smothered on the kicker's foot.

Wade was on the cover of *Time Magazine*. Peahead Walker, meanwhile, was just looking for cover.

The contest was a farce. Duke scored three touchdowns in the first ten minutes—one coming after Wake failed to cover a kickoff and Duke recovered it at the Deacon twenty-nine—and rolled to a 67–0 victory. Wade pushed his subs into the game early, but the not-so-kindly old "Bear"[20] never really let his foot off the pedal. Future Duke star George McAfee scored the last touchdown on a thirty-yard pass reception with less than a minute left to play.

Walker's men rallied to win their last two, beating Wofford 24–0 and Davidson 19–7, and wound up 3–6, which, as Walker had noted before the season began, was about the most that could have been expected. Of more importance to the long-term picture, Weaver and the freshmen from afar finished their season at 4–0-1 and handled the Deacon varsity roughly on several occasions. The Baby Deacs scored a whopping 146 points during the season, a total greatly enhanced by a 63–0 thrashing of the Naval Apprentice Academy in Norfolk, VA.[21] Wake beat the UNC and NC State frosh and tied Duke's "Blue Imps." A number of future stars were identified, including much-needed backs like Tony Gallovich, "Red" Mayberry, and Johnny Ringgold. "We really do have a very good freshman team," Walker told reporters at the end of the season. "The future looks bright."[22]

Walker's rebuilding plan for Wake Forest was simple: get better players. His opinion of the inherited talent, noted in a few brief public comments during the 1937 season, was made more explicit when he opened the 1938 season with a lineup consisting almost entirely of men from the 1937 freshman team. The starting backfield usually consisted of second-year men. Captain George

---

20 Although Paul "Bear" Bryant is far better known, he wasn't the first football coach with that nickname. He wasn't even the first Alabama coach. Wade, who became Alabama coach in 1923, was called the Bear by his players, and Carolina's Ray Wolf, a Wade and Walker contemporary, was also known as Bear.

21 The loss to the Wake frosh so demoralized the Apprentices that the Academy's Board of Trustees met the week after and voted to cancel the rest of the games scheduled.

22 *Charlotte Observer*, Dec. 5, 1937, but it is repeated in similar form in other journals.

Wirtz, a senior halfback who'd made all-conference at Mount Olive College before switching to Wake, sometimes opened in place of Mayberry, but Mayberry usually played more; both ends were freshmen once removed, as were linemen Lou Trunzo and Tom Tingle and line reserves Walter "Butch" Clark and Paul Waivers. The only upperclassmen who played at all were Wirtz, part-time quarterback Dave Fuller, tackle Rupert Pate, center (and sometimes end) John Pendergast, and tackle Allen Powers. Of these, only Pate and Fuller were true holdovers. Pendergast, Wirtz, and Powers were what today would be called junior college transfers, with Powers in particular taking a circuitous path. A Tennessee native, he went to the University of Tennessee in 1934, transferred to Tennessee Wesleyan, a two-year school, and graduated in 1936. He came to Wake in 1937 and was the best (and biggest) new player on Walker's first Deacon team. But when officials of an opposing Southern Conference team brought Power's Tennessee experience to the attention of league officials, a ruckus ensued.[23] Just prior to the game against NC State on October 15, a conference committee met and ruled Powers eligible. Its ruling was based, in large part, on an affidavit from the University of Tennessee's Neyland, stating he could find no record of Powers in the annals of Volunteer football. This more or less supported Powers's version of the story, namely that he practiced with the Tennessee freshmen but never played. Yes, he did receive the orange sweater awarded to all freshman team members. "But I never played for Tennessee," Powers told the *Old Gold & Black* in a heartfelt interview.

The team quickly became known as "Walker's Sophs," or, more often, as the "Flaming Sophs," a sobriquet often appended to teams fueled by an outstanding class of newcomers.[24] Time would demonstrate whether they were more smoke or flame, but a simple examination of the roster—or, for Deacon fans of the time, a simultaneous viewing of the upper and lower classmen on the

---

[23] The reporting school was not publicly identified, but Wake officials were certain it was Davidson. Athletic Director Weaver reported as much in letters to college alumni that are included in his personal collection at Wake Forest.

[24] The "flaming" adjective apparently meant they were "on fire," or "hot" in a competitive sense.

squad—highlights a major theme of Walker's talent upgrade: the new coach's quest for better Deacons usually meant bigger Deacons. In a sport dependent upon pushing, wrestling, and running into opponents, that was not exactly genius. But Walker saw to it that Wake got bigger. The holdovers from the Weaver era included players like 5'7", 165-pound end John Weaver (no relation to Jim Weaver) and brothers Jim and John Pittman, backfielders from Monroe, NC who'd come to Wake after a year at Wingate Junior College. The Pittmans were 5'4" and 5'7", respectively, both under 150 pounds, and went by the fitting nickname of "Rink and Dink." They didn't get much playing time after Walker arrived. By comparison, sophomore end John Jett, a rugged West Virginian, was 6'5", 210 pounds; new fullback Marshall Edwards was a 6'1", 190-pounder; and tackle Powers was a 250-pounder. And on and on it went, up and down the roster.

If nothing else, Walker's second Deacon team inspired greater hope in the hearts of the Deacon faithful. And, as was soon demonstrated, such hope was not ill-founded. Wake pummeled outmanned Randolph-Macon 57–6 in the 1938 opener at Gore Field, which had been upgraded for the season with a brand-new scoreboard.[25] Edwards starred with two long punt returns, but it was an overall whipping. Wake piled up 409 rushing yards—almost the season total for 1937—in its pasting of the Yellow Jackets.

That was Randolph-Macon—hardly a definitive test. But real affirmation of improvement was not far away. In week two, Wake traveled to Chapel Hill, where some 14,000 filled Kenan Stadium to see the Tar Heels kick off what was expected to be another solid season. Ray Wolf's third team was coming off back-to-back second-place finishes in the Southern Conference, and their neighbors from Wake Forest seemed to be useful early season sparring partners. The Deacons had been little more than that in the past decade or so of games against the Tar Heels, managing one tie, and no wins, in the past ten meetings between the teams.

---

25 The new contraption, some seven feet in diameter and spray-painted a snappy gold with black numerals, was built by Wake Forest physics professor Sherwood T. Githens for less than $100. It had balanced aluminum hands turned by a 7,200-rpm electric motor and a small white light that came on when the clock was stopped.

It was different this time. Early in the game a nice punt and Jett's second down sack of Tar Heel quarterback Jim "Sweet" LaLanne pinned Carolina inside its five. As was customary for a team pinned deep in their own territory in this era, the Tar Heels dropped into punt formation on third down. The towering Jett stormed in from the right side of the line to block Wally Winborne's punt. The ball bounced a couple of times in the end zone, hopped back across the goal line to the one-yard line and was recovered by a UNC player there. According to the rules of the day, Carolina retained possession at the one-yard line but it was now fourth down. Winborne lined up for another punt, and this time Rupert Pate bulled his way through to block it. Tom Tingle, the tackle from Peahead Walker's hometown, fell on the ball for a touchdown. Wake had an early 6–0 lead. That lead, however, would not last. The Deacons struggled to stop UNC's offensive juggernaut and couldn't get much going on their own—but the 14–6 final announced that the Deacons were back.

Wake followed up the near miss against Carolina with a 31–0 pasting of The Citadel and a narrow 20–19 victory over South Carolina, a respectable team but hardly a power. It was a very close game. Time was slipping away from Wake when USC's "Pinhead" Henson fumbled at the Gamecock twenty-three with USC clinging to a 19–13 lead. That gave Peahead's boys the break they needed. Three runs didn't move the ball much. Facing fourth down, the Deacons dug deep into Walker's bag of tricks. Fuller, on the receiving end of a triple pass (the second lateral on a play), sprinted toward right end and, while still on the run, lofted a pass to Paul Waivers at the USC five. Waivers scored untouched, tying the game. Walker fired Gallovich from his placement duties and ordered John "Goose" Pendergast to do the honors. His first kick of the season split the uprights and put Wake ahead 20–19 with less than three minutes to play. South Carolina didn't threaten after that and Wake Forest grabbed the win.

The 3–1 start attracted some attention and, as the *Old Gold & Black* noted, no shortage of "bandwagon riders." Inflamed with Deacon fever, Wake stalwarts began dreaming of a victory over Duke and possibly even a trip to one of those newfangled bowl games. Caught up in the hysteria, the Wake Forest Monogram Club announced plans to broadcast the upcoming game at Virginia Military Institute (VMI) to fans sitting in Gore Gymnasium on the Wake Forest campus.[26] The broadcast technology was crude to say the least. A special telephone line, leased at the Monogram Club's expense, would connect members of the *Old Gold & Black* staff in the press box at VMI to the public address system in the gym. Their youthful commentary would bring the game home to Wake Foresters who couldn't make the trip. To pay for this extravagance, the Club sold event sponsorships to local businesses and event tickets at fifteen cents each.

The outbreak of enthusiasm was tempered considerably when Wake stumbled against NC State the week after the South Carolina win. State was Wake's nearest neighbor among the four colleges in the Raleigh-Durham area, and the rivalry was already a bitter one when Walker arrived at Wake. School leaders met a month before the 1938 game to hammer out a joint proclamation decrying pre- and postgame vandalism on either campus. It was, of course, ignored. Wake Forest students (or someone) painted WFC and other black-and-gold slogans on a State dormitory wall.

Like Wake, State was attempting to jumpstart their program as well. The school had hired "Doc" Newton to replace Heartley "Hunk" Anderson[27] in 1937 after Hunk's rift with his players (and his losing ways, which ticked off some Wolfpack boosters) pushed him towards an assistant's job at the University of Michigan. Newton, like seemingly half the football coaches in the

---

26 Earl Gore was a star guard on Wake's first basketball team and an early benefactor of the athletic department.

27 Anderson, a standout during his playing days at Notre Dame, suffered through an ill-fated coaching career until finally catching a break at the end. The man Knute Rockne called the best lineman he ever coached started out as Rockne's line coach after Anderson's graduation in South Bend; he then followed Rockne as Notre Dame's coach after Rockne's death in 1931. Anderson' teams went 16-9-2 in three years—not bad, but somewhat short of Rockne's 105-12-5 record that included six national championships. Anderson resigned, was hired at State, failed there, and went on to Michigan as a line coach, where he was fired after one year along with Head Coach Harry Kipke. After that, things improved. Anderson moved to the National Football League and was part of the brain trust under George Halas when the Chicago Bears developed the new T formation offense that launched the modern game.

Southeast, was a baseball friend of Walker's and a well-known minor league umpire. A former high school coach in Birmingham and an assistant in football and baseball at Howard a few years after Walker passed through, Newton was known as an innovator—though not always a successful one. Newton's teams at Davidson, his post before arriving at State, had always run an assortment of trick plays, and his first State teams employed all that plus Newton's very own invention: a gizmo designed to ensure that the signals were called correctly, quickly, and out of earshot of the opposition. Just how serious a problem this was is hard to say, but Newton spent a lot of time developing (and manufacturing) the device, which was based on an umpire's ball-strike indicator and about the same size.

More time devoted to football fundamentals might have been wiser. The Wolfpack under Newton were, generally speaking, a mediocre bunch. In seven seasons, Newton produced one winning team and one that broke even. But the Wolves were good enough to whip Walker and his high-flying young Deacons 19–7 in 1938. Wake had the better of the play, piling up 247 rushing yards and 12 first downs to about half that much for State, but the Deacons couldn't make it count.

As Walker knew, the State loss was a double whammy. Wake missed beating a very beatable opponent (after beating Wake, State tied Furman 7–7, went five straight weeks without putting up a point, and finished 3–7–1), and the Deacons saw their momentum stopped cold. The schedule that followed didn't help. On back-to-back weekends, the Deacons faced Duke and Clemson. They lost both games by the same score: 7–0. That marked dramatic improvement from the year before when the combined count in those two games was 99–0, but they were losses all the same, cut from very similar cloth. In both contests, Wake's high-powered offense struggled against a quality defense and failed to capitalize on the scoring chances it did have—and the defense gave up crucial scores. Duke got its points in the first quarter and pushed Wake around much of the day at Winston-Salem's Bowman-Gray

Stadium.[28] Wake still had an excellent chance to pull out a tie, however, driving to the Duke seven with less than three minutes to play. Duke Coach Wallace Wade sent his first-team players back in at this point, including halfback Eric Tipton who was sick and hadn't played a down until then. Walker countered with some trickery, his favored tactic in tight situations near the goal, but it didn't work out so well. Fullback Edwards took the snap and handed the ball to Allen Powers, the burly tackle having lined up in the backfield for this play. Powers attempted to lateral the ball to Fuller, but it squirted backward, well out of Fuller's reach. Duke's Willard "Bolo" Perdue recovered at the Duke seventeen, ending the threat and the game. Just what Powers was supposed to do with the ball isn't clear. Reporters "confirmed" with Wake coaches afterward that Powers was supposed to be in the backfield. No one managed much of an explanation beyond that.

Powers's miscue short-circuited Wake's upset bid and kept the Deacons from being the spoilers of what turned out to be a historic season. Duke's victory over Wake was part of one of the last undefeated, un-scored-upon seasons in college football. It included a berth in the 1939 Rose Bowl (where California ended Duke's dreams of complete perfection by beating the Blue Devils 7–3).

A week later, in another defensive duel, Clemson completed the only two passes it tried, both on the same third quarter possession, as it marched to the game's lone touchdown. Wake was inside the Tiger thirty-five three times in the second half but couldn't score. "We played good," Walker told the press after the Clemson game, "but not good enough."[29]

More missed opportunities followed. Spellbound fans at Gore Gym listened to the student journalists describe a thrilling fourth quarter comeback against VMI and its hard-hitting

---

28 Wake, and other teams, regularly played contests in the state's bigger cities in an effort to draw bigger crowds and because city fathers were always looking for ways to drum up business. The Winston-Salem sojourn marked the christening of Bowman-Gray Stadium, a grand addition to the town's civic amenities even though there was no football team available to fill it on a regular basis until Wake Forest moved to Winston-Salem in 1954.

29 *Raleigh News & Observer*, Nov. 23, 1938.

linebacker-fullback Paul "Pounding" Shu. VMI was a strong team at the time and already had one impressive Southern Conference win on the season, having carved up Maryland 47–14 just a few weeks before. When Shu scored an early touchdown to give VMI a 6–0 lead and led another drive to the Deacon ten, it looked like Wake might suffer a similar fate, especially with the game-long downpour intensifying. The Deacons stiffened, however, kept the spread to a single touchdown, and then took control. As the fourth quarter began, Wake began a grinding, sixty-two-yard march through the Virginia mud that was capped by Gallovich's fourteen-yard dash to the one and Marshall Edwards's touchdown plunge. That knotted the score just as time was running out. Pendergast lined up to attempt the extra point on the sloppy field, but the snap from center Joe Kuchinski was bad, and Pendergast wound up running for his life, trying to throw a pass to a teammate. He never found one, and the game ended a tie.[30]

Although disappointing, the game the following week was downright disheartening. Possibly for recruiting purposes, and possibly because he had a lot of friends in Baltimore, Walker had lined up a game with the Green Terrors of Western Maryland College (modern-day McDaniel College) at Baltimore's old Municipal Stadium. Pregame intelligence suggested Wake should be a heavy favorite, and it was obvious from the outset that the Deacons were bigger, faster, and in most ways superior. They ran up and down the field on the Terrors, outrushing them 343–105, but the Deacons once again had all kinds of misfortunes in the kicking game, which was, in fact, a career-long curse for Walker. Western blocked a Mayberry punt for a score and a 6–0 lead.

Gallovich then ran sixty-three yards for a touchdown to make it 6–6. Then, after a fumble killed a Deacon drive at the Western Maryland eight yard line, Lou Trunzo broke through to block a Terror punt. Pendergast fell on it in the end zone, and seldom-used sophomore Irvin Byrd, who'd won another placekicking tryout the week before, nailed the extra point for a 13–6 lead at the half. It all fell apart after intermission, however.

---

30 Pendergast was Wake's starting center most of the year, but when he became place kicker he could, of course, no longer perform the centering task on kicks, which placed the less-experienced Kuchinski in that role.

A Western punt glanced off a Wake return man, setting up a short touchdown drive that tied the score. Wake retaliated with a fifty-five-yard drive to the Western ten. When that march stalled, Walker ordered up a field goal try, perhaps one of only two attempted during his Wake Forest tenure. Gallovich missed the kick, leaving the contest deadlocked.[31] In the final stanza, Western blocked yet another Deacon punt. The Terrors recovered on the Wake eighteen and drove for the winning score from there.[32]

Wake closed the bittersweet season by dominating Davidson in the Thanksgiving Day matchup in Charlotte. Trunzo, who along with fullback Marshall Edwards was named to the all-Southern Conference team, smashed through the line on the first play from scrimmage and yanked the ball away from the Davidson fullback, giving Wake possession at the Wildcat nineteen. Two plays later, Gallovich galloped in for a score, and Wake was on its way to a 21–0 victory, notable for its lack of blocked punts and Gallovich's surreal placekicking: he made all three he tried, pushing Wake's record on PATs to 11-for-26 for the season. "Why

---

31 Wake's official football statistical record extends only back to 1948, the very end of Walker's tenure, and isn't completely accurate even then. From a review of game accounts during the Walker years it's clear that the Deacons didn't make any field goals while Walker was coach, and they do not appear to have attempted many. A survey of game records shows only Gallovich's missed boot against Western Maryland and a similar miss by Gallovich from twenty-eight yards out two years later against UNC—this even though there were several occasions when a field goal would have helped the Deacon cause or even won a game. This was not much remarked upon at the time. Since the game turned away from the rounder, rugby-style ball in the 1890s, the field goal was not a point of major emphasis in college football in general or at Wake Forest in particular. Indeed, during the Deacon's first seventy-five or so years of football, field goals were few and far between, although in 1924 a player named Blaine Rackley may have drop kicked a fifty-two-yarder to beat Washington & Lee 10–8. Wake Forest's official record book lists Rackley's kick at forty-eight yards.

32 By my count, Wake had fifteen punts blocked during the 1938 season. That would be enough—more than enough—to get a special teams coach fired today. But at a time when blocked punts were fairly common—recall that Wake blocked punts on back-to-back plays against UNC in 1938 and two in one quarter against Western Maryland—no one seems to have been alarmed. And Walker had no special teams coach. He was the special teams coach.

can't we get a kicker like Carolina has?" moaned the *Old Gold & Black*'s Gordon Phillips in an early season column.

Well, maybe next year.

Indeed, prospects looked even brighter for 1939. Walker had the cream of two wondrous recruiting classes—nothing like them had ever before been seen wearing the Black and Gold—in the varsity fold. The Flaming Sophs Gallovich, Mayberry, Edwards, Trunzo, Jett, and company, who led Wake to the tantalizing 4-5-1 season in 1938, were now joined by the stars of the 1938 freshman team that was very nearly as good as the unbeaten frosh of 1937. A number of likely future stars were identified during the short freshman season, including linemen Carl Givler and Frank Kapriva, passer J.V. Pruitt, end Pat Geer, halfback Joe Duncavage and . . . a kid named John Polanski, a big, surprisingly fast bruiser from Buffalo, NY who was a real Deacon recruiting coup. A much-heralded three-sport star at Buffalo's Riverside High, where he earned the nickname the "Riverside Express," he was quickly identified by college recruiters in the area, including former UNC Coach Carl Snavely, who was now coaching at nearby Cornell. Snavely would have liked to have brought Polanski to Ithaca but apparently couldn't get him into school. So he, or perhaps Assistant Coach Jim Tatum, Walker's old baseball pal, clued Walker in. Receiving the news, Walker hurried to find Weaver. "C'mon, we're going to Buffalo to get us a player," Walker told his boss. "Great," Weaver supposedly said, "when do we leave?"[33]

Snavely may have put Walker onto Polanski simply as a favor to a friend—there was the Walker-Tatum connection, and Snavely and Walker seem to have had a warm relationship as well—but there may have been another motivation. *Greensboro Daily News* correspondent W.T. "Tom" Bost, a gossipy sort of journalist who churned out many interesting and possibly even true freelance stories during the 1930s and 1940s from his base in downtown Raleigh, suggested in a 1939 article that Snavely sent Polanski to Walker just to keep him out of Wallace Wade's hands. Snavely, UNC's coach from 1934 to 1935 (and again after World War II), was no fan of Wade's. The two men were embroiled in a

---

[33] Jim Weaver, personal correspondence, Wake Forest University archives.

cheating controversy in 1935 after Snavely (or his representatives) accused Wade and company of scouting UNC with a slow-motion movie camera. The charge sounds ridiculous today, when film studies are the backbone of scouting, but the technology was new then, and deploying it was considered an ethical breach (as well as another example of Duke flaunting its superior resources—who else could afford a fancy moving picture camera with slow-motion capabilities?). Whatever the case, Polanski headed south and became the gem of Walker's recruiting class in 1938. He scored five touchdowns for the freshmen, including a 102-yard return of the opening kickoff against NC State.

As Walker headed into his third season, the program was growing in both quality and quantity. The varsity included thirty-two players. A record forty were out for the freshmen team, including a speedy back named D.C. Walker Jr. Peahead Walker's oldest son was, by all accounts, a mirror image of his dad. He may have been slightly taller than his father, but he had nearly identical facial features and build. Also like dad, his chief physical attribute on the football field was his fleetness. His nickname—of course Peahead's son would have a nickname—was "Scooter."

D.C. Walker III, Peahead's grandson, says his dad told him that in his prime he broke 10 seconds flat for the 100-yard dash. That's very fast—just more than a half second off the world record of the day—but Peahead may have been faster. "Dad [D.C. Jr.] always said that even when he was older, Peahead could still beat him, or at least stay with him, in a race," D.C. Walker III said.

Scooter Walker didn't play much, if it all, for Weaver's freshman team and didn't last the year at Wake. D.C. Walker III says that his father was "miserable at Wake . . . mostly because his dad was so mean to him. He treated him very poorly."[34]

Walker's 1939 team was a much older and more experienced club than the sophomore-dominated club of 1938. In addition to all the sophomores-cum-juniors in the lineup, there were at least two senior linemen, Clem Crabtree and Eddie Woolbert, who were new additions (possibly transfers) or didn't play a big role previously, on hand to throw their weight around. Both

---

34 D.C. Walker III, interview with author.

started most of the 1939 season. Crabtree was good enough to get drafted by the Detroit Lions in the spring of 1940 and played two seasons there. The Deacons were much deeper, too. Ringgold, Gallovich, Mayberry, and Edwards were all back. Walker was trying to find a way to work sophomore tailback Joe Duncavage into the lineup to upgrade the Deacons' passing attack. And in what could be called an embarrassment of riches, Walker soon found himself benching Edwards, an All-Southern Conference pick, to make room for Polanski, the budding star. "[Marshall] Edwards is a fine boy and a good football player," Walker said. "He's good on pass defense and is a powerful runner. But once he's across the scrimmage line, he doesn't have the change of pace Polanski commands. You get John across the line he's liable to go ahead for a touchdown or a long gain."[35]

The Deacon coaching staff also had a new look. Fysal was gone, headed back to his native Wilson, NC to take a post as the Red Cross field director for that area. In his place, Walker hired ex-Duke star Tom Rogers as the Deacons' line coach.

Wake opened against Walker's old Elon club. The game, arranged in large part by Walker and his former boss L.E. Smith, was to be played in Greensboro. The idea was to move to a bigger city where football fans with no particular allegiance might swell the gate. With interest in Wake's team running high more than 8,000 paid to see the contest, more than might have been expected if the game were played at Wake Forest. A fair number of UNC students—including most of the Tar Heel football team—were on hand. What they saw was a thorough whipping of Elon by Walker's boys, although some overzealous campus pundits wanted more.

Beating Elon in Greensboro furthered the aforementioned bandwagon effect, with some new admirers coming from a surprising quarter. An article in *The Carolinian*, the student newspaper for the Women's College of the University of North Carolina (now UNC-Greensboro) several weeks after the game detailed how the school's all-female student body had latched on to the "underdog" Deacons during their recent foray into Greensboro. The women said they liked the Deacons' "exceptional

---

35 *Greensboro Daily News*, Sept. 11, 1939.

grit and spunk," so much that some even became "traitors" to the Carolina cause (Women's College and the University of North Carolina were both part of the state's expanding public college system). The stated cause of the Women's College's attachment may have been the grit and spunk the Deacs possessed, but co-ed comments in *The Carolinian* suggest the attraction also included carnal elements. Could some of the Women's College's co-eds have attended and been smitten? "Have you seen anything like the way Jim Ringgold blocks?" asked a dreamy co-ed after spending an evening with the players at a social event at the King Cotton Hotel. "Old Wake has its numbers and it can certainly have mine, too."[36]

Unaware of the swooning they were causing, Wake followed up the opening victory by beating South Carolina 19–7 at Gore Field. The 2–0 start set up a big early season matchup with UNC, which, with Snuffy Stirnweiss still in harness, again had high expectations.

As did Wake Forest. Although Walker's program was clearly on the rise, the Deacs had yet to post a signature victory over one of the acknowledged in-state powers (Duke or Carolina). The 1939 squad appeared to have enough strength and firepower to battle the Heels on even terms.

Appearances were deceiving, however. Carolina jumped on Wake for seventeen first quarter points and never let up. The final: 36–6. The Deacon demise started early. Stirnweiss, a heady improviser, sidestepped a Deacon tackler who looked to have him dead in his sights and heaved a forty-yard touchdown pass to George Radman on the game's fourth play. In the second half, Radman caught another long pass—perhaps intended for another receiver—when Gallovich batted it high into the air . . . and into Radman's waiting arms in the end zone. Some of those plays carried a flukish air, and Wake boosters continued to refer to the final result in those terms the rest of the season. But the Tar Heels' stifling of the theoretically potent Deacon offense was as legitimate as it could be. Wake couldn't move the ball against Carolina—the Deacons gained less than fifty yards and completed just one pass—

---

36 *The Carolinian*, Oct. 17, 1939.

and didn't threaten to score until the fourth quarter when the outcome had long been decided.

The Carolina loss was deflating, but smart scheduling—an October road trip to south Florida—proved an excellent salve. The Deacons headed to Walker's old Miami stomping grounds to face the University of Miami in a night game in the Orange Bowl. The contest drew more than 20,000 fans, most of them eager to cheer the Hurricanes on to victory in their belated season opener. But Walker's Deacons, and the speedy Gallovich in particular, wore the Hurricanes out. "Galloping" Gallovich scored touchdowns on runs of 18, 40, and 80 yards as Wake piled up 321 yards on the ground and whipped their hosts 32–0.

It was more of the same the next week in Raleigh, where Gallovich scored twice more on long runs (thirty-nine and sixty-six yards) and Polanski picked up two touchdowns of his own (one was an interception return—Polanski, like most regulars of the day, played both ways) in another 32–0 victory.

Next up was homecoming and a rematch against 1938 spoiler Western Maryland. This time Wake not only outclassed the Green Terrors in the stat book but did so on the newfangled electronic scoreboard as well, rolling to a 66–0 victory that included four touchdowns by Polanski and left Wake followers wondering what the heck happened the year before.

Wake was 5–1 and earned a national ranking of tenth according to the pseudoscientific strictures of the Williamson System, the Bowl Championship Series rating system of the day.[37] Polanski was the national rushing leader and ranked third nationally in scoring behind Butler University's Thomas Harding and a promising Michigan tailback named Tom Harmon. However, Polanski suffered a badly bruised arm en route to his four-touchdown day against the Terrors, and his availability for Wake's next game—against none other than its most hated rival Duke—was seriously in doubt.

---

37 The system, a mathematical formula based on comparative scores, was the work of Paul B. Williamson (some sources say Paul O. Williamson), a New Orleans sportswriter and football aficionado whose rating work was distributed by United Features from the early 1930s through World War II. As other polls involving voters developed, the Williamson system disappeared.

Rivalries change over time. Because of proximity—Wake Forest is essentially a suburb of Raleigh—NC State was always considered a natural rival for Wake. UNC was a more regular foe early on—the two schools are reputed to have played the state's first intercollegiate football game—and eventually the source of much Deacon frustration, in large part because of the Tar Heels' annoyingly successful basketball teams. But in the late 1930s and into the 1940s, the gold standard in Black and Gold rivals was Duke. Thanks to the Duke family fortune, the Duke campus in Durham towered (literally, thanks to the 210-foot-high bell tower atop the stately Duke Chapel) over its nearby competitors. Duke's students had already begun to carry their noses a little higher and, thanks to Coach Wallace Wade, Duke was on a level all its own when it came to Southern Conference football. The Blue Devils didn't always win the Southern under Wade, but they came close enough. Between 1933 and 1945, Duke captured the league title nine times in thirteen seasons.

Wade's 1939 team was another power—although not quite as strong as the 1938 bunch that went to the Rose Bowl. Not only had the Blue Devils already been scored upon before they met Wake in Durham in late October, they'd already been beaten. An early season trip to Pitt resulted in a 14–13 Panther victory. That did not seem particularly surprising at the time—Pitt was a longtime Eastern power. But this was the first Pitt team in a long time not coached by the legendary Jock Sutherland. The soft-spoken Scotsman resigned in early 1939 when Pitt's administration decided to end athletic subsidies (i.e., scholarships) and deemphasize football.[38]

Wake ascendant, Duke a little down, the Blue Devils looking past Wake to UNC—once again the elements were in place for a program-making upset for Walker and company. Beating Duke meant a lot to Walker for a number of reasons, not the least

---

[38] Sutherland, a certified and practicing dentist as well as a football coach, was a coaching star in his day. He replaced the better-known Glenn "Pop" Warner at Pitt in 1924 and went on to compile a 110-20-12 record.

of which was a personal rivalry with Wade.[39] Walker's eagerness to beat Wade created a certain enmity among Wake's players for the Blue Devils and their high-brow coach. The 67–0 whupping Duke laid on Wake in 1937 probably helped spur those feelings. Old-timers say Walker never forgot that game and that for the rest of his time at Wake Forest, Duke was his main target. Dewey Hobbs, who played at Wake in the mid-1940s, said "there was no bigger game for us because there was no bigger game for Walker."[40]

Walker's charges played with reckless abandon against Duke in 1938 when they cut the margin of defeat by 60 points (Duke won 7–0). A year later, Walker was determined to do all in his power to prepare his team for the big test. That meant long grueling practices that included extensive scrimmaging against another good freshman team. In fact, Walker appears to have just worn the freshmen out. After a week of scout team work against the varsity, the first-year men traveled to Virginia to play the William & Mary freshman and were pounded 26–6. A half-dozen regulars missed the contest because of injuries inflicted at practice the week before. It was neither the first nor last time that would happen to a Walker team.

***

Indeed, rugged, sometimes brutal practices were the norm for Peahead Walker football teams (and for that matter most football teams during the era, when the grueling and gruesome were commonplace). Walker's players often thought there wasn't a point

---

[39] Wade and Walker were solid acquaintances, if not exactly friends, and their paths had crossed many times. Wade was from Tennessee but coached the University of Alabama from 1923 to 1930. Walker was from Alabama, of course, and his brother, Erskine, played football at Alabama for Frank Thomas, Wade's successor. Thomas was close enough to Walker to visit him at practice once in the late 1940s, an event that stuck in several players' memories because Walker made a student manager go and get a chair for the old coach. As noted, Wade may also have coached Walker briefly at Vanderbilt, and he had a hand in Walker's coming to Wake in the first place, having written a recommendation on Walker's behalf.

[40] Dewey Hobbes, interview with author.

to much of what he did besides whipping them into shape by extreme physical exercise, and Walker himself really didn't disagree. Quizzed by a reporter one March about the potential length of spring football practice, he replied, "Well, I reckon we'll just stay down there [on the practice field] until we get tired."[41] Walker wanted his players to be in shape, but he believed the most difficult part of football to teach was the contact. As a player, and later, as a coach, he couldn't get enough of it. So Walker's practices involved a lot of contact.

A typical practice began with noncontact preliminaries. First up were calisthenics. Then a couple of laps around the field. Players at both Wake and Elon recall Walker spurring his charges to greater exertion by pelting them with small rocks as they ran.[42] The old shortstop had a strong and accurate arm and could hit a fanny half the time from forty paces. But that seemed to be more for fun (at least for the coach) than for any real purpose. Although Walker ran his players into the ground—Deacon Carl Haggard recalls being so tired after some practices that he'd just lie down in the shower until he had recovered enough to stand—what would today be known as conditioning was more or less left up to the player. There was no organized training program, in season or out, and players who lifted weights were considered an oddity. During Walker's closing years at Wake, he did have a few weightlifters, men like ex-paratrooper Bill Finnance, Buck Harris, and Ed "Bad News" Bradley. But anyone with a weightlifting interest brought it with them to school. Haggard recalled that roommate Harris brought his personal collection of free weights to school, causing their rickety dorm room floor to tilt towards Harris' side of the room.[43]

Walker occasionally boasted of his men's toughness or conditioning—when Georgia Coach Wally Butts complained after a 1944 defeat that he didn't see how Walker could beat his three-deep team with just twelve men, Walker replied that his boys could get after it all day and night—his main contribution to their fitness was a steady diet of full-contact football, a practice that ironically may have worn down his charges.

---

41 *Old Gold & Black*, Mar. 23, 1945.
42 Sources for this anecdote included a story in *The Chapel Hill Weekly* from July 22, 1970, the Elon Sports Hall of Fame program from 1978, and various interviews.
43 Carl Haggard, interview with author.

Players across the years remember forming two lines facing each other and practicing tackling to get things going after the calisthenics were over. Walker would make his way between the files, tossing a football to one man or the other in each pair. The player who received the ball would attempt to run over the player who did not. "There was no thought of dodging him or letting up," said Pride Ratterree, a Deacon lineman from the mid-1940s. "Peahead gave hell to anyone who tried that."[44] Each man had to drop his partner five times (some players recall that it was only three).

After the hard-hitting start it was off to position work. Depending upon the number of coaches available (during Walker's Deacon tenure he had as many as four assistants and as few as one), the squad would break up into two, three, or four groups and work on specific skills. Linemen would practice the blocking for a particular play through endless repetitions. Walker's love for power football during his early years at Wake meant forty-five minutes to an hour might be spent on the various permutations of the double-team block for the strong-side off-tackle play, the bread and butter of the single wing. The team also spent considerable time on aspects of each week's scouting report and game plan. Walker's players all say they felt well prepared and that they were seldom surprised in games. Walker's network of scouts helped some in this regard, but his intuition and detailed knowledge of the game also played a big role.

Backs spent practice time on ball handling, passing, and kicking (which also often involved some linemen) but were not exempt from heavy contact work. In addition to the considerable scrimmaging that ended most practices, Walker devised drills designed to simulate to critical points in the game. One drill encouraged runners to blast through a closing hole near the sideline. Another offered practice at "line plunges," a special running skill in which a ball carrier, realizing he is going to be tackled as he goes through the line, leaps forward in a near horizontal posture in order to pick up an extra yard or so.

---

44 Pride Ratteree, interview with author.

Several players recall a regular drill that went by the name "punt return" but which was really about practicing punt coverage, and more specifically, open field tackling. Willis "Doc" Murphrey, a rarely used sub on several teams just after World War II, says his main role was to catch punts in practice "and then get creamed by some Pollock or Wop that Walker had sent after me."[45]

Despite being a starter, Dickie Davis often found himself in the same role and said the problem (and it was only a problem from the player's point of view) was Walker's love of contact. There's no play in football that produces more hard hits than a kick return. So . . .

He'd let those SOBs [the players covering the punts] leave early [before ball was kicked]. He [Walker] loved it because of the hits, but if you were the one returning punts you didn't have a chance. I remember one day [Deacon lineman Ray] Cicia just drilled Bobby Stutts on a punt and Stutts came up bloody and ready to fight 'cause he thought Cicia had taken advantage. And he and Cicia did start fighting, and one of the coaches moved in. But Peahead got there real quick and said, "Aw, let 'em go. . . . Next!" Well, that meant the next man get out there and get killed. I was the next man and I wasn't having any part of that. So I caught my punt and, fast as I could, I ran backwards, sideways, wherever I could go, and up into the stands. Peahead was running after me, cussing me right and left. I just threw the ball back and we went on.[46]

Wily players devised ways of making drills, and even scrimmage plays, look—and sound—better than they were—the better to avoid add-on work that could rain down as a punishment. Ratterree recalls learning to slap his pads against another player in a way that really made a loud noise—much louder than what was merited by the actual contact: "He [Walker] would say, 'Yeah,

---

45 Murphrey, now deceased, was a well-known Wake Forest supporter and ribald raconteur. His ethnic slurs are, in part, a jab at Walker's fondness for immigrant sons from the Northeast, but his politically incorrect terminology may have been picked up from Walker himself. This quote is from a recording Murphrey made many years after his Wake Forest days.
46 Dickie Davis, interview with author.

goddamn Ratterree. That's how we want to do it. I like the sound of that!'" Ratterree said.[47]

Wake's practices were long and grueling because of the allegedly salutary effects of such a regimen, but many players thought the coach extended the workouts simply because he loved practice and squeezed every minute he could out of the practice day. His teams practiced—scrimmaged mostly—until dark . . . and even beyond. End Jack Lewis is one of several Deacons who recalled the managers wrapping stripes of white tape around the ball so that it could be seen amidst the gloaming. Later, after it was darker still, Walker's men would run plays with no ball at all.

"I don't know what the point of that was . . . just to hit people I guess," Lewis said. "You blocked anyone you could find, or tackled anyone who was running towards you."[48] Said Ratterree:

> *He thought the game was about contact and so you practiced that. The practices were tough. Sometimes you were just thankful if you were able to eat afterwards. But he was a tough guy. He was what? Mid-40s or so, when I played? He was very intimidating then. He had no problem just cussing you out, up and down, this way and that, or grabbing you by the throat and shaking you. People were terrified of him, understandably so.*[49]

Despite all the remembered rigor of a Peahead Walker practice, the occasional humorous recollection does crop up. Walker—perhaps more in hindsight than otherwise—was a funny man with a sharp wit. Long-time Wake Forest University Athletic Director Gene Hooks, who played baseball at WFC during Walker's last few years at the school, recalled that Walker "had this incredible needle. He was quick and you didn't want to be his target. I think that's one reason his players avoided him away from the field. They didn't want him to get started on them."[50]

---

47 Raterree, interview with author.
48 Jack Lewis, interview with author.
49 Pride Raterree, interview with author.
50 Gene Hooks, interview with author.

***

Davis recalls Walker harping on running back William "Nub" Smith's lack of conditioning one day. It was the usual stuff until after one particular lackluster bit of execution by Smith, Walker drawled, "Goddamn it, Nub. If you'd keep your ass out of the goddamn oyster bar and quit eating them goddamn oysters and screwing that gal of yours you wouldn't be so goddamn fat and maybe you could do something."

The tirade left players—Smith and others—slack-jawed in amazement. Smith did, in fact, have a girlfriend who worked at the famous 42nd Street Oyster Bar in Raleigh. The state of their relationship isn't known, but Walker's guess (or maybe he had actual knowledge) probably wasn't far off. But how in the world, Davis and others wondered, did Coach Walker know that, and how did he put all of that together in the middle of practice?

Johnny Majors, a colorful college coach in his own right at the University of Tennessee and the University of Pittsburgh, played for Walker in the Canadian Football League. He remembers that Walker had a great sense of humor and a fascinating mind. "I mean, he could come up with things—you know, coaches tend say a lot of the same things over and over, things coaches have said for years—but he'd some up with these things I hadn't heard before or since," said Majors.

Majors says when one of Walker's Montreal players missed the same assignment three plays in a row one day at practice, Walker spit the omnipresent cigarette out of his mouth and said, "Goddamn it, boy. They could put your brain in a celery seed and it would still rattle all around."

"A celery seed?" asked Majors. "Who'd think of something like that?"[51] In the late 1940s, while once again searching for a serviceable punter, Walker held an "all-call" tryout session in which nearly every team member was given a look at the task. Sophomore Bill George, a sensational placekicker, was one of the last to step in. Walker was fairly frustrated at this point, the punting candidates having put on a poor showing. So when George

---

51 Johnny Majors, interview with author.

took the snap and boomed one straight up—so straight that George had to duck when the ball came back down—Walker had had enough.

Arms folded, disgust etched across his face, Walker shouted, "Eureka! Eu-FUCKING—reka!"

Turning to an astonished group of players, Walker said, "For those of you who have not completed your studies in ancient Greek, that means 'I have fucking found it!'"[52]

Walker also broke discipline at least once, and possibly several times, near the end of his Wake reign to send one or more players in pursuit of Arnold Palmer and other Deacon golfers who had to walk around the football practice field, carrying their clubs, to reach the college golf course just through the woods to the west.

"They'd be lined up for a drill or a scrimmage or something, and he'd tell the guys to go tackle the golfers and they'd take off after us," recalled Palmer. "They were pretty far away and never caught us that I can remember, but it wasn't easy running and carrying those clubs."[53]

***

When Wake met Duke in Walker's second season, the Deacons battled the Blue Devils toe to toe, giving as good as they got and maybe giving a little bit better. The Deacons stopped Duke's offense in its tracks, outgained the Blue Devils 203–138, and registered 12 first downs to just 6 for the home team.

But they didn't win.

Duke kicked the ball a little better, didn't make quite as many mistakes, and was very good on defense—the usual Wade

---

[52] Ed Butler, interview with author.
[53] Arnold Palmer, interview with author. Throughout Palmer's career at Wake, Walker kidded the future professional golfer about switching to football, "or some other sport you can make a living at." Palmer, who came from Walker's hallowed western Pennsylvania recruiting territory, was a strong, barrel-chested young man who looked like he might have been a pretty good footballer. In fact, he was during his early high school years. But Palmer's father, Deacon, a golf pro, nixed that idea soon after when his son began demonstrating some potential as a golfer. Walker, who remained friends with Palmer long after both left Wake Forest, eventually saw the light as well.

formula in other words. The only score came late in the first half when Blue Devil star George McAfee capped a twenty-eight-yard scoring drive with a short touchdown run. Duke gained the short field by winning a lengthy punting duel that was the main feature of the first twenty or so minutes of play. Duke's 6–0 lead didn't seem decisive at the time, what with Gallovich and the Wake offense moving the ball with some regularity. But Duke made it stand up. Polanski, nursing the arm injury, was limited in playing time and ability despite cushioning provided by a special cast created by doctors at, of all places, Duke Hospital. Wake missed the extra pop his running could have provided, especially on their best chance of the day, which came early in the fourth quarter. Gallovich set it up with a forty-four-yard run from his thirty-seven-yard line that looked like it would be good for more. Gallovich broke through one side of the line and into the open, and in situations like that, the 5'9" 160-pounder was seldom caught. But on this occasion he was. Robby Robinson's diving tackle got just a piece of Gallovich's foot, just enough to bring him down at the nineteen. Wake picked up another first down to the nine and then pushed to the five, but the drive unwound there. Mayberry slipped on a reverse and was dropped for a seven-yard loss. Then, on fourth down, Gallovich tried the end and was hit for a three-yard loss. The Deacs didn't get another chance. Final score: Duke 6, Wake 0.

    The Duke loss left the Deacons in a depressed state. They boarded a train the next weekend for Huntington, WV, home of Marshall College. Wake was sluggish and Marshall jumped out to a 13–0 lead midway through the third quarter, and the visitors looked like they were sunk. But at that point, Polanski and Mayberry led a comeback. The Deacons drove sixty-one tough yards for a score, Mayberry and Polanski picking up all but eight of the yards. John Pendergast's extra point made it 13–7 with one quarter to play. With time winding down, the Deacons set out on another drive. This one covered sixty-seven yards. Polanski, bruises and all, capped it with an eleven-yard run that knotted the score. A crowd estimated at 9,000 on a cold and wet day in Huntington watched as Pendergast lined up what could be the winning PAT. The hold was shaky and the kick, while high, was not very strong. Associated Press sportswriter Dick Boyd reported that it "bounced almost squarely on top of the upright and fell over." It was an unusual—the Wake side might even say miraculous—play to say the least. Land a ball on top of the goal posts?[54] Pendergast couldn't do it again if he kept kicking the rest of his life. And what did it mean? The officials conferred and after some lengthy deliberations ruled it good. A narrow win for Wake and Walker.

The Deacons' overall success, coupled with its high-scoring offense that still ranked among the nation's leaders, put them in conversation for an invitation to one of college football's newfangled postseason bowl games. Bowls—named for the rounded shape of the large systems and in particular the formally named Rose Bowl in Pasadena, CA—had been around since the Tournament of Roses Parade attached a football game to its festivities in 1916.[55] But the 1930s marked the real beginnings of a bowl system, as several warm weather municipalities put together exhibition-style contests designed to boost local economies and promote local products (hence, the product-based names of many of the original contests). Wake's first-ever suitor was the four-year-old Sun Bowl in sunny (but not always all that warm in January) El Paso, TX. As was typical of the time, the Sun Bowl hoped to pit a local (meaning Southwestern) team against an interesting visitor from afar. Well-known teams that could draw a crowd were the first choice. Exotic teams—meaning those that could score—were right behind. Early talk for the 1940 Sun Bowl had Arizona State—coached by Alabaman Mildred "Dixie" Howell, a teammate of Peahead's brother Erskine Walker, and of Peahead's coaching pal Bear Bryant at Alabama—as the home team. Walker's high-scoring Deacons were in a group of a half dozen or so Eastern clubs under consideration as a foe.

The news electrified Wake Forest's fans, but Deacon officials were wary. It did not sound like a money maker given the

---

54 The event described seems unlikely, but would have been possible in that day. Goal posts were considerably shorter then than now.

55 A game associated with the Rose festival was held in 1902, but after Michigan routed Stanford organizers dropped the game in favor of other entertaining activities, such as a race between an elephant and a camel. Most Rose Bowl historians cite the 1916 game between Brown and Washington State as the official beginning of the "granddaddy" of all the bowl games.

extensive travel required, and El Paso's Kidd Field, on the campus of the University of Texas El Paso, was no gem even if it was brand new. A decision could wait in any event. Wake's worthiness depended upon its finish.

The biggest chore by far was a November 18 game at Clemson. Jess Neely's Tigers, 6–1 and in the hunt for both a Southern Conference championship and a bowl bid of their own, were led by Banks McFadden, a three-sport star now remembered as one of Clemson's best-ever athletes. On the football field he was a shifty runner whose powerful passing arm gave the Tiger offense extra oomph.

McFadden's passing was on display against Wake during a second quarter explosion of offense that was much remarked upon then but which seems quaint now, when such outbursts are commonplace. The explosion saw the two teams combine for twenty-one points in the space of about six minutes. McFadden was involved in two thirds of that total. He heaved a seventy-four-yard touchdown pass to Joe "Glue-Fingered" Blalock. Then, a few minutes later, he hit halfback Bru Trexler with a thirty-six-yard scoring strike. In between, Wake's Polanski set up a short Deacon scoring drive by returning a Clemson kickoff eighty-one yards.

McFadden's dazzling passing display illustrated the style and skill levels of the era. Game film from the Clemson game shows the star throwing a pass of about fifteen yards to Blalock, who is behind the Deacon linebackers but in front of two defensive backs. The ball was nearly overthrown, but Blalock leaped and tipped it just as Wake's "Red" Mayberry came rushing toward him. As an off-balance Mayberry brushed past him, Blalock caught his own deflection. Dodging another Wake player, who dove at his feet, he maintained his balance and ran unmolested to the end zone. The scoring toss to Trexler had a bit more of a planned feel, at least in the beginning. McFadden took a handoff from Trexler, the fullback, and rolled out to his right. He stopped, pivoted, and threw the ball back across the field to Trexler, who had run kind of a circle route out of the backfield following the handoff. Trexler was wide open around the Deacon twenty-five. He sprinted toward the goal line, pursued by several Deacons. One of them—probably center/linebacker John Pendergast—caught him near the ten and delivered a solid blow. The ball was knocked loose and tumbled into the end zone. But Trexler, still on his feet, managed to stumble forward and fall on it for a score.

Wake closed the 1939 season with 46–7 whipping of Davidson before some 10,000 at Charlotte's Legion Field. Polanski scored twenty-three points himself, and Walker showed little mercy in piling it on the Wildcats. Wake's first stringers were still hard at work well into a fourth quarter, during which Wake scored nineteen points. If that gave the proceedings a vindictive feel, so be it. There was some bitterness in the Charlotte air that afternoon—the last remaining vestiges of the running football feud between Wake and Davidson, a feud intensified by Peahead Walker's elevation of the Deacon program.

Davidson, like most schools, had been debating the football issue, with some camps in favor of escalating the school's commitment to the sport and others for deemphasizing it. It was a spirited dialogue, but by the late 1930s, the trustees and faculty had adopted a report requiring "that football or any other intercollegiate sport schedules be adjusted as necessary as to the size and relative strength of opponents . . . to minimize both the hazard of injuries and pressure to subsidize athletes, or over-empahsize any particular sport."[56]

The first schedule, or contract, to be adjusted, was, it turned out, the one calling for football games between Davidson and Wake Forest. In the fall of 1939, the Wildcats formally notified the Deacons they were, henceforth, dropping them in football (Davidson also dropped South Carolina from its 1940 slate, but that was a much shorter-lived rivalry). In place of those two contests, Davidson was picking up games with Sewanee and Washington & Lee.

The official logic behind the change seemed sensible enough, but the news was taken with some offense at Wake Forest, where Athletic Director Weaver moved quickly to retaliate. He lined up South Carolina, which was also miffed at Davidson, for the Thanksgiving Day game in Charlotte, cutting Davidson out of a prime date in the metropolitan market next door (Davidson was

---

56 Beaty, MD.D., *History of Davidson College*, 2013. Isha Books, p. 313.

about thirty miles north of Charlotte at that time; the city limits have expanded quite a bit in the years since). And later, when the Wildcats called looking to schedule the annual baseball and basketball games with Wake, Weaver told them his dance card in those sports was full.

Mary D. Beaty's *History of Davidson College* calls the severance of the Deacon–Wildcat football connection "symbolic," which suggests that it was more than just the implementation of some study's recommendation.[57] Wake was the only Big Five school that Davidson dropped at that time. The Wildcats continued to play Duke, NC State, and UNC teams until the onset of World War II. And Davidson and State continued a series into the 1950s.

Wake was apparently singled out because of the new tone of Deacon athletics, football in particular, since the arrival of one Peahead Walker. There were complaints from Davidson about the rough tactics adopted by Walker's men in the 1937 upset of Davidson. The *Old Gold & Black* (doubtless reporting information gleaned from Weaver and other athletic department sources) reported that Davidson officials were particularly offended by Walker's high-powered recruiting tactics. And, as noted earlier, Weaver believed that it was Davidson that turned in the Deacons over the Allen Powers affairs in 1937.[58]

That was the end of the season. The Deacons did not receive the rumored Sun Bowl bid. It went instead to Catholic University, which hopped a train to El Paso in late December and battled Arizona State to a scoreless tie—perhaps not what the promoters were after.

No matter. Back in North Carolina, Walker signed a second three-year contract with the school in January—with a "pay boost" according to some newspaper reports.[59] The increase was no more than $500 a year, and Walker's new salary was no more than $4,500 at the beginning of World War II.[60] College records put Walker's salary at $4,500 at the start of World War II. The raise, if there was one, recognized Walker's work in turning the Deacons'

---

57 Beaty, M.D., *History of Davidson College*. 2013. Isha Books, p. 309.
58 Jim Weaver personal papers, Wake Forest Archives.
59 *Raleigh News & Observer*, Dec. 11, 1939.
60 Wake Forest Board of Trustees Minutes, WFU Archives.

football fortunes around, but it was probably a wash for him personally since the new deal required giving up his summer baseball habit.

More important than the raise, perhaps, was the rising level of football facilities at Wake. Not only did school officials extend his contract after 1939 season, they also approved a significant enhancement of the school's football facilities just as the campaign was ending. The official action came at the November 1939 meeting of the Baptist State Convention, where a long-rumored stadium expansion was confirmed and announced. Gastonia textile tycoon Henry Groves, a Wake grad who'd already given $18,000 to build the old football stadium, agreed to cough up $15,000 more for an expansion and upgrade to 20,000 seats (and a new name, Groves Stadium, a name that, oddly, followed the school when it moved to Winston-Salem). The whole deal, complete with steel-and-concrete seats, an enhanced press box, and a souped-up field house, would cost $50,000 and would be ready for the 1940 season. When first announced, the stadium plan was pitched as an expansion of the existing field. When it actually began a few months later, it was a whole new stadium, about a half-mile away from the old one. Looking out a back window in Gore Gymnasium, Peahead Walker could make out the new site, a place call Rock Springs Ravine. It looked like a wonderful setting to him.

The 1940–1941 school year opened amidst an unsettling atmosphere filled with both hope and dread. On the one hand, the prospects looked pretty good for both Wake Forest and its student body, which had swollen to an all-time high of some 1,200. All kinds of construction activity was afoot or about to be. The new football stadium, a 20,000-seat bowl set among tall pines in a manner that caused more than a few to note the similarities with UNC's twelve-year-old Kenan Stadium, was nearing completion. Fundraising for a new chapel was nearly complete, meaning work could begin by spring.[61] And work was well underway on the new

---

[61] In a juxtaposition unlikely to be seen to today, the estimated cost of the chapel was $150,000, or about three times the cost of the new football stadium. In another anachronistic twist, the chapel campaign was at least partly a response to a student petition requesting that such a facility be built, whereas the stadium was the administration's idea.

Baptist Medical College in Winston-Salem. The school was closely affiliated with Wake Forest, and plans were for it to draw most of its student body from Wake's undergraduates. So there was all that.

And then, on the other hand, there was war.

Germany had just completed its conquest of France and the ejection of British forces from the continent. In hindsight, the involvement of the United States in the conflict was inevitable at this point, but it was not necessarily viewed that way at the time. Wake's enrollment (and the enrollments of most other colleges) rose in 1940 due in part to student reaction to conscription bills wending their way through Congress, but war hadn't arrive yet and there was still hope that it might never come. Clyde Erwin, head of the North Carolina Department of Public Instruction, greeted students and faculty in his address formally opening Wake's 107th session by telling them that they were "fortunate to live in a progressive country at peace in this time of international chaos."[62]

Peahead Walker hoped to create some Southern Conference chaos and had the horses to do it. If the 1940 Deacons could just add a little passing to their powerful rushing attack, they would be unstoppable. That was the thought anyway. And a livelier passing game did seem likely. Sophomore John VanBuren Pruitt (J.V. for short) appeared to be the best slinger Walker had ever had at Wake. He'd led yet another successful freshman team to great heights in 1939, and if Walker could find a way to get him on the field—the starting backfield from 1939 returned intact—Wake might have enough balance to finally whip some of the big boys. Even if there was no room for Pruitt, Wake might be better through the air. Gallovich had worked during the offseason to improve his passing. Sportswriters visiting early season practice noticed that the Deacons just "passed and passed and passed."[63] The *Charlotte Observer's* Jake Wade, who had, in prior years, made fun of Walker's boys for their poor passing, noted all this and made the inevitable if cavalier comparison between war and football. In a mid-September column, just before the opening of a new season, he wrote that, "This doesn't mean that this pretty running team . . .

---

62 *Old Gold & Black*, Sept. 13, 1940.
63 *Charlotte Observer*, Sept 19, 1940.

has been transformed into Goering's bombing act or an RAF. . . . Peahead says he's not sure if [Wake] will complete any, but says they will try, 'at least enough to shake up the defense.'"

Arguing against even more progress on the field for Walker and company was a more difficult schedule. In addition to the regular Southern Conference heavyweights, Weaver and Walker had put together a schedule that included road trips to Georgetown, which was a pretty good football team at the time, and Texas Tech, which was a logistical challenge even before considering the skill of the Red Raider team at that time, which was thought to be considerable. The only lightweight on the slate was William Jewell College, which Walker had lined up for the Deacons' season opener.

William Jewell was a small Baptist college in Missouri that seldom played football against big-time schools. William Jewell was coached by Henry Godfriaux, an obscure and unorthodox coach who used a metronome to help his gridders learn rhythm and timing. The steady tick-tocking of the device—it was normally used by musicians and music students—echoed across the Cardinals' practice field as Godfriaux's charges ran through their plays.

The Jewellers improved rhythm might have been a boon on the whole, but when thrown against Peahead Walker's strapping gridders, all the Cardinals got was a timely beating. Wake blasted the hapless visitors 79–0, gaining yardage and scoring points at will. The new aerial game was on display. Wake completed 9 of 18 passes for 170 yards. Whether that signified any real improvement was hard to say, however. The Deacons could have run backward with the ball and still picked up yardage against the Cards.

A truer assessment of this Deacon team wasn't long in coming, however. The second game was the annual early season tilt with UNC, and it was clear early on that Walker meant business. A budding fashion plate during the Zoot Suit era of the early 1940s, Walker strolled into Kenan Stadium wearing a pair of Tar Heel blue pants and some snappy, two-tone shoes along with a checked sports coat, standard-issue dark shirt, and a very loud tie. His players got the vibe. The defense, led by sophomore tackle Pat Preston, shut Carolina down from start to finish. Great field position helped. Deacon tailback John Van Buren Pruitt enjoyed a sensational day punting the ball, downing six kicks inside the Carolina fifteen-yard line. "[Pruitt] owned the coffin corner today," UNC coach Ray Wolf told reporters afterward.[64]

Wake kept Carolina bottled up throughout the first half and finally punched in a touchdown when Pruitt hit John Jett with a five-yard touchdown pass on fourth and goal. Wake iced the game with an impressive ninety-nine-yard scoring drive that began with back-to-back fake punts. Pruitt hit Gallovich for seven yards on the first fake and then ran eleven yards for a first down on the second. Polanski produced the breakout play, running fifty-two yards to the UNC twenty-two. Gallovich scored from there on a Walker favorite: the wingback reverse behind all the good blockers that could be found. Gallovich took the handoff from Polanski and romped into the end zone with Jett, Preston, and Jimmy Ringgold leading the way.

That was 12–0 and that was good enough. As an ecstatic Walker told reporters afterward, "Our boys have played one of the best games I have seen them play. I wouldn't say they were playing over their heads, but they were keyed up and out to avenge last year's one-sided score. . . . I still think we could lose 2–3 this year, though."

Said UNC's Wolf, "No alibis. We got beat. We knew we were going up against one of the stronger teams in the country."[65]

Wake followed up that victory with a 19–0 triumph over Furman in the first game ever played at Groves Stadium—although not the official opener (that would come several weeks later against Duke).

At 3–0 and with one handsome victory under their belts, the Deacons were looking good. That view was changed considerably during a mid-October trip to Clemson. The Tigers, under new coach Frank Howard, a long-time assistant to the departed Jess Neely, just wore Wake Forest out despite the Deacon debut of some snappy new uniforms: black pants and black jerseys

---

64 The term "coffin corner" refers, in general, to the corner formed by the sideline, the goal line, an imaginary line parallel to the sideline, and the five- or ten-yard line. The term probably originates in architecture, where it refers to dead space near the landings of Victorian Era staircases.
65 *Greensboro Daily News*, Sept. 29, 1940.

with golden yokes and sleeves. "Glue-Fingered" Blaylock, the 1939 nemesis, struck for two more touchdowns; backs "Booty" Payne and "Chippy" Maness (Howard, a well-known associate of Walker's, and possibly a close friend, was as much a fan of nicknames as was Peahead) ran wild, and the Tigers returned two interceptions for touchdowns. The result was a 39–0 Clemson defeat of a Wake Forest team that most sportswriters figured as the favorite in the contest despite the fact that it was at Clemson.

The disappointment of that loss was magnified a few weeks later when Duke ruined the official grand opening of Groves Stadium by beating the Deacons 23–0. Duke held a narrow 3–0 lead at the half thanks to a twenty-eight-yard field goal by Tony "the Toe" Ruffa. The crowd of 21,000 cheered during the halftime ceremonies when alum (and alumni group president) Henry Groves donated the stadium to the school. But the cheering died rather quickly after play resumed. In the first six minutes of the third quarter Duke piled up thirteen quick points. Steve Lach ran sixty-one yards for a touchdown, and then future college and pro coach Tommy Prothro blocked a punt that a teammate recovered for a score.

Wake's two big-game losses put a damper on the Deacons' momentum, but Walker drove them on. His basic plan at Wake— to get better players—proved to be successful despite the trying times. Senior Gallovich, for example, turned in several remarkable performances that kept the Deacons on the move. In between the losses to Clemson and Duke, he ran for a school record 226 yards, returned a punt 68 yards, punted six times for a 42.6-yard average, and scored 2 touchdowns as Wake beat Marshall 31–19. Two weeks after the Duke defeat, Gallovich's diving "you-see-it-and-still-don't-believe-it" catch of J.V. Pruitt's thirty-five-yard pass allowed Wake to rally and beat another rather weather-beaten NC State team 20–14.[66] The Deacs trailed 14–7 in that contest with just more than five minutes to play but rallied to win. The State victory made it two in a row and ran Wake's record to 6–2. The week before, with Polanski powering his way through the mud at Griffith Stadium, Wake had beaten George Washington 18–0.

---

66 *Raleigh News & Observer*, Nov. 10, 1940.

Long-distance logistics now became the Deacons' main concern. The next game for Walker and company was at Texas Tech. The machinations for obtaining a match with the Red Raiders were nearly as convoluted as the travel arrangements needed to make the twenty-four-hour train trip from Wake Forest to Lubbock. It began, oddly enough, when Wake signed an eleven-year contract with Charlotte city officials in 1939 and stole the Memorial Stadium Thanksgiving Day date away from Davidson. The plan seemed a good one because Wake had a ready-made foe—the University of South Carolina (USC)—all lined up for the game. With Columbia, SC less than two hours from Charlotte, the contest was guaranteed to be a good draw. But before the first Wake-USC Turkey Day contest could be played, USC announced it had signed to play Penn State on Thanksgiving Day in 1941. Not wanting to pay stadium rent for an intrasquad game, Wake officials began scouting around for a foe and somehow discovered Texas Tech. The common denominator was an open Thanksgiving Day date in 1941 for both teams and an opening on November 15, 1940. Wake lured Tech to Charlotte for the 1941 game by agreeing to come to Lubbock for a game in 1940.

The contest had a bowl-like atmosphere, starting with the novelty of a long train ride west and culminating in a heaping helping of West Texas hospitality. The Deacons were greeted at their hotel by a group of "Raiderettes" who presented all the players and coaches with ten-gallon hats. Dates had been lined up for the visitors as well—possibly a strength-sapping gambit by Tech coach Pete Cawthon—but Walker put the kibosh on any Lone Star hanky panky. Curfew was moved up. Bed checks were the order of the day. Liaisons—with Raiderettes or anyone else—were taboo. Walker knew his men would need their rest. Texas Tech was unbeaten and Wake was being served up as the main course for the school's homecoming festivities.

A crowd of 10,000, Tech's largest of the season, turned out for the contest and saw the hometown boys take one right in the mouth at the start of the game. With Gallovich running wild and J.V. Pruitt gaining ground on land and through the air, Wake scored a quick early touchdown and threatened to get another, driving sixty-two yards to the Tech three-yard line. The drive stalled there, however, and Tech roared back to cut the lead to 7–6 in the second quarter and then surged ahead 12–7 in the third. Wake worked hard at a comeback. Polanski, irritated at a third-quarter public address announcement noting that he'd been "held" to just seven net yards on the day, ran like a mad man as Wake pushed into Tech territory three times. Gallovich nearly slipped away on a twenty-yard run that saw him tackled by his shoelaces at the Raider thirty. Another drive reached the twenty before a fourth-down gamble resulted in a big loss of yardage—and loss of the ball. Close, but not close enough. Tech held on and a weary, big-hatted bunch of Deacons boarded the eastbound train and headed home.

They all made it safely, but not all at the same time. When the train stopped in Atlanta, Gallovich and end Herb Cline, the basketball star, got off to have a look around. They lost track of time and returned to the platform just in time to see the last car disappear from sight. An hour or so later, Coach Walker received a telegram, outlining the player's plight. He wired back some funds for two one-way tickets from Atlanta to Wake Forest plus enough for some food and told his players to make it back as soon as they could. Six hours after the Deacon Special chugged into the Wake Forest station, Cline and Gallovich rode in on the regular passenger service. No harm done.

Walker gave the team a holiday after the game for the stated purpose of letting the boys get their legs back after a long train trip. Maybe the coach needed a little "de-training" as well. Players recall that most of the team's lengthy road trips featured Walker, the other coaches, and any members of the visiting press traveling in a "refreshment car" that was off limits to the players.

Wake's season ender was almost two full weeks later on Thanksgiving Day in Charlotte. It was a defensive struggle against a mediocre South Carolina squad. Wake managed to pull out a 7–6 win thanks to a missed extra point by the Gamecocks.

So it was a win, but as President Kitchin noted in a speech at the postgame banquet for Charlotte alumni and college friends, a narrow one:

> *We must admit that it was mighty good to watch the Deacons feast on Palmetto Gamecocks, fresh from the gridiron.* . . . *[but] the fact is*

the game was so close that when it was over I felt like the man who went into the bank and cashed a check. He counted the money . . . and recounted it, and then counted it again. The cashier noticed this, of course and asked if had not given him enough. "Yes," said the man, "but by heck you just barely did."[67]

No recount was necessary to discover that Wake Forest had just put together its second straight 7–3 season. Yes, it was disappointing to lose again to Duke and Clemson, but repeating the accomplishments of 1939 was a sure sign of progress. And so, too, in a backhanded way, were the hits Walker and Wake were beginning to take in the press. During their late-season trip to Washington, DC, Bob Ruark, a columnist for the now defunct *Washington Daily News*, singled out the Deacons as a poster boy for the evil college football-as-business crowd: "If you should be looking for the perfect example of the professional football college," penned Ruark, "you might dash out to Griffith Stadium tomorrow night and cock an eye at Wake Forest . . . Wake Forest, that quiet, little sectarian Milquetoastish college, has a reputation for being one of the most brazen football foundries in the South, and that is covering a lot of ground."[68]

Ruark went on to accuse Wake of having too many out-of-state players, of bringing students to the school for the sole purpose of playing football, of offering players "unknown" inducements to come to the school, and of creating a huge athletic staff (thirteen people!).[69] The *Old Gold & Black* reported that the Deacons were saddened by the attack, but it is hard to imagine Walker being too put out.[70] The column confirmed that his work was being noticed and that his was a football program to be taken seriously.

Oddly, there were, at the same time, reports of alumni unrest in Deaconland. One report said some alumni had actually met to discuss a contract buyout and to consider possible

---

67 Thurman D. Kitchin, Presidential Papers, Wake Forest Archives.
68 *Washington Daily News*, Oct. 31, 1940.
69 Ruark stumbled over facts both big and small in his diatribe. Worse still (though hardly surprising from a Wake Forest point of view), he was a Carolina man.
70 *Old Gold & Black*, Nov. 8, 1940.

successors for Walker as the Deacons' head man (ex-Duke star George McAfee was mentioned).[71] A contract buyout—Walker had two years left on his new deal—would have been considered as fiscally unpalatable for an operation as big as Wake Forest's at that time, although it appears that at least one informal meeting was held to gauge interest in taking up a "buy-out collection."[72] Nothing came of that, but *Greensboro Daily News* columnist Smith Barrier related a story some years later (probably obtained from Walker himself) that suggested a dismissal in 1940 had been a near thing. According to Barrier/Walker, a trustees meeting scheduled to discuss the coach's firing was postponed when winter rains rendered some eastern North Carolina roads impassable. Too many trustees simply couldn't make it to Raleigh. By the time the meeting could be rescheduled, Walker had returned to the alum's good graces . . . or good enough anyway.

The reported unrest may not have been football-related. More probable was a case of alumni heartburn stemming from Walker's off-the-field behavior. Walker was called on the carpet at least twice, and perhaps more often than that, to answer for what today would be considered moral offenses. The instigators were always members of the Southern Baptist Convention (SBC), which, at the time, held considerable sway over Wake Forest's purse strings. When these SBC "commissions of inquiry" began is uncertain—SBC records are not public—but it is difficult to find a Wake player who didn't either testify in one of the hearings or know someone who did.[73]

Dewey Hobbs said he and Dick Kelly were called to a meeting in Raleigh once during his student days (1943–1946) and were quizzed for something like two hours.

---

71 *Charlotte Observer*, Nov. 29, 1940.
72 *Greensboro Daily News*, March 8, 1951.
73 The SBC records not only are not public but may not even be complete. Dewey Hobbs, who played for Walker who went on to become a prominent Baptist minister, and thus, had some access to the SBC archives, once spent some time searching for a record of a Walker "hearing" in which he participated as a student. "Couldn't find a word about it," Hobbs said. "They either didn't write it down or got rid of it." Source: Dewey Hobbs, interview with author.

> *I can still remember questions. "Have you ever heard Coach Walker use profane language?" "Yessir, if you count hells, damns, and Jesus Christ's name as profanity if used irreverently." I was 19 and I wasn't planning to go into coaching and wouldn't be depending on Peahead's support in my career. So I shot 'em straight. That's probably why they asked me to come in the first place. . . . Anyway, they asked me to compare Peahead with other Big Four coaches. I said I'd never played for the other coaches. "What about Peahead with women? Can you tell us what you've heard?" I didn't think that was a fair question, and I really hadn't heard much, so I said I didn't know. "What about drink? Ever seen him drinking?" I made them define what they meant. Beer, wine, liquor? They wanted to know if I had ever seen him drunk. I said, "I have seen times when I thought there was evidence of inebriation." That was that. I thought the whole thing was kind of a show to appease some members of the convention and that the votes for firing him weren't there. I guess that was right. Obviously nothing ever came of it.*[74]

Pride Ratterree, who played alongside Hobbs, said he was called to testify as well, either as a player or, just after his playing career, as a coach (he spent part of a year at Wake after graduation as what would, today, be known as a graduate assistant). The crucial subject then was Walker's morals—in particular his infidelity. "They called me, [Pat] Preston, and someone else, I forget who, who knew him pretty well, to some lawyer's office in Raleigh to be interrogated," said Ratterree. "We convinced [the attorney] that he was a pretty good coach and didn't say much about the other stuff. I think he got a new contract after that."[75]

Herb Appenzeller, who played two seasons under Walker in 1944–1945, agreed that the inquisitions were a regular event. "Every year the trustees would pick a few players to talk to about Peahead: 'Should we keep him? Does he drink? Is he profane?' That kind of thing. We always said everything was fine because he was a pretty good coach."[76]

---

74 Hobbs, interview with author.
75 Ratteree, interview with author.
76 Herb Appenzeller, interview with author.

Everything wasn't fine, of course, at least not by Baptist standards of the day, and everyone, except maybe the convention leaders, knew it. Walker's "immoral" activities were hardly a secret in the small, tight-knit college town. His profanity was more than just known—it was legendary. He smoked like a freight train and drank enough that most players saw him with liquor—or under its influence—at one time or another. Jack Lewis, a standout Deacon end from 1949-1952, recalled seeing his father and Walker return from dinner one night (the elder Lewis was, like Walker, a Birmingham native, and the two became close after Walker offered Lewis's son a scholarship) clearly under the influence of something. "Peahead was driving his car and twice he ran over reflectors trying to park. He just backed off them and kept going, all the while singing, in a fairly loud voice, 'My Wild Irish Rose.'"[77]

Womanizing apparently was a long-time hobby as well. Years after he left, Elon students were still pointing out campus hideaways where the young and dashing Walker had a liaison with this or that departmental secretary. And at Wake, Walker's relationship with his second wife-to-be Flonnie Horenthal Watts was well known to his Deacon players during the postwar years. More than one player recalled the team bus picking up Walker at the Sir Walter Raleigh hotel on Saturday morning for a road trip and seeing a nightgown-clad Flonnie stick her head out a hotel window to call out, "Good luck, Petie!"

Ratterree said Peahead's love life was common knowledge. "He was getting divorced," said Ratterree. "I sort of remember [Carolyne Walker, Peahead's first wife] being around a little bit. But he was obviously fooling around with some other women, too. We'd see 'em on campus every now and then. The president, I think, wanted him to get married. Or be married, or whatever. It was kind of a mess."[78]

While the details of Walker's romantic adventures remained essentially hidden, some public acts created perceptions that would have (and probably should have) set off trustee and/or SBC alarms. They certainly would today. Appenzeller, no shrinking violet himself, said that more than once he saw Walker hold court

---
[77] Jack Lewis, interview with author.
[78] Ratterree, interview with author.

with giggling coeds at a campus party. On one occasion, Walker wound up flat on his back, on the floor in a frat house, surrounded by beer bottles. He sang, laughed, and told stories from that position to an appreciative (or at least amused) crowd.

The group did not, apparently, include any members of the Southern Baptist Convention, who preferred to learn about such things by interrogating football players. Or perhaps they were just biding their time, letting the case against the successful coach build.

In the meantime, Walker was busy building an actual coaching staff—one that very nearly included Paul "Bear" Bryant. In time for the 1941 season, Walker added his younger brother Erskine, who went by the nickname "Bub" (which itself was a shortened version of Bubba) to the staff. Bub, who'd spent some time coaching the Deacon JVs in 1939, replaced Tom Rogers, who had flown the coop to take up coaching the baseball team at Clemson. Walker had also hired Herb Bartos as an assistant to go along with Greason, part-time PE instructor Phil Utley, and, of course, Jim Weaver. That made six, and it would have been seven if a promising new coach from Alabama had jumped on board.[79]

Walker's 1941 team appeared to have plenty of talent—freshly minted Alabama tailback Red Cochran was clearly the best passer Walker had ever had, better even than Pruitt—but with the class of 1940 (Gallovich, Jett, etc.) gone there was some uncertainty and some new men to break in. That led to a bumpy start. Wake pummeled a disorganized team from Camp Davis 65–

---

79 Walker offered a job to Bryant, a strapping teammate of Bub's at Alabama where Bryant had been known as Bear. Young Bryant was making a mark as a graduate assistant at Alabama, and Walker knew of him through Bub and through his association with Alabama coach Frank Thomas. Mickey Walker, Peahead's nephew, says his uncle told him that Bryant had agreed to come to Wake along with Bub in 1940 but backed out at the last minute when he was offered a similar but better-paying position at Vanderbilt. Bryant and Walker crossed paths again soon afterward, when the war finally arrived. Bryant served as football coach for the UNC preflight team (the Cloudbusters). The two men became close friends and stayed in touch throughout their careers.

0 in the opener,[80] but in week two the Deacons were manhandled by top-ranked Duke 43–14. The game was a disaster for Wake right from the start. The Deacons coughed up three turnovers in the first quarter (two interceptions plus a fumble by Polanski), all of which led to Duke touchdowns. When the gun sounded to signal the end of the first quarter, Duke had a 28–0 lead. It was 34–0 at the half, and Walker was ready to wave the white flag. By mutual consent of the coaches (but with no announcement to the crowd), the third and fourth quarters were reduced from fifteen to twelve minutes. Duke's Wade pulled some starters, and the final score turned a little more respectable. That didn't fool any in the crowd of 20,000 plus (including some 8,000 servicemen taking advantage of Wade's fifty-cent GI ticket). This was a superb Duke team, perhaps Wade's best. The Blue Devils were undefeated and outscored their opponents 311–41. As long-time Duke publicist Ted Mann noted, "this team simply beat the hell out of everyone." Part of Duke's success was Wade's good fortune in not losing any important players to military service (the call to duty was already beginning to affect many rosters).

Wake rallied from the Duke debacle to blast draft-depleted Furman 52–13 and then battled South Carolina to a 6–6 tie. Wake beat a poor NC State team 7–0 the next week to run its record to 3-1-1 heading into the annual showdown game against UNC, which had lost two straight. More than 14,000 filed into Groves Stadium for the tilt. The number would have been more, but a meningitis outbreak on the nearby campus of Meredith College, an all-girls' school in Raleigh where the students watched all-male proceedings on local football fields with great interest, led to a quarantine. The Meredith girls were confined to quarters and had to content themselves with listening to the game on the radio. The girls affiliated with the Wake side liked what they heard. The Deacons overwhelmed the Tar Heel offense, allowing them just two brief forays into Wake Forest territory. Meanwhile, Wake's improved passing game took flight. Early in the second quarter, Cochran hit Cline for a twenty-seven-yard score on fourth down.

---

[80] Military bases were beginning to pop up as the inevitability of war became clear, and their football teams would become regularly fodder for Wake and most colleges in the dark years ahead.

One possession later, Cochran connected with Johnny Perry on a fifty-yard pass and ran for another touchdown. That made it 13–0 and that's how it ended up. Cochran and Wake passed for 166 yards and ran for 122. Carolina managed just fifty-two yards total.

The UNC contest reflected Wake's early-season success. Cochran had already passed for six touchdowns in the first five games, an absolute aerial onslaught by the standards of Walker's teams up to this point. The 6'4" Cline, known mostly for his basketball rebounding and getting stranded on the Texas Tech trip, hauled in three of those. Meanwhile, Perry's touchdown was his sixth. He scored two against Duke, one on a ninety-five-yard kickoff return, and had the lone score against State. He and Cochran were clearly the stars of the offense. Mayberry, a standout from days gone by, was hurt. Pruitt couldn't get much time with Cochran in the way. And Polanski just couldn't get going, not in the way that might have been expected for a senior with his track record—his woes tied to ongoing problems with what Walker called "that trick stomach of his."[81] The pronouncement carried some undertone of suspected malingering, always an issue with Walker. Whatever the truth, Polanski's senior year was a dim copy of his earlier work.

Beating UNC turned out to be the Deacons' high-water mark. The season's momentum turned sharply the next week when Marshall upended the Deacons 16–6 before 10,000 in Huntington, WV. A pair of decisive defeats followed. Wake opened what was to be a long and grueling series with Boston College with a 26–6 defeat. It was a painful introduction to the Eagles' newfangled T-formation offense. A week later, Clemson's more conventional set was just as effective. The Tigers pounded out 341 rushing yards in a 29–0 victory that included another safety.

The Deacons were reeling, but fortuitous scheduling had them in the nation's capital to play George Washington, a mediocre program suffering through a poor season. Wake administered a 42–0 whipping to the Colonials, which included Cochran throwing three touchdown passes to Cline. Perry, one of the better kickers Walker ever had, booted all six extra points.

---

81 *Raleigh News & Observer*, Oct. 10.

With the bleeding stopped, Wake headed to Charlotte for its season ender with Texas Tech. The Red Raiders turned the long train ride into a three-day sojourn, stopping in Louisiana and Atlanta to practice and spend the night. They arrived in Charlotte on the Saturday after Thanksgiving a well-rested team and blasted the Deacons 35–6.

Walker's pass-happy 1941 team was through, and while it was considered a disappointment, it was interesting, some Wake backers noted, for a five-win Deacon team to be the object of scorn and disappointment. By Walker's standards the season was right in line with what he expected—he knew it would be something of a rebuilding year. And now, with Cochran, Perry, and tackles Pat Preston and George Owen all due back, the future looked bright.

Unless, of course, something unexpected occurred.

CHAPTER 6

PEAHEAD AT WAR

On December 7, just one week after Wake's loss to Texas Tech that concluded the 1941 season, the Japanese attacked Pearl Harbor, catapulting the Unites States into War World II. American life was turned upside down and life at Wake Forest College was not exempt from that turmoil. Like most American universities, Wake accelerated its academic program to help students graduate faster, just as soon as war was officially declared. Since Wake was on a semester as opposed to quarter system, that change was fairly simple. The school added a rigorous nine-week summer term between the regular fall and spring semesters. A student who attended year-round could finish a degree in three years (and, if really ambitious, less than that). In addition, like other schools, Wake became a site for a specialized military education program. The Army Finance School's branch for noncommissioned officers was located at Wake from August 1942 until the end of the war. The school was home, at the Finance School's peak, to more than three hundred students studying the intricacies of the Army payroll system.

The "Fighting Financiers" created numerous problems on campus. They sucked up dormitory, classroom, and even gymnasium space, dislocated fraternities, disrupted the housing of the college's newly welcomed coeds (see below), and made "the business of getting dinner and supper . . . into physical drudgery."[1] Students had to wait in long lines at the school cafeteria for food of a rather insipid nature. On the other hand, the government paid a handsome price for the space it rented. The financial windfall from the Finance School (plus some cost cutting) helped put college finances on a sound footing, even as normal college enrollment tailed off some thirty percent to around eight hundred. As

---

1 *Old Gold & Black*, Sept. 18, 1942.

numerous historians have noted, World War II was the ultimate antidote for the Great Depression, and that was true for economies both big and small.

Simultaneous to the war footing came another big change: the addition of some fifty women (admitted as juniors or seniors only) to the official campus roster. A handful of women—the daughters of faculty and prominent townsfolk—had attended some classes for years. But they weren't officially part of the school and couldn't earn degrees. Faced with downward enrollment pressure, however, the Board of Trustees and Baptist Convention approved the addition of bona fide female students for the academic year beginning in 1942. Though limited by strict college rules—the women had a 10:30 PM curfew, weren't allowed to smoke in public, and were prohibited from going on dates in cars (school and Baptist officials saw all kind of sinful possibilities there)—the coeds were still a big draw.

And there were still more changes. Courses aimed at beefing up war-abetting knowledge were offered, air raid drills were conducted (because, of course, the Nazis would want to strike Wake Forest, NC), calculations were made as to draft odds by academic major (science majors would probably be deferred), and shortages of fuel, auto parts, beer, and other collegiate essentials were felt and (more or less) tolerated.

A shortage of patriotism, at least as measured by financial gifts, also reared its head. The student council launched a war bond drive as soon as war was declared hoping to raise the funds needed to purchase a $1,000 bond from student donations. By the spring, with just $509 collected from the collegiate skinflints, the editors of the *Old Gold & Black* took to printing crude approximations of the Nazi swastika and Japanese rising sun above the masthead of each weekly issue. The enemy symbols would be removed, the editors said, when the students coughed up the war bound dough. Apparently times were tougher than the editors might have imagined. It took more than a year for the funds to be raised.

Out on the football field, the pace of "war losses" accelerated. End Jack Ciccarelli was an early draftee. A spring visit by a Marine recruiter saw six football players, including star Red

Cochran and regulars Jim Copley and Joe Duncavage, enlist in the Marine reserves. Guard Carl Givler joined the regular Marine Corps as a private. He wasn't any nobler than his reservist teammates—his draft number was up. Johnny Perry joined the reserves later that summer.

Wartime attrition struck on the sidelines, too, and Peahead Walker's expanding coaching staff, the one that drew the Washington newspaper complaints, fell apart in a hurry. Brother "Bub" left for a defense department position, and Hank Bartos signed on with the Army to teach P.E. classes at another school. That left Walker with what would be his wartime staff: Murray Greason and campus P.E. instructor Phil Utley. Jim Weaver was still around to coach the freshmen in 1942, but he accepted a Navy commission as a lieutenant in the P.E. program that winter. With Weaver gone, Walker accepted a "for the duration" commission as Wake's athletic director. The appointment came with an extra $1,000 for being the head man, a sum that didn't quite offset the $1,500 wartime reduction in pay implemented as part of a campus-wide austerity program. Effective January 1943, all professors and staff were dropped to no more than $3,000 per year, including Walker.[2] The freshman football team was suspended after 1942 when freshmen became eligible (and were needed) to fill the varsity ranks. Finance School students were also eligible, although it does not appear that Walker benefited from the new exception. There don't appear to have been any students from the Finance School on Walker's 1942 squad, and by the following year the Financiers were actually fielding their own, rather lackluster, team.

Baseball was eliminated in 1943 along with track and all other "minor" sports. That freed up Greason, the hardworking basketball/baseball/football assistant a bit, but wartime life was still pretty grim. Murray Greason Jr. said that the family survived on his father's meager salary thanks to a few perks, the most considerable of which was college-supplied housing. The family lived in a three-room house that belonged to the school (Walker and Weaver also occasionally lived in college housing). The Greason residence was situated a block from the gym (and about the same

---

2 Wake Forest Board of Trustees Minutes, Jan. 6, 1943.

distance from the football field), right next to the university steam plant. The short distance from the source of the college's heat made the house nice and toasty for most of the winter. But it was an icebox from mid-December, when the college closed for Christmas, until it reopened in early- to mid-January. "What I remember about Christmas mostly," said Greason Jr., "is that it was cold."[3] A few other living expenses were covered, and the innovative Greason managed to augment his salary in other ways.

One of his unofficial duties, which he certainly shared with Walker and Weaver, was to spend some time courting school boosters. What this usually meant was traveling to a booster's community and sharing a meal or maybe a day of hunting or fishing. At the end of the event, Greason would make the pitch, asking the sated booster for some cash.

While on one such adventure, Greason presented his closing argument. The booster paused and then shot back with the following: "I'll tell you what," he said. "I can give you maybe $200 in a few weeks, or I can give you this turkey I just bagged right here, right now," to which Greason responded, "Better give me the turkey. If you gave me $200 I might have to turn it in."[4]

The real wartime manpower crunch did not hit Wake until 1943. For the 1942 season, Walker had a roster of typical size: thirty-two players. Half that group were unproven sophomores, but they were the residue of another successful recruiting class and freshmen team, so there was plenty of reason for optimism. With the exception of Polanski and Cline, all the top skill-position players were back. He had the redoubtable Preston on hand to lead the line, and there was even the promise of a little depth.

What wasn't clear was just what Wake and Walker were up against. The situation at many of the regular opponents on Wake's schedule was up in the air. Both UNC's Ray Wolf and Duke's Wade had joined the Army (Wade returning to active duty as a major in an artillery unit). UNC, Duke, NC State, Clemson, and South Carolina all had large military training programs on campus that could, in theory, add tremendous manpower to their athletic teams. That infusion was already underway in 1942. NCAA

---

[3] Murray Greason Jr., interview with author.
[4] Ibid.

swimming champion Rene Chocteau, formerly of Yale, enrolled at UNC that fall, the harbinger of an athletic horde to come that would eventually include baseball Hall of Famer Ted Williams, future NFL star Otto Graham, and a coach in the making by the name of Paul "Bear" Bryant.

Just what the new coaches would have, and what they could do with it, was a mystery. And that was true not only throughout the Southern Conference but across the entire country as well. On the eve of his team's season opener, Clemson coach Frank Howard called his Tigers "terrible but promising." Walker's old pal Jim Tatum, UNC's new man, thought the Tar Heels had suffered in terms of recruiting during Wolf's last few years but was hopeful that the fortunes of war-driven enrollment would provide a boost.

No one could be sure just what would happen, but Walker and Wake knew one thing: it wouldn't take them long to find out. The Deacons opened with UNC and then had Duke the following week. Perhaps to distract his players during preseason practice, Walker penned a short story (reprinted in part in the *Old Gold & Black*) about a Rose Bowl showdown involving Wake and the mythical Great Western University. The Deacons didn't win the big game in Walker's fantasy world, but they did have a grand time on the big stage.

Back in the real world, luck favored Tatum's Tar Heels in Wake's 1942 inaugural contest. A driving rain—the remnants of a tropical storm—greeted Walker and company when they awoke on that late September day. The downpour never really let up. Raleigh sportswriter Dick Herbert called it the worst conditions for football at Chapel Hill since the Tar Heels battled Duke to a scoreless draw in 1930.[5] The heavy precipitation and soggy footing worked against both teams, but it handicapped Wake's Cochran (who was still available while awaiting his call-up) and the pass-happy Deacons more. Throwing a football in the rain was even tougher in those days, when resources were more limited and an entire game might be played with the same ball. Faced with those prospects, Walker and company ordered up just two passes; Tatum's boys tried only

---

[5] *Raleigh News & Observer*, Sept. 27, 1942.

three. The loss of Wake's potent air attack put the game on more even terms and turned it into a test of patience and punting. The two squads launched thirty-four punts, sixteen by the rubber-legged Cochran.

It was all decided by the inevitable kicking game error, of course. Late in the third quarter, Johnny Perry fielded a Tar Heel punt at his fifteen-yard line, darted up the middle of the field to the thirty, was hit, and fumbled. Carolina's Ralph Strayhorn fell on it at the twenty-eight, and the Tar Heels were in business with the break of the game. They pushed forward for a first down at the seventeen before Wake stiffened. On third and six, one of the rare passes of the day was incomplete, but a flag fluttered down onto the mud: holding, Wake Forest. How officials picked that infraction out of the muck and the mass of brown-uniformed players is unknown, but that was the call. The penalty gave Carolina a first down at the six and the Tar Heels took it in from there for a 6–0 lead early in the fourth quarter. That was all they needed. Wake couldn't move the ball at all and had already squandered its one shining moment. Earlier in the third, before Perry's fumble, Cochran had dashed up the middle for thirty-two yards to the Carolina forty, but he fumbled at the end of the run. The Tar Heels got that one too.

So the first act of the season was a disappointment. But the Deacons had no time for pity. Duke was next and Walker smelled an opportunity, if only because he'd be facing Eddie Cameron, Wade's long-time assistant, instead of the original "Bear" himself. There was more though. The war-induced coaching change in Durham had been matched by a good bit of turmoil on the Duke team itself. The Blue Devils lost a sizable senior contingent from the excellent 1941 team, and they had seen a fair number of men called off to military service as well. The Duke community also seemed distracted. The contest, played at Groves Stadium, did not attract the usual big crowd. Nonetheless, it was Duke, and Peahead Walker was in exceptional from, delivering a famous pregame speech that was, surprisingly, quite out of character. Despite his deserved reputation as an orator, Walker was not famous for his pregame or halftime speeches. Most players, in fact, recall him as quiet and low-key at those times and remember only rare occasions of motivational bombast. But this day was different, and his locker room speech (accounts differ as to whether it was before the game or at half) achieved a small measure of fame, primarily because of its basic premise. At a time when young men were expected to put their lives on the line for God and country, Walker asked them to think about what it would mean to die without beating Duke.

"Most of you will go off to war soon," Walker told his Deacons that day. "Some of you will get shot. I can't imagine that any of you want to get shot without being able to say, 'We beat those rich SOBs from Duke.'" Wake's Pat Preston recalled that the player sitting next to him—he forgot who it was—said, "Hell, I don't want to die without beating Duke."[6] Others murmured their assent, which quickly grew into a roar, and the team charged onto the field, ready to take their last desperate chance at gridiron glory.

Inspired or not, the Deacons, sporting new light-gray pants to go with their black jerseys, came out on fire. Kicker Otis "Bo" Sacrinty blasted the opening kickoff into the Duke end zone—a rarity in those days—putting the Blue Devils in an early hole and setting up an early Wake score. Johnny Perry got it, scoring from forty-nine yards out on a wingback reverse, Buck Jones's downfield block turning what was already a good gainer into a touchdown. The Deacons kept the pressure on. With Duke pinned deep in its own territory late in the first quarter, end Burnie Capps blasted through the line and blocked a Duke punt. Capps nearly carried the ball in for a score himself. He was knocked out of bounds at the two-yard line, however, and it was left to Russ Perry, Johnny's younger brother, to score the second touchdown. A few possessions after that, Preston, playing on a sore knee, duplicated Capps's feat. The second blocked punt set up the third Deacon touchdown, this one by Johnny Perry. Preston, Jones, and the rest of the Deacon defense held Duke to minus eight yards in the first half, and linebacker Elmer Barbour's hit knocked end Bob Gantt, one of Duke's best, out of the game in the opening quarter. The score at half was 20–0—and that was enough. Although Duke's offense got on track a bit in the second half, a late touchdown was all they could muster. When the final seconds ticked off the clock, Wake's

---

6 *Charlotte Observer,* July 22, 1970; Pat Preston, audio memoir.

players lofted Walker onto their shoulders and carried him off the field.

He had finally beaten Duke.

The victory lost some of is luster as the season progressed—Duke finished a mediocre 5-4-1 in the transition under Cameron—but it made quite an impression at the time. Alumni were delirious, and Walker was so taken with his accomplishment that at the team's postseason awards banquet he awarded himself most improved. "Beating Duke and all," Walker said, "I improved more than anyone."[7]

Beating Duke was huge, but it became clear shortly thereafter that Wake wasn't hitting on all cylinders. The defense, with Preston, Barbour, and Jones leading the way, was stout and would finish eighth nationally in yards allowed per game (just 160.8 per), but Cochran missed Cline, and there wasn't much thunder in the running game without Polanski. With points at a premium, the Deacons struggled through the middle of the season. Wake narrowly won a night game at Furman by a score of 14-6 and then battled NC State to a scoreless tie. Wake outgained the Wolfpack and had more close calls with the goal line, but State probably had the narrowest. On the last play of the first half from the Wake Forest thirty-two, Wolfpack tailback Eddie Teague hurled a pass to teammate George Burtner, who hauled it in at the two and tumbled into the end zone. Touchdown State . . . but no, the officials said his knee hit the ground at the two, meaning he was down there. End of play, end of half. Late in the third quarter, Preston recovered a fumbled punt at the State seven-yard line. The Deacons pounded their way to the two, but on fourth down Cochran was stopped for a loss. A field goal try apparently wasn't considered, even though both Sacrinty and Johnny Perry were serviceable kickers. Like many coaches of the day, Walker did not

---

7 *Durham Herald*, Dec. 1, 1942.

like the field goal. It was far from the certainty that it is today, and it really wasn't football.[8]

A trip to Boston College the following week brought Wake another nice paycheck—more than 20,000 saw the game at Fenway Park—but with it another sound Boston beat down. The unbeaten Eagles unleashed their Chicago Bear-style T on the Deacons again, piling up 329 rushing yards on the vaunted Deacon defense and winning 27–0.

The promising season seemed to be slipping away. But as was so often the case during Walker's career, he engineered a quick turnaround, beginning with a 19–6 homecoming victory over Clemson, Walker's first triumph over the Tigers. The performance was duplicated in the last three games of the year as Wake rolled over VMI, George Washington, and South Carolina. None of the contests was close.

Armchair analysts might note that the end of the Deacons' schedule wasn't as tough as the beginning, and there is certainly truth in that. But Walker's midseason turnaround was masterful all the same. He revamped the offense almost overnight, keeping Cochran at the helm but utilizing his running skills far more than his passing as the season headed down the stretch. The big line, led by Preston, Tony Rubino, and George Owen, gouged out big holes as the Deacons piled up 1,096 rushing yards over their last four games. That was more than half the team's season total (1,667 yards) and vaulted Wake to fourteenth in rushing nationally. Cochran, among the top ten in the nation in passing yards in 1941, finished seventeenth in rushing in 1942, surely a unique role reversal but also an indication of his overall ability and Walker's considerable tactical skills.

Wake's late-season surge led several rival coaches to anoint the 6-2-1 Deacons as the Southern Conference's toughest team by season's end. Toughest wasn't the same as conference champ though. Unbeaten William & Mary took that honor. The Tribe

---

8 The irony of football not being about kicking the ball with the foot was lost on coaches like Walker and Bear Bryant, who regularly passed up short field goals to win games. Although in the majority on the matter, it was by no means unanimous. Wallace Wade, in fact, was one of many big-name coaches whose teams regularly kicked field goals.

benefited from the disorganized loop's lack of scheduling requirements and won by playing a limited league schedule, mostly against the league's bottom tier. VMI, Virginia Tech, George Washington, and Richmond were the Tribe's conference victims.

Champs or no, Wake's performance fired up the Deacons' fan base. The Durham Alumni Club opened its pockets to host a black-tie postseason banquet where awards were handed out and many pounds of North Carolina's famous barbecue were consumed. Seniors were honored with the gift of a war bond. Walker announced that the ubiquitous Cochran, an All-Southern Conference pick along with Preston, had been elected captain for 1943.

It would be three long years before he would serve in that particular capacity, however. In the spring of 1943 the Marines called. Reserve Red Cochran had been promoted to Uncle Sam's starting lineup.

***

Maintaining a collegiate athletic team during World War II was no easy feat. Between two and three hundred colleges across the country dropped football (and most other sports) for one, two, or even three years during the war. Most did so because they found the hardships imposed by manpower shortages and fiscal constraints too much to bear, but there was an ethical aspect to the decision as well. With college-aged boys headed off to war and the perils war entailed, some thought that athletics—mere "sport"—seemed frivolous and thus wrong. Others saw it as a much-needed, perhaps even necessary, diversion. The merits of carrying on were debated everywhere.

Walker weighed in on the matter in an opinion piece for *Southern Coach & Athlete* magazine, in which he advocated the continuance of collegiate athletics as a morale booster for the home front. The Wake Forest administration backed Walker, providing, of course, that wartime sports didn't cause the university to blow a financial gasket. From a practical standpoint, that meant that Walker was once again asked to run a football program on a shoestring budget. The good news for Wake was that Walker was rather adept at that kind of thing.

Consider, for example, Walker's work in circumventing wartime travel restrictions. The rules, which assigned priority to military travelers on trains and the rationing of many automotive necessities, were complicated. That complexity was no problem for a lifelong finagler like Walker. Mary Arden Harris, wife of wartime footballer Dave Harris, was among the first full-time female students at Wake, coming to campus in 1942. Her interest in a football player—she and Harris met when he enrolled in 1943—brought her into Walker's circle. One day he saw her on campus, strode over with a big smile on his face, and began a friendly conversation. Eventually he got to the point: "Your daddy's a traveling salesman ain't he?" Walker asked. Mary Arden was stunned that Walker knew who she was, much less what her father did for a living.

"Yessss," she stammered.

"He got any of them rationing coupons? Traveling salesmen get some extra gas coupons and all, you know."

Mary Arden nodded.

"I need to do some recruiting and sure could use some coupons," Walker said.

Mary Arden Harris asked her father about the coupons. He did have some and "he did pass them along," she said. "We helped keep him [Walker] rolling until the end of the war."[9]

Walker's creativity in funding travel was remarkable enough that Wake could stand to play the entire 1943 season on the road. The opposition couldn't find enough gas (or train space) to travel to Wake Forest? No problem. Walker would find a way to meet them at their place (or, in several cases, at neutral sites along the way).[10]

---

9 Mary Arden Harris, interview with author.
10 Until the final years of his career, Walker's Wake Forest teams played far more road games than home games. The reason for this was fairly simple. With its small student body, Wake just didn't draw that well at home, at least in terms of gross numbers (a problem that still plagues Wake Forest athletics to this day). Road games, especially in big cities, produced bigger paydays that helped fund Wake's assorted athletic adventures.

Making do with limited funds was one thing. Fielding a team during a time of dwindling manpower was something else altogether. The draft was pulling in 200,000 men a month nationally, and Wake Forest was certainly sending its share. The *Old Gold & Black* ran regular stories on the young men called to duty. The windows of an office building in downtown Wake Forest, a few blocks from the school, displayed photos of the men taken into the service—local town boys but young men from the college as well. The numbers peaked and dipped, but the drain never stopped. Thanks to the draft, enrollment at Wake in the fall of 1943 was well under six hundred, a twenty-five percent drop from the year before. Walker's roster was decimated. Of the forty-nine players who wound up receiving letters or "numerals" (a lesser form of recognition, given to freshmen) following the 1942 season, only seven returned for the 1943 year. Not all of those absent were in the military, but the vast majority were.[11]

What was left at Wake and at most "pure" college programs—that is, colleges not benefitting from the addition of a military training school or camp on campus—were very young freshmen (now eligible after a mid-winter vote by the Southern Conference), players not yet drafted, and players deemed unfit for service because of physical or mental defects—i.e., "4-Fers." Members of this last group were often less than happy to find themselves available.

Among them was Dewey Hobbs of Wilmington, NC. A student commander of his high school ROTC unit, Hobbs had already signed up for officer candidate school when he and a group of friends drove to Fort Bragg, near Fayetteville, for their required military examination. The first doctor Hobbs encountered checked his vision and pronounced him 20/300 in one eye—well outside of accepted Army norms. The poor vision had never bothered Hobbs, however. Glasses allowed him to do all he needed to do, and for many activities—football for instance—the blurry vision in his one eye did not greatly affect him. He pleaded with the doctor to pass him, and eventually he did. "He [the doctor] said, 'Oh, if it means

---

11 It was worse elsewhere. For example, officials at Georgetown conducted a survey in the summer of 1942 and discovered that no freshman or varsity team members would return in 1943. As a result, the program was suspended.

that much to you, go on,'" Hobbs said. "But the next guy was a cardiovascular man. I had this defect in my heart and always had real high blood pressure. The systolic was over two hundred sometimes. He said, 'There's no way, son.' It may sound crazy today, but that was terrible news. I wanted to go. It was a real bad day for me. I was in a funk for a long time."

Wilmington attorney John Stevens, a friend of Hobbs's family and a Wake Forest alum, contacted the hulking Hobbs and asked him if he could write Coach Walker about him. Hobbs said okay, and a few days later he got a letter from Walker inviting him to come. "He knew a few things about me that surprised me," Hobbs said. "I was impressed by that, but the truth is I didn't have many other options." Stevens bought Hobbs a one-way bus ticket to Wake Forest—which wasn't against the rules back then—and drew him a map of how to get from the bus station to the gym. When Hobbs reported to Walker's preseason camp, practice had been underway for ten days and the Deacons still weren't up to full strength—full strength being defined in this case as having enough to hold a scrimmage.

"I was the twenty-first man in," said Hobbs. "They were having managers and townspeople and whoever fill in to make enough for practice."[12]

The season was never really in jeopardy, but it was an adventure. Walker was seldom certain as to just what he'd have until he had it. Days before Hobbs appeared, Walker was quizzed by a Raleigh newspaperman regarding the pending arrivals of lettermen Bill Starford and Jeff Brogden. "The last time I heard from them they said they were coming back," said Walker. "But the Army is grabbing them up pretty fast. . . . I'm not positive that they will show up."[13]

Starford and Brogden did eventually make it and Wake's ranks eventually swelled to twenty-eight. Included in that number were four varsity holdovers, five or six sophomores up from the previous year's freshman team, and a bunch of new guys. Most, like Hobbs, were freshmen, just out of high school. A few, like Dave Harris, were transfers from other schools. Harris, a star athlete in

---

[12] Dewey Hobbs, interview with author.
[13] *Raleigh News & Observer*, Sept. 10, 1943.

high school at Statesville High in North Carolina, spurned offers from UNC, Duke, and Tennessee to attend Appalachian State Teachers College, which was closer to his home and more economical. But after the 1942 season, Appalachian dropped football (it was revived with a four-game season in 1945). Hearing about the Appalachian decision, Walker scrambled to pick up some pieces. Harris, a rangy end with good speed, was one of the biggest prizes. So Walker borrowed some ration cards, drove to Statesville, and visited Harris at his home. "I'll have to say, I was pretty impressed," said Harris.[14]

Harris, who had chronically flat fleet, was not draftable. Neither was his former Appalachian teammate Pride Ratterree. Ratterree, who would become one of Walker's favorites, had already served some military time but was discharged because of a perforated ear drum (the Army would get less picky later on). He was working in a mill in his hometown of Cherryville, NC when Walker called him on a recommendation from Harris. Did he want to come to school and play some football? "Hell, I was working in a damn mill, going nowhere," said Raterree. "Playing football, going to school, it sounded like a pretty good deal to me."[15]

In an ironic twist, one of the eventual stars of the 1943 team, blocking back/linebacker Elmer Barbour, had been eligible for the draft but was knocked down to 4-F status after a knee injury suffered during the 1942 football season. He missed the war even though his was knee was strong enough for two more collegiate football seasons and a brief stint with the NFL's New York Giants.

There's no evidence that Walker facilitated Barbour's knee injury in any way, but the idea would certainly have intrigued him. At the end of the 1943 season, when Hobbs was summoned for another military exam, Walker took action to make sure his budding young star's blood pressure didn't improve. He approached Hobbs with a "one-dollar bottle of pills" that he told Hobbs was guaranteed to send his blood pressure skyrocketing. "But don't worry, Dewey," Walker said. "It's safe. It'll only go up for a little while. . . . "

---

14 Dave Harris, interview with author.
15 Pride Ratteree, interview with author.

Hobbs said Walker told him, "'Take one of these and then go see the doctor real quick. He'll check, it'll be high, and you'll be fine. . . . ' I think my blood pressure was 235 over 140 or whatever. It was way up there. But I lived through it and I was still in school."[16]

While Walker was scrounging for players and rigging medical tests to hold onto the ones he had, some colleges were enjoying an embarrassment of athletic riches courtesy of Uncle Sam. Among them were UNC and Duke, both of which were selected as one of 131 national sites for the Navy's V-12 officer training program. The Navy (and Marines) realized that although the draft was going to produce a mass of enlisted men, there would be an acute shortage of college-educated junior officers. So they set up special schools that could educate and train a passel of officer candidates in the quickest possible order. Candidates for the V-12 schools included college students already enrolled in Naval or Marine reserve programs, enlisted men recommended by their officers, and high school students who passed a special exam. Students went through three- to four-month-long semesters each year. A student with some college work already in place could be finished in twelve months—hence the program's name—and ready for his basic training and quick transition to cannon fodder.

Because the students were required to complete nine-and-a-half hours of physical training per week, sports teams were regular accompaniments. Whether they were necessary is another question. Calisthenics might have worked just as well. But the idea of powerful military football teams and military ranks populated with athletic stars was popular among Naval and Army brass. Beyond the V-12 work, both services employed recruiters who presented prospects with an offer that most couldn't refuse: join the service, and possibly face combat, or play service football and possibly face Navy/Army in a big game at the end of the season. The strategy was quite effective.

Duke's Navy V-12 program was one of the largest in the land, and a mass of talented athletes piled up on campus, producing an astonishing two-hundred-man football squad in

---

16 Hobbs, interview with author.

1943. It was studded with stars from across the country like Tiny Willoughby of Auburn and former Georgia star "Bulldog" Williams. It also included Pat Preston, Bo Sacrinty, and Jim Copley, most recently of Wake Forest. Preston had already played four seasons at Wake, but only three on varsity, so he was generously granted another season of varsity eligibility by the Navy if he wanted one. At first he didn't. In his audio memoir, Preston said the idea of putting on Duke blue seemed almost treasonous, especially after helping Walker beat the hated Blue Devils for the first time the year before. As Preston put it,

> *I thought I was being real loyal and all. And I wasn't on scholarship [at Duke]. I was in the Marines. So I didn't have to play. But right before I left, Coach Walker found me and said, "Preston, are you gonna play football over there at Duke?" And I said, "No sir. I'm not." "Preston," he said, "you oughta play football over there. The Bears have drafted you and if you play over at Duke it would help you, your salary, and everything." I said, "Coach, I don't want to play for Duke. We beat them over here last year. It would feel bad [playing against Wake Forest]. He said, "Well, Pat. You don't have to worry. We're not going to play them next year. We've just got a bunch of 4-Fs and young boys and all. So we ain't going to do that."*[17]

So Preston played—and starred—on the 1943 Duke team, which went 8–1, losing only to Navy, which fielded an even more star-studded team. Preston was named to the All-Southern Conference team, giving him the distinction of having made the team in back-to-back years while playing for two different schools. He was also named a first-team All-American.

Duke's 1943 team was so deep that it could absorb catastrophic losses with little or no effect. When a V-12 semester ended in late October 1943, Cameron lost eight starters and twenty-three others to military call-up or reassignment. No problem. He plugged in some more V-12ers, and in Duke's next

---

17 Preston, audio memoir.

game it whipped NC State 75–0 in an affair that, if possible, probably wasn't as close as the score indicates.

The power of V-12 football was not lost on a shrewd assessor of talent like Peahead Walker. His primary motivation in crafting the Deacs' 1943 schedule (Walker did all the work—Weaver, coaching at military base in Georgia by this time, had no input) was dodging V-12 schools. Walker feared that whatever he had scraped together at Wake would be overwhelmed by the talent and numbers of the military-aided schools. So Duke and UNC were off the schedule and replaced by Georgia and contests against various military-base teams that had the advantage (from their opponent's point of view) of not being particularly organized. The exception to the rule was South Carolina. The long-term Turkey Day contract with Charlotte was in effect, and Walker didn't see a way of getting out of it. A contract was a contract, and besides, it was a nice payday for a war-ravaged athletic department.

The wisdom of Walker's scheduling strategy was played out around the country as V-12 schools mopped up the field with schools that were without. The differences were dramatic and obvious. After a Navy-infused Notre Dame team pounded his Pitt Panthers 41–0, famed Pitt coach Clark Shaughnessy noted that "we are a pretty good high school team."[18]

Walker's Deacons were in a similar boat, and even without Duke and UNC Wake's schedule was daunting. Walker's young charges got a real baptism in their opener against Camp Davis. It wasn't that the anti-aircraft gunners, who Walker and company had embarrassed in 1941, were a great team. They were still indifferently coached and haphazardly organized. But they were all men and Wake was (mostly) boys.

"Heck," said Hobbs, "they had a fullback, I think his name was Goldberg, who had played for the Redskins or someone in the NFL. He was already bald. Most of us had never played against anyone like that before."[19]

---

18 Associated Press, Oct. 17, 1943.
19 Hobbs may have been referring to Marshall Goldberg, a former University of Pittsburgh star whose eight-year NFL career was interrupted by a three-year Navy hitch. Lineups for the Wake-Camp Davis game do list a Goldberg, but as an end.

Wake took a 20–12 lead into the final seven minutes against Camp Davis but couldn't hold it. Camp Davis marched to one touchdown and then forced and recovered a fumble deep in Wake territory with less than two minutes to go. From there they proceeded to punch in another touchdown—this one for the win.

The following week Wake was on more even terms, at least with regard to maturity, against Maryland in College Park. But the contest ended in similarly heartbreaking fashion. The Deacons failed to cash in on three trips inside the Old Liners'[20] ten-yard line in the second half and found themselves stuck in a 7–7 tie as time wound down in the final quarter. With just ten seconds to play and the ball on their own eleven-yard line, Joe Makar, Maryland's seventeen-year-old (and hence undraftable) freshman quarterback, dropped back into the end zone and fired a pass to halfback Dick Tushak, also seventeen years old, near the twenty-five. Tushak sped downfield, pursued by several Deacons. Russ Perry had him in his sights near the Wake forty and nearly pushed him out of bounds, but some nifty footwork by Tushak put him into the clear again, and he sprinted the rest of the way for the winning score in a 13–7 triumph.

Walker's squad dropped to 0–3 with another narrow loss, this time by a 7–0 count at Georgia. But all three losses were close, and Walker's young charges were rounding into shape. The next week the Deacons steamrolled NC State 54–6. Doc Newton's last Wolfpack team was a sorry bunch, but Wake's demolition job was so complete that in the aftermath State partisans groped for excuses. The Wolfpack couldn't compete with a "professional" team or one loaded up with transfers (the whining came from both fans and a Raleigh radio personality). The charges were unfounded. Wake didn't have professional players. It did, however, have a professional coach, and he knew how to pull rabbits out of his hat.

Against State, the Deacon star that day was a freshman fullback named Fred Grant who hadn't played a down up until the time he entered the State game, which was shortly after starting

---

20 Maryland's current nickname, the Terrapins, was introduced in 1933 but didn't catch on until the 1950s. Up until then they were often referred to as the Old Liners, a reference to Maryland's nickname, "The Old Line State," which probably dates to the American Revolution.

fullback Russ Perry went down with a first-half knee injury. Running through gaping holes in the Wolfpack line, Grant wound up rushing for more than 150 yards and scored 4 touchdowns. That performance, coupled with another touchdown a week later against VMI, put him atop the Southern Conference scoring stats midway through the season. By year's end, he was named to both the All-Conference and All-Region teams.

Wake had lots of breaks against State. The Deacons recovered three Wolfpack fumbles to set up scores. Nick Sacrinty, a budding star, returned a punt for a score (another example of Walker's kick return magic), and burly freshman Cliff Hobbs (no relation to Dewey) kicked six extra points and drove kickoff after kickoff deep into State territory. "Man, when he [Cliff Hobbs] got into one the ball looked like it would never come down," said Dewey Hobbs. "I don't know why we didn't try some field goals with him. He could have made them from a long ways out."[21]

Wake followed the rout of State with a trouncing of VMI in a game played in Lynchburg, VA and proceeded by more complaints about Deacon professionalism. The *Old Gold & Black* accused Walker of taking it easy on his old friend and fellow Alabamian Pooley Hubert, the VMI coach, and offered him a "sportsmanship award" in recognition of his humanitarian work.[22]

They didn't know the half of it. In bartering to obtain the contest, Hubert had stipulated that Wake couldn't play any transfers against the Cadets. The no-transfer clause in the one-game contract suggests Hubert didn't trust his old friend much when it came to recruiting—probably a wise stance—but Walker agreed all the same. Harris and Ratterree, transfers from the defunct Appalachian State program, didn't play.

Handicapped or no, Wake was rolling. The Deacons made it three in a row one week later when it laid another whupping on one of Walker's pals. The victim this time was Frank Howard, whose Clemson crew absorbed a 41–12 beating. Wake followed that up with a surprising victory of a service team called the North Carolina Pre-Flight Cloudbusters. A nifty lateral by Perry to Sacrinty turned a long run into an even longer scoring play. Coupled with a

---

21 Dewey Hobbs, interview with author.
22 *Old Gold & Black*, Oct. 29, 1943.

sensational game from Harris (a blocked punt, three recovered fumbles, and a touchdown reception), the Deacons managed to hold off the Cloudbusters. Although they did their best to wear the Deacons down, employing three different teams during the course of the game (compared with Walker's five subs and sixteen overall), the Cloudbusters could never completely break through. Walker's boys held on for a 20–12 win.

Wake's winning streak made them the subject of some postseason speculation—even with war going on there were still a few bowls being played—but Walker and company couldn't close the deal. They dropped a 14–0 decision to Basic Training Camp No. 10 before 10,000 in Greensboro and then fell to South Carolina 13–2 in the Thanksgiving Day contest in Charlotte. An oddity in the Turkey Day tilt: Wake went up 2–0 when Rick Farress's punt out of the Gamecock end zone went off the side of his foot and out of bounds before crossing the goal line.[23]

***

Peahead Walker's roster magic in 1943 was a marvel, but more would be needed the following year. If the pickings in 1943 had been slim, they were almost microscopic in 1944. Wake's roster for the opening of spring practice in March 1944 included twenty-five names, but only rarely were all of them available on a given day. When after weeks of grueling drills and conditioning the time finally came to hold a full-fledged intrasquad scrimmage, Walker and Greason, assisted by the team manager, swept through the men's dorms and fraternity halls looking for an extra body or two to guarantee two full sides of eleven men each. There wasn't much from which to choose. Winter enrollment at the college was just 328, the lowest in the century.

Walker's desperation in finding players of any description is reflected in the "recruitment" of one Herb Appenzeller, a diminutive eighteen year old from Newark, NJ who flunked both

---

23 The play is difficult to comprehend—how could he miss the ball that badly and still hit it hard enough to get it out of bounds?—without recalling that the hash marks were considerably wider then and a play, at that time, could originate within ten yards of the sideline.

the Army and Navy physicals while attempting to enlist in both in late January 1944. Dejected, Appenzeller wrote letters to several college coaches, including Walker, begging for scholarships. He enclosed newspaper clippings that described his performance in the most successful game of his high school football career (he scored two touchdowns) and, more importantly, in the previous year's state track meet, where he won both the one- and two-hundred-yard dashes despite running with a cast on one hand. That—plus the fact that Appenzeller was breathing and eligible—impressed Walker. He responded with an offer of tuition, room, and board. A brief negotiation ensued. Appenzeller's real aptitude was track. Would Walker allow him time off from spring football to run in the Southern Conference meet that year? Sure, Walker said. Come on down, boy. Play some football, run a little track. Appenzeller did, entering school at the start of the spring quarter (Wake moved to a quarter system for the 1943–1944 school year as part of its military machinations).

Appenzeller slogged away at practice for a month, then five weeks, then six. As the time passed, he began to worry that he might miss the conference track meet. One day after an April practice, he stopped his coach and asked if he'd heard anything about the dates for the meet. A small grin creased Walker's face before he quickly returned to the normal grumble mode. "Hell, boy," Walker said. "They ran that thing (that is, the Southern Conference track meet) back in March some time. Guess we'll give it a shot next year."[24]

As he assembled the 1944 squad, Walker suffered through more unexpected departures as players swirled about in the fog of war and the equally dense wartime regulations (or lack thereof). The coach never knew when a player might get the call. But helpful additions far outweighed subtractions. Gone from the 1943 squad were center Bill Starford, who had completed his eligibility, and fullback Russ Perry, who was off to medical school in Winston-Salem. Also missing was Fred Grant. The bolt-from-the-blue fullback had bolted again, transferring from Wake to the University of Alabama along with "Shorty" Robertson, a left-handed halfback

---

24 Herb Appenzeller, interview with author.

who had seen limited duty for the 1943 Deacons. Walker blamed their departure on the lure of Alabama's superior resources. "We just don't have the money to keep up with the big schools," said Walker.[25] In this complaint, Walker was lamenting the lack of funds and not the system that allowed pay for play. No doubt he would have paid Grant to play if he could've.

The loss of Grant (less so Robertson) seemed severe at the time. In the long run it was barely noticed. Grant lettered for three years at Bama but was hardly a star. And a far better fullback turned up in the form of Richard "Rock" Brinkley, a 210-pound bruiser from Norfolk, VA whose nickname came with him to college and was not, in his case, a Walker creation nor a comment on his scholastic ability. Just the opposite in fact with regard to the latter. Brinkley was an intelligent and complex young man. A deep and logical thinker and writer, he would go on to obtain a doctorate in philosophy. He smoked (but only during the offseason), worked incredibly hard, and wasn't afraid to stand up to Walker, which was no small feat. He was also almost certainly Wake's best fullback since Polanski, and he really might have been better because he was also an excellent defender and punter and didn't have Polanski's "trick stomach." Indeed, as events would show, his stomach (or heart) might have been his greatest asset.

Brinkley arrived at Wake after some brief military service and a side trip to the University of Georgia, where Brinkley played football in 1943. His size—at 6'2" and more than 200 pounds—was big for the day at any position, and his speed caught Bulldog coach Wally Butts's eye. But Brinkley couldn't crack the backfield lineup. Butts moved him to tackle—a position prized more for its speed in those days than it is now—but he couldn't break through there either. Disgruntled, Brinkley showed up at Wake in the spring of 1944.

The start of fall practice brought more help. Big George Owens, a starting lineman on the 1942 team, was back after a service hitch. And among the arriving freshmen were two backs of long-term note: Tom Fetzer and Nick Ognovich. Fetzer had been the heir to tailback Nick Sacrinty at Reidsville High School, a state

---

25 *Old Gold & Black*, Sept. 9, 1944.

power at the time, and then decided to stay on that same path in college. At 5'9" and 175 pounds, Ognovich was a fireplug of a man from Uniontown, PA, and a ferocious hitter who loved contact. Plugging those two into a backfield that already included Nick Sacrinty, Elmer Barbour, and Rock Brinkley gave Walker options.

He was eager to put them, and his newly acquired experience as a wartime coach, into practice. Watching the wartime college football world shake out, Walker had come to a greater understanding of just how it all worked. Hosting a military college program was becoming less of a boon than had originally been thought. Yes, players were still run through the schools by the bushel, but the operative word was "through." With the V-12 and other programs operating on the quarter system, and one of the quarters ending in mid-October, it was quite possible, even likely, to see massive midseason roster changes courtesy of Uncle Sam. That meant additions as well as subtractions, of course, but that kind of turmoil was never a good thing. A nice, stable, demilitarized roster often turned out to be the bigger benefit. With that in mind, Walker dropped the service teams in 1944—the Pre-Flight coach was furious at the change—and resumed contests with Duke and North Carolina, both of which were home to V-12 programs.

Walker's strategy for scheduling was laced with tactics that addressed the timing of call-ups. The two V-12 teams were scheduled near the quarter changes. Carolina was up first, in late September, just after the end of the summer quarter. Duke was set for an early November date, just after an expected round of late-fall call-ups.

The first half of the equation worked well. Wake traveled to Chapel Hill for its season opener and defeated the Tar Heels, under wartime coach Gene McEver, formerly of Davidson, by a 7–0 count. The game's only touchdown came shortly after intermission when the Deacons drove fifty yards for a touchdown. Sacrinty was injured early in the march, forcing freshman Ognovich to take over at tailback. He did just fine, completing two passes that led to a first down at the Tar Heel twenty-four. Ognovich dropped back to pass again on the next play, but it was a ruse—and an old one at that. As he reared back to throw, Ognovich froze. Wingback Bob Smathers, rolling around from the right end, plucked the ball out of his hand and galloped around the left end—it was the old Statue of Liberty play[26] for eighteen yards to the Carolina six. That was close—but still hard work from there. Three plays netted three yards. On fourth down, Walker sent Brinkley back into the fray, and Brinkley promptly bulled his way in for the score. Wake's defense took it from there, smothering the Tar Heels with the help of some nifty punting from an unexpected source, Russ Perry, who had taken time out from medical school to rejoin his old mates for the game. Although Perry did little other than punt and lead the team on the field to start the game, it was helpful. Just how Walker managed to twist the rules to allow Perry into the contest is unknown. The special dispensation must have been very specific because the only games the future doctor played were against UNC and Duke.

Wake's second game of the 1944 season included enough plot twists to make a writer like Rock Brinkley happy. He would also have enjoyed the fact that one of bigger twists involved him. As noted, Brinkley began his college career at Georgia, didn't fare well there, and transferred to Wake Forest. In the 1944 game against the Bulldogs, he scored both Deacon touchdowns in Wake's 14–7 victory. Meanwhile, Georgia's only touchdown in the contest was scored by Don Wells, an end who had played for Wake Forest in 1943. Wells's landing at Georgia is as mysterious as Brinkley's at Wake. Following the case, the *Old Gold & Black* reported that Wells simply "disappeared for several months before turning up in the Georgia camp."[27] Players bounced around like that during the war, although in Wells's case the movement seems to have had more to do with Uncle Peahead than Uncle Sam. Wake players in 1944 recall being told that Walker didn't like Wells and ran him off. That wasn't an uncommon occurrence under Walker, but he must have disliked Wells quite a bit to run him off at the

---

26 So named for the quarterback's pose at the point of the handoff, which more or less resembles the Statue of Liberty (particularly in regard to being still). It's one of the oldest trick plays in college football—its invention credited to Amos Alonzo Stagg and its popularity to the success of Fielding Yost's "point-a-minute" Michigan teams of the early 1900s. Walker adopted it for his Deacon teams in the 1940s and made liberal use of it.
27 *Old Gold & Black*, July 14, 1944.

same time he was trolling anywhere and everywhere for any possible enlistments he could find.

Brinkley's part of the double-alumni scoring fest was set up by a Walker coaching gem. Returning to the field after a scoreless half, Walker felt the humidity in the air—a Georgia thunderstorm was in the offing—and ordered his captains to tell the referee they wanted to kick off to start the second half. It was Wake's choice to open the third quarter, but the standard tactic would be to receive. Walker, however, figured that with the rain coming the ball might be hard to handle and that he might be better off making the other guys handle it.

He was right. Georgia muffed the second-half kickoff as the rain began and was pinned deep in its own territory. A punt set Wake up at the Bulldog forty-seven, and the Deacons repeated their grinding tactics from the UNC game: Ognovich completed a few passes, Smathers scampered several yards on the Statue down to the eight, and Brinkley punched it in from there. With the humid air turning into a full-blown rainstorm, Georgia fumbled the next kickoff outright. Wake recovered at the Georgia twenty-five. The Deacons ground out a couple of first downs before Brinkley rumbled in for another score on the first play of the fourth quarter.

Dewey Hobbs said that while Walker was a fairly methodical coach he was also intuitive in his own way. "That idea to kick off to start the half was pretty clever thinking. He was a football man. He was almost psychic when it came to figuring out what was going to happen."[28]

Wake did give up one touchdown—a sixty-nine-yard catch and run in the rain by Wells—early in the fourth, but the Deacons stopped Georgia on downs at the Wake forty a few minutes later to snuff out any remaining hope the Bulldogs had. The victory avenged the one defeat from 1943. And the week after that Wake took care of another. Playing their first home game midway through the 1942 season, Wake blasted Maryland 39–0. The contest was a rout from start to finish. While Wake ran and passed almost at will, piling up 434 yards, Maryland managed just 32. It was almost as if the Deacon defense knew what was coming. And in some ways

---

28 Hobbs, interview with author.

they did. Greason told the team beforehand that the signal for all of Maryland's pass plays began with the letter P, as in P-433 or P-200. The Old Liners' quarterback had a habit of spitting out the P with a little extra force so that the signal was overly loud. "You could hear it," said Hobbs. "It was very helpful. We were in their backfield all night."[29]

The tip was a product of Greason's scouting work, which basically involved snooping around a game featuring one of Wake's upcoming opponents . . . or sometimes a team that had played a team Wake was going to play. Greason took some notes on the formations he saw, etc., but the best information he collected came from outside locker rooms after a game (in the case of Maryland, Hampden-Sydney's, who the Old Liners lost to 12–0 in their opener). Greason would find some players as they left, butter them up with compliments, and then ask if their opponents were tipping off their plays. That's exactly how he learned how Maryland tipped their passes off and, as another example, how Miami's wingback's left hand would start twitching when a reverse was called. Warned of this trait, the Deacons were on guard. That was useful, but as events showed, foreknowledge wasn't everything.

Early in the third quarter of the 1944 game in Miami, with the Hurricanes pinned deep in its own territory, end Dave Harris thought he saw the twitch and whispered to Hobbs, lined up beside him, "Look! Look at his hand! Here comes the reverse."

Hobbs said he began salivating. "I figured, 'Oh boy, here's my chance. I'll just run right by my man, go in there, and hit that guy and either get a safety or force a fumble that I could recover for a touchdown. Either way, I figured I'd get my name in the paper."[30] Unfortunately, all didn't go as planned, and when Hobbs awoke—several minutes after he having been nailed by a Miami lineman—he found himself on the Deacons' sideline, a nasty gash in his right cheek, face to face with an Army doctor who was filling in as Wake's team physician on its South Florida sojourn. It hadn't been the reverse Hobbs and Harris had supposed. It hadn't been a reverse it all. It was just a twitch.

---

29 Ibid.
30 Hobbs, interview with author.

Still, Walker was a pioneer in the use of advance scouts and maintained a network of freelancers who helped his undermanned staff cover the necessary ground. The ranks of his part-time scouts included a man who owned a sporting goods store in Baltimore, a Wake Forest biology professor, and anyone else that fate might put in harm's way. For the Georgia game in 1944, Walker got a scouting report from his pal Jim Weaver, the former (and future) Wake Forest athletic director. Weaver was coaching at the Georgia Pre-Flight School near the university's Athens campus and was more than happy to take a stroll over to the practice field to take a look at the Bulldogs as they worked out before the Wake game.

Game film was available beginning in the 1920s but did not assume a large role until after World War II. Before then there had been some ethical discussion and debate over the use of film as a scouting tool (see chapter 5) and a general reluctance to exchange it with opponents or even friends, although some film was passed around after intensely negotiated compacts were made. The details were important lest a team send out a film of a game in which it played especially well (or poorly) and in which it used (or didn't use) particular plays and formations.

In any event the quality of the film was by no means great. Numbers were hard to read, the vantage point might be blocked by trees or light poles, and the action could be hard to follow. Dickie Davis, a Wake Forest quarterback and safety from 1948 to 1951, said Walker demanded that his players, especially his quarterbacks, watch film but that many found it difficult.

"They'd get you up in this little room over Peahead's office in the gym and you'd watch these old films. You couldn't see 'em and you weren't doing anything. No one was talking. And you'd get sleepy. I spent at least much time sleeping up there as watching them movies."[31]

It's likely that Wake would have worn out Maryland in the 1944 game, sharp scouting or no. Wake rolled to a 32–0 halftime lead. Walker and Maryland's Spears agreed to cut the third and fourth quarters to twelve minutes each, and Walker sent most of the starters to the showers at the half. "He told us to get dressed

---

31 Dickie Davis, interview with author.

and go sit with our girlfriends in the stands," Hobbs said. "We thought he was kidding but he said, 'Go on, git.' And so we did."[32]

Wake's early season onslaught continued with a 38–7 pasting of VMI and a 21–7 defeat of NC State, now directed by future NFL Hall of Famer Beattie Feathers. The Deacons followed that success with a 27–0 thrashing of Miami in the Orange Bowl (the game in which Hobbs didn't spot the reverse coming). The Hurricanes managed just eight yards rushing while surrendering 275 to the Deacons. Fetzer also returned a punt fifty yards to set up a score.

The victory was pyrrhic, however. Both Hobbs and Harris suffered severe facial injuries—Hobbs recalled a photographer grabbing them after the game to take a picture of their misshapen faces—and several other Deacons rode home with ice packs on their heads and limbs. As Mary Arden Harris, Dave's wife, starkly recounted, "They looked like they had been in a war."[33]

So that was six straight, the best start ever for a Wake Forest team. And it grabbed attention nationwide. The Deacons had climbed into the new national top twenty. Even more impressive, the Deacons had done all this without help from Nick Sacrinty, upon whom so much preseason hope was built. Sacrinty hurt his knee early in the second half against UNC, played briefly in the Georgia game, and then was shelved.

He was hardly missed. First Ognovich, then Fetzer, stepped in to fill his shoes. Ognovich, who would go on to fame as Walker's best-ever blocking back—better even than Ringgold or Barbour—got by on grit. Fetzer, Sacrinty's high school backup, was cut from the Sacrinty mold itself, albeit a slightly lesser version. He was not as big as Nick and couldn't pass quite as well, but he was pretty good all the same. Dave Harris said that Sacrinty, who went on to play professionally, was one of the best passers he ever saw, and in Harris's thirty-some-odd-year career as a player and high school coach, he saw quite a few. Although the statistical record is incomplete, Sacrinty probably completed better than fifty percent of his career attempts at Wake, an astonishingly high number during an era when passing was risky and not at all sophisticated.

---

32 Hobbs, interview with author.
33 Mary Arden Harris, interview with author.

Most coaches were satisfied with completion percentages in the low forties and tolerated what would today be considered a lot of interceptions.

Sacrinty should have been sorely missed, but early on the Deacon offense chugged right along without him. Brinkley and Buck Mabry pounded away inside, Smathers ran the Statues and the trademark Wake Forest reverse, and Ognovich and Fetzer piled up the passing yards. The Deacon line was a constant concern for Wake opponents, and receivers like the rangy Harris could make a lot of passers look good. Walker's part was bringing the youngsters up to speed . . . and cobbling together a schedule filled with easy targets.

As part of his scheduling magic, Walker was building momentum toward a big finish. The Deacons closed with Clemson, Duke, and South Carolina. Sandwiching the two sandlapper schools around Duke may not have been ideal, but he was obligated to the date for the South Carolina game, and contemplating the end of the academic quarter and the potential for V-12 reassignment, he may have figured he got that about right, too.

First came Clemson though. The Deacons controlled play, and Fetzer directed two scoring drives that built a 13–0 lead after three quarters. Clemson drove to an early fourth quarter score, but Wake responded with a sixty-five-yard march that consumed clock despite not scoring points. Clemson never got close, and Wake was now 7–0. New Year's Day bowl scouts were knocking, Sacrinty was back in the harness, and the Deacons had moved ahead of Duke, which was sporting an unusual 2–4 record. The records didn't faze pollsters much, however. Duke was still Duke. The Blue Devils entered the game ranked twentieth in the wire service poll, whereas Wake was seventeenth and eleventh in another.

The Wake-Duke game, played before 28,000 at Duke Stadium, started in promising fashion for the visitors but quickly went awry. The Deacons took the opening kickoff and moved easily down the field—Sacrinty accounting for most of the yardage. A first down on the Duke five looked like the drive most certainly would end in a score, but the Blue Devils held the Deacons on downs. A few minutes later, Duke's George Clark fielded a Perry punt at the

Duke six and headed up field—aided by a nifty block on Deacon end John Bruno. Clark blew past a mass of Deacons around the thirty and found himself in the clear, save for one out-of-shape med student, the much-surprised Perry. Wake's part-time punter whiffed, and Clark sped to the end zone. The ninety-four-yard return for a score was just one touchdown, but it seemed like a backbreaker. Wake tried to storm back with a drive into Duke territory but couldn't convert. And it all slipped away after that. Near the end of the half, a Sacrinty pass deep in his own territory was picked off by Ed Sharkey, Duke's middle linebacker. Sharkey lumbered to the sidelines and into the end zone to make it 12–0.

After the break, the teams brought out their trick plays. Duke's worked. Wake's didn't. On a play from his own forty-two, the Blue Devils' Tom Davis starting running right and then held out the ball to give it away on another reverse, a play Duke had been running with some success in recent weeks. But this time it was a fake. Davis pulled the ball away and hid it on his hip as he turned up field. Safety Fetzer was the only Deacon to notice, but he noticed too late. Davis sped down the sidelines for a touchdown. Duke quickly stopped Wake again and then scored on a sixty-six-yard drive. On their next possession the Deacons drove to midfield, and Walker, sensing perhaps his last opening, called for the old Statue of Liberty play again, their secret weapon of the early season. The Duke defense, however, led by Ernie Knotts, had been ripping through the Deacon line all day. They hit Smathers hard, jarring the ball loose and recovering the fumble at their own forty-nine. Clark then burst up the middle for a long gain on the first play after that. Fetzer grabbed Clark at the thirty, but Clark alertly lateraled the ball to Davis, who went the rest of the way for a score. Duke 32. Wake 0. And to make it worse, Duke tackled Fetzer for a safety on the game's next-to-last play for a 34–0 final.

The loss was disheartening, of course, and early in the finale against South Carolina it seemed debilitating. But after falling behind 7–0 after some early lethargic play, Wake bounced back and rolled past the Gamecocks 19–13 to complete an 8–1 season.

The loss to Duke, however, sent the big bowl scouts scurrying elsewhere.[34] But Wake wasn't completely out of the picture. The Deacons' old pals from the Sun Bowl were interested. Would Wake come down to El Paso for a game against the Second Air Force team?

No.

At a meeting called to discuss whether or not to accept the bowl bid, some players essentially asked, "What's in it for us?"

The answer: the Sun Bowl would cover travel expenses and every player would receive . . . a blanket.

"A blanket?" said Appenzeller. "We were all looking around going, 'What the hell?'"[35]

So no more football . . . and no blankets. The Deacons would have to find another way to stay warm for the winter.

***

Football, especially winning football, was fun, and it provided a diversion to the grim business of war. But it was only a diversion. The war, even though it appeared to be heading toward an end in the winter of 1944, was still there. For anyone who forgot, personal reminders were never more than a sudden telegram or an unexpected phone call away.

Peahead Walker didn't forget, but was reminded all the same. His own personal dose of wartime tragedy arrived via messenger in mid-January 1945 in a busy Atlanta railroad station. His friend Paul "Bear" Bryant, who at the time was Lt. Bryant, assistant coach of the NC Pre-Flight football team, was the messenger, revealing to Walker that his son had been killed in combat training. The depth of Walker and Bryant's relationship is not entirely clear, but clearly they had a number of connections

---

34 To Duke, for instance. The Blue Devils, who were clearly rallying late in the year, snagged an appearance in the Sugar Bowl against Alabama, the Navy having decided that bowl games were okay for V-12 schools after all. That game might have been Wake's game had the Duke game gone differently.

35 Appenzeller, interview with author.

from their shared Alabama backgrounds. Family members are certain it was Bryant who delivered the message.[36]

Walter Hill Walker, Douglas and Carolyne's youngest son, was not even twenty before he died. He had joined the Air Force in 1944 and was training as a turret gunner in the B-24 Liberator bomber. He had not been overseas but was a casualty of war all the same—killed in a plane crash at the end of a training mission flown out of Mountain Home Army Air Station, a base located about an hour's drive southeast of Boise, ID. His plane may have hit some power lines during its descent—that's what the family heard later—but whatever the cause, the bomber crashed and burned. Walter Hill was one of three members of the crew who died.

The news crushed Peahead. Hill was clearly his favorite, possibly because his oldest son D.C. was more his momma's boy, and the Walkers were in the process of splitting up during the war, heading toward an official divorce in 1950.

Carolyne Walker went back to Birmingham at some point to live with her family, possibly when the war began. Certainly it was before it ended. When footballer Herb Appenzeller arrived on campus in the spring of 1944, Peahead Walker was already ensconced in his bachelor pad in the basement of Gore Gym. It's unlikely either of the boys lived with him there. Hill may have lived briefly back in Birmingham with Carolyne. He's listed as a Birmingham boy in the official Army dispatch on the accident. D.C.'s relations with his dad had been strained for some time.

Walker's players didn't know what to make of a grieving Peahead. It was a side they had not seen before, and they found him in places he had seldom ever been seen. Dewey Hobbs, Baptist Student Union leader and aspiring preacher, recalled spotting Walker one Sunday morning in the Wake Forest Baptist Church not long after Hill's death. It was not a usual Walker haunt, although when quizzed on the subject he always claimed a strong Baptist heritage. Walker had sponsored a massive spray of gladiolas for the baptistery that morning and was sitting in the front row. Hobbs, who had some churchly duties—he was a

---

36 D.C. Walker III and others, interview with author.

chaperone for the college coeds and usually sat in a special row in back—moved up front to sit next to his coach.

"I never pushed myself on him in terms of religion," said Hobbs, "and I didn't that day. I was only a ministerial student. But he looked like he needed some company. So I sat there with him. I don't recall that we said much."[37]

***

Spring practice that year came and went. Some new faces showed up; a few old ones disappeared. Walker, still in a decidedly melancholy state, did not really care either way. The war, though fast drawing to a close, still had the power to shuffle personnel without warning. Walker would wait until fall before making any pronouncements.

One who would not be back was Johnny Perry, the shifty back who was one of the stars of the 1941 and 1942 seasons. He had become a corporal in the Marines since that time and was killed in June during fighting on Okinawa.[38] It was one of the last big battles of the war, a messy slugfest across a volcanic island that made battle information hard to come by. But Wake Foresters would eventually learn that Perry had died a hero.

A month earlier, while leading a rifle platoon from Company H of the Third Battalion of the 29th Marines, Perry, according to the official medal citation, "made his way to a vital ridge through an avalanche of grenades." From his new position, Perry figured out which enemy position was holding his unit up. He then returned to his unit, positioned his machine gun squad, and directed it to fire until the enemy strong point was neutralized. For his leadership and valor he was awarded the prestigious Navy Cross.

No Perry, but Walker's 1945 squad was loaded with veteran starters—every regular except tackle George Owen returned. But Peahead had no proven reserves, indeed no real reserves period.

---

37 Hobbs, interview with author.
38 Perry was one of three players Walker coached who were killed in combat. The others were fullback Frank "Red" McCarthy from Walker's first Wake team and tailback George Wirtz from his 1938 and 1939 teams.

There was a wide gulf between the first teamers and the rest, even the backups who had been around awhile and played a little.

"They [the second and third units] are a bunch of freshmen, just ordinary boys, and we surely would hate to put them in a ball game," Walker told Smith Barrier of the *Greensboro Daily News* in mid-September. But then, reported Barrier, Walker smiled and added, "Maybe we could rest 15 minutes between quarters. Then my first team, and oh what a first team, could play the whole game."[39]

In fact, as starting guard Pride Ratterree recalled, Walker's 1945 squad was really two teams in one:

> *One team was a team with a bunch of old men, and then there was another team of boys. The team with the men did all the playing. There were about twelve or thirteen of us. I was twenty-three. Bo Sacrinty was a Marine lieutenant and about twenty-four or so. Nick [Sacrinty] was pretty old too [twenty-one actually]. I'm pretty sure Elmer Barbour was twenty-seven or twenty-eight. [Buck] Garrison was up there too.*[40]

As the season began, Walker had forty-three men on varsity (a few more would be added as the season went on). Of those, twenty-four were freshmen. The freshmen were a mixed lot. Many were "all-call" players of the Appenzeller class, players Walker signed up in the spring when the exact end date for the war was far from certain. A small proportion represented some solid recruiting work, although it must be said the Walker's wartime recruiting classes bore little resemblance to the groups he brought in before and after. No surprise there, of course. Walker was on his own during the vital winter and early springs when most of his solicitations were made because Greason was coaching basketball. And with a war going on and players being sucked up left and right into the service or to some military college program, the pickings were slim.

No matter. Not in 1945 anyway. The freshmen, such as they were, were there as practice fodder. Walker could play a pat hand,

---

39 *Greensboro Daily News*, Sept. 18, 1945.
40 Ratterree, interview with author.

embellished only by the addition of wingback Bo Sacrinty, back from the front.

Knowing he had a veteran club, Walker lined up a difficult schedule for his team. The first three games were against Tennessee, Duke, and—Deacon fans could hardly believe it—Army. Walker had no illusions about the schedule. He told the local press corps that Wake would likely start 0–3, the only real possibility for victory being the third game, a home contest against Duke.

On the other hand, Wake's bank account would look a lot better. Both Tennessee and Army would produce good paydays for the Deacons, and money was surely on the minds of Walker and the-just-back-from-the-war Weaver. The Board of Trustees restored Walker to his prewar salary of $4,500 a year in September.[41] That was an effective raise of just $500 since he lost the $1,000 a year received as Weaver's stand-in. No hard feelings there. Walker was happy to palm off some of his wartime duties—at home games he'd often been found in the ticket booth less than an hour before game time trying to peddle a few more passes—in exchange for a little cash.

With regards to scheduling, Wake was also struggling a bit with the residue of its recent success. A lot of teams just didn't want to play the Deacons. They were tough to beat and didn't pay well either in gate guarantees or prestige. Both Army and Tennessee were above such considerations at this point. Tennessee was nearing the end of Robert Barnhill's solid stand-in work for Major-cum-General Robert Neyland, the legendary Volunteer coach who'd been called up to service in 1941. Barnhill went 32–5–2 in five seasons and took the Volunteers to two major bowl games—not the worst interim showing ever. The Volunteers were a bona fide national power.

The 1945 Army team, meanwhile, was a team from another planet. Stocked with all-star talent culled from the nation's best teams via the fight-or-football recruiting pitch, Army was all but unbeatable. Legendary coach Red Blaik and company were shameless in their plunder of the rest of the nation's football teams. Virtually the entire first team started their collegiate careers at

---

41 Wake Forest Board of Trustees Minutes, Sept. 4, 1945.

other schools, the exception perhaps being massive tackle DeWitt "Tex" Coulter, who enlisted in the Army as a teenager and then was shifted to the academy football team when word of his size and prowess moved up the chain of command. At least Blaik didn't pick on just one school for his roster raids: All-American end Hank Foldberg started his career at Texas A&M, fellow end Barney Poole first starred at Ole Miss, Herschel "Ug" Fuson was once a Tennessee player, Ted "Shorty" McWilliams began at Mississippi State, and tackle Al "Bear" Nemetz was a former Walker recruit at Wake Forest.[42] Even the Cadets' most famous players, fullback Felix "Doc" Blanchard and halfback Glenn Davis, were imports. Davis played two seasons at California State Polytechnic University, Pomona while Blanchard played a season of freshman ball at North Carolina. A native of tiny Bishopville, SC, the life of a football mercenary ran through the Blanchard blood. Felix Sr. (or "Big Boy" Blanchard as he was known) played at least three seasons of football at Wake Forest during or shortly after World War I. He just missed playing a game with Peahead during his singular appearance in black and gold back in 1920 (see chapter 1 for details). Later, he played at Tulane under an assumed name, a common ploy in football's formative years.

With all those stars, the 1945 Cadets went 9-0 and were seldom threatened. Their closest game was a 32-13 victory over Navy, and their starting team gave up only one touchdown all season.

It wasn't against Wake Forest, although the Deacons arrived on the banks of the Hudson in September of 1945 brimming with confidence and only a few stars in their eyes. A few more appeared when the Army team, all seventy of them, ran onto the field. Herb Appenzeller remembers teammate Dick Foreman watching the stampede of chiseled athletes go by, his mouth agape. "My God, Herbie," Foreman told Appenzeller. "Just look at them. What a team."[43]

---

42 A second former Deacon, Bill Webb, was also on the Cadet squad but didn't play much. His Army teammates did nickname him "Peahead," however, which suggests how well Walker was known around the country.
43 Appenzeller, interview with author.

Foreman wasn't completely bedazzled, however. The hard-hitting linebacker rocked Blanchard on the opening kickoff, giving his teammates a shot of confidence and a play they'd remember all their lives. But the Cadets were, as it turned out, every bit as good as they looked. Five plays into their first possession, backup halfback Herschel "Ug" Fuson, who later in the season moved to the starting center position, rolled around left end, picked up some blocking, and coasted fifty-one yards for a score. Four plays after that, future Heisman Trophy winner Glenn Davis ran sixty-five yards for a touchdown. And so it went. Wake played Army to a draw on many plays, only to see the Cadets break a big one. Blanchard, perhaps bridled by Blaik, was not a complete terror on offense, but he did run an interception back fifty-two yards for a score. McWilliams, the former Rebel, ran eighty yards from scrimmage for another. Army managed just eleven first downs in the game—the same as Wake—but piled up a whopping 538 total yards, the most ever against a Walker-coached team, and beat the Deacons 54–0.

Scribes made something of the fact that Army won easily despite playing its second and third teams much of the game. But as Walker pointed out afterward, there really wasn't much of a drop-off: "The second team is really just as good. How can you beat them?"[44]

Although a good bit short of Army's depth, Walker didn't leave his starters in to the bitter end. After one of Army's late touchdowns, he sent Appenzeller in for the hobbled Sacrinty to return the kickoff. The ball rocketed skyward, then fell, end over end, into Appenzeller's arms around the ten. He looked at the Army behemoths bearing down on him and raced up for the left sideline, making all the yards he could until purposely running out of bounds. Upon returning to the bench he was greeted by a furious Walker. Appenzeller had run left. The return was set up to the right. What the hell was he thinking? Walker wanted to know. Appenzeller had no answer at the time, but later recalled, "What I was thinking was I was just hoping to stay alive and that was the closest sideline I could find."[45]

---

44 *Greensboro Daily News*, Oct. 14, 1945.
45 Appenzeller, interview with author.

Despite the final score, the Wake players who participated in the contest generally recall it with some fondness. The Deacons traded a lot of good licks with the Cadets and gave as good as they got on many plays. Several players pointed to the draw in first downs as a sign that the game was closer than it seemed. "They really only beat us a few plays," said Ratterree.[46]

And only by fifty-four points.

Lopsided defeat and injuries aside, Walker was actually feeling pretty good about his team after two games. The Deacons really had outplayed the Vols in the first week, knocking out their All-Conference tailback, Buster Stephens, on the game's first play and outgaining them by more than a hundred yards. Wake came close to at least two touchdowns over the first three quarters but couldn't put points on the board. The contest was still scoreless in the final quarter when freshman tailback Bob Lund led Tennessee on a drive that produced a touchdown and a 7–0 lead. Wake stormed back behind Nick Sacrinty, marching sixty-seven yards for a touchdown that Brinkley got from two yards out. That cut the lead to one with three minutes to play. Bo Sacrinty lined up the extra point but pushed it wide left. Wake didn't get the ball back and ended up departing Knoxville on the short end of a 7–6 margin.

The Duke game in week three was a classic. The Blue Devils' George Clark awoke unpleasant memories of the 1944 debacle when he ran sixty-nine yards for a touchdown on the first play from scrimmage. But that play didn't seem to rattle Wake the way Clark's longer punt return had the year before. Sacrinty led the Deacons back down the field, capping a long drive by hitting John Bruno on a third-and-ten pass from the Duke thirty-six. Bruno picked up twenty yards to the sixteen before being hemmed in. Just before he was tackled he lateraled to Dave Harris—it was a legal lateral, but just barely—who ran the rest of the way for the score. That tied the game at 6–6. A few minutes later, after Sacrinty's sixty-one-yard punt return pinned Duke deep in its own territory, Wake scored again. This time Sacrinty hit Harris with a pass, and this time it was Harris who lateraled to a teammate, in this case halfback Nick Demetriou. The played covered thirty-three

---

46 Ratterree, interview with author.

yards and put Wake up 13–6. The seesawing continued, Duke coming right back with a long scoring drive capped by another Clark touchdown.

The game turned in the third quarter when Duke's Gordon Carver intercepted a Deacon pass and returned it to the Duke forty-two. On the next play, Clark blasted through the line and into the Deacon secondary. The hobbled Sacrinty nearly pushed him towards the sideline at the twenty-five. Sacrinty thought he'd knocked the Blue Devil back out of bounds, but Clark tiptoed along the boundary and made his way to the end zone. 20–13 Duke. Wake roared back one last time. Sacrinty's passing drove the Deacons to the Duke seven. After being held to no gain on two consecutive runs, Wake trotted out the old Statue of Liberty play again on third down. Duke was expecting it, but Walker was expecting that they would expect it and had put on a fake instead. Sacrinty pretended to handoff to Smathers, who was immediately swarmed by Duke tacklers. Sacrinty then flipped a pass over the Duke secondary to backup end Carroll Worthington, who was standing alone in the back of the end zone. The score put Wake within one, but alas—Bo Sacrinty's extra point failed once again. This one was too low and was blocked by Fred Knotts, Duke's middle linebacker.

Wake got the ball back one final time and picked up a first down or two on more Sacrinty passes. But Duke's Jim Larue intercepted his next attempt and returned it to the Wake twenty-four. The fading Deacons gave way slowly, but Duke eventually scored to make it 26–19.

And that was that. Wake was 0–3 for the first time since Walker's inaugural season. But here, almost a decade later, it was a vicious schedule, not Deacon ineptitude, that was the cause. Good, if not easy, times were right around the corner, starting with a dramatic 19–18 victory over NC State. Nick Sacrinty scored all three Wake touchdowns, including one on an eighty-nine-yard kickoff return. But Beattie Feather's Wolfpack nearly pulled it out at the end. Winston Naugher finished a long drive with a short touchdown run that cut the Deacon lead to one with three minutes left. An extra point would tie it, but Dave Harris blocked Art Klock's boot. That seemed to save the day and preserve the Deacons' first victory. But State held Wake after the kickoff and forced a punt that was blocked and recovered at the Deacon thirty-nine. State star Howard Turner hurled three straight passes into the end zone from there. All three hit State hands before falling incomplete. By a margin as narrow as that, Wake gained its first victory of the season.

A needed breather followed. Walker had corralled Presbyterian College from Clinton, SC for a home match, and his Deacons steamrolled the Blue Hose 53–0, even with players from deep on the bench seeing significant time. Charles Medlin scored the only touchdown of his career. Herb Appenzeller, a notoriously inexpert passer (see more later in this chapter and in chapter 7), managed a touchdown pass.

Carolina was next. The Tar Heels, coming out of war mode, had rehired Carl Snavely, the "Gray Fox," to restore some luster to the program. In time, he would do just that, applying all his foxiness, and no small amount of recruiting resources, to the task. For the time being, however, the Tar Heels were short on men and talent. Even so, on this day they nearly played the more experienced Deacons to a draw. Wake wasn't at its best and needed two goal-line stands, several Tar Heel fumbles, and a blocked extra point attempt to come away with a 14–13 victory.

Wake battled South Carolina to a 13–13 tie on Thanksgiving and then headed to Clemson for the season finale. Frank Howard had put together a surprisingly good team at Clemson. The Tigers had defeated Tulane and Georgia Tech, two traditional Deep South powers, coming into the game and were ranked sixteenth in the nation. A crowd of almost 20,000—roughly ten times the population of the town of Clemson at that time—filled brand-new Memorial Stadium for the contest. They roared their approval when Clemson dominated early play and gained a 6–0 lead. But Wake held the Tigers at bay the rest of the half, and after what Rock Brinkley described in his *Old Gold & Black* column as a "brisk halftime talk" by coach Walker, the Deacons stormed to a 13–6 victory.[47] While Brinkley considered Walker's locker room oratory brisk, Dewey Hobbs recalled it as just plain miraculous. He wasn't

---

47 *Old Gold & Black*, Dec. 7, 1945.

playing close attention—Walker usually didn't have much to say beyond his tactical/technical fixes, and he usually didn't direct those at the entire team—when suddenly his ears perked up. "Men," Hobbs heard Walker say, "life is tough. We can't be perfect. The only perfect man there ever was got crucified. All we can do is the best we can. Do your best and remember: our plan is the win it in the fourth quarter."

Said Hobbs, "I was sitting next to Nick Sacrinty. He turned to me and whispered, 'Dewey, the Head's gone crazy.' I mean, no one had ever heard him talk about religion or anything close to it, and to work it into a halftime speech . . . well, a lot of us were surprised. But I was kind of impressed, too. For Peahead of all people to make appropriate references to the second person of the deity . . . well, that was remarkable."[48]

Dredging up his religious knowledge may have impressed Hobbs, but it was Walker's hard-nosed strategy that probably won the game. Based on some of Greason's sleuthing, Wake went into the game gunning for Clemson tailback Butch Butler, a gifted player but something of a prima donna who was known to turn on his linemen if he felt he wasn't getting the protection he deserved. By hitting Butler early and often, Walker hoped to upset Clemson's team chemistry. The ploy seemed to work. After the early touchdown, Clemson's offense was stopped cold and eventually just fell apart. "We could hear him [Butler] complaining," said Hobbs. "All was going according to plan."[49]

Walker exacerbated Clemson's offensive woes with a few halftime adjustments that shut off Clemson's inside running game, but that still left Wake with the problem of how to crack a tough Tiger defense. Walker met fire with fire, setting his offense on a one-track course. The Deacons would spend the second half, or most of it, running over right tackle where Walker had detected a weakness in the Clemson line, a strength in his, or some of both. That bit of tactical focus worked as well. Nick Sacrinty eventually broke an off-tackle play for fifty-two yards and the go-ahead score and then ripped off a series of shorter gains behind the strong-side crew—Hobbs, Ratterree, Harris, and a rejuvenated Nick

---

[48] Hobbs, interview with author.
[49] Ibid.

Ognovich—in the drive that allowed Wake to hold on for a gritty 13–6 triumph.

All in all, the season ender was a sweet victory that tickled Walker's fancy. Players recall that on Sacrinty's long touchdown run, Walker leaped off the bench to cheer him on and then, in his excitement, attempted to sit back down without realizing his initial leap had taken him several feet away from where he had been sitting. He landed hard on his tailbone but was a happy man all the same.

The victory knocked Clemson out of a share of the Southern Conference title and pushed Wake into second, the Deacons only league loss coming in the barn burner against Duke. They were 4-3-1 overall and 4-0-1 since the hellish start. It was a nice way to end the season.

Except that it wasn't the end. The Deacons were going bowling.

Wake had several suitors, but the game that finally grabbed Walker's attention was the Gator Bowl in Jacksonville, FL. Although a new bowl in 1946, it had been in the works for years—and then the war came along.

Wake's bid, officially extended around the first of December, was stronger than any postseason possibility the Deacons had ever had before. Civic boosters promised a big crowd (and payout), and the trip from Wake Forest to Jacksonville wasn't nearly as onerous as the slog to El Paso. The opponent was attractive too, at least to Walker. Officials with the Jacksonville Lions Club, the bowl's sponsor, lined up South Carolina for the game, creating a rematch of the teams' 13-13 Thanksgiving tie. The strategy seems odd today—why replay a game that was just played? South Carolina's lackluster 2-3-3 record makes the choice seem stranger still by modern standards.

Bowl promoters offered no clear explanation. The matched apparently seemed promotable to them, although it's clear they had another matchup in mind. Initial overtures went to Wake and Georgia. The Bulldogs owned a better record than South Carolina, and many of their partisans were just across the state line from Jacksonville. But while a Wake-Georgia matchup was the bowl organizers' first choice, the same could not be said for Wally Butts, the Georgia coach. Recalling the Deacons' hard-nosed play in 1944, he wanted no part of a rematch. So, the Gator matchmakers turned to old South Carolina.

Walker liked the idea. It looked like a win to him, and he wasn't happy with the way the first game came out. He'd gone around for days afterward grumbling about how Wake should have whipped the Gamecocks. At least part of his disgust was the fact that he'd been beaten—tied to be exact, but it felt like a loss—by a mere boy. Young John D. McMillan, who turned twenty-six during the season, was the Gamecocks' wartime coach in place of Rex Enright, who had been called to military duty. Enright was actually discharged in time to attend the bowl and could have installed himself as coach if he had wanted because the administration had promised to hold the post open for him. Enright declined, which was either a classy gesture on his part or a practical evaluation of the situation facing the Gamecocks.

So a Gator Bowl bid for Wake Forest was all lined up. All that remained was to convince Wake's players that they ought to do it. As with the Sun Bowl deal a few years before, the Deacons certainly did not feel obligated to play an extra game, scholarship or no, and when the idea was first broached enthusiasm again was not high. At an early December meeting at the Wake Forest bookstore, the assembled players voted "something like 30–1" against playing in the extra game.[50] The only player voting for it, as best anyone can remember, was sophomore Dick Kelly, who happened to live near Jacksonville.

"To everyone else it just seemed like a huge chore," said Appenzeller. "Hell, we'd been at school since August. We were ready to go home and we sure didn't want any more of Peahead's practices."[51]

And the player compensation issue was still on the table. Most of the players had jobs over the month-long winter break. It was how they made their spending money.

"That was the real issue," said Hobbs. "Most of us didn't see how we could afford to go."[52]

---

50 Appenzeller, interview with author.
51 Ibid.
52 Hobbs, interview with author.

Walker was recruiting at the annual Shrine Bowl high school game between the North and South Carolina all-stars in Charlotte when the bookstore meeting took place.[53] Greason relayed the results of the player vote to Walker by phone. How much are the players going to earn over the break? Walker wanted to know. Greason said an informal survey suggested it was something less than $80 apiece. "Well," said Walker, "then let's give 'em a $100 bill and a train ticket home and be done with it."[54]

Just where the money came from is a mystery, but the bargain was struck. Walker didn't have much choice. He had already committed Wake to the contest and needed his players to join him.

As the idea sunk in, and certainly years after the fact, Walker's men came to appreciate their coach's efforts in making them Wake Forest's bowling pioneers. A photo of the Gator Bowl team, and the commemorative pin given to all the players, would, in the years ahead, adorn the walls of many a 1945 Deacon. But at the time, the magnitude was not fully appreciated, although some got it sooner than others. As fullback/scribe Rock Brinkley crowed in his December 14th *Old Gold & Black* column, "The Demon Deacons have finally hit the big time in the football world."

A few loose ends remained in getting the entire team to Florida. Dave Harris and Nick Sacrinty had been selected to play in the East-West all-star game, which was played on the same day as the Gator Bowl. After the team voted to take the money and go to the game, and after Walker returned to campus, Harris sought him out to say thanks and goodbye. It was necessary, Harris figured, what with him being a senior and all and with his schedule preventing him from joining the team in Jacksonville. But as Harris recalled, Walker had other plans:

The Gator Bowl really wasn't that big a deal to me, but the East-West game . . . now that was something. So I said, "Coach, I sure wish you guys well, but I won't be going. I'm going to the East-West game with Nick, you know." He said, "You're not going anywhere

---

53 Among the Tar Heel state stars was John Hobbs, Dewey's younger brother.
54 Appenzller and Hobbs, interview with author. Both men heard the story Greason years after the fact.

but to the goddamn Gator Bowl." "Well what about my invitation?" I asked. "I called 'em yesterday and told 'em you didn't want to play," said Walker. "And believe me, you don't."[55]

Thanks to his sensational year as Wake's center/middle linebacker, Dick Foreman also made an all-star team. He had a berth in the North-South all-star game in Mobile, AL. Unlike Harris, Foreman would get to play in his game even though it was being held just two days before the Gator and was a day-long train ride away. Walker was willing to let Foreman join the team in progress in order to placate the hard-hitting linebacker and keep him in the lineup. But Harris and Sacrinty were out of luck. There was no way to be two places at once.

The Gator Bowl team was a generally classy and well-intentioned group—the contrast with some of Walker's postwar teams is striking—and after negotiating their bowl fee, they displayed a magnanimous bent. Led by Harris, who didn't want to play in the East-West game after all, they decided to chip in some of the $100 and pay for one of their student managers, Tommy "Dynamite" Creed of Greensboro, to make the trip.[56] Walker had cut Creed from the travel party. What with forking out $3,300 in player "salaries" and all, Peahead's bowl budget was straining at the seams (Wake's guarantee for participating was only $10,000). But the players decided the game just wouldn't be the same without Dynamite.

As it turned out, the first Gator Bowl was all that a bowl should be. The locals were enthused and the atmosphere was festive. A train car full of sportswriters accompanied Walker and his staff, which was beefed up with the postwar addition of Hank Bartos and Bub Walker (who had spent part of the war coaching at his brother's alma mater Howard). Stories and spirits flowed as the Sun Queen Express rumbled southward. Players recall plenty of laughter coming from the club car. The source of it all was a mystery. The car was off limits to them.

---

55 Dave Harris, interview with author.
56 Creed was one of at least four people upon whom Walker bestowed the "Dynamite" nickname. As noted earlier, this was generally not a compliment.

Upon arrival, the colorful Walker was the toast of the town and proved to be as much a draw as the team itself. The Jacksonville Lions presented him a gaudy necktie upon his arrival (it had a fish motif and fit in with the rest of Walker's famed cravat collection), and his quotes provided excellent pregame copy.

Walker yukked it up, but he drilled his club pretty hard for the game and had done plenty of planning and preparing for the rematch. His idea, based on the team's November meeting, was pretty simple. The Deacons had passed the ball too much in that game he thought, especially given the fairly decisive advantage in size and strength they had. In the bowl game, the Deacons would tweak the blocking on some of their favorite running plays and run the Gamecocks into the ground.

The plan worked perfectly. North Florida was cold that first morning of 1946, and a brisk wind began to blow across the St. John's River and into the stadium. It picked up as game time neared and was strong enough by kickoff to all but end either team's thoughts of a big day in the air. That was fine with Wake, of course. Passing wasn't in the Deacons' plans. The same could not be said for the Gamecocks.

And they couldn't stop Wake either as it turned out. With Brinkley and a rejuvenated Bo Sacrinty leading the way, the Deacons piled up 368 rushing yards and 23 first downs. South Carolina managed to take an early 7–6 lead, but Wake pushed ahead 19–7 after three quarters. The Deacons put the contest away when Foreman, fresh off the train from Mobile, blocked a Gamecock punt early in the fourth quarter, and Bob Smathers scored untouched on a wingback reverse on the very next play. That made it 26–7 and Walker cleared his bench, although not without some prompting. In the huddle after Foreman's blocked kick was recovered at the South Carolina twenty-five, Nick Sacrinty told the boys that "we need to run this play for Smathers perfectly so he can score and the other guys can get in, have some fun, and finish the game." What Sacrinty had suggested transpired, and when the starters came off the field after the extra point, iron man Pride Ratterree went to Walker and said, "Coach, we've got this one. Why not let some of those boys who've never played, and probably never will, get in for this one?" Walker thought for a moment, then nodded. "All right, Ratt-er-ree. If you think so."[57]

The regulars kicked off and the new men poured in. The Sacrinty brothers, playing what they believed was their last game together, came off the field arm in arm. The celebration was on.

For a time, it looked like the subs might keep up the Deacon avalanche. They drove deep into South Carolina territory before losing the ball on downs at the South Carolina nine-yard line. But they got it right back when Pee Wee Jones intercepted a pass from Dutch Brembs and returned it to the South Carolina twenty-five. He lateraled to Appenzeller, who moved forward for ten more yards to the fifteen. Less than a minute remained. The Deacon reserves smelled blood.

Appenzeller, in for Nick Sacrinty at tailback, called a pass. He dropped back and lofted one toward the left sideline. It was intended for a receiver near the goal line, but the wind, coupled with Appenzeller's lack of velocity, held it up. The Gamecocks' Brembs ran under the dying quail, snared it, and raced ninety yards for the score, slicing Wake's lead to 26–14. There were only eight seconds left when Brembs crossed the goal, so Appenzeller's gaff didn't mean much, and Walker, uncharacteristically, didn't say much about it. At least not then.

The following spring, however, when the noodle-armed Appenzeller essentially recreated the play during a scrimmage, floating a goal-line pass to a defender who ran it back for touchdown, Walker wrinkled up his face and let Appenzeller know that all was not forgotten.

"Goddamn it, Appenzeller," Walker roared, "that's the same shitty pass you threw against South Carolina in the goddamned Gator Bowl. Ain't you ever going to improve?"[58]

He wouldn't, but Walker's Deacons would.

High times were right around the corner.

---

[57] Ratterree, interview with author.
[58] Appenzeller, interview with author.

CHAPTER 7

IN ALL HIS GLORY

A national giddiness—part relief, part hubris, part hope—ran rampant across the United States at the end of World War II. It rolled in with the great tide of soldiers and sailors who washed ashore during the weeks, months, and years that followed. Some sixteen million men had served in the conflict, more than one out of every ten Americans, and as fast as the Army, Navy, and Marines could muster them out they were coming home to start life anew or . . . to pick up where they had left off.

Among that latter group were thousands of still unspoiled (that is to say not tainted by professionalism) college football talent, a fact not lost on Peahead Walker and many of his collegiate coaching brethren. A new recruiting front opened in the summer of 1945, with the real fighting beginning the following spring when the trickle of player-soldiers turned into a torrent. Viewing this coming onslaught, Dick Herbert of the *Raleigh News & Observer* predicted with his characteristic simplicity that "there will be a dogged fight for football talent and the teams that come up with the best men will have the best teams. That fight started a long time ago."[1]

The recruiting war would be fought on many battlefields, but the first one was procedural. What rules, if any, would govern the placement of players returning from duty? That is, would they be obligated to return to the schools they'd left when duty called? Or would they be "free agents"? For much of the nation, it was not a difficult question. The vast majority of the organized, athletic conferences took a laissez-faire approach. The chips, and the athletes, would fall where they may.

In the South, however, there was some resistance to such a plan. Both the Southeastern and Southern Conferences had

---

1 *Raleigh News & Observer*, Dec. 3, 1945.

installed temporary restrictions against free-ranging movement. But if they were the only ones doing it, wouldn't that put them at a competitive disadvantage? And weren't there legal matters to consider? And beyond all that, what was fair to the vets? And on and on it went.

The matter was brought to a head in the Southern when Curly Byrd, the University of Maryland's aggressive president, snatched up NC Pre-Flight football guru Paul "Bear" Bryant to coach the Terrapins/Old Liners for a cool $10,000 a year. Bryant was tickled to take the Maryland job but felt some tenderness toward the Pre-Flight boys he was leaving behind—after all, they'd been through the hell of war together. Yes, their hell had been Chapel Hill, NC, not a steamy Pacific jungle or the flak-filled skies above Polesti, but there was still a bond there all the same. And besides, they were a carefully constructed all-star football team chockfull of useful talent. Who could think of breaking up an outfit like that and not have a tear well up in their eye?

Certainly not Bryant. The Bear balked at having to leave all that talent behind. Was it possible, he asked his new employer, to bring his Cloudbusters with him? If not the whole bunch, then at least the biggest, fastest, and meanest ones? Surely that could be arranged.

The gung-ho Byrd, a former coach and ever the player's friend, said sure, why not? And the game was on. Bryant made plans to bring what was essentially a full team—some twenty-eight players—with him to College Park. Southern Conference officials, naturally, went berserk. Byrd was called on the carpet and Maryland was threatened with expulsion. Byrd responded with a blistering letter in which he threatened secession if the mass transfers were not allowed.

It was a tricky question. NC Pre-Flight wasn't an NCAA institution even if it had been based at one, so the players really weren't transfers in an administrative sense. Instead, they were coming from the individual schools where some (but not all) of them had played before the war. It was as if suddenly, at once, dozens of players from all over all decided to transfer to the University of Maryland. That's what they wanted to do. What, if anything, was wrong with that? The official answer was a befuddled mumble, and although a principled debate was held on high, just as had been the case with the prudish Graham Plan before, the outcome was seldom in doubt. The conference's power schools—Duke plus the big state schools—all wanted an open-door policy. Maryland might have twenty-eight Cloudbusters lined up, but all the rest had an eye on their very own slice of the appetizing, postwar talent pie.

Coaches at the two Southern Conference schools that had benefited most from becoming war-time training sites, Duke's Wallace Wade and North Carolina's Carl Snavely, both embraced a "fairness" doctrine that endorsed unhindered movement for the returning vets. It was by far the majority view.

A dissenter was Wake's Peahead Walker. He certainly didn't mind diving into a recruiting fight with the big boys. He was an accomplished proselytizer after all and had shown he could go toe to toe with the best of 'em. But he thought the end of regulations, coupled with the big schools' carryover advantages from the war—and their massive war chests for example—would be too much. And besides, the big boys always seemed to get the breaks. How about a change for once?

"These big schools like Duke and Carolina had the Navy units [V-12s] all during the war, which meant good football players, and now they want to change the rules so that they can continue to have all the breaks over us little fellows," Walker moaned. "[Changing the rules] will do nothing but open [them] up so that the rich schools [can] buy all the good returning servicemen."[2]

Walker's logic seemed sound, but when the rules were, in fact, overturned and the floodgates opened, it didn't quite work like that. The scope of operations was just too great for the big boys to have it all. Great resources were employed to upgrade facilities and chase the big names. But thousands of players—several years worth of recruiting classes—were coming home, and even at the big schools coaching staffs weren't big enough to keep up. Nobody had the manpower to go after everyone, much less keep up with them all. And not every coach figured things out as fast as they could have.

---

2 Ibid.

For instance, Duke and Carolina, Walker's two biggest proselytizing rivals, might have done more damage had they not become preoccupied with the pursuit of one Charlie Justice, a high school phenom from Lee Edwards High in Asheville, NC who'd been slated to attend Duke when the war broke out.[3] Justice's college career was forestalled by war and a nice piece of recruiting by the Navy, which corralled him before he could set foot in Durham and sent him to its Bainbridge Naval Training Station in Port Deposit, MD just as the war began. As fate would have it, Bainbridge had just formed a base football team—and a solid one at that. It included professional players from Washington, DC and elsewhere and would become one of the best in the nation. The slightly built Justice—5'8," maybe 160 pounds as a fuzzy-cheeked 17-year-old—made the team as a punter (it was always his best skill). But after several dazzling runs on fake punts, he became the starting tailback. His second year at Bainbridge, the squad went undefeated while Justice averaged twelve yards per carry. A sailor/fan at Bainbridge is credited with comparing Justice to a train, or, more specifically, a choo choo train. Sportswriters covering Bainbridge picked up on it, and the name "Choo Choo" Justice was born.

Justice's Bainbridge exploits validated the promise he'd shown in high school and didn't do anything to lessen the collegiate interest in Justice as his service commitment came to an end in late 1945. Neither did the possibility that he had already signed a professional contract.[4] As the war ended, Duke's Wade sicc'ed Assistant Coach Dan Hill on Justice. Hill wasn't recruiting, of course—Duke didn't do that—but he was awfully dogged, in his effort to "bump into" Justice from one end of the United States (and

---

[3] The Justice teams at Lee Edwards, which also featured speedster Billy Britt, were marvels. They were undefeated for two straight seasons and all but unscored upon. During Justice's senior year, Lee Edwards outscored its opposition 442–6, and Justice averaged eighteen yards per carry—twenty-five by some accounts—and scored twenty-seven touchdowns. Source: Quincy, B., Scheer, J., *The Choo Choo Justice Story*. 1958. Cambridge, MA: Bentley Publishers.

[4] Justice apparently did sign on with the Philadelphia Eagles in 1944 or 1945, but NFL officials declared the contract void based on Justice's youth. The NFL told Southern Conference officials investigating the matter in 1947 that Elmer Layden, the NFL commissioner during the war, had cancelled the document because Justice was, in Layden's words, "just a high school kid."

future United States) to the other. Indeed, Hill may have set some sort of recruiting mileage record when he followed Justice on a cross-country trip from North Carolina to Hawaii and back, capping off the junket by greeting a surprised Justice just as he debarked the Asheville train station. Justice was impressed by Hill's detective work if nothing else. He later claimed he only told his wife about his itinerary, which suggests either intimate betrayal or an elaborate Blue Devil spy network.[5]

Duke was not alone in its pursuit. More than two hundred schools sent Justice scholarship offers. The affable Justice may have been overwhelmed, but guidance form his older brother Jack helped him through the maze. Though Justice himself was impressed by South Carolina's Rex Enright, a Navy man, Jack Justice thought his little brother should stay in North Carolina (meaning Duke or UNC—Wake and State were never in the picture). The rumors swirled and the proselytizing continued. Enright had Justice come down to Jacksonville, FL to sit on the Gamecocks' bench during South Carolina's Gator Bowl loss to Wake Forest, a spectacle that could have depressed Justice or encouraged him with the prospect of ample playing time. The Gamecocks were in the hunt, but Duke and UNC kept the pressure on. Brother Jack, who wasn't a fan of the imperious Wade, pushed Charlie toward UNC. That wound up being Justice's choice, although Snavely was less than impressed after seeing him in person during his recruiting visit. While driving Justice back from campus to the airport for his departure, the Gray Fox asked the prized recruit just one scintillating question: "How much do you weigh?"

Wake's Walker didn't spend time on Justice, and it was probably just as well. He was plenty busy in the winter and spring of 1945–1946. After the conference rule change in early 1946 (and quite possibly before that), he began contacting prospects who'd been at Wake before the war—and some who hadn't. Walker wound up piling up so many players—the squad eventually leveled off at a robust sixty-six players after starting with many more—that eventually he had to run some off. Among the casualties was Herb

---

5 *The Choo Choo Justice Story.*

Appenzeller, who figured to be about the ninth-string tailback if he stayed.

Official word of his demise came by campus mail.

> *About a dozen of us, maybe more, got a little postcard that said our scholarships weren't any good anymore. They didn't even put it in an envelope. But that was okay. I understood. They had Sacrinty [who had decided to postpone med school for a year] coming back [at tailback], plus Fetzer, and Cochran back from the war. And then they'd signed some more guys coming back. Hey, I could see it. The war was over. The good players were coming back. Who needed a 4F tailback?*[6]

To soften the blow, Walker and company tried to help the lost lettermen find new gigs. Appenzeller said Assistant Coach Tom Rogers showed up at his dorm a few days after the postcard arrived to tell him he'd lined up a football-playing, scholarship-earning opportunity for him at Glenville State (West Virginia) Teachers College.

"He [Rogers] said, 'I even got you some laundry money. You know, you never had that here,'" said Appenzeller. "I told him I appreciated it, but I said, 'Coach, I'm a junior. I'm taking Latin from maybe the best Latin teacher in the world [Dr. Hubert Poteat]. I've got friends here. I think I'll just stay. Don't worry about me. I'll find a job.'"[7]

The industrious Appenzeller did find a job. He landed a post as a dry-cleaning deliveryman for the son-in-law of a Wake Forest College alumnus, receiving a small hourly wage plus commission on any new jobs he could pick up. Peahead Walker heard about this, as he did most things that went on around campus. He sent the job of cleaning the football team's uniforms Appenzeller's way, earning him a big sale. "Then he got the players to help me," Appenzeller said. "I'd go by the dorms and pick up their personal laundry, too. I guess you could say I finally did get my laundry money."[8]

---

6 Herb Appenzeller, interview with author.
7 Ibid.
8 Ibid.

Walker succeeded in talking many prewar Deacons into coming back to school—most seemed to have quite eager to return—but also landed a handful of players from other schools. Fullback Clay Croom, end Ed Hoey, and tackle Ulysses "Jim" Cornogg had all been at UNC. End Jim Duncan spent a year as a V-12er at Duke. Walker and his newly refurbished staff stayed busy hunting down players. Line coach Tom Rogers, along with ex-Deacon John Jett and Pat Preston, former Tulane star Bobby Kellogg and, of course, the irreplaceable Greason, beat the bushes in areas both new (Georgia and Virginia) and old (Alabama, New Jersey, and New York). Winning that competition meant coming up with the best offers and, just as importantly, getting there first. In that regard, Walker's legmen were no less impressive than Wade's. Ed Butler, who had starred on a sensational Reynolds High School team in Winston-Salem before the war, recalled that Pat Preston was knocking on his door the morning after Butler was discharged from the Army:

> *I mean, I hadn't been back a day when Pat came knocking on the door. It was Friday, about 8 AM, and I'd been out pretty late celebrating getting back and all with the boys. He said, 'Why don't you come to Wake Forest?' I said, 'Well, maybe.' He was insistent. He said, 'We'd like you to come visit today.' I said, 'Well, I can't—I've got a date.' 'Don't worry,' he said. 'We'll take you down there and get you back in plenty of time.' So I went and talked to Peahead and he seemed okay and he told me what he'd give me and I said okay. And that was about it. And I did make it back in time just like they promised. But the date didn't turn out. I did wind up marrying a Wake Forest girl though, so it was a good decision. I had been planning to go to Duke.*[9]

Ed Hoey, from the hardscrabble western Pennsylvania town of Clairton, had followed star Andy Bershak from Clairton to UNC in 1942. After three years in the service, plus marriage to his newfound sweetheart, he went back to UNC, where Snavely had

---

9 Ed Butler, interview with author.

promised that apartments for married students would be ready for occupancy. They weren't.

"And that upset me tremendously," said Hoey. "To be honest, I didn't much like him [Snavely] anyway. He was kind of an executive coach type, a sort of pompous ass really. . . . When I found out the apartments weren't ready, I called a friend of mine at Wake [Jim Camp] and told him all about it. He said, 'Why don't you come here?' I told him, 'Well, you tell Peahead that I'd be interested. If he's interested give me a call.' And he did."

Hoey said Walker's pitch was impressive.

"He was very personable, would look you right in the eye, tell you what he thought. I thought he was a good guy, a good human being, right then, and that turned out to be the case."[10]

Hoey was hardly the only word-of-mouth recruit added to the roster. The 1946 and 1947 rosters were littered with groups of players from the same high school or hometown. The fact that current players were recruiting for Walker reflects well on the morale inside the program. It also helped him compete against schools with more resources for scouting. Bernie Hanula, a tackle from Vineland, NJ, brought teammates Anthony DiTomo and Mike Gagliordi with him. Rock Brinkley, home for a visit, ran into the recently discharged Carl Haggard, a fellow Norfolk native, and talked him into coming to Wake. That led to a meeting with Walker that didn't include much buttering up on the coach's part. Haggard was billed as a fleet halfback, but he didn't look like one to Walker.

"I was kind of fat, what from being on leave and all," said Haggard, "and [Walker] said, 'Boy you look like a damn lineman to me.' I said, 'No, Coach, I'm a backfield man,' and I told him about some stuff I'd done and how fast I was. He nodded and said, 'Well, you're going to have to come in here and run and get in shape. Are you willing to do that?' I said I was. He told me what he could get me [monetarily] and that was that."[11]

Creativity on Walker's part, and on the part of college officials, helped make the pay-for-play competition more even than it might have been. Returning GIs like Hoey and Haggard could attend school for free in most cases. The legislation, technically

---

10 Ed Hoey, interview with author.
11 Carl Haggard, interview with author.

known as the Serviceman's Readjustment Act of 1944 but commonly referred to as the GI Bill, provided $50 per month toward an education, a princely sum in that day. Wake's bill for a semester of tuition and fees totaled just $150 in 1949. That made the GI Bill a windfall for Wake Forest (the government paid the full amount, regardless of actual tuition). Enrollment for the 1946 school year swelled to above 1,500, a record. The majority, some nine hundred, were ex-servicemen, meaning the largest part of Wake's tuition income came from Uncle Sam. The cash-strapped college was suddenly rolling down Easy Street.

That was good news, but since the GI Bill's benefits were good at nearly every college in the country, the ability of a school to offer/provide a scholarship ceased to be much of a lure. Hoey said that in his case at least, Wake came up with the novel (and lucrative) approach of cutting Hoey a check equal to the scholarship funds the school didn't have to provide. College records don't offer much clarity on the matter, but if Hoey's entire GI Bill supplement went to the school, Wake came out ahead on the transaction, writing Hoey a check for less than the $50 per month the government provided. Whatever the accounting realities, Hoey said his football days were definitely the good life.

"[Walker] arranged the housing for us, lined up our groceries [Hoey and his wife simply charged their purchases to a special account at a designated grocery in downtown Wake Forest] and gave us a check that was equivalent to the tuition the school would have paid," said Hoey. "I guess you'd call it a salary. It was quite a deal. It killed me when college was over. I wasn't that well off again for years."[12]

The apartments where Hoey and the other married guys stayed were former Civilian Conservation Corps dorms that had been snapped up by the Army for barracks at nearby Camp Butner during the war. Approximately fifty three-bedroom units were placed in an activity field between the college tennis courts on Faculty Drive and the college steam plant. The area was known informally as GI Town. The grocery store was probably Hollowells. The owners of the downtown establishment had a long and cozy

---

12 Hoey, interview with author.

relationship with the college, its athletic department in particular.[13]

Wake was hardly unique when it came to GI Bill shenanigans. Rivals were certain that Justice received untold riches for going to UNC, but all Choo Choo would ever admit to was some GI Bill legerdemain, similar to what Wake did with Hoey. Since Justice was going to school at the government's expense, Carolina officials simply transferred his athletic "scholarship" to his wife Sarah.[14]

Such a transfer of benefits—much less a cash-in-lieu arrangement—skirted the line for fraud if it didn't cross it outright. It was certainly contrary to the intent of the NCAA's new "Purity Code" (later called the "Sanity Code"), which was passed by member organizations in 1947. The code called for limited, need-based subsidies for athletes, most of which were to be generated by work-study programs. Laundry money was limited to a set amount (beginning at $10 a month), and training tables were restricted to a single daily meal in season. The rules passed even though hundreds of colleges—quite likely a majority of the NCAA membership—were not in compliance. The gross hypocrisy of voting for a rule even while violating it was not much discussed in public—although surely it was well understood. Historian John Sayle Watterson suggests that member schools were of two minds. Some believed in the rules but couldn't bring themselves to comply. Others just figured that with the toothless NCAA as the only cop in town they could get away with it.[15] Loss of NCAA membership might have kept a school out of a bowl game or, at worst, put it on some sort of competitive blacklist, meaning member schools might have refused to schedule it. It was never put to a real test.

---

13 Shaw, B., *The History of Wake Forest College*. 1988. Winston-Salem, NC: Wake Forest University; Murray Greason Jr., interview with author.
14 Justice's version of his inducements at UNC is recorded in both *The Choo Choo Justice Story* and in various newspaper interviews long after the fact. In these accounts he admits to an offer of $10,000 from another, unnamed school plus a checking account of unstated size.
15 Watterson, J.S., *College Football: History, Spectacle, and Controversy*. 2000. Baltimore: Johns Hopkins University Press.

The Southern Conference included more cynics than true believers. Few if any Southern Conference teams, public pronouncements aside, were anywhere close to complying with the Sanity Code. But with the rules still being developed (the Sanity Code was reformed several times after it was written) and no resources available for investigation or enforcement, there was little motivation to abide by them. The NCAA's only official initiative for catching violators was to send an annual form to its four hundred-plus members asking if they were in compliance. The schools that replied tended to report that they were.

Cheating, or what would be called cheating in today's game, was widespread, and the astonishing allocation of resources to football reached levels that would be considered absurd even by modern standards. The University of Oklahoma, for instance, had a fleet of twenty-two corporate planes (courtesy of Halliburton Oil) available for recruiting.[16] And a national scandal erupted in 1946 when "Shorty" McWilliams, the former Mississippi State back who helped Army lay waste to Wake Forest in 1945, tried to transfer back to his old school. Army officials threatened to hold McWilliams in eligibility bondage—he hadn't completed his required military duty after all—and intimated that Mississippi State boosters had offered jobs, cash, and cars. After everyone's eye was blackened, McWilliams ended the ruckus with a magnanimous gesture: he agreed to attend Mississippi State "just on scholarship."

The era's lawless excess engulfed the Southern Conference as well. Maryland, even with the Bear off to Kentucky after just one year, was giving out close to eighty scholarships. At William & Mary it was discovered that coaches had altered the high school transcripts of recruits in order to slip them by admission officials, who apparently hadn't gotten the memo canceling institutional morality. The detective story surrounding the uncovering of the scandal centered on a typewriter with a defective, telltale key. William & Mary officials denied it all until the unique instrument, miscreant key and all, was found in the football coach's basement office.

---

16 Dent, J., *The Undefeated: The Oklahoma Sooners and the Greatest Winning Streak in College Football.* 2002. New York: St. Martin's Press.

North Carolina officials all but formally announced a full-time return to the land of subsidy and recruiting by offering Snavely an annual salary in excess of $12,000 to return to the school as football coach.[17] With Snavely back in the harness, it was clear that any debate about whether to recruit and offer scholarships was over on the UNC campus.

It was over at little old Wake Forest, too, and had been for some time. Peahead Walker had seen to that.

A golden era for Wake Forest football was dawning, a time in which Deacon teams were regularly ranked among the nation's top twenty, and Deacon players took pride in the fact that they were just as good as anybody else. Hoey, a 1946 recruit, said, "While I was there, we could play with anyone. We just had so much talent. It wasn't the old deal at Wake where they didn't have enough depth. We had plenty of everything."[18]

Larry Spencer, a freshman in 1949, said, "Our players were just as good as anyone's and we played the best teams in the country." Like several players in the class of 1949, Spencer took pride in the fact that he and seven other classmates were drafted and went on to play professional football.

"I think that's a record at Wake," he said. "Probably at a lot of other places, too."[19]

After twenty-some-odd years in the saddle, Walker's recruiting work was finally taking hold. And while it was the stuff of legend and barside fable, there was nothing magical or mysterious about it. He worked hard to find the prospects,

---

17 The increased funding of the UNC football job was approved at a meeting of the University of North Carolina system's Board of Trustees in late 1945 and included a similar increase for the coach at NC State. At the meeting, Trustee Benton Stacy complained that Carolina had no chance against powerful teams like Army, Navy, Georgia Tech, or Tulane. North Carolina Governor J. Melville Broughton, a Wake Forester through and through, and a de facto member of the board, was heard strangling in the background during Benton's complaint and was recognized by the chairman for comment. "And Wake Forest," Broughton coughed, adding another team to Stacy's list of schools UNC and State had no chance of beating. The addition was noted in the official minutes. Source: *Raleigh News & Observer*, Dec. 3, 1945.
18 Hoey, interview with author.
19 Larry Spencer, interview with author.

managed to dig up the resources needed for competitive inducement, and was a whiz at making the sale.

Walker's signature addition to Wake's talent procurement process was the expansion of the recruiting base. Early on, he pulled in players from an area that ranged from Alabama to New York. His eventual expansion covered the entire East Coast, plus an occasional foray into the Deep South and the Midwest. In 1946, Walker's expanded sixty-six-man roster included players from thirteen different states. During his Deacon career his recruiting web spanned nineteen states, although remarkably he never landed anyone from South Carolina.

North Carolina, Wake's home state and Walker's for most of his adult life, was naturally his favorite recruiting ground and produced the most players, but Walker also drew a lot of players from Pennsylvania, particularly the coal mining country in the west. In this regard he was hardly alone. That part of the country was vibrant and demographically rich in the 1940s and 1950s, and football was a local tradition. Consequently, the hardscrabble mining towns were a target for football coaches from throughout the East and Southeast—Walker's friend Bear Bryant being just one of many who delved deep into mining country for talent from far away. Southern Conference rivals North Carolina, NC State, and Clemson also did business there, but Walker did especially well in Pennsylvania. Seven of the thirty-seven All-Conference players during Walker's Wake tenure came from Pennsylvania, as well as one of the two All-Americans. Rival Frank Howard, the Clemson coach, quipped that if Peahead coughed within earshot of any western Pennsylvania mine shaft, someone down below would reply, "Is that you, Coach Walker?"[20] Willis "Doc" Murphrey, who played for Walker in the 1940s, joked that Wake had several players who couldn't play unless Walker bolted a lamp onto their football helmets.[21] A refugee from another steel-and-coal region (Birmingham, AL), Walker shared a similar world view with the keystone state. Pennsylvanian Hoey said, "Peahead was a blood and guts guy. He worked his players hard, beat the hell out of you to be honest. He kind of reminded me of Jock Sutherland [the

---

20 Perkins, V., *Howard: The Clemson Legend*. 1990. Brentwood, TN: Howard Books.
21 Doc Murphrey, audio recording.

former Pittsburgh coach] and I think that did play well [in western Pennsylvania]. There were a lot of tough guys there, and he [Walker] came across as another one."22

Walker's western Pennsylvania stomping grounds spilled over into northern West Virginia and western Maryland. He also maintained the Birmingham pipeline and seldom was without a good player from around Baltimore. New Jersey and, later in his career, Connecticut, also proved to be fertile ground. He ranged north to Buffalo to land the great fullback John Polanski as well as Buck Jones, an All-Conference tackle.

Walker's distant forays were driven by the realization that he couldn't find enough of what he needed in North Carolina. The best Tar Heel boys wound up at Duke (first choice) or North Carolina, although here and there, and especially near the end of his Wake career, Walker did make inroads in his, and Wake Forest's, home state.

Walker found players through a network of "informants" who helped point him in the right direction. They included other coaches, sporting goods salesmen (and even executives—Claude Carr, one of Walker's teammate's at Howard College, later held a post in upper management with Rawlings Sporting Goods), former players, store owners, sportswriters, and other contacts. Nephew Mickey Walker recalled that his uncle had hangouts in several big cities where he said he went to recruit.

Among Walker's favorite recruiting hangouts was the iconic Mama Leone's restaurant in New York City. The 1,200-seat emporium on West 48th Street was known for its homemade pasta—served in gigantic portions that would have been right up Peahead Walker's alley. Among the regulars (aside from Walker) were Bear Bryant, President Dwight D. Eisenhower, and later, Bryant's brightest New York star, "Broadway" Joe Namath, who was, originally, one of those Pennsylvania guys.23 Mickey Walker said that his uncle told the family he'd meet people there all the time to gather as much info as he possibly could on potential recruits from the area.

---

22 Hoey, interview with author.
23 Namath went to Mama Leone's to celebrate after leading his Jets to a huge upset win over the Colts in Super Bowl III. Source: *New York Times*, Sept. 19, 1907.

Walker's detective work in locating players must be placed in context. There were no recruiting services in the 1930s or 1940s, and even for a hardworking coach with borrowed gas ration cards in his pocket, there wasn't time to travel to see many games or visit many recruits. As a result, a lot of recruiting was word of mouth, and wise coaches didn't pass up many of those opportunities either, even though sometimes the "word" wasn't always good. Clemson's Howard wrote that while he was working as an assistant to Jess Neely in the 1930s he was sent to Charleston, SC to track down a rumor of a 240-pound tackle—huge by the standards of the day. Howard located the boy's address and was greeted by an unimposing youth of about 130 pounds. When Howard discovered that this was, in fact, the recruit he'd been sent to find, he told the young man that he was selling subscriptions to the *Saturday Evening Post* door to door. "Would you like to buy one?" Howard reputedly said. The lightweight tackle did not.

Walker regularly signed players sight unseen. He brought in some real duds that way, including several he had to run off. But he landed a number of important players off the cuff as well, including Jack Lewis, an excellent end who played for Walker in 1949 and 1950. Lewis had excelled in high school sports in Birmingham and was good enough to play in a national high school football all-star game in 1948. Walker may have heard of him but was not actively recruiting him until Jack's dad (who'd gone to Wake) brought his son to the campus while on their way to visit the U.S. Naval Academy in Annapolis, MD.

"We walked into the gym and there [Peahead] was," said Lewis. "We introduced ourselves and he took time to show us around. We weren't expected, but he did a pretty good sales job on the whole family, just off the cuff. He talked to my younger sister, who was interested in going to college to study music, about that; he even took her to the music building. I realized later it was probably first time he'd ever been there."[24]

Walker's spiel—and Lewis's worries over his existing college possibilities, Auburn and Navy—eventually led him to choose Wake.

---

24 Jack Lewis, interview with author.

Ed Kissell, who played a key role as Wake's quarterback in the Deacons' excellent 1950 season, didn't receive even that much attention. Former Deacon Bob Leonetti was playing professional football with Kissell's older (and considerably bigger) brother Vito when it came time for Ed to go college. Kissell was a fine basketball player and an excellent all-around athlete, a gritty sort with a nose for the game. But he was short—barely 5'7" his senior year in high school—and wasn't attracting much attention from colleges. Leonetti wrote Walker, telling him he ought to recruit the latest gridder from the Kissell clan. Walker knew the family well: John Kissell was one of the star bruisers on the Boston College teams that tormented Wake and Walker in 1946 and 1947. Walker offered Kissell a partial scholarship—and the chance to earn more—if he'd come down and try his luck. Kissell did and eventually made good, although Walker' first impression of the unseen recruit wasn't positive. He'd expected something more along the lines of Kissell's four football-playing brothers—all beefy linemen. "Kiss-ell," Walker said upon first laying eyes on the stubby recruit, "you know there's a runt in every litter. I do believe that in your litter you are the runt."[25]

Ironically, Leonetti, who started Kissell on the road to Wake, was himself a product of some word-of-mouth recruiting. A star athlete in Mount Carmel, PA, Leonetti played for George Washington in 1942 before going off to war. After thirty-two months in the service, he was part of the hordes of returning athletes that drew the recruiting attention of most of the serious football schools. Duke's Eddie Cameron spent a considerable amount of time chasing him, and he appeared to be headed to Durham. But on his spring visit to the school, Leonetti decided/was persuaded to visit a couple of high school buddies at Wake Forest during a southern swing in which he was supposed to visit Duke. His Deaconville welcoming party included, in addition to his Pennsylvania friends, one Peahead Walker. Somehow Leonetti never made it to Durham—except when Wake played the Blue Devils. The story may bear the real-life seed of the famed Bill George recruiting tale (see the

---

[25] Ed Kissell, interview with author.

Introduction), although there's no evidence that Leonetti visited the "West Campus."

Walker used that sort of haphazard recruiting to pad rosters and fill in the many gaps created by the less-than-scientific recruiting of the day. Actual tryouts before scholarships papers were signed—legal during this time, or, if illegal, then unstoppable—also helped. Appenzeller, one of Walker's fastest if not necessarily best players, remembers running wind sprints against prospective recruits so Walker could figure out how fast they were. If they were faster than Appenzeller, who took pride in not getting beat, they were pretty fast. That crude athletic metric was used at many schools. Dickie Davis, a Deacon quarterback in the late 1940s, said he was paired against Charlie Justice at UNC during a visit there, but missed the start of the race because it was signaled by a coach dropping his hat to the ground. "I'd never seen that before," said Davis. "I was waiting for a damn whistle to blow or something."[26]

Coaches had to be careful though. Bringing a player in for a tryout could backfire, especially if that coach was Peahead Walker, a man whose competitive intensity only had one setting: high. Pride Ratterree said players would come to Wake and go through a practice, or a part of a practice, with the team . . . and never come back. One of Ratterree's high school teammates attended such a session at Wake and came back saying, "That man is crazy. I'll never go there."[27]

Walker was also very adaptable on the recruiting trail.

Dickie Davis, part of a ballyhooed Wake recruiting class in 1948 that included all four members of the Associated Press' All-North Carolina prep backfield, was wooed by Walker in a most unusual way.

An All-State tailback at Wilson's Charles L. Coon High with coveted triple-threat skills, Davis was an obvious recruiting target for collegiate programs in the state—and beyond. He'd already been to visit North Carolina, South Carolina, and Duke. And he had offers of interest (and more) from Clemson and several other colleges. But there was a problem: his grades weren't good. UNC's

---

26 Dickie Davis, interview with author.
27 Pride Ratterree, interview with author.

Snavely wanted him to spend a year at a prep school such as Fork Union Military Academy. That would give him time to improve his grades, and it would time his arrival to UNC better. He'd be coming in just as Justice was going out. Actually, Davis's problems were more than just poor grades. He'd failed a course his last semester at Coon and hadn't graduated from high school. Walker knew all this when he met Davis but didn't care. He had a plan to get him to Wake despite his academic shortcomings.

"He told me to get in the car, and we did," said Davis. "We drove back towards Wilson and he laid it out. He said, 'I need you for the football team. Here's what we'll do. We'll get you up to Wake right now, get a tutor, pay for your room and board, get you ready to come in with this freshman class where we really need a quarterback.' Hell, as I found out later, they had quarterbacks coming back, and coming in, out the butt. But he told me flat out it'd be me."[28]

Walker's idea sounded pretty good, but Davis had basically already made up his mind to do something else. He had a summer job and was figuring he'd return to high school where he could have an easy year, pass the necessary class, and maybe do some things he'd missed in his first "senior" year, like playing in the East-West Shrine Game.

"So, I said, 'Well, Coach, I don't know. I'm going to be a lifeguard for the summer and . . . ' Walker broke in and said, 'Goddamn boy, I'm offering a free education. A lifeguard job? Damn boy. Are you really that stupid?'

"I said, 'Well, suppose I can't get out in four years'—English had always been trouble for me and the requirement for it at Wake was bothering me—and he said, 'Son, you come to Wake Forest, you got a place to stay for life if need be.' That sounded pretty good to me because the way things had gone for me in school, that's about how long I figured I'd need to get out of college."[29]

That was a sale, but there was still the matter of Davis's graduation from high school. Officially, he was still a course short. Walker asked Davis which teacher had flunked him. Davis told him, and Walker asked the Deacon alum who'd brought him to see

---

28 Davis, interview with author.
29 Ibid.

Davis if he knew where the man lived. He did. And so, in what is surely one of the more unusual recruiting expeditions ever, Walker, Davis, and the alumnus rode to a small town near Wilson to find the man. They did—and Walker, says Davis, talked a very surprised teacher into changing the grade.

Walker would go to great lengths to land a player he thought important. He helped Davis graduate from high school, persuaded Bill George that Wake's campus looked just like Duke's, and wasn't above hiding a player so that rivals couldn't find them—a common recruiting practice in that era. While working to land Pat Preston, the superb tackle from the Baptist orphanage, Walker allegedly brought him to Wake Forest in the summer after his senior year in high school and let him stay in a room above the gym (possibly Walker's future apartment) for several months. One day, Walker's friend Herman Hickman, then an assistant coach at NC State, came by to visit Walker to impress/depress him with tales of the Wolfpack's impending rise to football prominence. The talk quickly turned to recruiting.

"Let me tell you, Peahead," said Hickman. "I've got a line on the greatest tackle you've ever seen—played at a little school and not too many heard of him—but when we get him there'll be no stopping us."

"Oh yeah?" said Walker. "What's his name?"

"Preston," said Hickman. "He's from the orphanage near Thomasville."

"Shhhhhhhh!" hushed Walker.

"Why?" said Hickman in an alarmed whisper.

"Waall," said Walker, "that Preston boy is asleep upstairs. He needs his rest and I don't won't you to wake him."[30]

Tom Donahue, a big, fast center from Altoona, PA, met Walker in the winter of 1948 one day after basketball practice at his Catholic high school. Walker, who was beginning to fatten up by this point in his career, didn't make a great physical impression—"He was kind of this squat little guy," Donahue said—but it was a sale all the same.

---

30 *The Herman Hickman Reader* and various interviews.

"You could tell right away he was a sharp guy and a very likeable person," said Donahue. "We talked and talked. He finally said, 'How'd you like to come to Wake Forest?' I said I'd think about it." Although Donahue was a Catholic at a Catholic high school, he eventually signed with Baptist Wake. "I liked the place—and I did visit the actual Wake campus by the way—and, hell, I liked Peahead."[31]

On a trip to woo potential Deacon Terry Senogle, it was Walker's "quiet" charm that won the day. Throughout the meal, Senogle's sister referred to Walker as "Mr. Pearhead," or just "Pearhead." Walker just smiled and nodded as though he'd been called Pearhead all his life.[32]

Walker's recruiting of Bill George, famous for the campus switcheroo caper, illustrates one of Walker's very real recruiting skills: his ability to project talent. George was a big man, a naturally gifted athlete with "the body of a Greek god and the ability to do anything."[33] But he really wasn't much of a high school football player. He was an excellent wrestler, however, a two-time state champ in Pennsylvania, where high school wrestling was and still is a big deal.

"He had a lot of wrestling offers," said Biff George, Bill's son. "He was a state champ, very quick, very naturally strong. I think it came down to Oklahoma State for wrestling and Wake for football. Dad told me once that it came down to laundry money, which they could give then. Oklahoma State offered $20 and Wake Forest offered $25. Now that seems silly today, but that's how he would have looked at things, especially back then when they were struggling. The $25 was more than $20, so that was better. That's what clinched it."[34]

Walker also promised George a dual wrestling-football career to help lure the big man South. It was sound thinking except for the fact that Wake had no wrestling team. But, as Herb Appenzeller learned (see Chapter 6), that was no obstacle for Walker. George's extraordinary abilities may have made him a

---

31 Tom Donahue, interview with author.
32 Appenzeller, interview with author.
33 Davis, interview with author.
34 Biff George, interview with author.

special case because no matter Walker's preferences, Wake had a wrestling "team" in the late 1940s and early 1950s. It consisted solely of George and the coach who accompanied him to the Southern Conference meet, where George captured the league's heavyweight championships in 1948, 1949, and 1951.

Walker turned a number of wrestlers into crackerjack football players at Wake. He was also able to see past a player's alleged physical limitations or the pigeonholing of previous coaches. His series of mighty-mite blocking backs—Jimmy Ringgold, Ray Manieri, and Nick Ognovich—repeatedly won awards even though their stature left them off the recruiting lists of many bigger schools. And he developed skill position stars from high school linemen like Rock Brinkley and Red O'Quinn. O'Quinn, who never caught a pass in high school, led the nation in receiving in 1948, caught more than five hundred passes as a professional player, and was inducted into the Canadian Football League Hall of Fame, primarily as a receiver.

Just as there's no doubt that Walker was a clever and energetic recruiter, there's also no doubt that he broke rules and crossed ethical lines to stay competitive in the recruiting wars of the day. Although the Sanity Code that had been created to rein in recruiting abuses was in place, it was not in force. Walker and company could do just about whatever they wanted . . . or could afford. That included cash for individuals and some special facilities for the betterment of the team.

Walker and the athletic department seemed, for a time, to have run their own bookstore, where athletes could come and borrow the books needed for class. Ministerial student Dewey Hobbs recalled that when he graduated, Walker told him to go find team manager "Daddy" Behm so that he could give Hobbs his helmet (which he used for four years) as a memento. "And tell him to give you all those damn high religion books, too," Walker said. "We won't be needing those again."[35,36]

---

35 Actually he would. Wake Forest, with its Baptist backing, was always a ministry mill, and it was a rarity for Walker to have a team without a future preacher in the ranks. Future reverend Bob Auffarth followed in Hobbs's footsteps just two years after Hobbs left, and John Gibson came along shortly after that.
36 Dewey Hobbs, interview with author.

The Wake athletic department also operated a boarding house for athletes. Generously called the "Colonial Club," it was a ramshackle affair just across Highway 98 from the campus proper. It may have been a hotel originally or a public boarding house. Whatever the case, the structure became the athlete's dorm and mess hall at least by 1942. It was operated by the Strouds, an aging Christian couple (he was a retired Baptist minister) who took care of basic maintenance and served up three hearty squares a day. Although players remember the Colonial as a borderline fire and rat trap with intermittent showers—only certain rooms had hot water, so it wasn't uncommon to find a player from another floor showering in someone else's room—they appreciated the intimacy of the overall experience and the heartiness of the food. Backed by athletic department funds, the Strouds served up daily feasts. The meals, served family style, weren't fancy, but they were copious. Platters of meats and huge bowls of vegetables were served. Every player received a whole bottle (a quart?) of milk to drink at least twice a day; at supper there was a loaf of bread for every two to three players. Hijinks were part of the daily rations. The good-natured Strouds insisted upon a blessing for every meal, a tradition that often turned into a spoof when team captains or other leaders called on a particularly dimwitted or inarticulate gridder (there were usually several from which to choose) to deliver the benediction.

"[The Colonial Club] was kind of rough," said Dave Harris, a Deacon from 1943 to 1945. "But it was some pretty good eating at a time when there wasn't that much to go around."[37]

The Colonial Club was very real. An oft-repeated story about Walker facilitating the construction of another recruiting aid—a Catholic church in Wake Forest—is not. The tale was spawned by the arrival of John Polanski at Wake, a New Yorker whose name suggested he was Catholic, and the fact that St. Catherine of Siena Church was built in Wake Forest just as Polanski's tenure was drawing to a close. Was coach Walker trying to bring in more hard-hitting Catholic boys from up North by building them a church of their very own? The idea is intriguing

---

37 Dave Harris, interview with author.

and certainly Walkeresque, but the official church history tells a different story. St. Catherine's was the work of Greenwich, CT benefactor Katherine E. Price, relative of the noted Bishop of Raleigh, Eugene J. McGuiness, but not of the noted football prelate, Peahead Walker. While visiting the Bishop in the late 1930s, Price was appalled to learn that a college town like Wake Forest had no Catholic church. She thus donated a large sum of money for the purpose of constructing what became Saint Catherine of Siena Catholic Church.

"Laundry money" was cold hard cash and was much appreciated. But it was doled out in odd lots. Amounts differed according to skill and perhaps negotiating abilities. Bill George, according to intra-team rumors, got $60 per month in laundry money (not the $25 he told his son about, or the more typical $15 to $20). Whether all the funds were actually characterized as laundry money is unknown, as is the accuracy of the claim that George got more. But the rumor was widespread, and it made sense to most.

"Whatever he got," said Dickie Davis, "that S.O.B. was worth every penny of it."[38]

Davis, a Walker favorite despite never quite matching his high school reputation while a Deacon, was on a special "laundry" plan all his own. Walker told him early on to take his meals at one of two downtown eateries where he could just sign Walker's name to the check. He was also promised three free suits of clothes per year at Ed's, a haberdasher in downtown Wake Forest. And he and other favored players—Jack Lewis was one—sometimes rode to nearby "away" games in Walker's car instead of the team bus. Sometimes the future Mrs. Peahead Walker no. 2., Flonnie Horenthal, rode with them. "Now *that* was kind of weird," said Lewis.[39]

Davis's "royal" treatment sounds like great stuff, but he quickly found it uncomfortable. He didn't like the questions he got from the other players about his eating habits, so he started eating with the rest of the team at the Colonial Club. As for the suits . . .

---

38 Davis, interview with author.
39 Lewis, interview with author.

well, he figured that wasn't going to work as soon as showed up in the first one.

"All I heard was 'where'd you get the suit?' 'Is that suit new?' And a bunch of stuff like that," said Davis. "The rest of the guys, they all paid attention. I didn't want any more of that. I think I got one more suit while I was there and I didn't wear it."[40]

Players remember Walker having a roll of cash in his pocket or in his desk drawer at almost all times. He disbursed money from this "fund" on demand and as he saw fit. Ken Bridges had to beg for his laundry money, which he usually didn't get, and Herb Appenzeller couldn't get his broken teeth fixed (or couldn't get Walker to pay for it). But Walker's favorites, which mostly meant his best players, received free dental work, regular laundry money, and cash for an assortment of living expenses, including fraternity dues, cigarette money, and a few extra dollars, as needed, for a date. (Davis said that when he went out he'd regularly hit up the coach for a couple of bucks.)

Pride Ratterree, whose playing career ended before the growing largesse of the postwar years, said everyone was aware of what everyone else was getting. But he thought Walker's payouts were based more on need than anything else. There's no doubt that Walker, a Depression survivor, coached with a paternal interest. His recruiting spiel to Pat Preston's caretakers at the orphanage—"I'll treat him like a son"—contained some exaggeration designed to sway and impress. But it was also the way Walker, and many others of his generation, lived. Help was provided when help was needed, and nobody asked whether it was within the rules.

"I can remember him giving some guys who were struggling a twenty in the dining hall and thanking them for busing the table," Ratterree said. "Of course, they did no such thing."[41]

Walker's most egregious financial inducement went to the highly touted halfback William "Nub" Smith, who was part of the famous 1948 freshman class. Smith, said several teammates, had use of a slightly used car and . . . a house. Smith shared both with his sister, Rose Fulmer, and a man that Davis and other Deacons always thought was her husband. The living arrangement seems

---

40 Davis, interview with author.
41 Ratterree, interview with author.

odd, but it was actually just a continuation of Smith's high school plan. An Alabama native, Smith was recruited to Fayetteville, NC by town officials who wanted to build a powerhouse high school football team and who had heard about Smith from his former coach, who was a friend of the incoming Fayetteville football mentor. Smith stayed with the family of a prominent Fayetteville businessman for a month or so before his sister and her husband moved to North Carolina to live with him. The idea of recruiting players across long distances to build high-octane high school teams may be thought of as a modern construct, but it's nothing new and Smith's case wasn't unique. Dickie Davis said he had feelers from coaches or other interested parties in Durham and Greensboro following a sensational sophomore year in Wilson. The practice, he said, was fairly common at that time.

Smith was the linchpin to Fayetteville High's outstanding team in 1947. The Bulldogs went undefeated, won the state public school championship, and beat Children's Home in a postseason "bowl game" and a Jacksonville, FL school in a rare interstate matchup. Smith scored twenty-nine touchdowns in two seasons at Fayetteville. In 1947 he scored fifteen of them, including four on kickoff returns. Some might say the actual numbers were sixteen and five. In the state title game against Charlotte Central, Smith ran the second-half kickoff back for a score only to see it called back because of a penalty. On the ensuing redo, Smith caught the kick and once again zipped downfield for a touchdown. "Do you want us to do it again?" Smith supposedly asked the referee as he handed him the ball.[42]

Paying players in college wasn't exactly illegal and didn't bear the stigma it does today. Bringing players of less-than-shining academic ability to a school did draw some attention, however. Walker was known for doing this, and while his work in this area was probably exaggerated—he also recruited many fine students—there's no doubt he'd cut an academic corner or two if the situation demanded it. Ken Bridges, an honor student and future law school grad, as well as a football player in the late 1940s at Wake, said it

---

42 *Fayetteville Observer,* Sept. 25, 1999.

was pretty clear that there "were some who were just there for football and not much else."[43]

Davis, who teetered on the edge of the cirumstance described by Bridges, was more blunt in his assessment: "We had some real dumbasses in school while I was there."[44]

**

As the 1946 fall semester began at Wake Forest, the atmosphere was electric—and not just because of Peahead Walker's football team. A series of stunning events the previous spring and summer had everyone abuzz. The college was—literally—on the move.

At its summer meeting in early August, just before Walker's new football army began to assemble, the Baptist State Convention voted to accept an offer from the Reynolds Foundation, the charitable arm of the family that built the R.J. Reynolds Tobacco Company, to move the college to Winston-Salem, some 100 miles west of Wake Forest. The foundation was offering land (some three hundred acres of a family estate) just north of the bustling twin city (Winston-Salem was a merger of two cities that grew together) plus a fantastic amount of money: the ongoing and seemingly unending flow of cash from a $10 million endowment. That amounted to something like $350,000 per annum, a tidy sum in that day. There was some opposition to the idea, of course. Tradition is tradition, and nobody really likes the idea of being bought, but when all was said and done it was just too much for an institution that had struggled for so long to ignore. The Board of Trustees and the Convention's general board recommended acceptance of the offer, and on August 1, the Convention voted overwhelmingly—twenty to one—to move to Forsyth County.

The motivation for the offer was simple. Reynolds's chief rival in the tobacco world was James B. Duke's American Tobacco Company, which already had its own endowment-funded university (Duke) in the same town where its headquarters were located (Durham). American had funded the college's move from Trinity, NC to Durham near the end of the nineteenth century. The

---

43 Ken Bridges, interview with author.
44 Davis, interview with author.

Reynolds, whose start in the business trailed American by a couple of decades, were eager to get on even footing in the educational world. And with the industry prospering like few others during the 1930s and 1940s, Reynolds had money to burn.

For Peahead Walker, a man used to shoestring operations and a lack of depth, the view in the fall of 1946 was hard to believe. He had, the winter before, just two weeks after the Gator Bowl triumph, been rewarded with a new four-year contract that included a salary bump to $6,000 (half of what Snavely made, just more than a third of Wallace Wade's salary, but still a nice increase and the most he'd ever made) and the right to hire two full-time assistants of his own choosing. And he would soon be in charge of a program in a new city, with new resources and a tremendous amount of potential.

Walker appreciated opportunity, the money, and the sudden operational largesse. But what really made him smile was the horde of talent descending on Wake in the late summer of 1946. For a long-time pauper it was an embarrassment of riches. Players poured in from everywhere. At the height of the assemblage he had something like twenty ends and twelve tailbacks in camp, nearly half of whom were capable of starting. Those were the deepest parts of the team, but the other positions were nearly as well stocked.

That was good news, but even with an expanded staff Walker and company couldn't keep up with everyone. Some wheat needed to be separated from this field of gridiron chaff. So one hot summer day a scrimmage was organized. A very long scrimmage.

Carl Haggard, the "fat" wingback plucked away from Georgia, recalled that "we had these recruits coming in from everywhere and so, at our first scrimmage on a Saturday in August, we had something like 120 players. I don't know how many. They covered the field, were just everywhere.

"Well, we started playing along about 1 PM and went on till, well, I don't remember how long. A long time. It was hot. It was just brutal, the worst thing you can imagine, just play after play after play," said Haggard.

The result was just what Walker hoped. Players began to cut themselves from the roster—right and left. Old-timers all recall a memorable scene: dozens of strapping young men toting suitcases, hitchhiking their way out of Wake Forest throughout the weekend.

"When we got to practice on Monday," said Haggard, "there were only sixty-seven players there, and that's about how many we had all season. It was like that then. Things after the war were real confusing."[45]

Peahead Walker may have run off some useful players, but he still had plenty of guys left, far more than any other point in his career. The real problem now was how to keep everybody happy. This was especially true when it came to the backfield, where the prospects were lined up three and four deep. Brinkley, the All-Southern Conference fullback, was being pushed hard by ex-UNC star Clay Crooms and twenty-five-year-old "freshman" Anthony DiTomo, a bruising 220-pounder from Vineland, NJ. Nick Sacrinty, newly married and having decided to postpone medical school for another year of undergraduate study and gridiron work, was back at tailback. But could he beat out the sensational Red Cochran, star of the 1942 victory over Duke, now a grizzled vet? Might Tom Fetzer, who showed great promise on the 1944 team before the Navy called, best them both? Haggard was in an eight-man group at wingback that also included Nick Sacrinty's brother Bo along with a promising ex-paratrooper named Harry Dowda. Dowda, twenty-one, possessed extensive military ball experience but was classified as a freshman. Nick Ognovich was back at blocking back, but so was twenty-six-year-old Ray Manieri, a prewar Walker favorite from way back in 1941.

***

The relatively advanced age of some team members—twenty-three players were twenty-three or older—plus the infusion of the now worldly vets created some interesting team dynamics. Freshmen tackles Gene Hitchcock and Tom "Hogjaw" Palmer were nine years younger than Manieri. The chain-smoking servicemen,

---

45 Carl Haggard, interview with author.

some of whom had seen extensive combat experience,[46] were not much impressed by threats from screaming coaches. Peahead Walker may have been a practice field terror, but how scary was that, really, to a guy who'd stormed Pacific beaches or faced down Nazi Stormtroopers?

"You know, after the war, football practice, while it was still very demanding, just didn't seem so tough," said Ed Hoey. "You'd have these veteran guys, standing around smoking cigarettes, and then some guy starts hollering about hustle and 'get your butt going' and all. It just didn't make much of an impression."[47]

Walker, figuring his club would be pretty good, lined up a difficult schedule, highlighted by another road game against Tennessee. The Deacons opened with two big-city road games at Boston College and against Georgetown in Washington, DC.

Boston College, resuming serious football after fielding informal teams during the war, was a tough club loaded with future pros like Art Donovan, Ernie Stautner, Art Spinney, and Butch Songin. But early in their first season back, they were not well organized. Wake took advantage—grinding out a 12–6 victory before a crowd of almost 40,000 at old Braves Field.

---

46 DiTomo was a veteran of Okinawa and Saipan, Cochran flew the perilous "Hump" routes in the China-Burma-India theater, Bob Leonetti and Dowda (a paratrooper with the famed 101st Airborne) were in the thick of the European campaign, etc.

47 Smoking, anathema of course to athletes today, was not encouraged by Walker and company, but it wasn't discouraged either. On-campus cigarette giveaways were still a regular event—for all students, not just athletes—and many players smoked. Walker, a chain smoker himself whose ability to dangle an ash-laden butt on his lip was legendary, had very few rules. None of the players remember anything being said about smoking, although Pride Ratterree recalled that fear of Walker's wrath led to some self-enforcement. "He didn't need rules because players were so worried about what he might do that they didn't so some things just in case he didn't want 'em to do that," said Ratterree. "Smoking was one of those. Most of the guys didn't smoke around him, even though he smoked around us all the time." Herb Appenzeller said that Brinkley, as fine a physical specimen as Wake had during the war years, was a regular smoker but that he usually quit smoking during the season as kind of a concession. Others observed a special smoking regimen as well. Many only smoked only on off days, like Sunday. Source: From various interviews with the author.

Cochran set up the clinching touchdown with a sixty-eight-yard punt return in the fourth quarter but nearly scuttled Wake's first score with some addled play calling, possibly because of a concussion, or concussion-like event. Wake recovered a fumble on the opening kickoff and was driving for a score when Cochran ordered up a trap play for Brinkley. It was a poor call near the goal line because the defenders played differently in that part of the field, diving to the ground to avoid being blocked out of position. That tactic all but eliminated the effectiveness of a trap block, which is designed to take advantage of a defensive lineman charging up field. It also created penetration problems at the spot from whence the trapper came.

Dewey Hobbs called Cochran on the error:

I said, "Red, that's a trap play. They'll be coming across on hands and knees." He said, "Oh hell I forgot," but he'd been hit and was bleeding from the nose and maybe a little confused. And so on the next play he called a trap again. I said something again, and he said, "Shut up—I'm captain of this team. I'll kick you out." Brinkley scored [on the trap play] anyway, but he had to run over a defensive player and a blocker, too.[48]

Hobbs went to Walker after the game and told him what had happened. The coach didn't say much, but the next week, before the Georgetown game, Walker told the team prior to the coin toss that "there's a fellow on the other side of field with a frock on [Georgetown, a Catholic school, always brought a priest to the game] and considering that, this might be a good night for the Reverend [Hobbs's nickname] to be one of our captains. Now, Dewey, you know the coin has two sides, a head and a tail. Just pick the one you think is best." Then, Walker added, "For the rest of season I'm making Dewey the line's quarterback, and if you got anything you want to say to the tailback, you tell Dewey and he'll take care of it."

Said Hobbs: "He was pretty smooth dealing with problems like that."[49]

---

48 Hobbs, interview with author.
49 Ibid.

Led by their new captain/minister in training, Wake whipped Georgetown 19–6. The Hoyas lost six fumbles and three interceptions. Given that, a dynamic offense might have produced a rout, but Walker played it close to the vest.

Walker uncorked the passing game in the Deacs' home opener, paving the way to a 19–7 victory over Clemson. Sacrinty hit freshman phenom John O'Quinn of Asheboro, NC with a fifty-seven-yard touchdown pass less than three minutes into the game. Then Red Cochran connected on four passes in a long drive that produced Wake's second score and a 13–7 lead. Rain dominated the second half. Wake scored once more when Croom pounced on a fumble at the Clemson five. Croom, staying on with the offense, scored the touchdown on two running plays.

Wake was 3–0 even though Walker was still feeling out his team (and even adding players—tackle Ulysses Cornogg arrived just before the season opener). The Deacons did pass for 155 yards against Clemson but for the most part had played good old-fashioned Walker football—the "Walker power system" North Carolina sportswriters called it—in getting off to their fast start. The Deacons ran the ball with authority, stoned the opposition with a stout defense, and made off with three victories. Although the squad wasn't firing on all cylinders yet, especially not on offense, things were shaping up nicely for the October 26 trip to Tennessee, which Walker had scheduled strategically. The Deacons would be catching Tennessee the week after its big homecoming game against Alabama, just ahead of a high-profile intersectional contest with North Carolina and its new tailback phenom Charlie Justice—a "trap game" for Tennessee in modern parlance.

It was a good plan, but the would-be trapper wound up getting trapped himself. With his squad confident after a 3–0 start and doubtless looking ahead to Tennessee, Wake stumbled in its own homecoming contest against NC State. An ongoing case of fumbleitis—the Deacons coughed it up four times the week before against Clemson despite pulling out the win—did them in against the Wolfpack. Wake lost three fumbles in the game and had four passes intercepted. Two of the interceptions came in the desperate final minutes of the 14–6 Wolfpack win and could be partially discounted. But the fumbles were all deep in State territory and cost Wake dearly.

Down 7–6 at the half after State blocked an extra point, Wake pounded the Pack, driving inside the ten. But Brinkley fumbled at the six. A few minutes later, after forcing a State punt, Wake was closing in again when Croom, now handling the fullback duties (fumblers often found themselves benched by Walker), fumbled one himself.

The seven turnovers were more than Wake could overcome against a pretty good State team that already had a win over Duke under its belt and a ten-foot-tall good luck charm on the sideline. The latter was a faux robot wolf, constructed by some aspiring engineers and manned from inside by a student by the name of Ira Helms via a series of ropes and pulleys. The Wolfbot was part of a student protest against an administration push to change the school's athletic nickname from the Wolfpack to something else. The name bothered some because it called to mind the Nazi U-Boat groups during the recently concluded war. Just how the robot wolf fit into the protest isn't clear, but the contraption was a smash hit with the capacity crowd at Groves Stadium. Even the Deacon students howled. Less enthused was Helms, the monster's operator, who nearly passed out while working inside the robot's steamy interior. The Wolfbot's young engineers neglected to proper ventilate their creation.

The loss to State was a real downer, especially for student sports columnist and hard-charging fullback Rock Brinkley, whose "Covering the Field" column the week after the game was essentially a mea culpa. Brinkley reported he had "played the game over a million times in my head," and his only conclusion was that "Brinkley" (referring to himself in the third person) was a negative force on the two biggest plays of the night. One was the critical third-quarter fumble. The other was a missed assignment on the extra point following Wake's lone touchdown. If Brinkley had stepped to the correct spot and blocked State's Paul Gibson, Bo Sacrinty's kick might have been good and the game would have been tied. As it was, the mistake "put pressure on the Deacons throughout the game," wrote Brinkley.[50]

Brinkley's already considerable distress was compounded during film review on Wednesday night following the game. Assistant Coach Bobby Kellogg, running the projector during the team's film study, showed the blocked kick over and over again. More importantly, he showed Brinkley apparently snapping his finger after the play, a seeming admission of guilt that carried a casual, lackluster feel. About the fourth or fifth time the film was run, Kellogg said something like, "Well, damn. We keep running the same damn play and Brinkley misses his block every time." Brinkley leaped up at that point and shouted at Kellogg. He may have threatened him physically. Walker told his star fullback to sit down, but Brinkley didn't listen . . . or maybe didn't hear. Brinkley was a 4-Fer because of a perforated ear drum and teammates on hand that night speculated he missed Walker's command. Whatever the case, Walker threw Brinkley out of the meeting and suspended him for the upcoming Tennessee game. The team boarded the train and left for Tennessee without Brinkley or Dewey Hobbs, who had separated his shoulder against State.

Hobbs said Brinkley took the suspension badly and began to drink. He was so soused by Friday that he had to be rousted from his bed by Walton Kitchin, the former Wake player and son of the president . . . and, on this day, secret emissary from Peahead Walker. Kitchin told Brinkley to get his stuff—he was flying him to Knoxville in his private plane for the Tennessee game. Brinkley arrived just as the team was going on to the field to start the game. Miraculously, his uniform was waiting for him in the locker room. He got dressed and wound up playing a key role in one of the biggest victories of Peahead Walker's career.

Tennessee, with General Bob Neyland back in command, was rounding back into its prewar form as a regional and national power. The Vols had just polished off Alabama's defending Rose Bowl champs 12-0 and, heading to the encounter with Wake, were ranked fourth in the nation by the various polls and rating services then in place. The Deacons were confident all the same. They'd

---

50 *Old Gold & Black*, Oct. 25, 1946.

played Tennessee tight the year before (losing 7–6), and while this wasn't the same team—only four Tennessee players from 1945 played in the 1946 game—Wake wasn't overawed by the orange and white.[51] Tennessee was under no illusions, or shouldn't have been, as to the quality of its opponent. Scout Ike Frost had seen Wake twice and warned the Volunteers that the Deacs were one of the best in the nation. Whether the message would sink in with a bunch of twenty-year-olds who'd just beaten Alabama was another question.

Wake served early notice to the 25,000 on hand at Shields-Watkins Stadium that it was not fooling around, blunting an early Tennessee drive thanks to a fourth-down sack by Hobbs's replacement Bernie Hanula and then driving sixty-six yards for a touchdown in just eight plays. Two of the six passes Nick Sacrinty completed on the day (Cochran was injured and played only three plays in the contest) did most of the damage, the real killer being a thirty-five-yard toss to Burnie Capps that carried Wake to the Tennessee four. Neyland, disgusted by the reversal in momentum, rushed a whole new team onto the field at that point, but it was too late. Crooms, in for the semi-suspended Brinkley, pounded it over in two tries from there, giving Wake a 6–0 lead.

Tennessee got the score right back when George Kelly picked off a Sacrinty pass and ran it back to the Deacon twenty-six. On the very next play Bob Lund hit backup end Jim Powell for a touchdown and the game was tied. With a little wind back in its sails, Tennessee nearly took the lead near the end of the half, rushing downfield behind the passing of freshman J.B. Proctor. But Sacrinty's diving tackle stopped Orvis Milner at the Wake ten on the end of a twenty-three-yard play as the clock wound down to the end of the second quarter. The halftime gun sounded with the Vols rushing to line up to run another play.

At the half, Walker found Brinkley, who hadn't been in yet, and asked him if he was ready.

"Try me," Rock said.

Walker did.

---

51 Tennessee benefited from war returnees and the free transfer rule just like Wake and others. Among the Volunteer starters in 1946 was fullback George Baltisaris, an ex-Duke player.

Following a rare kicking game blunder by Tennessee—tailback/punter Walt Slater sliced a punt off his foot for just four yards, giving Wake the ball at the Vols' thirty-four—Walker sent Brinkley in and gave Sacrinty instructions to call Rock's number.[52] He called Harry Dowda's first, softening up Tennessee with a little wingback reverse action. But after that it was Brinkley on five straight blasts up the middle. The plays were all the same. Brinkley would run off right tackle, and O'Quinn, Wake's right end, would block down hard on Charley Mitchell, Tennessee's top linebacker. Brinkley and the Wake offense bulldozed their way to the twenty before Tennessee's defense tightened. With the defensive backs creeping up in support, Tennessee slowed Brinkley down, setting up a pivotal fourth-down play from the Volunteer fourteen. As the ball was snapped, Brinkley faked taking it from the center, who had actually passed it to Sacrinty, who was lined up to Brinkley's left. Brinkley plowed into the line, carrying out the fake, while Sacrinty dropped back and lofted a perfect pass to O'Quinn, who had faked his by-now-monotonous block on the linebacker and then run to the end zone. With Tennessee crowding the line to stop Brinkley and cut down on O'Quinn's blocking angle, O'Quinn was wide open—newspaper accounts varyingly credited him with having five or ten yards of open space—and hauled in the pass easily for the go-ahead score. Bo Sacrinty's extra point made it 13-6.

Three plays after the kickoff, Tennessee violated another Neyland maxim when George Balitsaris fumbled at the Volunteer thirty-four. Wake's Ed Bradley recovered. Throwing another wrinkle at the Vols, Walker had Bo Sacrinty run a reverse from the right wingback spot—the right-handed Deacs usually went the other way—and he romped thirty-one yards to the Tennessee three. It was back to Brinkley from there. He pounded inside the one on first down and then bulled over for the score on second.

That was enough. The defense, which held Tennessee to just eighty-six rushing yards, continued to dominate. Walker's men

---

52 The punting error was notable because of Neyland's famed emphasis on fundamental football. To hear some modern coaches tell it, Neyland had all but invented the kicking game.

ran out the clock, leaning heavily on the inside thrusts of Brinkley, who carried eighteen times—all, of course, in the second half.

Wake's players hoisted Walker on their shoulders in the locker room where he (and they) posed for pictures. Walker told reporters his line deserved most of the credit for the win. He feared beforehand that Huffman and the Tennessee front might cut his boys to pieces but said afterward that "our line decided it didn't want to be eaten up."[53]

Walker was magnanimous in victory—at least in public. He took a slightly different tack later. In a purported wire to his buddy Herman Hickman, the ex-Tennessee star (and current Army assistant coach), Walker crowed, "I just captured me a General."

The victory made the Deacons and their coach the talk of the nation, or at least that part with a serious interest in college football. Walkerisms were printed in papers up and down the East Coast, the *New York Times Sunday Magazine* listed him in a feature on the nation's best coaches, and he was heard nationwide on United Press International's "Coach of the Week" radio broadcast. On air, Walker allowed that the victory was the biggest of his career and that Wake was pretty good.

Others agreed. *Knoxville Journal* sportswriter Ed Harris noted the following postmortem: "Last Saturday we believed Tennessee had the greatest football team in the world. Today we believe the same of Wake Forest."[54]

Wake's big victory vaulted to the Deacons into the national rankings. They debuted at number twelve. After returning to Tennessee the following Friday to thump Chattanooga 34–12, they dropped one place to thirteenth.

The apparent slight didn't bother Deacon fans, who were just happy to be riding such a wave and who, if they had been paying attention to football in general, were used to the vagaries of the polls, as silly then as they are now. What was more important was an impending showdown with arch-nemesis Duke. The Blue Devils, in Wallace Wade's first year back from artillery duty, had lost four of the first six coming into the Wake game. Wade hadn't matched Walker's success in pulling the prewar Devils back into

---

53 *Knoxville News Sentinel*, Oct. 27, 1946.
54 *Knoxville Journal*, Oct. 28, 1946.

the fold—just three such men were on the Duke roster—and was fielding what he considered to be a "freshman team," albeit with many freshmen who were in their early- to mid-twenties.

The moaning coming from Durham was music to most Deacon ears, but the head man of the Wake camp heard in it a siren song: would a shipful of overconfident Deacons be lured to their doom in Durham? On the eve of the game, Walker noted that "Duke still has the players and they're going to take all these defeats out on somebody this year."[55]

The Blue Devils took it out on Wake as it turned out. With a promising new defensive guard named Al DeRogatis wreaking havoc in the Wake Forest backfield, Duke blanked the Deacs 13-0. It was a very near thing. Duke needed to block a Sacrinty punt late in the game to set up a short drive for the clinching score. Sacrinty was doing the punting after Walker had made a gamble of sorts and started the battered Cochran at tailback. Red had injured his leg against Clemson and then suffered a separated shoulder during his brief appearance against Tennessee. Cochran earned Walker's undying love and admiration in the game against the Vols. On one of the handful of downs he played that day he launched a sixty-yard punt from his own end zone. That was always a useful contribution, but what really caught Walker's eye was the fact that Cochran's big boot came one play after his shoulder popped out of joint. For a tough guy like Walker, there was little that impressed more than playing hurt.

And the opposite, too.

Walker had no use of malingerers. His disgust with injuries and the whining is reflected in the famous "you're a doc, make him breathe" story (see introduction). The anecdote is humorous and was employed by Walker and others on the banquet circuit for years, but it's clear that malingering was no joke to Walker. No small part of his coaching life was spent coaxing and badgering the

---

[55] *Greensboro Daily News*, Nov. 5, 1946.

sick and lame back into the lineup, and kicking the oft-injured off his teams.[56]

Walker's dislike of injury and illness was intense, but not necessarily uncommon. The hardscrabble football days of the 1910s, and 20s produced a generation of hard-boiled coaches with similar attitudes.

Bear Bryant, Walker's long-time friend, stayed in against Tennessee despite a broken leg (but only after a Crimson Tide assistant coach shamed into the act, Bryant wrote later in his life). Adam Walsh, the center on Rockne's famed "Four Horsemen" team at Notre Dame in the early 1920s, made every snap without a hitch in a game against Army despite *two* broken hands. And Alabama star W.T. "Bully" Vandegraff suffered a severe cut to his ear—the bottom lobe was nearly severed from the rest—in a 1913 game. Feeling the ear and realizing it was hanging down in full view beneath his helmet's ear flap, Vandegraff purportedly ripped it the rest of the way off so that officials wouldn't see it and remove him from the game.[57] The list goes on and on and even included Peahead Walker himself, who played against Auburn and several other teams during his junior year at Howard—and played well— despite a broken nose. Apparently he learned to make himself breathe.

Walker's upbringing was certainly part of his disgust with malingering, but the bigger part may have been the sheer inconvenience it caused. Rarely could Walker's teams afford to have a good man down, and if he could just get a boy out of bed and moving, well, he could probably have him playing, too. Hence, Red Cochran, two weeks removed from a separated shoulder, got the start against Duke. Blocking him for that day was Dewey Hobbs, back at right tackle, just three weeks after a more severely

---

[56] Murray Greason Jr., son of Peahead's long-time assistant and a regular visitor to Deacon practices as a child, says he has a vague memory of the actual incident behind the "breathe" tale, but admits he may be remembering the story as much as the event. Herman Hickman, who chronicled many stories about his good friend Peahead in his memoir/story collection *The Herman Hickman Reader*, places the event during Walker's high school coaching days.

[57] Danzig, A., *Oh, How They Played the Game: The Early Days of Football and the Heroes Who Made It Great.* 1971. London: Macmillan.

separated shoulder suffered against NC State. According to Hobbs, the limb dislocated so badly from the joint that the top of his arm bone hung down beside his rib cage.

He missed the Deacons' great upset of Tennessee as well as the following game at Chattanooga, but that was all Walker would allow. Before the big game against Duke, he sent Hobbs to see (ironically) a Duke Hospital doctor who rigged up a canvas-and-chain undergarment—kind of straightjacket with a few extra adornments and no wrap-around arms. In theory, the device prevented Hobbs from lifting his shoulder past horizontal.

"I put it on and there wasn't too much pain so I played," says Hobbs. "The chains and what not all broke during the game though, meaning I could move [my shoulder] any which way. But it turned out all right I guess. I didn't hurt it again, and I wasn't crippled for life."[58]

Going to such lengths was no surprise to Hobbs. He'd been clued in to how things would be early in his career at Wake. At practice during his freshman year, Hobbs knocked out a tooth during practice. It sheared off right at the gum line. That didn't seem too bad until Hobbs opened his mouth to suck in a breath of air.

"Then the cold air hit [the nerve] and I said to myself, 'Well, I'd better not do that again," said Hobbs. "Anyway, I went over to coach and said, 'Coach, ah knocked out mah toof. Wha' do you wa' me to do?' [Walker] spit into his hands, looked at his watch, and said, 'Son, we've got thirty more minutes of practice. What do I want you to do? I want you to get back in there and block."[59]

Carl Haggard received essentially the same message during his first season at Wake (1946). A wingback, Haggard was trying to finish off a block in practice when hard-hitting senior Rock Brinkley slammed his shoulder pad, full speed, into Haggard's face.[60] Haggard never saw it coming and took a real blow. Two teeth were knocked out and his nose was broken. Sixty-some years later,

---

58 Hobbs, interview with author.
59 Ibid.
60 Ironically, it was Brinkley who talked Haggard, a fellow Norfolk native, into attending Wake.

there was still evidence of the hit on Haggard's face and nose, which slants slightly to the left.

"I was lying there, bleeding and all, and the trainer came up to check me out and help me, and next thing I knew, there was Peahead over me, shaking his head," said Haggard. "Aw, shit. Get him off the goddamn field," Haggard remembers Walker saying, "he can't help us anymore today."[61]

Sometime after his broken tooth, but before his separated shoulder, Hobbs developed a set of boils and sores on his arms. Black dye from the team's brand-new jerseys got into the wounds and an infection developed. It was so bad, in fact, that Hobbs had to go to the infirmary with a fever and other symptoms. Walker came to visit him the first night, which seemed like a touching gesture—for a minute or two. Hobbs remembers the coach consoling him and then saying, "You know, Hobbs, you got to keep your legs in shape. There's a back door on this here infirmary. When it gets about three o'clock [the time practice started] slip out, tell them you'll be back, and come down here and join us [the practice field was in sight of the rear of the infirmary, several hundred yards away]. You can do a few things to stay in shape."

"I did it," said Hobbs. "I came down and ran, even got in on a few plays. And I played the next week with rubber pads on my elbows to pad the sores, but during the game the boils all burst."[62]

In the fall of 1945, as Walker and company were preparing to leave for a game against North Carolina, Walker asked "Daddy" Behm, the team's legendary, long-term manager, if everyone was present and accounted for. "Nope," said Behm, who could rival the selectively taciturn Walker for vocal economy.

"Well, who's not here?" said Walker.

"Garrison," said Behm.

"Where is he?"

"Infirmary," said Behm.

"Well," said Walker, "go get him. Tell him to put his goddamn clothes on and get over here in ten minutes. He's got a football game to play."[63]

---

[61] Haggard, interview with author.
[62] Hobbs, interview with author.
[63] Hobbs, Ratterree, interviews with author.

Pride Ratterree, who played guard on that team, recalled that when the player in question, a strapping tackle named Buck Garrison, arrived a few minutes later, he looked terrible:

I mean, he had been in the infirmary with a 103 temperature and some kind of infection or something most of the week. But he went with us over to the game and got dressed and all. He was sitting next to me in the locker room, shivering and sweating and all, and Coach Walker came over and said, real nice and friendly like, 'Now Buck my boy ... how ya' doin,' Buck? Feeling a little better? Now, Buck, I want you to just try the kickoff and see how it goes. Maybe you'll get out there and feel better.' He played sixty minutes of course. I was picking him up and all but carrying him back to the huddles at the end. But he got to feeling okay afterwards. Playing actually seemed to do him some good.[64]

Although Walker-era players generally agree that the size and speed of the modern game make it more violent, facemask- and mouthguard-free football was no picnic.[65] Nearly every player who played any appreciable amount of time suffered one or more dental and/or facial injuries during their careers. Some were worse than others. Hobbs was hit so hard in the Miami game his sophomore year that his teeth were knocked through his cheek, creating a bloody mess that left his fellow Deacons gawking in wonder as they huddled over the stricken Hobbs on the field. As Hobbs recalled,

I could hear [teammate] Dave Harris and some others talking, but I couldn't say anything. I must have been a mess 'cause they were saying, 'Oh my God, he's bleeding out of his eyes. . . . No, wait, it's his nose. . . . No, it's his mouth!' They got me off the field and our team doctor, an Army Air Force guy [this game was played while World War II was in full swing, so military personnel were

---

64 Ratterree, interview with author.
65 The molded plastic teeth protectors that are now a requirement at all levels of football—a player can incur a penalty if he doesn't have his mouth guard in while a play is live—weren't introduced into football and other sports until the early 1970s. "Mouthguard?" said Dewey Hobbs. "We couldn't even spell it." Hobbs, interview with author.

everywhere], stitched me up right there on the sideline like we were in a field hospital. I remember this because [teammate] Tom Fetzer caught a punt and made a long return and the doc stood up to watch and I had to come with him because he was still holding onto the needle and thread."[66]

The game was played on a Friday. The next Monday at practice, Hobbs's face was badly swollen and Walker was in a conciliatory mood: he let Hobbs sit out the majority of the drills. This was partly out of compassion but mostly because Hobbs didn't have a helmet. Walker had sent it off to "the prison bar company" to have it fitted for a facemask. It came back in time for the next game, giving Hobbs's jaw minimal new protection via one vertical and one horizontal iron bar, each a half inch or so in diameter. Both were crudely riveted to the sides and forehead of the helmet and were welded together where the bars met. Walker gave Hobbs the headgear when Hobbs graduated and he kept it all his life. Somewhat weathered, it looked like a piece of used medieval battle armor.[67]

Hobbs recalls being the only one on the team with a facemask, but teammate Dave Harris recalls earning one in that very same game against Miami. He lost all four of his front teeth and had the orbital bone below his eye smashed all on the same hit, a high-speed collision while covering a punt.[68] Harris says the trainer came out on the field to take a look, followed soon after by an anxious Walker who didn't want to lose his best end and who offered advice that lends credence to the more famous "make him

---

66 Hobbs, interview with author.
67 Hobbs's helmet and other artifacts from his playing days were eventually donated to the Wake Forest Birthplace Museum, shortly before Hobbs' death.
68 Wake won the Miami game 27–0 but suffered a real physical beating from a Hurricane team that Deacon players said had a reputation for brutal, illegal play. Hobbs recalls that he and Harris looked so bad that a Miami photographer had them pose together on the sidelines and took a "battle casualty" photo. Harris's wife, Mary Arden, remembers almost fainting when she saw her boyfriend and husband-to-be get off the train after the trip. "He looked like he'd been to war," she said.

breathe" tale. Peering at Harris, Walker growled, "Aw, hell. It ain't gonna kill you. Let's go."[69]

Harris finished the game. He wound up getting a facemask similar to Hobbs's soon after but quickly ditched it after Walker made fun of the contraption.

Facemasks didn't catch on in football until the 1950s and weren't mandatory until 1958, by which point it could be made of plastic and hence not nearly the burden that Hobbs's prison bar get-up was. Players who played for Walker in Canada in the 1950s said he still wasn't much of a fan of the device. In this regard he reflects the general attitude of old-line coaches who were always slow to adopt equipment advances. Helmets, for instance, weren't a requirement until 1939, although it's hard to find photos or other records after the 1920s where a player's head is uncovered. Old-timers weren't easily persuaded, however. In a 1912 instructional manual, written when some players wore helmets and some did not, legendary coach Glenn "Pop" Warner graciously allowed that while he didn't see much benefit in headgear, he wouldn't interfere with any player who wanted to wear it.[70]

Walker wasn't against all technical breakthroughs, however. Painkillers were just fine. Ratterree remembered that when fullback Russ Perry broke a collarbone one week Peahead told equipment manager Daddy Behm to get a doctor, tape him up, and get him a shot. And he did. He played the rest of the game pumped full of drugs and with a broken collarbone.

If Walker's attitude seems harsh today, it was somewhat less in the context of his times. The young men who excelled while playing for Walker quickly learned not to report injuries unless serious and proven.

"Walker just didn't *believe* in getting hurt," recalls Ratterree. "The only thing you reported was having your teeth knocked out or something. And the only important thing there was to kind of document it, you know, so that the next week you could get the money from him to have it fixed."

Ratterree says he first heard about "Peahead's dental plan" when Garrison, the sickly tackle, bragged about his new—and

---

[69] Harris, interview with author.
[70] Warner, G.S., A Course in Football for Players and Coaches. 1912.

free—teeth one night at dinner. "So I figured I'd go try [Peahead] out on that and went to see him. 'Coach, can I get my teeth cleaned and fixed up?' I said. He growled back at me, 'Ratt-er-ree, d'jou damage 'em playing football?' 'No sir,' I said, 'But I heard you did it for Garrison.' 'Well,' he said, 'go ahead and do it and put it on my bill.' I never did though."[71]

Walker's willingness to pay for Ratterree's teeth likely reflected some value judgment, a sort of return-on-investment calculation. Ratterree was a tough, dependable lineman who seldom came off the field. Herb Appenzeller, the diminutive tailback with the spaghetti arm, had a different reception when he went to see Walker about a legitimate dental expense.

"I broke a tooth in practice," said Appenzeller. "I went to Peahead to see if he'd pay for the dental work. He said, 'App-en-zeller, you may help me here and there but you'll never help me beat Carolina [meaning, in other words, that he wasn't worth the cost]."[72]

As it turned out, Walker was wrong about Appenzeller, a fine student who went on to serve for decades as Athletic Director at Guilford College in Greensboro. His contribution to the Deacon war effort never amounted to much on the field, but after finishing at Wake, Appenzeller helped tutor some of Walker's less academically gifted recruits in the years right after World War II. Some of those players did, in fact, help Walker beat North Carolina, so Appenzeller always figured he should've received some credit for that feat. "But of course I never told him that," Appenzeller said.[73]

Although plenty of Christians, Deacons, and Alouettes were broken up in various ways under Walker's command, he managed to avoid the crippling or mortal blow that can taint a coach forever. No one died or became a cripple on his watch. But on at least one occasion he did run into a controversy connected to a football injury. It happened in 1946 when backup Malcolm "Mack" Grandy suffered a serious knee injury in Wake's game at Chattanooga College. Perhaps because they really didn't take the injury seriously enough, and perhaps because it was just difficult to find

---

[71] Ratterree, interview with author.
[72] Appenzeller, interview with author.
[73] Ibid.

another solution, Walker and team doctor George W. Paschal put Gandy through quite an ordeal. He was left in his room after the game for several hours while the team completed a scheduled postgame buffet at the same hotel and then was given what Gandy later claimed to be minimal pain relief for the long train ride home to Wake Forest.

When Gandy finally got home, Paschal, the son of a longtime Wake Forest professor, operated on Grandy's knee. The surgery, and a follow-up operation, did not go well. Grandy's sports career (he was also a talented baseball player) was done, and he was left with what he portrayed as a lifelong disability.[74]

***

Wake's difficult 1946 schedule didn't ease after the loss to Duke. Next up was a game with North Carolina in Chapel Hill, where momentum was building with Carl Snavely's Tar Heels. Snavely had assembled a superb collection of talent, including ends Art Weiner and Ken Powell, tackle Lee Szafaryn, fullback Walt Pupa . . . and, of course, Charlie Justice.

The officious Snavely had done his best to downplay Justice's messiah-like arrival on campus. Asked about the freshman's impact once Justice announced he was coming to Carolina, Snavely deadpanned, "I hope he comes out for football."

He did. And once the ball was in his hands there was no way to hide him. Justice was an absolute sensation, that rarest of rarities, a massively hyped player who actually lived up to all the talk. The pile of statistics that clutter Choo Choo's collegiate resume probably don't do him . . . well, justice. One example gives the general tenor, however: he scored a touchdown every thirteen times he touched the ball. This would be a remarkable feat in any

---

[74] Grandy went on to be a lawyer, and while learning that trade, filed suit against Walker and Paschal in Wake County court in May 1949. He alleged that the two men had not offered proper care on the night of, or in the days following, the injury. The meat of the suit, however, was mostly a malpractice case that accused Paschal of botching the operation. But Walker was cited for delaying treatment and possibly aggravating the situation. A post-World War II judge wasn't moved. Grandy's case was dismissed in June 1951, and Grandy was ordered to pay the court costs. His appeal was also denied.

era, but in a day when teams regularly punted the ball away on first down deep in their own territory and when four touchdowns by a team was considered an offensive explosion, Justice's quick-strike abilities were astonishing. It is no wonder that a new Tar Heel cheer was born—"All the way Choo Choo, all the way" they'd chant as the opposition prepared to punt or kick off—or that his exploits spawned a song. Classmate Orville Campbell's corny lyrics, pushed along by a peppy swing band tune, turned "All the Way Choo Choo" into a brief hit in the late 1940s. Strained though they may be, Campbell's words do get at the heart of Justice's unique football skills. A 170-pounder (that was his official weight—he may not have been that heavy), Justice was not an overpowering runner. He wasn't the fastest player on the field either (though he was fast enough). But he possessed an uncanny ability to cut and turn, to stop and start, that made tackling him in the open field a complicated process. On film, his long runs have the feel of choreography. Surely opposing tacklers could not miss Justice, collide with one another, or fall down at just the right time without practice. And, yet, they regularly do it more than once on a single play.

Justice's trademark was reversing his field. Stymied at the right sideline, he'd feint, dodge, and cut until he found room to circle around to the left. Once there, it was not uncommon for him to repeat the whole process over again.[75]

Several Wake Forest players recall Walker offering a bounty on Justice on the opening kickoff of a Wake-UNC game, possibly the 1946 affair. It was $5 for the man who tackled him and $10 if

---

75 The final stanza of "All the Way..." includes this bit:

> A football field is a hundred yards long,
> Check these figures, they ain't wrong;
> He took the ball, poured on the coal,
> Ran a thousand yards from goal to goal.

he really laid him out.⁷⁶ Ed Bradley, the Deacons' aggressive end, swore he'd get the kickoff cash, and sure enough, as Justice cut and sped toward the Wake sidelines, Bradley appeared to have an angle on him. But at the last second Justice stopped and reversed field. Bradley, his eyes set on Justice's midsection and Walker's cash, dove . . . but it was too late. He went flying into the Deacon bench, landing at Walker's feet.

"Almost got him, Coach," Bradley said. As he clambered to his feet, ready to resume pursuit of his elusive prey, Walker put his hand on the player's shoulder and said, "Just wait here, boy. I reckon he'll be back this way in a minute or two."⁷⁷

Walker waxed poetic, and romantic, when describing Justice in the real world. He told the *Charlotte Observer*'s Bob Quincy that Justice "reminds you of a beautiful woman. Everybody's reaching out to grab—and it looks like it won't be too difficult. But just when you get your confidence up, you get the slip and are left there standing all alone."⁷⁸ Walker was speaking from experience. He had plenty of experience . . . coaching against Justice.

By the time the Wake-UNC game rolled around, Justice's bona fides were well established, and Carolina was on the way to a Southern Conference title and postseason bowl. The Tar Heels had tied a mediocre Virginia Tech team in their season opener and lost at Tennessee 20–14 the week after Wake beat the Vols. But they were otherwise unbeaten against a tough schedule. The Carolina-Wake game was a big one for both programs, and a football-perfect November day produced a carnival-like atmosphere for the 30,000 or so in attendance at Kenan Stadium. The Carolina fans were in

---

76 Bounties were illegal, of course, if only because they circumvented the subsidization rules set up by the NCAA and Southern Conference. But they seem to have been fairly common nonetheless. Clemson players say Frank Howard always had an opening kickoff bounty, and Walker and others paid for hard hits on certain players as well as for major accomplishments, like blocked punts and fumble recoveries. Sources: various interviews.

77 This story is almost certainly apocryphal. Duke footballer George Clark told the same tale, substituting teammate Lou Allen for Bradley and Duke's Wallace Wade for Walker. Source: Bowling, L., *Wallace Wade: Championship Years at Alabama and Duke*. 2006. Durham, NC: Carolina Academic Press.

78 *The Choo Choo Justice Story*.

fine fettle, with their "Choo-Choo" chants echoing through the pines along with the whoops of "Tarzan" Morris, back from a wartime absence. The Farmville, NC native wowed crowds with his authentic Tarzan yell, which could be heard stadium wide.

Wake's Walker served notice that it was an extra special occasion, too, showing up at a packed Kenan Stadium in a "loud shirt and tie that made a rainbow seem modest and pale."[79] Such outfits were his trademark.

The game, perhaps to Walker's chagrin, quickly turned into a freewheeling affair. Even a first-quarter exchange of punts was electric. Justice, whose best skill might actually have been his punting, launched a sixty-nine-yarder from deep in his own territory. A penalty negated the play, so he hammered out a seventy-one-yard boot on his next try. Wake's Cochran answered with a fifty-nine-yarder, and then Justice answered that with a sixty-two-yard boot.[80]

The next time Carolina got the ball, Justice crossed up the Deacs, faking a punt and running sixty-two yards to the Deacon twenty-five. Two plays after that, Pupa hit Justice with a pass in the left flat. He snared the toss and outraced the Deacon defense to the end zone for the game's first score. Wake answered with a long scoring drive and looked like it would take a 7–6 lead to the locker room at halftime. But Carolina struck with just forty seconds remaining in the half. Pupa faked a handoff to Justice and hit Weiner, running behind Cochran, with a fifty-three-yard touchdown bomb. Wake almost got the score back with a good kickoff return and a Sacrinty pass to Gordon Studer, who ran free in the Carolina secondary. Emulating Justice, Studer bobbed and weaved some forty-six (all downhill) yards to inside the Tar Heel twenty before Billy Myers yanked him down at the ten just as the first half clock expired.

An interception set Carolina up at the Deacon thirty-seven midway through the third, and Pupa used the fake-to-Justice

---

79 *Charlotte Observer*, Nov. 17, 1946.
80 These kicking distances are inflated to some degree because several of them were quick kicks over the defense that did not deploy a deep back to return the kick. Hence, the ball not only flew a great distance in the air but also could roll for significantly more yardage. Still, that's some pretty good kicking.

action again to freeze Wake's defense a second time. On this occasion, the open man downfield was end Bob Cox, who hauled in Pupa's throw for a thirty-seven-yard touchdown and a 19–7 lead.

Wake rallied with some aerial fireworks of their own. Sacrinty, who combined with Cochran to throw for 257 yards against the Tar Heels, dusted off the Statue of Library play but faked the handoff to Studer. Pulling the ball away from the circling back, Sacrinty stepped back and flung it to a wide open Ed Bradley for a forty-six-yard score. That made it 19–14, and the Deacon faithful were whooping it up. But Wake just couldn't stop the Tar Heels. Jim Camp's thirty-yard run on a reverse brought the ball to the Wake twenty, and Justice cruised around left end from there for the clinching score. Cox's extra point made it 26–14, and that was the final. The teams combined for more than 700 yards of offense, a remarkable figure for the time.

Wake closed its season with a 35–0 shellacking of South Carolina on Thanksgiving Day, a sweet finish to a kind of sour season. Sour? Yes. There was the big win over Tennessee, but for the first time since 1938 the Deacons had been swept by their Big Four brethren.

Pondering the scenario many years later, Dewey Hobbs suspected the season was a disappointment for Wake fans.

"Beating Duke, Carolina and State meant a whole lot more than beating some team like Tennessee," said Hobbs. "I'm sure most of our fans would rather have seen us do that than beat Tennessee any old time."

***

Wake's 1946 season was an exemplar of the latter stages of the Walker era—sustained success that raised grand hopes never quite realized. His last five seasons featured a succession of five-, six- or seven-win seasons more notable for what might have been rather than what was.

There was some agony in that, but what Walker had built was no small feat. He had brought Wake Forest College football to an utterly unexpected spot. The Deacons were serious players in both the Southern Conference and the country, and they were doing it on the cheap. Walker was, as Athletic Director Weaver noted on many occasions, the "best coaching bargain in the South."

Could Walker scavenge another bargain basement winner in 1947? Fans wondered. The Deacons' once overcrowded backfield was suddenly thinner than the padding on a Baptist church pew. Gone were fullbacks Brinkley and Croom, both off to semipro football in Charlotte; wingbacks Bo Sacrinty and Gordon Studer; Ray Manieri, the hard-hitting, almost thirty-something blocking back; and, of course, the twin tailback terrors Nick Sacrinty and Red Cochran, who both landed in the NFL, a unique feat for first- and second-teamers at the same position on the same team. Sacrinty was drafted by the powerful Chicago Bears, where he backed up Hall of Famer Sid Luckman in the Bears' T-formation offense. Cochran signed with the Chicago Cardinals, where he starred for three seasons, mostly as a defender and kick returner.

Filling those shoes would not be easy, but Walker had of course been on the recruiting trail. The twenty-nine-man freshman class included twelve backfield candidates, half of them tailbacks. The most promising of these was Bill Gregus, a rare Ohio recruit who'd been voted the Buckeye state's player of the year as senior at Toledo's Waite High School.

One line of thought was that if Walker could find anyone to carry the ball they'd do well behind what figured to be a talented and mammoth Deacon line. Bob "the Box" Leonetti (the name a reference to his squatty stature—the 230-pounder was well under 6'0") was back, as was Ed Royston, center Harry Clark, and the aggressive Bernie Hanula, who'd eclipsed the banged-up Hobbs at tackle late in the 1946 season. But what caught most casual observers' eyes was the sheer size of the Deacons. Walker had twenty-plus players listed at 6'2" or taller and seven linemen (most of them tackles) who weighed 220 or more. Two even tipped the scales at 250, which was considered quite big at the time. Among the whoppers was a strapping freshman from Pennsylvania named Bill George.

This beefy assemblage impressed practice visitors immensely—Peahead Walker less so. During a mid-September press visit, Walker acknowledged the lineman's considerable girth but thought it said more about poor conditioning than anything else: "They're so big and fat that maybe those other teams will have trouble running around them," he said.[81]

Wake started well, at least from a bottom-line point of view. The Deacons beat a mediocre Georgetown team 6–0 in a contest that featured twelve turnovers, eight of which were interceptions, and then was just about that sloppy again on a week two trip to Clemson, where they escaped with a 16–14 victory. Red O'Quinn blocked a Tiger punt out of the end zone for a safety, fullback Tony DiTomo capped the go-ahead drive in the fourth quarter with a short touchdown dive, and Carl Haggard and Tom Fetzer intercepted passes late in the game to stop Clemson drives. Haggard's gem was a redemptive play. Earlier in the game, woozy from the heat and a long stretch of two-way play, Haggard lined up on the wrong side of the field. Clemson threw a pass into the area where he should have been and scored a touchdown. "But I got some smelling salts and got better," said Haggard. "And I got 'em back in the end."[82]

The Clemson win set up an early-season showdown with UNC, which floundered out of the gate despite the return of Justice and lots of other lettermen from the excellent 1946 team. Wake raced out to a 19–0 halftime lead and then sat on the ball for the last two quarters for a surprisingly easy 19–7 victory. Fetzer and the Deacons sliced through the Tar Heel defense by air, completing 14 of 22 passes for 251 yards, and some sharp game planning stifled the Tar Heel attack. Walker and his staff considered which tracks Justice most preferred and did their best to keep them blocked. Although he often wound up running outside (and then all over the field) after he'd cracked the line of scrimmage, Choo Choo's preferred running lane was off tackle. Walker ordered his guards, tackles, and ends on both sides to slant to the outside, shutting down that hole and forcing Justice to the middle. Waiting for him there was Nick Ognovich, Wake's finest tackler and a player, said teammate Haggard, "who would just knock the fool out of you."

Justice wound up with just seven yards rushing on the day. Incredibly, he only carried the ball eight times, which might have

---

[81] *Greensboro Daily News*, Sept. 17, 1947.
[82] Haggard, interview with author.

been a blunder by UNC's Snavely or simply another effect of Walker's game plan. Snavely countered Walker's tactics by using Justice as a decoy to the outside and running other (lesser) backs up the middle. That took the Heels' best weapon out of the game as effectively as the Deacons' defense might have done.[83]

The plan was clever, but timing may have mattered as much as tactics. Carolina eventually recovered from its 0–3 start to win its last seven games, averaging twenty-seven points a game in the process. Although neither Snavely nor anyone else would admit it, off-the-field problems may have distracted the team early in the season. A story in *Pic Magazine* in the summer of 1947 accused Justice of being a professional because he had signed a pro contract several years before. The Southern Conference announced a special meeting of its executive committee shortly before the Wake-Carolina game. Held the week after the contest, the meeting "cleared" Justice to play the rest of the year, but the controversy continued. Evidence uncovered by Southern Conference leaders showed that Justice had, in fact, signed a contract with the Philadelphia Eagles in 1943 while playing for Bainbridge Naval Station. Elmer Layden, the ex-Notre Dame star who was the NFL's commissioner at the time, told Southern Conference officials that he'd voided the document at the time because Justice was in high school and thus too young to be signed. But the news caused a kerfuffle all the same, and for a time there was some question as to whether or not Justice would finish the season.

The now fourteenth-ranked Deacons flattened George Washington 39–7 at Griffith Stadium in the nation's capital to run their record to 4–0, matching the start of the 1944 club. The Deacons were on a roll, which meant, of course, that the Duke game must be right around the corner.

This one was in Wake Forest on homecoming weekend—and it was a dilly. Smith Barrier, the Greensboro sportswriter sometimes prone to hyperbole, called it "the finest game a spectator has witnessed in this state in several seasons."[84]

Peahead Walker's postgame sentiments are unknown but likely less sanguine. Long after the game was over, reporters found

---

83 Ibid.
84 *Greensboro Daily News*, Oct. 27, 1947.

him sitting in the Groves Stadium field house, unable or willing to say a word—the silence the result of another narrow defeat to Wade's Blue Devils.

The pivotal sequence in the nip-and-tuck contest came early in the fourth quarter with the game tied 6–6. When it began, the 25,000 or so at Groves surely must have thought things were pivoting Wake's way. The Deacons' Bud Wedel burst through the Duke line on fourth down to block Fred Folger's punt at the Duke thirty-eight. Wedel grabbed the bouncing pigskin and was on his way to a score when Folger caught him from behind and dropped him at the Blue Devil eight. A short run and offsetting penalties moved the ball to the six. The hard-hitting Gregus—the freshman had quickly become one of Wake's tailback mainstays—ground out two yards to the four, and then fullback George Pryor picked up a couple more. Facing fourth and goal from the two, Walker eschewed a field goal and sent Pryor into the line again. The 200-pounder surged forward but was stopped just inches short of the goal line. Duke was safe for the moment but not out of the woods by any means.

Folger punted out on first down, the textbook call for that situation in that day and age, and Gregus returned it all the way to the thirty-one. Two plays later, however, a Fetzer pass was tipped and intercepted by Ben Williams, who returned it to the twenty-six. Duke couldn't move, but the Blue Devils' sharp kicking game helped flip the field a few minutes later, setting the Blue Devils up at the Deacon forty-five.

The winning score didn't come easily. Folger, scooping a low snap from center, ran for his life and turned a mess into a twenty-yard gain to the twenty-five. He passed for nine yards to the sixteen and then got some help when officials whistled Wake's Jeff Brogden for pass interference at the Deacon four. Wade, perhaps understanding the power of karma, inserted long-time Deacon killer George Clark for Folger at this point and watched him romp around left end for a touchdown.

Less than a minute remained. A pass interference call and a Fetzer-to-Haggard pass brought the ball down to the Duke thirty-seven. But on the next play, Folger snared Fetzer's pass and ran it back deep into Wake territory, sealing the Blue Devils' 13–6 victory.

The effects of the loss carried over to the next week—like a "hangover" noted the *Old Gold & Black*. Wake lost to a good-but-not-great William & Mary team 21–0 in Williamsburg.

The next week, Wake made its now annual pilgrimage to Boston and took one from Boston College that it had no business taking. The Eagles and their powerful T-formation offense ran over the Deacons for 272 rushing yards. But Nick Ognovich and the rest of the Deacon defenders hit the Eagles hard when they finally caught up with them, forcing seven fumbles that stopped drive after drive. Wake sputtered on offense, but Fetzer hit Ed Hoey with a long pass for one score, and after a fumble gave Wake the ball inside the Boston College thirty, Walker pulled some backfield speed out of his hat to get another. Freshman Lou Pollaci, who had played all of one play to that point in the season, went in for an ailing Harry Dowda and ran twenty-six yards for Wake's second touchdown. It would turn out to be the Deacons' longest run from scrimmage of the year. The two touchdowns, plus the two extra points from freshman George, who, to everyone's surprise, was also a pretty fair kicker, was just enough. Wake beat Boston College 14–13.

At 5–2, Wake was hanging on as a possible bowl participant. But the Deacons' record was better than their condition. Injuries—Ognovich, Pryor, and Leonetti all missed significant time—were wearing the Deacs down. The offense just couldn't quite kick into high gear, and, try as he might, Walker never found a way to mesh all his talent.

Bad luck with the weather didn't help either. The pass, with O'Quinn and Dowda on the receiving end, was Wake's best weapon. But the Deacons played two of their last three in miserable conditions that all but eliminated that tactic. The annual rivalry game with NC State was played on a cold and wet afternoon at Riddick Stadium, where the proceedings slowed to a crawl. Two weeks later, the annual Turkey Bowl contest against South Carolina was played on a Charlotte Memorial Stadium gridiron that one witness thought "closely resembled a hog wallow." Wake managed to complete just two of eight passes in a 20–0 loss to State. Against South Carolina, Fetzter completed six—two to his teammates and four to Gamecock defenders. That was all South Carolina needed for a 6–0 victory.

The loss to the Gamecocks left the Deacon brain trust livid. Although it had been a wet fall, no rain had fallen in Charlotte since the previous weekend, and not much had fallen then. Nonetheless, the field was a mess. Managerial greed, or incompetence, seemed to be the culprit. Charlotte officials had been milking Memorial Stadium for all it was worth, opening its gates to high school games (including one memorable contest featuring a future Deacon running back named William "Nub" Smith) and to professional contests featuring the Charlotte Clippers. The grass had disappeared from most parts of the field by the end of October. Cleats had churned the soggy earth throughout the month of November, leaving the Deacons and Gamecocks to do battle in a swamp. Wake athletic director Jim Weaver told the Charlotte Touchdown Club the night after the game that the conditions were deplorable and announced the end of the annual Wake-South Carolina duel in the Queen City. Wake and South Carolina continued their season-ending game into the mid-1950s but returned to Charlotte on just one other occasion.

The Deacons were full of mud-caked excuses, but both State and South Carolina were eminently beatable in 1947 (a rejuvenated North Carolina squad had embarrassed State 41–6 the week before the Wake game, for instance).

The late-season stumble turned into to postseason grumbling from Wake's faithful. And there was some soul searching in the Deacon football office. Maybe it was time to try something new.

What, Peahead Walker thought, about that T-formation offense that was all the rage? How would it look in black and gold?

He and his boys were about to find out.

CHAPTER 8

A STRANGE ENDING

The T-formation rage swept across the country during and after World War II, one of those occasional but highly influential, evolutionary bursts of innovation in the sport.

In some ways it was nothing new. Historians of the game—Peahead Walker among them—recognized some old turned new again in the T, or at least in its most distinguishing feature, the direct handoff between center and quarterback. That had been around a long time.[1] But here it was again, with several new wrinkles, most related to rules changes in the 1930s affecting the size of the ball and restrictions on passing.

The precise origin of the modern T is foggy and controversial. The University of Minnesota excelled with a T-formation offense in the late 1930s. Stanford stunned the West Coast football world in 1940 when it abruptly converted to the T under new coach Clark Shaughnessy, an acknowledged T-formation innovator. And the Chicago Bears stood the professional football world on ear that same year with their world championship T-formation team.[2] As is always the case, success bred imitation. College and pro teams quickly imitated the (mostly) successful T pioneers. Numerous innovations followed, including the I-formation, and split T formations. All presaged modern usage like the triple option and assorted backfield combinations.

---

[1] In fact, it might be one of the game's oldest formations. Some sources claim that Walter Camp, the volunteer Yale coach who is credited with all but inventing the American game, used a center-to-quarterback handoff system as early as 1882. And it appears that Peahead Walker himself took handoffs in that manner for at least part of his collegiate career.

[2] The fight song "Bear Down, Chicago Bears," written by Al Hoffman after the Bears' 73–0 victory over Washington in the 1940 NFL title game, commemorates the formation along with the team with these inspiring lyrics: "We'll never forget the way you thrilled the nation / with your T formation."

The origin may have been a mystery, but the allure of the T was clear for all to see. Teams employing it piled up yards and points in an unprecedented manner, and fans loved the deception it employed and the enhanced opportunity for long runs that it produced. Single-wing and other power offenses, based on massed blocking at the point of attack, occasionally produced long runs as well, but the misdirection of the T made big gainers commonplace, especially early on while defenses were still adjusting.

The T formation was built around its now-you-see-it, now-you-don't ball work on nearly every play. The single wing included some misdirection and some fancy ball handling, especially on the "spinner" series, but it was nothing like the T. Backs, lined up closer to the line than in the old power offenses, darted this way and that at the snap, zipping by the quarterback who handed off or faked with both hands. Run correctly, the T offense forced defenses to react to, and even tackle, two to three different ball carriers on nearly every play. Of course, only one of them had the ball, and because of their position near the line and the ability for all of them to start at the snap, the plays hit the line much faster. Light blocks, known as brush blocks because the blocker merely "brushed" the defensive man, pushing him briefly in one direction or another, were all that was needed to spring a flying back through a hole and downfield on a long run.

Peahead Walker was intrigued by the T for several reasons.

First, his teams had struggled against good T-formation teams. Early East Coast T adopter Boston College had tormented Walker's Deacons for years, and most other games against other T teams didn't bring back pleasant memories either.

Walker also understood the value of a good show on the field. As his Deacon troops readied themselves to head out before a 1949 game, Walker said, "Boys, remember: these people came to see a show. Let's go out and give 'em one."[3] The T helped him do that.

Finally, but perhaps mostly importantly, it looked like a way to beat Duke.

---

3 Dickie Davis, interview with author.

Early in the 1947 season, Missouri Tigers and split-T innovator Don Faurot ruined Duke's homecoming 28–7, embarrassing Wade's normally tough-as-nails defense with 302 rushing yards. So deft and deceptive was the Tigers' ball handling that some press box wags wondered if Faurot had "recruited a band of magicians" to play in his backfield.[4] For a coach who had been bedeviled by Duke for a decade, that may have been all that was needed. He'd run anything if it meant beating Duke.

The timing was also right. Wake would be the first T team in the Big Four in North Carolina, and hard-hitting blocking back Nick Ognovich had graduated. Walker had been pondering a switch to the T for several years apparently but was unwilling to change to an offense that would have effectively taken Ognovich off the field.

"The T-formation ran through my mind week after week [in 1947]," Walker told the press in September 1948, "and then, about the time I figured we should change over, Ognovich would walk by. . . .

"In the single wing, Ognovich is a great little player. He could really block those big men. But if we went to the T formation, where could Nick play? The T has no position for a blocker. . . . Ognovich would be without a job. So we stuck with the single wing."[5]

To prep for installing the modern T at Wake, Walker went to the Cleveland Browns' annual winter seminar; contacted his old stars Nick Sacrinty and Red Cochran, both now playing in T attacks in the pros; brought in Pat Preston, who played tackle on the same Bears team as Sacrinty as a part-time assistant coach; and even enlisted the help of ex-Duke star George McAfee, who played some T ball in the NFL.

And then there were family ties. Walker's brother Archie had recently been installed as head football coach at Mebane High near Wake Forest and had just put in the T. Mickey Walker, Archie's son and Peahead's nephew, said his dad learned the new offense from a sporting goods rep who knew the professor who

---

4 Raleigh News & Observer, Nov. 9, 1947.
5 Greensboro Daily News, Sept. 13, 1948.

helped Faurot develop the split T at Missouri. Uncle Peahead invited himself up to practice to see it in action for himself.

"I've heard that [Peahead] didn't take any notes [at the practice]," Mickey Walker said. "He just came by and picked it all up by watching."[6,7]

Walker's mastery of the T was a work in progress, but his players sang a merry tune about the offense when quizzed by reporters in the late summer of 1948. It would improve the Deacon passing game, they said, the players were actually better suited to the T than the single wing, the assignments were easier, etc.

To what extent this was true remained to be seen. The idea that the Deacons' personnel was better suited to the new offense was particularly suspect. Whoever manned the quarterback post—Fetzer was the most likely candidate—would have to learn it from scratch. Walker did have a fine collection of pass-catching ends, but their role might be reduced in the T, which emphasized passing to backs, especially backs in motion before the start of the play. And the critical fullback position, which set up some plays by maintaining a consistent inside threat and led the blocking on many others, was undermanned. This problem was greatly aggravated when Tony DiTomo, a war-toughened 220-pounder (he'd entered Wake in 1946 at the age of 23), was declared ineligible. As the start of the season drew near, the best candidate appeared to be Bud Lail, a converted tailback. Hard-hitting Bill Gregus, the ex-single-wing tailback, might have made a good fullback, but Walker wanted to save him for halfback duty, where his power and speed would create a real threat.

There were several good fullbacks in the excellent freshman class entering school in the fall of 1948. Walker could have chosen from at least three newcomers for help at that position. But thanks to a new Southern Conference rule that required freshmen to play on a freshman team, they were no longer available for varsity games. Wake's varsity squad dropped to under fifty the first year

---

6 Mickey Walker, interview with author.

7 The advantages of implanting the "Mebane T" at Wake were not immediately clear. Mebane lost its first T game 39–0. Archie Walker would eventually compile a brilliant record, but his early days with the T were rough—a "conversion experience' his brother, and many other converts, would share.

the new rule was in place, a significant reduction after the almost seventy-man squads of the postwar years. Of course, Walker had made do with less than thirty men during the war, so forty-seven in uniform wasn't too bad.

The good news in terms of personnel, however, was that the line was very good, which suggested that, if nothing else, Wake could be pretty stout on defense. George, the budding superstar, was back at tackle along with Bernie Hanula and several promising younger players. Youngsters Ray Cicia and Gene Pambiachi had proven themselves tough and dependable players at guard from 1947 on.

Things went well enough in the team's home opener. The new offense churned out 260 net yards on the ground and popped two long gainers. Gregus was, as expected, the star, piling up 178 yards from scrimmage. Fetzer hit Ed Hoey with a seventy-three-yard touchdown pass and the Deacons beat George Washington 27–13. The final spread might have been bigger, but the Deacons lost four fumbles and had three passes intercepted, one of which was returned for a score. Early in the second half, GW also managed to pull off the old "sleeper" play. Halfback Jim Kline "hid" along the sidelines, disguising himself as one of two players apparently leaving the field for substitutes before a play began at the Wake thirty-six. Only one new man came in, however, and when GW quarterback Andy Davis hustled his men to the line, Kline was all by himself along the right sideline, unguarded by the less-than-vigilant Deacons. Davis took a quick snap and heaved a long one that Kline ran under around the twenty. He scored untouched and Deacon fans, like *Old Gold & Black* columnist Bill Hensley, were left with nothing but sanctimonious indignation. "Most modern coaches consider the play just a little too amateurish for college play," Hensley declared.[8]

---

[8] *Old Gold & Black*, Sept. 24, 1948. Hensley's opinion calls to mind a similar complaint from Clemson's Frank Howard following a loss to Maryland in the mid-1950s. The winning touchdown came on a trick play. Howard said afterward, "Maryland used a high school play to beat us." Apprised of Howard's critique, Maryland Coach Tom Nugent replied, "When you play high school teams, high school plays seem to work best."

Peahead Walker, his now twenty-plus years of coaching and ever-expanding waistline aside, was certainly a modern coach. But his latest innovation, the Deacon T, looked like less of a solution in week two when Boston College pounded the Deacons 26–9.

The offense was a little sharper the following week as Wake stopped William & Mary, but it was the defense that really did the job. Ed Bradley recovered two William & Mary fumbles in Indian territory—both inside the Tribe twenty to be exact—which paved the way to two of Wake's scores in the 21–12 victory. George continued his solid extra point booting—he was easily the best kicker Walker ever coached—and a new offensive weapon debuted. Sophomore Carroll Blackerby, a Birmingham boy who'd played for Walker's brother Bub while in the V-12 program at Howard, split time with Fetzer at quarterback and lobbed his first touchdown pass, a six-yarder to O'Quinn for Wake's last touchdown.

So much for preliminaries. Wake's season started in earnest in mid-October when Snavely's Carolina boys came over for a game at the expanded—the seating now totaled 27,500—but still-sold out Groves Stadium. The Tar Heels were never a picnic, but the Deacons' assignment in 1948 was particularly daunting. Carolina was at the peak of the Choo Choo Justice era. They came to Wake Forest riding a nine-game win streak, dating back to the 1947 season when Snavely turned his 0–3 team around, guiding it to a 7–3 finish. The 1948 team would go undefeated before dropping a Sugar Bowl heartbreaker to powerful Oklahoma.

Justice was still the difference maker on this Tar Heel team, but the Choo Choo now pulled a full-fledged train. Snavely had thirty-three lettermen back from 1947, many of them men in their mid-twenties who'd been through a war—and now two or three years of football. Twenty-five Tar Heels were age twenty-two or older. Many of the vets were also excellent football players. More than a dozen players off the team eventually played professionally. That figure doesn't include giant tackle Bill "Earthquake" Smith, who quit before the season due to "trouble with both books and professional greenbacks."[9] Even without Smith, listed in some journals as a 280-pounder, the Tar Heels were a big, bruising lot, perfect for Snavely's single wing-based offenses. His teams generally just pounded the opposition with simple plays, although he was known for a succession of innovations, including a single-wing variant known as the A formation offense; various refinements to the sweep; and a host of ideas related to his legendary obsession to detail. Snavely used to handwrite every player a note at the end of the season, critiquing their season and offering suggestions for improvement. He is also one of several coaches credited with popularizing the use of game film for studying football. His wife, his first videographer, and dog Barnaby (and a large bowl of vanilla ice cream) were his standard film-watching companions.[10]

Snavely, nicknamed the Grey Fox and Dutch Master by sportswriters desperate for copy and as addicted to nicknames as Peahead Walker, was perceived as something of a cold fish. But he had a wry sense of humor (he and Walker were fairly close) and enjoyed a successful coaching career.

The burly Tar Heels steamrolled the almost-as-burly Deacons 28–6. Carolina ground out 236 rushing yards and limited the Wake Forest ground attack. Walker's boys once again took to the air, but the Fetzer/Blackerby combination struggled to make much headway. The game did feature some early excitement, however. George blasted the opening kickoff six yards deep into the Carolina end zone, where Justice grabbed it and started weaving his way out. Some fifty or so vertical yards later—many more were covered as Justice cut from side to side—Justice was nearing midfield with but one man to beat: the Deacs' Fetzer. He faked, juked, and then cut toward the Deacon sideline. Fetzer wasn't fooled and gave Justice a shove into the Wake Forest bench. Bud Lail came flying in to finish the job, and some Deacon

---

[9] *Greensboro Daily News*, Sept. 11, 1948. Smith had apparently been receiving cash from one or more pro teams while still in college. When found out, he quickly became an above-board pro, although his career with the Chicago Cardinals was quite brief.

[10] Ironically, during his first stint at North Carolina, Snavely had accused Duke's Wade of cheating by using game film, which was considered a rules violation at the time.

benchwarmers appeared to have "helped" Justice to the ground as well. Justice had to be carried to the Carolina sideline and was out of action for awhile. Afterward he blamed it on the effects of his long run, coupled with a bad cold, but added that he'd never been tackled as hard in his life as he was tackled by "those Wake Forest men."[11] Snavely didn't seem to think anything was amiss, but Walker, sensitive to postgame complaints from the Carolina faithful, launched a public relations campaign several weeks after the fact. He drove his brand-new Cadillac—a gift from Deacon alumni—to the Greensboro Touchdown Club and showed clips from the game that proved the Deacons didn't take any cheap shots. The crowd, dazzled by Walker's command of modern projection technology and his Kelly green shirt and tie, seemed convinced, but the uproar bugged Walker for a long time. He told Charlotte sportswriter Bob Quincy several years later, "We played 'em four years and were able to tackle Justice [just] once. And everybody raised hell! You'd think they were at a tennis match."[12]

***

The Deacons and their new T formation finally began rounding into form at midseason. Not playing a bunch of bruisers like Boston College and Carolina helped, but Walker's boys were getting the hang of it, too. Fetzer passed for two scores and Blackerby one as Wake blitzed Duquesne 41–15. Two weeks later, following a week off, the Deacons rolled over an NC State teamed noted for its defense 34–13. The Wolfpack's new red helmets must have been spinning as Wake rang up twenty first quarter points. Bradley recovered a fumble and ran twenty-two yards for one of those scores, while O'Quinn dazzled offensively. He took a halfback pass from Gregus forty-one yards for a score and then hauled in a Blackerby toss for fifty-eight yards and another. Walker called him the best receiver in the nation afterward, and by season's end that was more than just a coaching boast. His 39 receptions and 695 yards (neither total would be much in today's pass-happy game)

---

11 *Greensboro Daily News*, Oct. 11, 1948.
12 *Chapel Hill Weekly*, Sept. 22, 1970.

led the country. State's head coach Beattie "the Chief" Feathers was impressed with both O'Quinn and the Deacs. Wake, he said after the whupping, was the best T-formation team he'd ever faced.

So the Deacons were 4–2, and in the bowl conversation. It was a pivotal point in the season. As usual, Duke was next.

It was. The Duke game was, by this time, known as "the jinx" on the Wake campus. Walker had faced Wade eight times without beating him (the 1942 victory against Duke, as Wade liked to point out, came when Eddie Cameron coached the team), and the quest was beginning to assume mythic aspects. But Walker was making progress. As Wade's program faded—the Colonel wasn't long from retirement and his zest for certain aspects of the business, such as recruiting, was sagging—Walker quickly made up ground. Since a 34–0 pounding by Cameron's V-12-infused squad had ended the 1944 Deacon squad's unbeaten dreams, Wake had battled the Devils on even terms for three straight years. Two of the contests had been real thrillers and the Deacons could easily have won all three games. But . . .

The 1948 game topped them all as far as excitement goes. The teams battled to a 13–13 halftime tie, Wake knotting it up on the last play before the end of the half. Then, the Deacons surged ahead at the end the third quarter when Carroll Blackerby found O'Quinn behind the Duke secondary and hit him for forty-eight yards and a Deacon score. That made it 20–13. Duke was in trouble.

Wallace Wade was a fundamentalist when it came to football. If he mentioned the Statue of Liberty to his players, he was probably talking about the tourist attraction. But with a tight game slipping from his grasp on this day, he reached into a not-so-very-deep bag of tricks and pulled out all he had. In this case, it was a brand-new offensive formation, a slight variation of the T. Wade called it the punt T, an unusual formation that featured a quarterback under center with three backs lined up behind him, one of whom would line up as far as eight or ten yards deep—deep enough to punt. Walker and company hadn't seen it and Wade hadn't intended on using it—he had been saving it for the Carolina game. But with the Wake game in the balance, he rolled it out, and lo and behold, it worked even better than expected. Duke's Jack Frielland broke an eighty-two-yard run through the surprised

Deacons D for a touchdown that tied the game 20–20 with four minutes left. Momentum had turned a deep blue.

And then, just as quickly, it turned gold again. Gregus grabbed the ensuing kickoff, plowed up the middle behind a four-man blocking phalanx, and then cut to the right sideline and raced seventy-seven yards to the Blue Devil seventeen. The Deacons were in business, but the business wasn't quite complete.

Duke's defense rose up and stonewalled the Deacons, forcing Wake to turn the ball over on downs at the Blue Devil nine. A tie seemed likely, but on the very next play the Deacons forced a fumble. Wake's Pee Wee Jones recovered it at the Duke ten with just under two minutes left.

Using Gregus as a decoy, Blackerby pitched the ball to Mike Sprock running outside. He bounced off a couple of tacklers at the five and dove into the end zone for the go-ahead score. George booted the extra point and Wake led 27–20.

It was enough—but just barely.

Duke completed a long pass out of the punt T—Wade reportedly drew up the play on a piece of paper on the sideline—to carry the ball to the Wake twenty-four.[13] Three more plays, including a long pass into the end zone that bounced off end Mike Souchak's hands, kept the Deacons holding their breath.[14]

"I was worried every time the ball was in the air," Walker said afterward. His anxiety was confirmed by neutral observers. A *Charlotte Observer* sportswriter noted that Walker smoked enough cigarettes during the contest to "use up all the extra inventory in this tobacco town [Durham]."[15]

When it was finally over, the joy and relief were palpable. Walker, clad in regal attire (purple shirt, gold tie), rode on his

---

13 *Greensboro Daily News*, Nov. 7, 1948.
14 Souchak was a pretty good football player who not only played end but also kicked for the Blue Devils. He was an even better golfer though. After college he won fifteen PGA Tour events during an eighteen-year career and in 1955 set a tournament record at the Texas Open with a seventy-two-hole score of 257. The record stood for nearly fifty years. In 2001, Mark Calcavecchia broke it at the Phoenix Open with a 256.
15 *Charlotte Observer*, Nov. 9, 1948.

players' shoulders to the locker room. He later declared the afternoon the happiest of his life.

After all the disappointments against Duke, he'd finally won one. And in many ways the Deacons were fortunate. The late Duke fumble was an outrageous bit of luck, one that some Duke players weren't sure was entirely deserved. They thought Jones stole the ball out of the pile after the whistle blew. Several other breaks went the Deacons' way, notably Jim Duncan's spectacular catch of Blackerby's touchdown pass in the closing seconds of the first half.

But the Deacons' jinx-breaking luck was also a product of some seriously hard work. Wade's team, while not among his best, was still a tough, stingy lot. Duke surrendered just ninety-two points all season. Wake Forest and North Carolina (which beat Duke 20–0) accounted for more than half that total. A big part of the Blue Devils' defensive success was Wade's use of captain Al Derogatis, a rugged senior lineman known for his ferocity. Wade regularly aligned Derogatis, a guard, over the opposition's center. The ploy, unusual at that time, wrecked many an offense—and many a center—as Derogatis teed off play after play against his hapless, overmatched opposition.

Walker was well aware of Derogatis. While at Duke, Walker regularly used the Derogatis bogeyman to chastise Wake Forest linemen during practice. "Hell, boys," the Deacon coach would say after a display of mediocre effort or technique, "do that against De-row-got-us and somebody's gonna get killed."

Noting Wade's new use of Derogatis as a center smasher, Walker came up with a simple solution to get his boys ready: he'd toughen up his center, senior Boyd Allen, with some extra practice. "What Peahead did," said Ed Hoey, an end of the 1948 team, "was line everyone up at practice to take their shot at Boyd Allen, one after the other. Three days straight like that. It was terrible for Boyd, but I think by the time Saturday rolled around he was pretty happy to be facing Derogatis."[16] Relieved or otherwise, Allen, with help from guard Ray Cicia, a player almost as ornery as Derogatis, handled the Blue Devil star, and Wake's offense enjoyed a banner day.

---

16 Walker used a similar technique the next year to toughen up linebacker Ed Karpus for a special Duke running play. Ed Hoey, interview with author.

To that banner another was soon added. Two days after the victory, the Deacons accepted an invitation to the newly founded Dixie Bowl in Birmingham. Walker was going home to coach in a postseason game. Baylor, another Baptist school, would be the opponent.

The early bid put Wake in an odd place as it closed out its season. The very next week it faced an unbeaten Clemson team—which was hoping for, but did not currently have, a bowl bid—and it closed at South Carolina, which had some postseason aspirations as well. The effect of the bid—did it spark ire among the Tigers or complacency among the Deacons—is hard to discern. Clemson beat Wake 21–14 in Winston-Salem, but it was a tight, hard-fought game. The Tigers perhaps got the better of the overall play, but as noted, Clemson was unbeaten, so the result can hardly be considered an upset. The following week Wake demolished South Carolina 38–0 to finish the regular season 6–3.

The bowl matchup looked like an even battle. Both Wake and Baylor ran the T—a major marketing plus thought bowl game organizers at that time—and both finished with three loses (Baylor was 5–3-2, losing to Texas and the two national powers of the day, Tulane and Southern Methodist). The Bears' schedule was probably the more difficult of the two, but Baylor still had some defects, the most obvious being that coach Bob Woodruff's team couldn't stop the run, having yielded something like 175 yards per game on the ground over the course of the season. That figure wouldn't be good even today. It was terrible in the more conservative, offensively stunted 1940s. Wake was a team capable of exploiting such a flaw. Gregus finished the 1948 regular season with 635 rushing yards, among the nation's best, and Walker fielded a powerful collection of backs beyond him. But for some reason, Walker and the Deacons ignored that tantalizing matchup during the cold New Year's Day matchup in Birmingham—probably costing them a second bowl victory.

The narrative of the contest, witnessed by a little more than 20,000 fans at the newly constructed Legion Field, was that Baylor took advantage of several Wake Forest turnovers, and maybe a couple of officiating miscues, while rolling to 20–0 halftime lead that culminated with a 20–7 victory. But the deciding factor was

Wake's inability to run the ball until the second half. The Deacons rushed for 150 of their 191 rushing yards after intermission, by which time it was just about too late. Wake drove the ball with some effectiveness all five times it had it in the second half but was stopped on downs twice and by fumbles two other times. One of those fumbles, which came early in the fourth quarter, halted Wake's increasing momentum and ultimately turned out to be the death knell. On first down from the Baylor 37, Blackerby fired a short pass to Duncan. Observers noted that the ball bounced off Duncan's chest but was ruled a fumble and, more importantly, Baylor's ball since the Bears' Jack Southern recovered it. In the press box, Baylor quarterback coach Frank Broyles stood up and shouted, "No! We don't want to win that way!"[17] Walker agreed afterward that is was a bad call, but opined that Wake did itself in more than did the men in stripes.

"We were just too late in getting started," Walker said. He also credited Baylor with devising the "perfect pass defense against us," which specifically no doubt meant the Bears' double-teaming of O'Quinn most of the day, preventing him from catching a single pass. But given Baylor's problems against the run, Walker's pass-heavy strategy itself seems suspect.

The defeat, though disappointing, did not leave the Deacons with all that bitter a taste in their mouths. In fact—quite the contrary. At the postgame banquet at the Tutwiler Hotel, every player received a lapel pin that was presented by a female member of the Dixie Bowl court. Egged on by bowl committee chair Holt Rast, the prizes were accompanied by a kiss. Several players attempted to make their kiss more memorable still and pretty soon the whole thing devolved into a kissing contest. Most of the crowd howled in delight, though the wives of some of the married Deacons—there were several—were less amused. Feminists in the crowd, had any existed, would likely have been appalled. Walker, who was neither a feminist nor a Deacon wife, put his stamp of approval on the proceedings.

---

17 Broyles's remark was noted by several sportswriters. He later went on to fame as a football coach and athletic director at Arkansas, and later still, as ABC's primary color commentator for college football games.

"Oh, you Bears," he told the Baylor team when his turn at the podium came, "you hug as good as you tackle."[18]

***

Kissable or not, Walker and his men viewed the 1949 season with some optimism. Much of it derived from the most-publicized recruiting coup of Walker's career. The freshman class that had enrolled at Wake in the fall of 1948 included the entire backfield from the Associated Press's 1947 first-team All-North Carolina prep team. It was a stunning upset, but not as mysterious as it might seem. As fate would have it, Walker had inside tracks with all four players. He and Dickie Davis, the Wilson, NC quarterback, shared a number of friends and acquaintances from Walker's baseball days in Wilson. A relative of Charles "Bobo" Roberson's was a secretary in the Wake Forest athletic department. Bobby Stutts was from Burlington, in between Elon College and Mebane, where Walker maintained influential family connections. And the star of the class, running back William "Nub" Smith, was from Fayetteville . . . by way of Birmingham. He'd spent his first two high school seasons in Leeds, Alabama, an industrial town just outside Birmingham, but was recruited to Fayetteville in 1946 as part of a major escalation of the football at Fayetteville High.

The special connections helped Walker land the famous foursome and, as is still the case today in similar situations, the class helped build itself. Davis had met Smith when their teams played in 1946 and 1947 and recalls Smith "calling or maybe even coming to see me, to try to get me to come to Wake."[19] Roberson applied similar pressure. The all-star backfield moved as one into Deaconland.

Walker's coup eventually turned out to be something less than what it appeared at the time. Stutts and Roberson were slowed by injuries (an especially serious turn of events in the case of Stutts) and never amounted to much. Davis and Smith were clearly gifted—old-timers still rank Smith among the best players in North Carolina prep history—but both players were flawed in

---

[18] *Raleigh News & Observer*, January 1, 1949.
[19] Dickie Davis, interview with author.

other ways. Neither was an academic star for one thing. That actually helped Walker land the twosome, or at least Davis. Since Wake was hardly an elite academic school in this era, it could admit a less-than-scholarly athlete from time to time. Duke had somewhat higher standards and a much stuffier coach. Wade knew Davis was a whale of player but didn't think he could cut the academic mustard. He told Davis as much on a recruiting visit, advising him to try junior college or prep school for a few years before coming to Duke. Bluntly, Wade told Davis that he couldn't get into any Southern Conference school. Said the feisty Davis, "Yeah, well I bet I can."[20]

Carolina may have had some doubts as well, but Snavely's plan to farm Davis out to a prep school was based more on depth-chart considerations than anything else: it would work better if he enrolled after Justice left. In any event, although marked by flashes of greatness at times, Davis never really became a star.

Smith may have been an even greater academic risk than Davis and apparently wasn't even recruited by Duke despite his high school fame. Handsome and happy, Smith was a gifted musician who played the cello and bass in the Wake Forest orchestra and in a traveling swing band as well.[21] But he was, at best, an indifferent student who was lost to academic ineligibility after three football seasons at Wake. Jack Lewis, a teammate, said Smith's collegiate academic woes began "when they ran out of music courses he could take."[22]

Academic stumbles were nothing new for Smith. His well-known nickname "Nub" was purportedly derived from an unfortunate incident with a power tool in a high school woodworking class. The injury was not as serious as the nickname implied—the mishap with a table saw just sliced off some skin and a bit of fingernail—but the moniker stuck to Smith like glue, perhaps because it fit an already budding reputation. No one called him Bill.

---

20 Ibid.
21 Later in life, after going back home to Alabama, he had his own country and western group.
22 Jack Lewis, interview with author.

Good-natured, if something of a loner, Smith was the butt of jokes in high school[23] and a natural target for Walker's lacerating needle. On the bus ride to a game against Boston College in 1949, the Wake Forest team drove past Harvard and its famous school of medicine. Walker, sitting up front in his usual seat, jumped up in mock alarm. "Quick boys," Walker said, "grab Nub and stick him down in the aisle where no one can see him. If them boys at the medical school seem him they'll want to take him and study his brain in the name of science." Jack Lewis recalled that, as was often the case, Walker's humor flew over the heads of many of the players. A couple of teammates sitting near Smith actually grabbed him and covered him up as the coach had instructed.[24]

On the field, Smith never lived up to the considerable potential of his high school days. He was a highly skilled, old-fashioned, do-everything triple-threat back but did not work hard and showed brilliance only in flashes, such as his (then) school record 246-yard rushing day against William & Mary. That was great, but it accounted for almost half his rushing yards that year and roughly a quarter of his career total. In other games, he barely scratched the plus column.

Noted his teammate and fellow classmate Davis:

He just didn't seem to take football all that seriously. He didn't work real hard, wasn't in real good shape, and seemed to be screwing around more than anything at practice. We'd be waiting for the next play or something and he'd come up to me and say, "Hey, Dickie, watch this new move I've been working on." He liked football okay. He liked being with his girl and playing his fiddle [cello] more."[25]

Other teammates recall Walker demoting Smith on a regular basis—he often wound up on the scout team with the

---

[23] An English teacher in Fayetteville purportedly chastised him for stumbling through verb conjugations one day. "If you were as smart in class as you are on the football field, you could make A's," she said. "If I had ten men a helping me here, I bet I could, too," Nub supposedly replied. Source: *Fayetteville Observer*, Sept. 25, 1999.

[24] Jack Lewis, interview with author.

[25] Dickie Davis, interview with author.

scrubs—and seeing to it that he took a beating in practice. It didn't seem to have much effect. Smith's potential still got him playing time, but Wake was deep enough by then that it didn't guarantee him much more than an occasional look.

Indeed, he may not even have been the best back in the freshman class. Walker's good work in the spring of 1948 didn't stop at the North Carolina border. He actually brought in the equivalent of almost three full starting backfields. Behind the famous four from North Carolina was a group that included Ed Kissell, halfbacks Dick Travaligne and Francis Scarton, and powerful fullback Bill Miller. Travaligne was an All-State back in Maryland, and Kissell, Miller, and Scarton all played prominent roles for Wake over the next three years. Kissell said the talent in the class was astonishing:

I got there and there were all these freshmen. Millions of them. And of course they had the four backs from North Carolina. A big deal. I know Travaligne didn't like that, didn't like not starting. I think he was all-world or something in Maryland. It was kind of crazy. All I know is players kept disappearing and here'd be some new ones. I don't know where they all came from. I don't know what Walker was thinking.[26]

Wake had plenty of good linemen in the fall of 1949 as well—Walker had three excellent tackles in Bill George, Jim Staton, and Tom Palmer; tough guards in Ray Cicia and Bob Auffarth; and enough good ends that Walker could divide them into offensive and defensive units. The backfield, however, was a worry. If the freshmen-cum-sophomores could give the Deacs a lift—if they lived up to their clippings—Wake might really have something. But would they? That was the question as preseason camp opened in late August.

It was temporarily forgotten when a summer roster crisis reared its head. As practice was beginning, Gregus and Cicia, two of Wake's most talented players, left the team. The pair showed up for the start of practice on September 1 and then disappeared a few

---

[26] Ed Kissell, interview with author.

days later, leaving most of their belongings behind. School officials played it cool—Athletic Director Jim Weaver told reporters that the two boys were on "an extended Labor Day vacation"—but the fact was they had gone AWOL. The *Raleigh News & Observer* reported that they had quit the team. The truth trickled out later, well after their college careers were over: Gregus and Cicia left Wake to play semipro ball in Canada. What threats, sweet talk, or brutal realities brought them back (and what rules they might have broken while they were gone—like being paid to play) are lost now to the mists of time. The bottom line is that they left, disrupting the team's preseason preparations and setting a fractious tone for what would be one of the rockiest seasons of Walker's Wake Forest tenure.

The many problems encountered1949 squad all centered on team chemistry. The hotshot sophomores didn't mix well with the older boys. The team's northerners didn't blend well with the native sons. The academically minded team members were at odds with those who were . . . not so inclined.

"There were definitely several camps," said Ken Bridges, a lesser light (at least in terms of football talent) in the great 1948 freshman class. "You either wanted to go to school and saw an athletic scholarship as pretty darn near the only scholarship available, or you only wanted to play football and couldn't care less about going to class and all. There were plenty of those. They figured they'd make it rich in the pros or coaching or something."[27]

The various divisions probably didn't matter as much as the simple fact that Walker's "football-first" cadre include some rough, hard-edged guys, "the kind of guys you wouldn't seek out as a fraternity brother, and maybe would cross the street to avoid," said Bill Hensley, sports editor of the *Old Gold & Black* (and high-stepping drum major for the marching band) in the late 1940s.[28]

Davis confirmed the personality conflicts of those days while thumbing through the 1949–1950 *Howler*, Wake Forest's annual, during an interview decades after the fact. Davis pondered a page of football team mugshots and noted a long list of problem cases:

---

27 Ken Bridges, interview with author.
28 Bill Hensley, interview with author.

"Now that guy was a real asshole," Davis said, pointing to one ex-teammate. "And he was too. . . . And so was he." Davis's work picked up speed. Bouncing through the photo array, he fingered every third or fourth photo. "Asshole. . . . Asshole. . . . Asshole. . . .

"You know," he said, pausing from his brutal assessment, "we just had a bunch of guys who were hard to get along with. We didn't like each other very much. If we had, we might have done a whole lot better."[29]

Walker understood he had a problem with the 1949 team but didn't admit to it until well after the fact. A theme that dominates the early-season reporting of the 1950 team is that some addition had occurred via subtraction when a dozen or so members of the 1949 squad didn't return for the 1950 season for one reason or another. The talented Gregus was one of those players. Getting rid of him was "like bouncing the worst apple out of the barrel," wrote Bill Currie of the *High Point Enterprise*.[30] That may have been clear in the fall of 1950, but in the fall of 1949 what Walker knew for sure is that he had a lot of talent at his command, perhaps as much as at any time in his coaching career. Figuring out the best way to deploy it on the field was another matter.

In the season opener, Wake overpowered Duquesne 22–7, dominating the game after the Dukes' John Duchess returned an intercepted Blackerby pass seventy yards for a score just four minutes into the contest. Next up was a stiffer test. So confident was Walker in the potential of the 1949 team that he felt relatively safe in scheduling a week two matchup against top-ranked Southern Methodist University in Dallas. Walker and Weaver arranged the contest after a scheduling conflict forced Southern Cal to back out of a late-September date with the Mustangs. That Wake was enough of a draw to fill the void says something about what Walker had wrought by this point in his career. SMU officials seemed delighted with the pairing. Wake was delighted with the notoriety and the big check they'd get for playing in front of a sold-out crowd at the Cotton Bowl.

---

29 Dickie Davis, interview with author.
30 *High Point Enterprise*, Sept. 7, 1950.

SMU coach Maddy Bell had assembled an excellent team in 1949, but most of the buzz in Mustang land was generated by Doak Walker, a Dallas-area prep phenom who'd gone on to college stardom in his hometown. Walker won the Heisman Trophy Award, given annually to the top college player in the country, in 1948.[31] Walker was much like Carolina's Justice, a flashy, multi-skilled player with a less-than-overwhelming physique. Doak Walker was listed at 5'11" and 175 pounds, but seeing him in team photos of the day, it is hard to imagine that he fulfilled either boundary. He was a short, slightly built man with good looks and uncanny athletic ability. Walker also lettered in basketball and baseball at SMU and after his professional football career became an excellent snow skier. Like Justice, he did everything for SMU: run, return kicks, punt, place kick, and throw and receive passes (though, generally, not on the same play). Said Coach Walker of Wake Forest on the eve of facing him, "We've heard all about him."

The September 24 game was a Wake Forest landmark in many ways. Among other things, it marked the first time in school history that the entire Deacon team flew to a game. Coach Walker told reporters that he dropped more than twenty pounds over the summer in preparation for the flight to Dallas and for another one scheduled the following week to Boston. The reasoning: he didn't want to overburden the planes with any unnecessary strain.

A little payload slack might provide enough capacity to carry home the Deacons' loot. The SMU contest paid a whopping $60,000. That was a lot of laundry money and had everyone's attention. The spring before the Wake Forest bursar had called the trustees' attention to the fact that athletics, thanks mostly to football, had grown into a $200,000 per year business. But that might not last the bursar's reported noted. The budget was built on revenues from "fat" years, which included big pay days from SMU and Boston College, among others. Budgeting based on that kind of revenue might create problems when the inevitable down year rolled around. "A very fine football team might have a few bad breaks in early season which could reduce gate receipts by

---

31 Walker, just the second junior to win the award, did not repeat in 1949. He also didn't win the Doak Walker Award, given annually to the top running back in college football, either.... That award wasn't established until 1990.

thousands of dollars," the bursar wrote. What then? The bursar's recommendation: set aside an athletic reserve. His recommended amount was $50,000, or just about what the SMU game brought in. The trustees did not immediately take action.[32]

The matchup in Dallas also put Wake squarely in the national spotlight. That was worth something in itself, but even if it did not, Walker was clearly enjoying the moment. The team was greeted at the Dallas airport by Mustang cheerleaders and a covey of newsmen. The latter descended on the visiting coach, who was easy to spot thanks to an outfit that was garish, even by Peahead Walker's sartorial standards. Walker arrived wearing "a green coat with a red shirt, blue pants and a pink necktie speckled with bright figures."[33] Later, in what is remembered as one of his better pregame speeches—one of the few that most players could even recall in fact—Walker reminded his team of the once-in-a-lifetime opportunity that lay before it. "Beat SMU and Doak Walker," Peahead said, "and they will remember you forever."

They almost did. Up and coming tackle Jim Staton blocked a Walker punt in the first quarter, Ed Karpus recovered it on the SMU two, and Gregus scored on the next play to give Wake a 7–0 lead. That was just the kind of start an upset-minded team needed, and for a time it looked like it might be enough. Coach Walker's defensive tactics—he sent all six of his linemen, including the ends, barreling into the SMU backfield on every play—kept Doak Walker under wraps. SMU had minus-five rushing yards at the half and needed a pair of long Walker-to-John Milam passes to produce a scoring drive that cut the Deacon lead to 7–6 at the break.

The contest eventually turned on a couple of very near Deacon misses in the second half. With SMU pinned deep in its own territory in the third quarter, Wake's Francis Scarton stepped in front of Walker's pass to Kyle Rote Jr. at the Mustang twenty-five. The ball was on Scarton's hands and an open field beckoned, but he couldn't control the ball. Worse still, from a Deacon point of view, it popped into the air where Rote grabbed it and headed the other way. He finished with a thirty-one-yard gain to the Wake forty-nine. Two plays later, Walker used Wake's aggressive rush

---

32 Wake Forest College Board of Trustees Minutes, May 31, 1948. WFU Archives.
33 *Dallas Morning News*, Sept. 23, 1949.

against it, flipping a screen pass to fullback Dick McKissack in the middle of the field. Escorted by most of the offensive line, McKissack rolled up the right sideline and into the end zone for the go-ahead score.

The Deacons, hampered by 110 yards in penalties and a wave of injuries at the tackle position, struggled offensively most of the night. But they had one good chance in the fourth quarter. Blackerby strikes to Jim Duncan and Nub Smith pushed the ball from Wake's thirty-nine to the SMU twenty. On second down from there, Blackerby dropped back and spotted O'Quinn speeding toward the end zone all by himself. Before he could get the pass off, however, SMU's Jack Halliday buried him after blasting through one of the injury-depleted tackle spots in the Deacon line. The result: a ten-yard loss. Blackerby's third down pass was incomplete, and Wake kicked the ball away on fourth—never to reach SMU territory again.

And so it ended. Wake had played well but didn't get the breaks it needed to pull out the win.

"We got beat," Walker said, referring back to Scarton's near miss, "on a pass we intercepted."[34] More flying—and more losing—followed. Wake flew back home and then out to Boston four days later, where it dropped a 13-7 decision to Boston College. The pass defense was a problem again. Boston College scored twice in the last six minutes to take the win, moving the ball on those drives almost exclusively through the air. A debilitating home loss followed. Wake moved the ball all over the field at Groves Stadium but fumbled five times and fell to a modest Georgetown club 12-6.

That was three losses in a row, the first such skein since 1945 when Walker's club opened against the Tennessee-Army-Duke murderer's row. A 28-14 loss to another powerful UNC team made it four straight, Walker's worst string since his first Deacon season.

What was wrong?

The chemistry was poor and injuries were a problem, too. George had a broken foot. Staton, Palmer, Karpus, and Ed Listopad—all tackles—were hobbling around on various strained

---

34 *Greensboro Daily News*, Sept. 26, 1949.

muscles. Blackerby, it turned out, wasn't whole either—his suddenly wild passing a byproduct of an aching shoulder. The logical replacement, Davis, injured his foot against Boston College, so Ed Kissell, the "runt" of Walker's quarterback litter, became the starter. He was a capable ball handler and field general—probably better than either of the others at handling those responsibilities—but was a poor passer, his range limited by an old baseball injury as well as his small stature. Kissell's meager passing even earned him grief from his teammates, including fullback Bill Miller, who taunted Kissell by reminding him that he (Miller) was his leading receiver.

"Because he was a fullback, that meant all I was throwing was little screens and short passes," said Kissell. "He laughed at me, so I just stopped throwing it to him. He'd say in the huddle, 'Hey, throw me a pass.' And I'd say, 'Sure, coming right up.' But I don't think I threw him another one all season."[35]

Wake looked like it was in for a long season. The Deacons were dragging after the Carolina loss. Sports columnists in the state were writing about Peahead Walker's impending demise, and the schedule didn't offer much respite. A game against a decent William & Mary team was followed by contests against Clemson, Duke, NC State, and South Carolina. Some wondered whether the Deacons would even win one more the rest of the way.

They would. On a chilly October afternoon at Groves Stadium, the Deacons' potential turned to reality, at least for an afternoon. Nub Smith made some some sweet music on the ground, running for a school record 246 yards; O'Quinn, whose decision to return for a final season as a graduate student had, to this point, appeared to be a big mistake, caught three touchdown passes; and the Deacons buried William & Mary 55–28. Rube McCrary, shell-shocked William & Mary coach, said, "My God, they had everything." Said Wake's Walker: "I think the boys were mad."[36]

The out-of-the-October-blue result reinvigorated the Deacons. Wake stormed into Death Valley and pounded Clemson 35–21, rolling up 556 yards of total offense (which didn't include Dickie Davis's sixty-yard punt return for a score). Then they

---

35 Ed Kissell, interview with author.
36 *Richmond Times Dispatch*, Oct. 23, 1949.

marched into Durham and blasted Duke 27–7. It was a complete role reversal. Duke couldn't stop Wake's inside running, meanwhile, Wake stopped the Devils whenever it counted. The Deacons' third quarter goal line stand while nursing a 13–7 lead all but decided the game. Wake took over on its seven and drove ninety-three yards for a touchdown to put the game away. Walker credited brutal practice work for the victory. To whip linebacker Ed Karpus in shape, Walker ran a fullback at him about fifty times one day in practice. "It was a terrific workout for Karpus," Walker said, "but it paid off. He made the key tackle on the goal line."[37]

And for the third week in a row Peahead Walker rode off the field on his players' shoulders. It looked like the beginnings of a storybook finish—bumbling team closes with five straight victories—but it was not to be. Just as quickly as the Deacons' light switch came on it flicked back off.

Before a packed house at Raleigh's Riddick Stadium, NC State scored three touchdowns in the first eleven minutes of play and held on for a 27–14 victory. Wake rallied from the early deficit and was driving for the go-ahead touchdown when Blackerby was sacked and fumbled at the State forty. Moments later, the Wolfpack's Bob Bowlby stepped in front of a Blackerby pass and ran it back thirty-nine yards for State's last touchdown. The result didn't sit well with some Deacons. George Sniscak and Bill George were both ejected for fighting during the waning moments. George and NC State's Tom Morse got tangled up on the interception return. They were sent to the sidelines, but George—now minus his helmet and bare-chested—was prepared to resume the brawl after the game and headed toward the State locker room to do just that. Only the intervention of NC State's wrestling coach, a friend and admirer of George, prevented additional extracurriculars.

The story—minus the fighting—was similar two weeks later in Columbia, where South Carolina jumped out to a 13–0 lead and then scored twice in the fourth to go ahead 27–7. Davis, displaying what would become his standard operating procedure, came on as quarterback and rallied the Deacons to two late scores to close the gap to 27–20, but that was all the damage Wake could muster.

---

37 *Greensboro Daily News*, Nov. 11, 1949.

Despite piling up the yards again—Wake outgained the Gamecocks 284 to 190—the Deacons couldn't close the deal, done in the for the most part by failures in the shadow of the goal and, one again, those pesky turnovers.

Wake finished with a whopping thirty-eight turnovers in just ten games. Their opposition combined to commit only twenty-two. Blackerby, who began his career by going his first seven games without an interception, was picked off sixteen times in 1949—one out of every ten times he threw.

A season that had begun with much promise finished with the abject disappointment afforded by a 4–6 record, Walker's first losing season since 1943.

Surprisingly, that resulted in not punishment but reward. In the spring of 1950 Walker signed a new contract that extended his term for three more years and upped his salary to $7,500 a year. Once again Walker gained some leverage from rumors of his candidacy for other jobs (Texas Tech, Baylor, and West Virginia were among his supposed suitors this time around). He may even have received an actual offer. But the main push behind the new contract was that Wake's brain trust—meaning, for the most part, Jim Weaver—thought that Walker was a brilliant coach. The Wake Forest football program, Weaver believed, was in good shape.

That seemed a concensus opinion until the second week of January when fate delivered a stunner to Deacon doorsteps: six members of the football team had been either expelled from school or placed on probation after being convicted of cheating on a chemistry exam. The dirty half-dozen included three stars—the former AWOL kids, Gregus and Cicia, and Bill George—plus three others. George, Cicia, and tackle George Sniscak—old "Anthracite Head"—were all expelled. Gregus and two seldom-used reserves, Dick Medlecot and Bill Whilelmy, were placed on probation but barred from participating in any extracurricular activity—no glee club, debate team . . . or football for them. The distinction between those who received probation and those who were expelled had to do with prior offenses. Cicia, George, and Sniscak all had been caught for the same offense previously. Gregus, Medlecot, and Whilhelmy were, as far as the student honor council knew, first-time cheats.

That those particular players would cheat and get caught was no surprise. All were northerners from the "football-first" camp who found the school part of the Wake Forest assignment a chore, a bore—or both. Several were noted for a certain lack of academic interest or ability. Gregus and Cicia were just "dumb, dumb guys," said Davis. "They had no chance to graduate and they knew it. The only reason they cheated was to keep playing I guess."[38]

Gene Hooks, a baseball player at Wake in the late 1940s and later the school's athletic director, said Gregus was "about the least academic guy I knew. A pretty good guy, I thought, but you couldn't carry on much of a conversation with him. There was nothing to talk about."[39]

Hooks recalled that Gregus came out for baseball one year. Part of the tryout included a rapid-fire batting drill in which a player took three swings and then, following his third swing, was instructed to run to second no matter if or where the ball was it. The idea was to give the coaches a look at the player's speed out of the batter's box. Gregus was the first one up after the instructions were issued. He took his three hacks and then blasted out of the batter's box . . . and straight toward second base via the pitcher's mound. "He just about ran [pitcher] Moe Bauer down," said Hooks.[40]

Gregus' lack of academic stardom received additional validation in an oft-cited, but almost surely fanciful, tale in which a Wake Forest dean told Walker that he had incontrovertible proof that Gregus had cheated on tests in a history class. What, asked Walker, was the evidence? Well, said the dean, Gregus had the exact same score on the semester's first two tests as the best student in the class: a 100 and a 96.

"Now Dean," Walker said, "that don't mean a thing. Old Bill could have done all that himself."

"Maybe," said the Dean, "but there's more. They both missed only one question and it was the same one."

"Still sounds like a coincidence to me," Walker said hopefully.

---

38 Dickie Davis, interview with author.
39 Gene Hooks, interview with author.
40 Ibid.

"We don't think so," said the Dean. "The top student's answer for that question was, 'I have no idea.' Your boy's was 'me neither.'"

There was some sentiment on the football team that the honor council was making an example of the football players because they were football players. Ken Bridges, a "school-first" footballer who was a member of the honor council, said he doubted that was so. He didn't know for sure, however, because he recused himself from the case from the outset, hoping to avoid both conflicts of interest and hard feelings from his teammates. Sound though this strategy might have been, it didn't work. As Bridges, who when on to a career as both a military and civilian attorney, recalled:

> *I had nothing to do with the case. I made that clear, and anyone with any sense would have known that. Who'd want to deal with all that crap? But it didn't matter. A lot of the players thought I was involved. So my meals became real quick affairs. I went down to the Colonial Club three times a day—that free food was important to me—but I never stayed long. They were pretty rough on me for awhile there.*[41]

Bridges's sad story of football hazing had a happy ending though. He was standing in line at graduation when Bill George came up to him and apologized. "He said, 'You know I know, and those other guys know, that you weren't involved,'" recalled Bridges. "He said, 'I'm sorry about all the stuff that happened over that. You were right.' Well, him apologizing, that meant a lot to me."[42]

That George was ever at a Wake Forest graduation ceremony was a surprise to many. He wasn't a great student, and hadn't he been expelled as part of the cheating scandal? He had. But aided by intercessory work from Walker, he was allowed to come back—the only member of the dirty half-dozen to do so.

The cheating scandal appears to have been transformative for George, shocking him into a realization of what football and a

---

41 Bridges, interview with author.
42 Ibid.

free education meant—and, conversely—what it would have meant to throw that all away. No doubt much of Walker's lobbying on George's behalf was due to his extraordinary abilities on the field, but at least some of it was fighting for a young man he believed was good at heart. And besides, he'd promised him a chance to see that West Campus.

When the verdict was handed down, Gregus and Cicia headed north again. Both landed Canadian Football League (CFL) jobs for the 1950 season, Cicia in Montreal and Gregus in Hamilton. Both were named to the All-Big Four (eastern Canada) All-Star team in their rookie seasons. Cicia went on to have a solid Canadian career, eventually reuniting with his old college coach. Gregus didn't last as long in the CFL. He was drafted by the NFL's Chicago Bears in 1951. He didn't make that team, bumped around the CFL for a few more years, and then began a long career in the low-level semipro ranks. Former Wake Forest teammate Larry Spencer, who settled in Gregus's hometown of Toledo after college, said he ran into Gregus in the mid-1960s and that "he was still playing for some semipro team there in town. . . . He really liked football, I guess."[43]

The student honor council may not have singled out the footballers for unusual prosecution or punishment, but the idea of football players bending rules or getting an extra break stretched no imaginations on campus or around town. For good and bad, the Walker system was entrenched. The benefits that football players received were so common, the strings Walker could pull so numerous, that the line between right and wrong became a blur for some. Dickie Davis, who narrowly missed a dust-up with the honor council himself, recalled that:

> *At the time, it was hard to know if some of that stuff we were doing was cheating or not. We always had real smart guys available to us for tutoring and . . . whatever. They had to be compensated and I know we [the players] didn't pay them. They just showed up and*

---

43 Larry Spencer, interview with author.

our grades got better. It was just like if you got traffic tickets. That was bad, but Peahead could get that fixed.[44]

Even so, the football cheating case arrived on the honor council docket at an inopportune time. A debate over the effectiveness of Wake's honor code was in full swing in the winter of 1949–1950. Part of the uproar was over the general ineffectiveness of the existing honor code, which put students "on their honor" not to cheat on tests (which were not proctored), on papers, or in any other way. A poll taken at a mandatory chapel in late 1949 showed an almost even split on the subject. Some 865 thought it was not effective; some 833 thought it was. At the same time the student council began advocating for more strenuous penalties for convicted code offenders. Some were incensed that certain students were still able to participate in activities, like varsity athletics, after being caught.[45] More ominously, the gridders' case went before the council while the school was in the midst of an ugly scandal involving the murder of WFC student Roy Coble by classmate Raymond Hair over a gambling debt. The Hair case was a sensation because murder was quite rare on the Wake campus, and because Hair eluded authorities for almost two weeks after the killing—he was eventually captured in California. Interestingly, the gambling connection raised almost as many embarrassing questions about the reality of campus life at a small Baptist school than the murder did. What in the world were they teaching them over there? And now the football players were cheating? It was not the best of times for school president Thurman Kitchin, who was already on his way out, having announced his retirement at the end of the 1950 school year months before.

For Peahead Walker, who'd have to stay around and pick up the pieces, things weren't too rosy either. Reached at a coaching convention in Atlanta the day the punishments were announced, Walker sounded both hopeful (and misinformed) when he told reporters that the Wake school year ended in June and that a new one started in September. In fact, regular privileges were not restored. Five of the six were gone for good and George was in what

---
44 Dickie Davis, interview with author.
45 *Old Gold & Black*, Dec. 16, 1949.

turned out to be a one-year purgatory. The roster and depth chart for 1950 were dealt a severe blow. The team's two best linemen and its most dynamic back were gone.

But, there turned out to be some pluses in those minuses. The honor council action may have excised a cancerous cell from the football body, and the scandal blew over quickly enough to avoid toppling the program (similar incidents helped to take down at least two other Southern Conference football programs in the early 1950s). Talents like Gregus, George, and Cicia would be missed, but help was on the way.

For all the ballyhoo over the freshman class of 1948, Walker's class of 1949, which became eligible for varsity work in 1950, was actually better. It contained less flash—the best players were lineman and defensive players, not offensive backs—but more substance. Of the seventeen sophomores on the 1950 roster, four would fill key roles on that team, nine would become important players at some point in their career, and seven would be drafted by the NFL. The exploits of the ballyhooed 1948 class paled by comparison.

Heading into the 1950 season, Walker had three quarterbacks with some playing experience; a powerful fullback in nasty Bill Miller; and some halfback punch with speedy sophomore Larry Spencer, shifty Frances Scarton (nicknamed "Guido" by the always politically correct Walker), and a beefed-up Nub Smith. Smith, for all his failings, had led the 1949 team in rushing and upon entering his junior year was in the best shape of his collegiate football life, having spent the previous summer digging coal in his native Alabama.

The Deacons stumbled—quite literally—in their opener. Playing Boston College at Braves Field, Wake dominated play and piled up the yards but struggled to score points. Four times they drove inside the Eagles' twenty without scoring. On one of those sorties, sophomore end Jack Lewis broke into the open on a pass pattern. The ball was on target, but a few steps from grabbing it he tripped over . . . the pitcher's mound, still in place because the Boston Braves' baseball season was not yet over.

"Most of the mound and the infield were still there," said Lewis. "You had to watch your step, which is hard to do at full speed."[46]

Later, Deacon guard Bill Finnance burst into the Boston College backfield and scooped up a fumble. With a cordon of blockers around him, he headed for the end zone just eighteen yards away and . . . slipped on his first step. Finnance made up for that gaff late in the game, pulling the ball away from an Eagles' player inside the Wake three-yard line. That stop saved the day, preserving a 7–7 tie, which looked better at the time than it did later on. As it turned out, it was the only game Boston College didn't lose that season.

That inauspicious beginning was followed by routs of some Virginia fodder. Wake blitzed Richmond 43–0 and then went up to William & Mary and pounded the Indians 47–0. All that was not in sync the first game was fixed in games two and three. The defense, boosted by newcomers like Lewis, Bob Gaona, and Larry Spencer, stopped both foes cold. The offense, despite continued uncertainty at quarterback, rolled down the field almost at will. Peahead Walker was a happy man.

And not just because of football. The day after his boys whipped Richmond, he was married again. The ceremony was held at the Raleigh home of George and Beth Paschal, second-generation Wake Foresters, and attended by a small group of friends. Flonnie Horenthal Watts looked good in a fancy blue dress and hat. The groom stunned observers by showing up in a dark blue suit, white shirt, and (relatively) sedate tie. The wedding formalized a long-time arrangement, although just when the Walker-Watts (her maiden name was Horenthal, this was her second rodeo too) relationship began is not certain. Players from the late 1940s recall her as a constant in Walker's life. A Raleigh resident, though not a native, Watts had been installed as hostess and manager of the bar at the Sir Walter Raleigh Hotel since the end of World War II, if not before. She was a natural in that post, her gift of gab and considerable skills at the piano charming guests week after week. Given that position and a predisposition to good

---

46 Jack Lewis, interview with author.

times after dark, her meeting up with "Petie" was unavoidable. The Sir Walter Raleigh, near the halls of the state government, was a capital hotspot, and Peahead Walker found hotspots almost as easily as he found hard-hitting blocking backs.

That Flonnie and Petie weren't married sooner—school, or at least Baptist officials, had been pressuring him on this for some time—is less of a mystery. Walker couldn't remarry because he wasn't *unmarried* yet. Proceedings in the divorce case of D.C. and Carolyne Walker didn't wrap up until mid-September, roughly two weeks before his marriage to Watts. The action had been in the works for the better part of 1950, and when all was said and done, appeared fairly amicable. The grounds for the divorce were a two-year separation, a circumstance that had been in effect unofficially for a longer period than that. The divorce documents list the official separation date as June 15, 1943, and the split may have happened before that. Most Wake Foresters remember Walker living in a room under the gym, and Carolyne Walker was seldom seen in the community. "She just never seemed to fit in," recalled Jennie Brewer, who grew up with the Walkers and later served as an athletic department secretary.[47]

The divorce settlement was simple. Peahead Walker gave his first wife $2,500 cash plus $150 a month for the rest of her life—or his. He also agreed to pay her medical expenses, up to $500 per year. The Wake County judge handling the matter thought it was fair—and that was that. Walker was free to get hitched again, which he soon did.

Back on the football field, Walker was trying to find a steady quarterback to lead his offense, but that was proving difficult. Carroll Blackerby, the once-promising freshman, was now a battered senior, recuperating in the fall of 1950 from a broken collar bone. Dickie Davis, now a junior and a regular as the team's defensive safety, had a certain flair but was erratic. He completed just six of twenty-two passes against Boston College and had three picked off. Sophomore Joe Koch, a superb athlete who supposedly once knocked out the take-on-all-comers wrestling bear at the county fair in Franklin County, next door to Wake Forest, got a

---

47 Jennie Brewer, interview with author.

look but, as his alleged bear-baiting days suggest, was better suited for other gridiron pursuits.[48] The only other serious possibility was . . . Ed Kissell.

Kissell had, of course, turned in some acceptable quarterbacking in 1949, but he wasn't Peahead Walker's first choice. He couldn't throw the ball like Davis or Blackerby and couldn't run like Davis or some other signal callers of days gone by. So when the season started he was on the bench. He didn't play against Boston College but then started against Richmond when Davis missed most of the week's practice with an ear infection. Kissell threw three touchdown passes (all short tosses, of course) and handled the offense well. "That was his proving ground," Walker said. "We needed some help there and he gave it to us."[49] On the trip to William & Mary, Kissell opened at the Deacon helm and, helped by a defense that forced five turnovers and also blocked a punt, led the Deacons on five scoring drives. Davis directed two more in the fourth quarter as Walker's boys piled it on in a 47–0 victory.

Reflecting on his play years after the fact, Kissell said, "I was just a guy who worked and who could run the offense. I wasn't great and I knew it."[50]

Whether a guy who wasn't great was good enough to solve the Deacons' quarterback dilemma remained to be seen. There was no doubt, however, that Kissell could make the Deacon T go. He was a deft ball handler, which he attributed to his background as a very good basketball point guard. He also naturally understood the game, a byproduct, perhaps, of growing up in a football-loving family. Coach-like knowledge of an offense was just as much a requirement for quarterbacks then as it is now, and in some ways

---

48 Once upon a time, man-vs-mammal matchups were a regular attraction at fairs and the like, with bears being the most common choices. Muzzled, de-clawed and often drugged, the massive beasts were still quite formidable and easily bested most of their foes. Among the best known ursine grappler of recent vintage was Victor the Wrestling Bear, whom the Associated Press reported had a 15,000–0 (that is, 15,000 wins vs. zero losses) record in 1977. In truth, Victor occasionally lost so Koch's alleged feat is not impossible. Bear wrestling is now against the law in many states.
49 *Greensboro Daily News*, Oct. 2, 1950.
50 Ed Kissell, interview with author.

it was more important in the years after World War II when offenses became more sophisticated but when most coaches still let the quarterbacks call the plays. The T formation, with its fake handoffs and option-play possibilities, worked best when a quarterback understood not only individual plays but also their place in sequence. A straight dive to the fullback set up a handoff sweep to the offside halfback, which opened up the defense for a counter play from the play-side half . . . and so on. Kissell's keen understanding of all this—indeed, of what could and couldn't be done on the football field—was demonstrated from the very start of his time at Wake. Arriving at practice amidst the horde of freshmen in 1948, Kissell went with the group of boys working out at end, his high school position. Noting the size of the competition—he was very much the runt of *that* litter—Kissell immediately decided a switch was in order.

"I saw all those big guys at end and I said, 'Ed, you're a quarterback now,'" Kissell recalled.[51]

He was the Deacons' number one quarterback as they took on the Choo-Choo-less Tar Heels at Kenan Stadium in mid-October. For the first fifty-five or so minutes, the contest could hardly have been considered a classic, but from there it turned into a doozy.

With the score tied 7–7 late in the final quarter, Carolina had the ball and a first and goal at the Wake seven. The Deacons yielded nearly all that ground and almost gave up the score, but on fourth and goal from the one, Wake's Bill Finnance and Jim Staton knocked UNC tailback Dick Bunting to the ground and jarred the ball loose as he tried to rumble into the end zone off right tackle. Staton alertly pounced on the fumble, the threat survived.

Both brain trusts then pursued desperate gambles to grab a win, eschewing the safety of a tie. Instead of punting immediately from the one, the standard procedure of the day, Walker ordered fullback Miller to try to batter his way out. He did, picking up a first down to the eleven. Scarton broke a long one from there, carrying the ball out to midfield. The Deacon drive stalled, but the improved field position allowed them to kick the Heels into a

---

51 Ibid.

corner. Undaunted by their own poor position and the waning time—less than a minute now remained—Snavely ordered up a series of passes. "We didn't play for a tie," he said afterward. "We gambled and we lost."[52] The first two efforts from tailback Billy Hayes fell incomplete. The third did not. Wake's Larry Spencer ran snared it at the Carolina thirty-six, reversed his field, and brought it back to the Tar Heel twenty-five. It was his third pick of the still-young season. A roughing penalty on Wake on the return—the blunder could have decided the game—pushed the ball back to the Carolina forty-one. Accounts vary as to the exact time left, but it was something just under twenty seconds.

The chances of scoring from a little more than forty yards out in a play or two were unlikely, but Walker had worked up a play for a situation just like this. He'd told Kissell to run it earlier in the game, but Kissell wouldn't make the call, possibly because he wasn't sure he could throw the ball far enough. It was just as well. Now, when Walker needed something up his sleeve, something was in fact there, unknown and undiagnosed.

Walker pulled Kissell and put in Davis for his only play of the day at quarterback. He also added reserve end Ed "Congo" Butler to the lineup. The senior was not a great defender but was an excellent receiver, much better than any of Wake's other ends. He'd already caught two touchdown passes on the season.

Davis and Butler ran into the huddle, drawing surprised looks from their teammates. "All right, boys," said Davis, "we're going to run . . . um, you know, that play we've been working on in practice." Recalling the moment years later, Davis said, "Hell, I just couldn't remember the name of it."[53]

Said Butler, "I couldn't believe it. I said, 'You mean 633 pass?' And he said, 'Yeah, that's it.' I guess everyone knew what we were talking about it. It worked."[54]

Scarton ran a short crossing route that pulled in Carolina's linebackers and briefly froze the safety, future NFL coach Bud Carson. Butler sped past Bunting, the Tar Heel cornerback, and quarterback Davis, biding his time behind good protection, lofted

---

52 *Winston-Salem Journal*, Oct. 14, 1950.
53 Dickie Davis, interview with author.
54 Ed Butler, interview with author.

the ball high into the October sky. It dropped perfectly into Butler's arms at the five. He skipped into the end zone with ten seconds left. Wake had pulled off a miracle.

A wild scene ensued. Wake fans stormed onto the field and began tearing down the goal posts in the end zone. They'd snapped off one pole and brought down the crossbar when Carolina fans rushed to its (that is, the helpless goal post's) defense. A melee erupted. Several students from both schools were injured—one of Wake's student managers was knocked out cold when the broken goal post whacked him on the head—and authorities needed nearly an hour to restore order.

In the Southern Conference it could not be restored. There, Wake Forest was on top and still undefeated.

Momentum was building in Deaconland and the newlywed coach found himself a very popular fellow. This was not something new. Walker had always been popular in town and on campus. His infrequent appearances as guest speaker for the school's mandatory chapel series were always packed, said Mary Arden Harris, a student in the mid-1940s, "and not just because he was funny; he told us some important things, too."[55] Even among the school's many Baptist backers in the hinterlands of eastern North Carolina, Walker was a much-admired figure. Gene Hooks, Wake's athletic director in the 1960s, 70s, and 80s, said Peahead's hold on the school's alumni and supporter base in the state (and beyond) was complete:

> *Despite some occasional grumbling, the Baptists basically loved Peahead. They all thought the school was without resources and were very proud of what he did under those circumstances. If he did something . . . well, when he did something, that was . . . un-Baptist-like, they made an exception, at least most of them did. Now when we moved to Winston-Salem, we lost a lot of those eastern Baptist folks. I think if Peahead had still been [in Wake Forest], we could have brought most of [the easterners] along.*[56]

As noted earlier, Walker's "morals" were the subject of some intra-

---

55 Mary Arden Harris, interview with author.
56 Gene Hooks, interview with author.

Baptist debate, but moves to oust him never got very far.

Walker's fame and good standing with the Deacon partisans took on tangible form at the 1950 homecoming game against George Washington. At halftime, the Wake Forest band, along with three visiting high school bands, marched onto the field and spelled out P—E—A- H—E—A—D. The bands then morphed to spell T—R—I—B—B—L—E, the name of the newly appointed school president Harold Tribble. Observers report distinctly different reactions to the two spellings. When the band spelled Peahead, the crowd roared its approval. A few minutes later, Tribble drew polite applause. The disparity can hardly be considered surprising—who, after all, roots for college presidents, especially one so newly minted?—but may have been galling to Tribble all the same. The new president, appointed in June 1950 after Kitchin's resignation and retirement the previous summer, was never on the same page with Walker. Although an accomplished athlete—he played collegiate basketball and tennis at Richmond University—Tribble arrived at Wake with a reputation as something of a sourpuss when it came to big-time college athletics. Eventually, his alleged ruining of Deacon athletics during the trying years of Wake's move and transition to Winston-Salem, was among the factors that nearly cost Tribble his job. His lasting reputation was as an administrator who tolerated athletics, but who wasn't going to let it run the show. Tension with popular coaches was bound to follow from such stance, but in the fall of 1950, that kind of controversy seemed far away. As time would tell, it was not.

The antics of the WFC band and the boisterous homecoming crowd produced a festive atmosphere for the George Washington game, but for Coach Walker the day was more frustrating than anything. Although he brushed aside the idea afterward that his club was suffering from a post-Carolina letdown, the Deacons weren't sharp against the Colonials. Despite intercepting six passes, Wake struggled to a 13–0 victory. Kissell threw a fourth-down pass to Scarton for a third-quarter score, and sophomore Spencer, on his way to a brilliant season, intercepted a pass and ran it back eighty-three yards for the clincher in the final period.

No masterpiece, but Wake was still undefeated.

And the pressure was mounting. Next up was Clemson in a game that was as hyped as any conference game of Walker's career. Both teams were unbeaten (though both had been tied) and both were ranked in the national top twenty (Clemson was sixteenth and Wake seventeenth). The victor would have the inside track to the Southern Conference championship. Wake Forest's Jim Weaver was positively giddy at the interest in the game. He had to ship temporary bleachers from Wake Forest to the game's site in Winston-Salem to accommodate a crowd expected to exceed the 17,500-seat capacity of the concrete bowl at Bowman Gray Stadium by several thousand. "We're just tickled any time we can get that many people to a game," Weaver told the *Winston-Salem Journal*.[57]

While the contest captured the imagination of the fans, its import was not fully understood by the players. Dickie Davis, who admittedly was not always the most astute observer, said the team had no idea the game had such import until after the fact. Kissell, Jack Lewis, and other team members agreed. The Clemson game was the Clemson game—a point of emphasis because years of familiarity had bred some contempt and because of the Walker-Howard rivalry, but nothing more than that.

Of course, that was significant, especially the personal aspect.

The exploits of the Walker-Howard banquet circuit tandem, and their apparent chumminess after Walker landed in Montreal, suggest a genuine friendship. But Deacons around at the time were never sure. Howard just seemed too unlikeable, and Walker's interest in beating Clemson seemed too intense for a friendly rivalry.

"I don't think [Walker] really liked [Howard] much at all," said Bill Hensley, the student journalist. "They were supposed to be friends and all, but the way he acted about that game, I just didn't see it."[58]

Dewey Hobbs said tensions were always high when Clemson was on the schedule. Howard was a tough guy for many to like. His antics-during his younger years—he was known to turn

---

57 *Winston-Salem Journal*, Oct. 22, 1950.
58 Bill Hensley, interview with author.

cartwheels on the sidelines when the Tigers scored—came off as boorish or bullying. And he possessed both a mean streak and an arrogance that didn't sit well. One year, before a game at Clemson, as Hobbs recalled, Howard visited the Wake Forest dressing room and almost started a fight.

> *I can't remember if it was before the game or before practice the day before. He just walked in and he knew us all. He was making comments and little jokes. He was like that, kind of came across as a bully or something. Anyway, he came up and slapped Dave Harris on the back and said something, I forget what, and if we hadn't held him back, I think Harris would have fought Frank Howard right there. . . . I don't know. Peahead always told us before that game that Howard is "nothing but a damn clown." You'd hear what they said about each other and their families and all, and I'd have to say that that didn't sound very friendly to me. I don't know, but I never believed (they were friends).*[59]

Bitter friends or bitter enemies, the 1950 Wake-Clemson contest was a humdinger with many twists and turns. Clemson's two best backs, fullback Fred Cone and wingback Ray Matthews, were put out of action early in the game by Wake's hard-hitting defense. But it was the Tigers who drew first blood. In a two-minute span midway through the second quarter, Clemson scored on two long touchdowns, both of which were on reverses around Wake's left end. Frank Kennedy, a little-used sophomore subbing for Matthews, scored the first from twenty-two yards out. The slightly more experienced Jim Shirley got the second on a fifty-seven-yard run. Shirley's scoring play, which included a pass fake by Clemson's tailback, was similar, if not identical to Kennedy's jaunt; and it made Walker wonder if his old coaching pal had psychic powers. Just before both plays, Walker had subbed a new man into the game at end, sophomore Ken Bridges. On both plays, Bridges bit on the pass fake, leaving the Deacon flank uncovered.

---

59 Dewey Hobbs, interview with author.

"It was just a dumb mistake," said Bridges. "After the second one, he [Walker] called me an idiot and quite a few other names, but by then the damage was done."[60]

Walker didn't call Bridges out publicly after the game—coaches were even less likely to do that then than they are now—but did note that his team "just made two mistakes on defense and they cost us touchdowns. . . . I don't know how Clemson guessed it, but we had just made substitutions at those spots where they chose to run it."[61]

Wake was behind 13–0, and with Clemson's defense bowing up every time Wake threatened to score, it looked like that would be more than enough until midway through the fourth quarter when tackle Jim Staton blocked a Clemson punt. Wake recovered at the Tiger eight-yard line and punched in a play later from there on a Miller run. That cut the lead to 13–6, but Kissell's extra point sailed wide, leaving the Deacons a touchdown and a point after away from a tie. The missed kick didn't look like it would matter until Walker decided he'd give the Davis-Butler duo a shot at another late game miracle. He pulled Kissell and one of the regular ends and put Dickie and "Congo" in to see what they could do.

Wake had the ball at its own thirteen with just more than ninety seconds to play, but Davis quickly drove the Deacons into Clemson territory. A forty-five-yard completion to Butler put the ball at the Clemson twenty-eight. Davis followed that up with a twenty-four-yard strike to Jack Lewis, who made a leaping catch at the four. With time winding down, Davis dropped back again, was mobbed by Clemson rushers, danced around, and finally lobbed one to Butler, who'd used Davis's scrambling to locate a quiet and solitary spot for himself in the back of the end zone.

Now it was 13–12, and Kissell came on again—this one for the tie. He got the kick off this time, but it was low and a Clemson player smothered it. Clemson's victory was secure.

The quality of kicking at the time was such that not much was made of the two missed extra points—those things just happened back then—but years later Kissell said that at least part

---

60 Bridges, interview with author.
61 *Greensboro Daily News,* Oct. 29, 1950.

of the blame rested on the team's equipment manager, Jesse Haddock, who left Kissell's kicking tee back in Wake Forest:

> *Or someplace. I don't really know where. I don't know what was up with that. He was supposed to have it but didn't. Every time it was time to kick, the tee was nowhere to be found. So I had to kick it off the ground, which I hadn't practiced. Later on, I learned to do that, but I didn't know then and it was kind of upsetting. I don't know, I guess I should have called time out. But at the time you felt like you were just a little guy and didn't really have authority to call timeout for something like that. So you did the best you could. I tried. I missed. We lost.*[62]

Walker, as noted, was more inclined to blame the two defensive lapses for the defeat. The "old country sonofabitch" on the other sidelines credited his defense for the victory but gave an assist to a gold-plated tiger tooth charm he had taken to carrying in his pocket. "That's the luckiest thing in the world," Howard told reporters during a postgame briefing and whiskey sampling back at his suite in the Robert E. Lee Hotel. "I almost rubbed the skin off my hand [while] rubbing it on that [last] extra point."[63]

It is instructive of the mentality of the era that Walker, Weaver, and company did not regard Wake's first loss of the season in tragic terms. Indeed, the primary postgame view was that the game was an artistic and—more to the point—financial success. Standing-room-only tickets were sold up to and beyond kickoff time and the crowd swelled past 22,000. It was easily the largest home crowd in school history for a contest not involving one of Wake's well-populated nearby rivals. At the time, that seemed like consolation enough.

A clever (at least in hindsight) piece of scheduling gave the Deacons time to recover. They had a week off before traveling to Durham for the annual war with Duke.

---

62 Kissell, interview with author.
63 *Winston-Salem Journal*, Oct. 29, 1950.

The Blue Devils were fading in what would be Wallace Wade's last season, although they were still a fine team.[64] Duke brought a 5–2 record into the game, having lost to Tennessee and Maryland, the latter of which was turning into a national power under Walker's old baseball pal "Big" Jim Tatum.[65] The contest was played on a cold and rainy day on a muddy field and was the low-scoring affair that might have been expected under such conditions. Wake took a 13–7 lead when Davis hit Lewis with a forty-two-yard touchdown pass in the last two minutes of the first half. The Deacons made it stand up, using the running of Miller and Scarton and the punting of Davis to control the ball and the field position after intermission. Duke crossed midfield just once after the break and didn't really come close to scoring. Walker slowed Duke with some special anti-Blue Devil strategies. He unveiled a new defense—an unusual 4-3 alignment—that dropped an extra player off the line of scrimmage. Walker assigned that man—sophomore Tom Donohue for the most part—to the special duty of whacking Duke end Mike Souchak on every snap. The contact threw off Souchak's passing routes and kept him from double-teaming Wake's defensive tackle, a key component of Wade's single-wing attack.

"He (Walker) was always a pretty good game coach," said Donohue. "I always felt like he had a good plan, something different, something special, for every team we played."[66]

Teammate Jack Lewis agreed with Donohue's assessment and recalled a game in which his standard assignment was altered radically to confuse an opponent. An end, Lewis usually had the essential responsibility for containing the opposition's outside running game. On this particular day, Lewis's task was to crash

---

64 Wade didn't resign until December. He got married right after the season, went on a honeymoon, and returned to announce that he was leaving coaching to become the first full-time commissioner of the Southern Conference. Ironically, in that role, Wade presided over a major breakup of the league when seven schools, including his beloved Duke, left to form the Atlantic Coast Conference.
65 Notably, Walker never scheduled a game against Maryland while Tatum was the head coach.
66 Tom Donahue, interview with author.

into the backfield, disrupting whatever play was in progress in whatever way he could. Said Lewis:

> *It was unusual. I didn't have contain. I was so worried that my dad would think I was goofing up the whole game. So I told coach before the game, 'I've got to find Dad for a minute,' and he let me go. . . . He [Walker] was forever trying new things. Once against UNC he had me backing into pass coverage. Oh man was I lost. He didn't do that again. But he wasn't afraid to try new things and I think it made us better. We were among the best in the nation that year in total defense and I think keeping other teams off balance was part of that. I know after he left it wasn't like that. It was just the same week after week.*[67]

The victory over Duke was Walker's third straight over the Wade dynasty. Even with Duke slipping a bit, that was something to savor, especially given Wake's long-suffering record against the Blue Devils.

Less savory was Walker's late-career work against NC State and Coach Beattie Feathers. After dominating Feathers's predecessor and giving Wake control of that rivalry, Walker's postwar teams sputtered against the college's closest (geographically speaking) rival. Walker was 1-3-1 against Feathers from 1946 to 1950, and this while the Wolfpack were in a decided state of decline. Feathers and company, struggling to recruit top-notch players and lacking even some basic resources or organization—sportswriters noted some Wolfpack wearing beige "practice pants" during games—managed just one winning season from 1948 until Feathers was canned after the 1951 season. And that despite salting the schedule with regular gimmes like Davidson, Richmond, and Duquesne. But when it came to Wake Forest, the Wolves were ready. The matchup seemed to be just one of those things that happens in sports. The Wolfpack had the Deacons' number, and Feathers, who often seemed overmatched on the sidelines, regularly got the best of Walker.

---

67 Jack Lewis, interview with author.

The 1950 meeting between the two schools was typical of the late-Walker-era contests. The underdog Wolfpack played conservatively while hoping to capitalize on a mistake, and Wake simply tried to overpower the outmanned Pack. Statistically the Deacons did just that—running 84 offensive plays to just 37 for State and piling up 339 total yards to just 177. But when all was said and done, the contest finished in a 6–6 draw. Despite driving deep into State territory time and time again, the Deacons could not muster anything on the day other than Scarton's blocked punt and return for touchdown. For its part, State did very little with the ball until pulling off a trick play in the waning moments.

With the ball on the Wolfpack thirty and less than two minutes to play, Feathers ordered up a clever little gambit he'd installed on Wednesday. Tailback Ed Mooney dropped back a couple of steps and flipped a pass to fullback Jim O'Rourke, who'd circled into the right flat. O'Rourke caught it in the clear, took a few steps toward the line of scrimmage, and then stopped and fired a long pass downfield to wingback Jimmy Smith. Smith, well behind several confused Deacon defenders, hauled in the pass around the Wake forty and raced in for the score.

The play could have sealed the deal—Wake had failed yet again to convert a point after, this time on a planned but incomplete pass after Walker once more had given up on kickers—but Ray Barkouskie, the Wolfpack's normally reliable kicker, missed badly. A sore ankle on his kicking foot was cited as a postgame excuse.

Perhaps it was just as well. The play was tinged with controversy. If the first pass in the play, Mooney's sideways toss to O'Rourke, was actually a legitimate forward pass, then the second pass would have been illegal. That, of course, was the trick. The first pass had to look like a forward pass without actually being one. Most of the Wake defenders were fooled. They ran forward to tackle O'Rourke and uncovered Smith in the process. As a result, he was wide open when O'Rourke stopped to throw the second pass on the play. Whether it was legal or not is impossible to say. Officials made no call at the time, and the grainy game film doesn't provide the proper angle to make a determination. Wake's players were upset, but Walker didn't make a big deal of it.

"We had other chances to win," he said.[68]

In the afterglow of the moral victory and actual tie, Feathers said he hoped that "movies" didn't show the play to have been illegal. "I wouldn't want to tie a team as good as Wake Forest with an illegal play," he said.[69]

Wake wrapped up the 1950 season with a 14–7 victory over South Carolina on a bitterly cold Thanksgiving Day in Columbia. The tough Deacon defense held the Gamecocks to less than ninety-five total yards, and the offense did enough to get by, which, in a nutshell, was the story of the second half of the season. Notably, Wake made two extra points against USC, both by center Jimmy Zrakas, the fifth Deacon to try his foot at the task during the season. Even with Zrakas's closing onslaught, Wake finished the season a dismal eleven for twenty-four on point after touchdowns. As it turned out, the biggest pain inflicted by the January academic scandal was the absence of Bill George's educated toe. George made twenty-four of twenty-nine extra points in 1949. A year later, Wake was just a couple of successful boots away from an unbeaten season.

Clemson was the chief benefactor of the Deacons' inaccuracy. The Tigers' near escape in Winston-Salem allowed them to complete an unbeaten season and land an Orange Bowl berth. They did not, however, win the Southern Conference championship. That honor, such as it was, went to Washington & Lee, which went 6–0 in league play, although it was a very different league from the one in which Wake Forest, Clemson, Duke, and North Carolina played. The Generals played none of the league's powers.

Some Deacon fans may have found the 1950 season a little disappointing—it was just inches away from perfection after all—but in the Deacon locker room there was a satisfying glow. Walker and his boys overcame the cheating scandal of the winter before, smoothed over the internal turmoil of 1949, and put together an excellent season. The 6-1-2 mark was one of the best in school history. The team was not as flashy as some of Walker's other teams, but it did the unglamorous things well. The Deacons gave

---

68 *Greensboro Daily News*, Nov. 20, 1950.
69 Ibid.

up just 69.1 yards per game on the ground, second-lowest figure in the country; rushed for almost two hundred yards per game; didn't give up big plays in the kicking game (missed extra points aside); and made the plays needed to pull several close games out of the fire. All good enough to cause *Old Gold & Black* sports columnist Wiley Warren to declare it the end of an era, "the end of the days of easy pickings in the football land of the Magnolia and Deacons."[70]

***

Warren turned out to be prophetic, though not in quite the way intended. A few months later, just as spring practice began, Deacon fans awoke one Monday morning to discover that an era in Wake Forest football had indeed ended.

The Peahead Walker era.

The best coach the school had ever had was leaving.

It was a bolt out of the blue. On a Thursday in late March, Walker was guiding a draft-depleted Deacon squad through spring drills (conscription for the Korean War was instituted in the fall of 1950, and several footballers were called up). By the following Monday he was on his way to Yale to assist long-time friend Herman Hickman in coaching the Bulldogs.

That seemed an astonishingly fast turn of events, but some moves had been in the works far longer. The clear starting point was the previous September when Harold Tribble was installed as Wake's new president.

Publicly, Walker left over a dispute over a pedestrian sum of money—$1,000, or the difference between a raise of $500 versus $1,500 per year. But there was much more to it than that. The crux of the matter was a conflict between Walker and the new president.

The most telling evidence for this conclusion is the fact that Tribble felt the need to issue an official statement during the departure denouement declaring that there was "no friction" attached to the coach's resignation. The release may have seemed

---

[70] *Old Gold & Black*, Nov. 20, 1950.

necessary, but officially calling attention to the lack of friction implied that some almost certainly existed.

There was very little contact between Walker and Tribble as things fell apart, but the relationship between new president and popular coach was anything but friendly. Tribble's actions clearly played a major role in forcing Walker to accept the Yale post, even if Tribble didn't order it directly (and there's absolutely no evidence that that was the case). The newly minted president faced a hailstorm of criticism from Wake's alumni/booster crowd after the fact. Walker said that the telegrams he received on the matter numbered in the hundreds. Tribble was likely inundated, too. He realized the need to get his side of the story out, so a rare press release was prepared, the thesis of which was that Walker willingly left Wake for New Haven, CT for a lesser post (i.e., he would be an assistant coach) at an equal salary, in a "foreign" part of the country, and with a school that was in the process of de-emphasizing the sport of football. The scenario seemed as far-fetched to observers then as it does, when considered in retrospect, now.

The Yale job may have held some allure for Walker. The biggest reason to go, quite literally, was Herman "Half Ton" Hickman. The chance to pair up with his fellow trencherman and king-sized backwoods raconteur may have actually interested Walker, although subsequent events suggest otherwise. Hickman, who had gained the post in 1948 after posting a sterling record as Army's line coach during West Point's glory years just after World War II, claimed to have begun courting Walker as an assistant shortly after that.

No serious offer was made, however, until late February or early March 1951, after both of Yale's line coaches left for other jobs (Alva Kelley took the head job at Brown while Wyatt Posey left for an assistant's post at Texas Tech).

The timing was either wonderfully fortuitous or strangely coincidental. Walker had been waiting throughout the winter for confirmation of a contract extension and raise at Wake. The athletic committee, basking in the glow of the 1950 season's record-setting football box office, had met in December and approved a new four-year contract with a salary boost from $7,500 to $9,000 per year for Walker. But the pact had not been consummated because—said sources at the time—it lacked the approval of the university's administration, specifically Tribble. With the Yale offer in hand, Walker forced the issue, informing both Athletic Director Jim Weaver and President Tribble of his offer of a new position at Yale. Was the president going to approve Walker's new WFC contract, with its 20 percent raise, or not? A Friday deadline for a decision was set—Walker needed to give Yale an answer—but Tribble requested a one-day delay. It was granted, but when the appointed hour rolled round on Saturday, Walker still hadn't heard . . . or what he had heard he didn't like. Tribble would approve a new contract, but only with an increase of $500 per year to $8,000. Coincidentally or otherwise, that was just what Hickman was offering Walker to come to Yale. Walker called Hickman and Bob Hall, chair of Yale's Board of Athletic Control, Saturday afternoon and told them he'd take the job.

Word spread quickly. Newspapers in Raleigh, Durham, and Greensboro reported the startling news in their Monday editions. Wake's sporting alumni, informed by newspaper or backchannel phone calls, were up in arms. Walker was quitting over a pittance? And how, some not in the know asked, has Wake Forest gotten away with paying Walker half as much as the coaches he was beating on a regular basis? Wade and Snavely were both making (or in Wade's case had been making) more than $15,000 a year at that point. Walker was, at best, in the bottom third of the entire Southern Conference in salary. He may have been at the very bottom.

Alumni had quickly agreed they'd make up any difference between what the president would approve and what Walker wanted, and although having their support felt good he noted later, it really became a matter of principle. He thought the school ought to be the source of the funds—not friends of the program who had already been taking care of him (recall the new auto of two falls before). It didn't seem right for the school to hijack that resource for its own purposes.

Something more was at stake as well, however. According to both Walker and Weaver's accounts, Tribble had informally okayed the $1,500 raise in December. It was, in Walker's mind, a done deal. The subsequent reduction, however necessary Tribble believed it to be given school finances and some consideration about the relationship between faculty and coaching pay, looked like backtracking.

And then there was the question of commitment. Was Tribble really behind football or not? More specifically, was he behind Walker's style and brand? His public pronouncements were not promising. Introduced on campus in late September, Tribble submitted to an extensive interview with the *Old Gold & Black* in which he weighed in on a number of topics, including football and athletics. He lauded Wake's success under Walker, but the compliments sounded forced and backhanded—especially in hindsight. More credible was Tribble's "very strong conviction [that football] must be kept in line with the central purposes of the college. I think the football players ought to meet every mental and moral requirement that every other student has to meet." Tribble added that he was "especially glad" at the outcome of the 1950 football cheating scandal and was happy that "students took such a vigorous and positive part in this moral discipline of themselves."[71]

Whether these sentiments were expressed in private meetings between the two men—and again, it's not clear that there were many of those—is impossible to say. That some strain developed early on in their relationship was plain for observers at the time to see. Walker didn't have the personal connection with Tribble that he'd enjoyed with Kitchin—he wasn't Tribble's man. And the new president, an ordained minister and the president of a theological seminary prior to coming to Wake Forest, was made of sterner, some might say more sanctimonious, stuff. Edwin O. Wilson, a Wake Forest faculty legend whose career began as Walker's was ending, put it this way: "Tribble had kind of a stiff neck. He and Peahead did not get along. I think Tribble's attitude towards athletics was part of that. And he didn't think much of Peahead's behavior at all. I'm sure it was a surprise you might say for Tribble to find him as the coach at WFC."[72]

---

71 *Old Gold & Black,* Sept. 25, 1950.
72 Edwin O. Wilson, interview with author.

Not a complete surprise, however. Tribble had been briefed about the various improprieties of Coach Walker and his occasionally rowdy players long before he took the job. In a separate letter accompanying the one inviting him to Wake Forest to interview for the job, Dr. Casper C. Warren, chair of the search committee, told Tribble that as the new president he'd have substantial backing if he wanted to lead a fundamentalist takeover of the college. The problem for Warren et al. was the spirit of cynicism, liberalism, independence, etc., that had crept into the school. That spirit didn't exactly jibe with North Carolina Baptists. Among the worst manifestations of this new spirit? Coach Peahead Walker.

In a letter to Tribble, Warren wrote:

> *The most disturbing thing during the past five or six years has been the drinking of Coach Peahead Walker and his most outstanding football players. Complaints were repeatedly made to the trustees [but] investigating committees seem to major in explaining away rather than eliminating the evil. Since Peahead could still go to S.M.U., for example, and bring back $50,000, alumni groups protest bitterly against the expulsion of football men for cheating on the basis that it could wreck the team.*[73]

Tribble, more of a scholar than a fire-and-brim-stoner, does not seem to have taken either Warren's words, or his offer, to heart. The fundamentalists never took control (ironically, a group of trustees that included some "fundie" remnants, nearly managed to get Tribble fired in the mid-1950s) and the increasingly prickly Tribble became ever more his own man as his tenure progressed. It's difficult to say whether Tribble's famed reputation for moral

---

[73] Wake Forest University Archives. Papers of Harold D. Tribble. As noted elsewhere, official sources say the $50,000 sum Warren cites in this passage was closer to $60,000.

uprightness[74] or just a general disconnect with Walker was the biggest cause of their rift. What does seem certain is that both men realized they were going to struggle to see things in the same way and that conflict was bound to ensue. Walker had made football that big at Wake Forest. Tribble, evidence suggests, wished it were smaller.

Tribble was certainly no Thurman Kitchin, a stalwart supporter of both Walker and big-time football. Tribble was a different guy. Put to the test, early in his tenure, he didn't back down.

In the immediate postmortems, Weaver stepped up and took the blame for the technical problems, saying he was responsible for giving Walker the impression that Tribble would sign off on the $9,000 deal. "It's been a bad misunderstanding. . . . I'm just sick about it," Weaver said.[75]

No doubt he was, but later events suggest it wasn't mere miscommunication. Three years later, Tribble pulled a similar bait-and-switch stunt while hiring Pat Preston to fill Weaver's shoes after Weaver had announced he was leaving to become the leader of the newly formed Atlantic Coast Conference. Preston, an assistant coach at Wake under Walker and then under Walker's successor Tom Rogers, was a reluctant athletic director. But as a man with a young family, he couldn't afford to pass up the job, and the accompanying $3,000-a-year raise, when it was offered. He discussed the matter with Weaver, met the trustees, and, like his old coach three years before, thought the deal was done. A week into his new job, however, Tribble called him in for a meeting and told him the school couldn't afford the promised salary.

---

74 In a story well-known to old Wake Foresters, Tribble is walking home from his office late one night when he spies a male student and coed dash into some bushes up ahead of him. Alarmed, Tribble hurries quickly to the site where he observes various pieces of clothing being tossed over the shrubbery. Soon, the shrubs began to shake and moans of pleasure can be heard. Tribble can take it no more. "Ah-hemmmmm," he says, clearing his throat. "This is President Harold Tribble. Just what is going on in there?" After a brief silence a male voice replies, "Well, Dr. Tribble, we were just smooching a little." A long pause. And then—from a clearly relieved Tribble—"Oh, thank goodness. From the way the bushes were shaking I was afraid you were dancing."

75 *Raleigh News & Observer*, March 7, 1951.

"He said, 'Pat, you know you've never been in administration before. Our full professors don't make an AD's salary. We can't afford that.' I didn't know what to do," said Preston. "It was already in the papers that Preston would be the new AD. I'd look dumb if I quit then. People would say, 'Why not look into that before?' But the salary had been set. The trustees had set it and I sure thought the president had agreed.

"I won't say the president lied . . . well he did lie," said Preston. "He went back on his word. A lot of preachers [Tribble was an ordained clergyman] are like that."[76]

Tribble's stated reasoning in the Walker case—as related without attribution by sports columnists of the time—was similar. Walker's new salary would have placed him above all the professors on campus, and it would have been an unusually robust raise during a new era of campus-wide fiscal austerity caused by decreasing enrollment, war worries, and the expected cost of the impending move to Winston-Salem. So $500 more—but not $1,500. Such penny pinching eventually became Tribble's administrative calling card. He may have been predisposed to such an attitude, but Wake's budgetary struggles forced it upon him as well. Wilson recalled that not long after Peahead's departure, a faculty colleague of his went to Tribble with a Peahead-like proposition. He'd received a better offer from another institution but told the president that he really wanted to stay at Wake. "I'd really like to stay, Dr. Tribble," the suffering professor said, "but my salary here is not very good and I do have this other offer. I just don't know what to do and would really value your advice."

"Well," replied Tribble in Wilson's version of the tale, "if you have a better offer, I would advise you to take it."[77]

He probably did not phrase his answer to Walker in just those terms, but the tone sounded, or felt, the same to the school's football-loving alumni. The athletic council, led by Greensboro businessman Henry Liles, called a special meeting for Monday night, the day after the news broke. More alums than usual were present. At least two current members of the football team were also there. All were of the same mind—the school needed to find a

---

76 Pat Preston audio memoir, courtesy of Andy Preston.
77 Ed Wilson, interview with author.

way to keep Walker—and they voted to encourage Tribble and the college to meet the $9,000 salary figure. A post-vote statement noted that the vote had been unanimous, "with President Tribble concurring," for offering Walker a new four-year deal with a salary starting at $9,000 a year. The new offer was made, said the council statement, "without any thought of trying to outbid Yale but as an expression of appreciation of Coach Walker's work and in a desire to express the wish of the council and administration to retain him."[78]

Of course.

Weaver delivered the news to Walker late Monday and Walker seriously considered reversing his decision.

"I just about changed my mind," he said later.[79]

But Tuesday he was on a plane to New Haven for what may have been his first actual visit to Yale, a sign that the whole saga was not much more than a bargaining chip gone wrong. He told Weaver before he left, however, that he was unlikely to change his mind, a verdict he confirmed the next day after a campus tour, a dinner with Hickman, and an evening spent watching the Ezzard Charles-Jersey Joe Walcott heavyweight title fight on the Hickmans' fancy new gizmo. It was called a TV.

Leaving Wake was not an easy decision. Walker had put down real roots in North Carolina.

"When you've lived in a state as long as I have it's hard to break all the ties and leave all your friends," Walker said. "But we hope we can make the same kind of friends up here."[80]

Walker's farewell sounds like something less than a friction-free departure. Why leave "home" voluntarily for a job that paid less? Weaver's valedictory comments belie a certain tension along those lines as well. In his address he all but called out Tribble for his penurious intent and his inability to spot a true bargain.

"Since 1937," Weaver said, "Wake Forest has had more coaching at less expense than any institution in the United States."[81]

---

78 *Raleigh News & Observer*, March 9, 1951.
79 *Greensboro Daily News*, Mar. 8, 1951.
80 Ibid.
81 Ibid.

CHAPTER 9

LA TETE DU POIS

Yale was already one of America's great university's when Peahead Walker arrived in the spring of 1951. But just what it was athletically, well, that was another matter.

The famed Connecticut college was home to one of the foundational programs of big-time college athletics in America and it had the trappings to prove it. The Yale Bowl, home to Bulldog football, seated 70,000 in the nation's prototype, bowl-shaped stadium. Payne Whitney gymnasium was a nine-and-a-half story neo-Gothic tower that housed two basketball courts, a swimming pool, twenty-eight handball courts, and countless locker rooms and exercise spaces. It astonished all who saw it, include Yale's newest assistant football coach in the spring of 1951. "It's 14 stories high and cost $14 million when they built it back in 1932," Walker gushed [and exaggerated] when reporting back to his Boswell, Smith Barrier of the *Greensboro Daily News*. "Man, they have got the facilities."[1] Yale also had the tradition, the alumni, and the money. Walker bumped into all of those early and often. For instance, the center and best player on the first, and only, Yale line he coached was one of the DuPont heirs.

What the Eli didn't have in 1951 was the athletic ambition of the Walter Camp days. Back then, Yale had more than the trappings of athletic power; it was a strong advocate of professionalism, proselytization, and all that went with it. That was Yale's long-time legacy. But during the debates of the 1930s, sentiment at Yale had began to turn. When other "Ivies" pressed for athletic retrenchment after World War II—what they wanted was an end to the direct subsidization of athletics and to all recruiting—Yale didn't put up a fight. By the time Walker arrived, the Bulldogs, and the Ivy League in general, were in a strange

---

1 *Greensboro Daily News*, July 3, 1951.

athletic limbo—headed toward athletic obscurity but still jousting with big-time football. Princeton, with All-American Dick Kazmaier in tow, remained a ranked team through the mid-1950s, and other league members still played national heavyweights. But with athletic scholarships at an end and recruiting officially at a standstill, the atmosphere was . . . different. It was, Walker confided to friends not long after his arrival, "amateur football."[2]

For a professional coach like Walker, this was agonizing. He didn't quite know what to do. He spent the summer of 1951 traveling in North Carolina with Flonnie and visiting old friends rather than beating the bushes for fresh talent. It was, he said, his first summer off since . . . well, he couldn't remember. Walker did have a recruiting area—the South—but no real authority to pursue talent within it. If an alumnus pointed a Southern player Yale's way, Walker could follow up. But that was it. And once a player arrived at Yale, the coaching staff's hold just wasn't the same. Chemistry labs and family trips took precedence over mundane chores like spring practice. "We got more accomplished in a week (of practice) at Wake Forest," Walker said after his one and only Yale spring season was over, "than we did here in two months."[3]

Mitigating against this assault on Walker's professional sensibilities was the conditions under which he worked. He was being paid a nice salary for a much-reduced workload; he got to spend time with his friend Herman Hickman; and for all his moaning, the watered-down football at Yale really wasn't much of a surprise. Although the public pronouncements of Hickman and other Yale officials at the time of Walker's signing suggest the ex-Deacon head was being brought in to help create a new national power, Hickman's actions and record make it clear that he understood what this posting was all about. To put it bluntly, the Yale job—and this was especially true for someone familiar with serious college football like—was something of a lark. In that regard, it was a near perfect match for Hickman's entire coaching career, which always seemed something of a sideshow.

In addition to coaching football at Wake Forest, NC State, and Army, Hickman also wrote and recited poetry, had played pro

---

2 Bill Hensley, interview with author.
3 *Greensboro Daily News*, July 3, 1951.

football, and had been a prolific professional wrestler with more than three hundred matches under his sizeable belt.[4] And, by the time Hickman arrived at Yale, he was already a burgeoning radio and television personality.

Hickman seems to have been as much a character as a coach during his stay in Eli-land. Accounts of his time there are taken up more by one-liners and anecdotes than accolades and events. Hickman said early on that his task was to make sure that the alumni were "sullen but not mutinous," and he generally succeeded in bringing that plan to fruition. His teams were mediocre but not horrible. He won often enough to make his post-victory practice of saluting the bust of the great Coach Camp—"Well, Walt, we got another one," Hickman would reputedly say—into something of a Yale tradition.

Sportswriters in search of copy and color found all this funnier than alums and players, but Hickman did seem to have a chummy rapport with the young men on the squad. Upon arriving at Yale directly after coaching massive lines for Red Blaik at Army, Hickman told the press he was calling his first Yale line "the Seven Dwarfs" because of their slight stature. A day or so after that, the starting line showed up at practice with new names taped across their helmets: Dopey, Sleepy, Doc, etc. Levi Jackson, Yale's first black player but not a lineman, got into the spirit of things and wore Snow White.

Ed Carricolo, who played at Yale from 1949 to 1953, said, "Hickman was a pretty nice guy and all but it was clear we needed someone who'd put a little more into it."[5]

Hickman did possess bona fides as both a coach and a player. He was a brilliant All-American at Tennessee, where, as a 5'10", 245-pound guard, he drew copious praise from Volunteer coaching legend Bob Neyland. The General called Hickman the best guard he'd coached—or ever seen play. Hickman went on to enjoy a brief professional career as well and through the first ten to fifteen years of his coaching career was still good enough to terrorize his

---

[4] Some sources list Hickman's grappling experience at closer to six hundred bouts. Since many of the matches were quite informal and held in outposts of civilization like Bluefield, WV, the real number is impossible to compute.
[5] Ed Carricolo, interview with author.

charges in practice. Army's Blaik eventually banned him from participating in practice—as a player—because he was injuring so many of West Point's actual squadmen.

Just how astute a coach he was is hard to say. He is credited as being one of the pioneers of dedicated special teams play, a subject of which Peahead Walker was also fond,[6] and at Army, Coach Hickman churned out All-American linemen one after the other. But given Army's ability to stock its roster with military "draftees" during Hickman's days at West Point (see chapter 6 for more on this scheme), Francis the Talking Mule could have coached the line and Army would still have been reaping laurels right and left. Hickman, who played at Tennessee in the early 1930s, was certainly an old-school coach. Unlike Walker, he was not quick to adopt modern tactics, although Yale did eventually run some T-formation plays under his tutelage. Hickman later wrote that all the "faking we did in the backfield [as part of the T] was designed more to distract alumni from the awful things that usually happened when we had the ball than anything else."[7]

Although part of his after-dinner (and later television and radio) patter was telling stories about backwoods life in his native Tennessee, Hickman was, in fact, an intelligent and learned man. He was a well-read son from a family of affluent jurists and businessmen, a man who loved literature and could recite long passages from Shakespeare. He came to the University of Tennessee from the prestigious Baylor Preparatory School, perhaps Tennessee's premier secondary school in that day, where he won the state oratorical competition for his recitation of "Spartacus to the Gladiators," as well as the shot put event at the state track meet. Surely it was a rare double.

Reputedly, Hickman dusted off the Spartacus speech—"If ye are beasts, then stand here like fat oxen, waiting for the butcher's knife! If ye are men, follow me!" is the critical line—before his first Harvard-Yale game.

Walker fell into, and survived, this strange situation because he and Hickman were friends long before Walker got to

---

6 M. West, *Legends of the Tennessee Vols.* 2005. New York: Sports Publishing.
7 *Herman Hickman: The Tennessee Terror,* University of Tennessee News Service, 1997.

Wake. The exact nature of the connection isn't clear, but the fact that a bond was created is hardly surprising, for they had much in common. Both men liked to eat, especially at big city restaurants. (Hickman, like Walker, was a fan of Mama Leone's in New York city, where serving size was more notable than culinary brilliance.) They both enjoyed telling and being the butt of a good story, and both were sons of the South who played their "hick" card for all it was worth. Indeed, during his Yale and New York years, Hickman's Cadillac even sported a HICK license plate,[8] which of course was also a play on his name. It was not an accurate representation of either man. Walker was slick and worldly, Hickman erudite, almost scholarly. He was a member—and probably a founder—of an informal group called the Village Green Reading Society. The name suggests great pretension but was dripping in sarcasm. The members gathered semiannually to consume enormous meals and to read and recite poetry and various writings. Other group members included sports writing legends Grantland Rice and "Red" Smith, famed sports cartoonist Willard Mullins, and Yale sports publicist Charley Loftus.[9]

Hickman's Army football pedigree, coupled with the "personality" created by his intimate association with the nation's sports writing literati, is probably what got him the Yale job, awarded, in his case, to a non-alumnus for the first time in school history. More surprising is how well the non-alum got along in New Haven despite his squads' less-than-inspiring performances. After his first season at the Bulldog helm, a 4–5 campaign that was every bit as mediocre as the record implies, Athletic Director Bob Kiphuth extended Hickman's contract to five years. It had been increased again—to a whopping ten years—by the time Walker showed up, even though Yale's performance had shown only slight

---

8 *The Harvard Crimson*, Nov. 20, 1948.
9 The sports publicist position was a more prestigious job then than it is now. Especially in the major markets of the Northeast, a good publicist could go a long way in making the reputation of a player, coach, or team. Loftus, long-time promoter of Yale fortunes, was proud of his school, perhaps overly so. Greeting a new sports editor one day, he introduced himself as "Charley Loftus of the University." "Which university?" asked the sports editor. "Oh, for goodness sake," said Loftus, "when they play *God Save the King* they don't ask 'which king,' do they?" Source: *The Herman Hickman Reader*.

improvement. Hickman's salary may have been generous—available Yale records do not specify it—but that probably didn't matter. About the time he moved to Yale, Hickman's career as a "celebrity," or "personality," took off, boosted by the new medium of television which allowed better public appreciation of both his mirth and girth. One was about as notable as the other. Hickman's imposing size (he was well over three hundred pounds during his coaching days) seemed an important part of his charm and appeal for big-city audiences. In cartoons of the period, including those penned by his Village Green pal Mullins, Hickman's bulk is grossly exaggerated. In some sketches he envelopes the vast majority of the panel and appears to be inflated with some highly pressurized gas. It is somewhat grotesque and might have made a lesser man angry, but Hickman understood it was part of a bankable image. In an interview shortly before his death (he passed away in 1958 from complications during ulcer surgery), he said that he made more (between $12,000 and $30,000 a year) as a speaker and entertainer than he did as a football coach.[10] So not only did he suffer fat drawings and comment without complaint, he joined in the fun. Perhaps a third of his jokes and one-liners dealt with weight and/or his apparent appetite ("I'll eat anything that's not a threat to eat me" was an oft-reported line). The rest of his stories were reserved for dumb football player tales and anecdotes about bumpkins in the Tennessee hills.

Eventually, Hickman landed a deal with the Robert Burns Cigar company as a sort of spokesman/endorser. Robert Burns sponsored Hickman's weekly radio show and later *The Herman Hickman Show*, a half hour of cornpone comedy and assorted skits that was broadcast live on TV.

Walker and Hickman's lone year at Yale was not funny and certainly not worth televising. The Bulldogs went 2–5–2, beating Bates and Colgate and getting pummeled by Cornell and Princeton. The ties came against Navy early in the year and in "The Game" against Harvard at the end. The Bulldogs' matchup with the Crimson Tide was a nail-biting thriller, if not necessarily a classic. Neither team was very good, but on this day they kept everyone on

---

10 *Sports Illustrated*, Nov. 1958.

edge. Hickman's boys jumped out to an early 14–0 lead. But Harvard tied it in the third quarter and went ahead 21–14 in the fourth on a return of an intercepted pass. With time running out, Hickman called quarterback Ed Molloy, a talented passer who many Yale observers felt was underutilized in the Half-Ton regime, to his side. "You start pitching and I'll start walking," Hickman reportedly said. What he meant was that Molloy should use the pass to drive Yale down the field, while Hickman used his sturdy legs to propel himself toward the exit ahead of the postgame mob. Both plans were executed to perfection. Molloy threw for the game-tying score with less than two minutes to play, and Hickman beat the crush off the field.

Dramatic finish notwithstanding, it wasn't much of a season for the Hickman-Walker tandem. The team wasn't any good and, the newly created duo wasn't all that funny or colorful either, which, as noted, some believed was the real aim. Yale player Ed Carricolo said that Walker's arrival was "no big deal." He said that while it was obvious the new coach knew his football, he was a "low-key" guy around his new team:

> I knew he'd been a head coach before—Wake Forest or Clemson or some place down South. It was also clear that he came from a different place with different expectations. He didn't coach me directly [Carricolo played end], but he did throw me out of practice once. Some guy I was in line with or something said something funny, and I was laughing, and I guess he didn't like it so he said, "Carritch-o-lo"—he had trouble with names, as did Hickman—"get off the field!" Well, it was hot and I was kind of tired so that was fine with me. Herman came down to the field a few minutes later—I'm not sure where he'd been—and he said, "Car-ratch-ilcolo, what's going on?" I said, "Well, I guess I said something that Coach Walker didn't appreciate so he asked me to leave."[11]

Walker's suddenly forgettable personality may simply have been a matter of deferring to the head man, but it might have been sign of some sulking, too. Bill Hensley, the old Wake Forest sports

---

11 Carricolo, interview with author.

columnist/drum major, wound up in Connecticut for graduate school while Walker was there and, on a whim, decided to call up the old coach to see how he was doing. The contact turned (naturally) into a dinner date. Hensley found Walker eager to talk to someone about the good old days.

"He was in good spirits," recalled Hensley, "but was absolutely disgusted with the players. He couldn't believe they'd go off to Bermuda for fall break."[12]

Said Walker in a later interview, "They [Yale] put classes on a higher priority than football practice and we didn't do that where I came from."[13] As a result, said Walker, "I didn't do much coaching there."[14]

Walker's disgust turned to wanderlust shortly after Yale's season ended. The fact that Bulldog football was taking an even more amateurish turn with the elimination of spring ball for 1952—"That meant we'd just be hanging around up here half the season," Walker moaned to Barrier—pushed him along.[15] He surveyed the college scene but didn't see much that attracted him—or maybe didn't want to see it. His eyes were mostly on pro football, which had piqued his curiosity for some time.

Walker's investigations led to a rapid-fire courtship with the Montreal franchise of the Canadian pro league that quickly blossomed. On Valentine's Day 1952, Walker signed a one-year contract to coach the Alouettes of the Canadian "Big Four."[16] In a post-signing interview with Barrier, Walker said the Montreal post was "a good job" that paid more than he'd ever made at Wake or Yale. Alouette records were lost when the franchise folded in the

---

12 Hensley, interview with author.
13 *Washington Evening Star*, Sept. 10, 1968.
14 *The Chapel Hill Weekly*, July 22, 1970.
15 *Greensboro Daily News*, Feb. 15, 1952.
16 Because of geography and the travel issues it created, Canada still had two professional leagues in 1952. The Big Four, consisting of Montreal, Toronto, Hamilton, and Ottawa, played in one league, the East Division, whereas four, or sometimes five, other teams made up the other league, the West Division. Teams from the two leagues often met in the preseason but not afterward until the winners clashed in the Grey Cup, Canada's Super Bowl. Aside from the title tilt, the two leagues were separate. They had separate schedules, some different rules, and even a separate collegiate draft.

1980s, but press accounts of the time peg Walker's pay at $12,000 a year. The Associated Press, never much of a source of inside information, reported that Walker would get $12,000 a year for just four months of work and would be "free to pursue other interests the rest of the year."[17]

"It [Montreal and the Canadian pro league] is certainly worth trying," said Walker. "I had made up my mind to leave Yale if something good came along. I wasn't exactly happy up there anyway."[18] Some of Walker's unhappiness was job related, and some of it might have been personal. Years later, Walker complained that he just couldn't take the change, especially Yale's failure to embrace his famous nickname. The New Haven crowd just couldn't bring themselves to call a grown man Peahead, and Walker, now in his early 50s, couldn't imagine being called anything else (except by Flonnie, who still got by with Petie).

"You just don't go through life being called 'Peahead' and all of sudden turn up as 'Doug,'" Walker moaned. The fact that it came from "them Yale boys who had some pretty funny nicknames themselves," didn't help.[19]

So it was off to a new place, but still a foreign Yankee land with which strange customs and entirely new sporting institutions. Walker knew little about any of it. Barrier noted that on signing day in Montreal, his old friend couldn't name the rest of the teams in the Big Four, a notable information gap (if literally true) for someone heading into a four-team league. The Canadian press may or may not have asked Walker to name the Big Four but were amused by his introductory interview all the same. Their source of delight was two-fold: Walker's all-but-indecipherable Southern drawl and his grasp of strategy—or lack thereof. Asked how he'd handle the twelve-man lineups allowed in Canadian football versus the eleven allowed in American football, Walker responded that he'd just "stick one man way out yonder on the flank," and then play "regular" eleven-man football with the rest.[20] Some Canadian writers appeared to think Walker was serious. He was not. But he

---

17 Associated Press, Feb. 24, 1952.
18 *Greensboro Daily News*, Feb. 15, 1952.
19 *Washington Evening Star*, Sept. 10, 1968.
20 *La Presse*, Feb. 14, 1952.

was proud of his flanker-and-eleven line—so much so that he used it on the offseason banquet circuit throughout his Canadian career. Some American audiences may have thought he was serious, too.

In another non-laughing matter, Walker was now completely and permanently known as Doug. The appellation was consistent throughout his north-of-the-border tenure, although the French-language papers in Montreal took some apparent delight early on in translating his nickname into the native tongue: in French Canada he was *la tête du pois* (literally, the head of the pea).

Walker's arrival was a bolt out of the blue, for there as no obvious connection. The Alouettes wanted Jimmy Phelan, who was working as an assistant at the time with the moribund New York Yanks of the NFL.[21] But when that franchise was sold to a Texas millionaire and moved to Dallas, Phelan went with it as head coach, leaving Montreal General Manager Lew Hayman and company holding an empty bag.[22] Hayman turned to Walker to fill the position, a typical move for a Canadian franchise at the time. While some locals (like Hayman himself and Toronto's Frank Clair) held Canadian coaching posts, the trend in the early 1950s was to hire American coaches. Nearly all the top coaches during Walker's Canadian career—Carl "Dutch" Voyles, Frank "Pop" Ivy, Bud Grant, Clem Crowe, Eagle Keys—were Americans who crossed the border to play, coach, or both. They typically knew more football and, even more importantly, had more contacts to American football players than their Canadian counterparts. The Big Four allowed eight American "imports" on each roster (the number grew and varied throughout Walker's Canadian tenure), so possessing a coach who could find the right "foreign" stars was critical.

There were some top-flight Americans to be had. In that era, Canadian teams had no trouble competing with the NFL on salaries. The NFL was decades away from today's almost unfathomable wealth, and CFL only had to pay top dollar for a

---

21 *New Haven Herald*, Feb. 24, 1952.
22 The 1952 Dallas Texans were a miserable team that won but a single game and were moved to Hershey, PA by the league halfway through the season. Phelan stayed on to the bitter end but retired when the season was over.

handful of American players. The Canadians on the squad came were paid at a cut rate. Most held down full-time jobs while they played. So a coach who knew where to put his team's dollars was invaluable. Doug Walker figured to be a whiz at this business. Didn't he find one bargain after another at Wake Forest?

Meanwhile, back at Yale, Hickman quickly followed Walker out the door. He'd begun to feel the heat and had better things to do with his time. The last few years of Hickman's life were busy as he whirled his way through a multimedia career. In addition to his radio and TV shows, he wrote two books, was hired to the original staff of *Sports Illustrated* (many of his stories were ghost written, a sore point with some other members of the staff), and appeared in a movie with Tony Curtis and Mamie Van Dorn called *The All-American*. Hickman, much to his dismay, was cast as a football coach.

"I shouldn't have been surprised," he said. "I'd been playing one for 18 years."[23]

Hickman's old friend Peahead Walker had played a coach even longer—some twenty-seven years—and was going to try it for a few more under an assumed name in a different country. The head of the pea faced an uphill task in Montreal. The Alouettes had won the 1949 Grey Cup under Hayman, but star quarterback Frankie Filchock had returned to the NFL the next year (he'd moved to Canada after being banned by the NFL for not reporting an attempted bribe), and Montreal went into rebuilding mode. Hayman, a part owner as well as the coach, sold his shares after the 1951 season, in which the Als finished last in the Big Four. The new owners brought in Walker to rebuild the team.

His first task was finding some new Americans. Not surprisingly, Walker looked South, and in particular, to some of his old Wake Forest players. He signed end Red O'Quinn away from the Chicago Bears and pried Jim Staton from the Washington Redskins. In the Big Four draft,[24] Walker selected, among others, quarterback "Slinging Sam" Etchevarry from the University of

---

23 Legends of the Tennessee Vols.
24 Technically, the Canadian East Division was known, until the formation of the merged Canadian Football League in 1958, as the International Rugby Football, but it was commonly referred to as the Big Four.

Denver. Etchevarry, whose parents had immigrated to New Mexico from Spain, was an unusual pick to say the least. He had piled up a mountain of passing stats for the University of Denver, but it came against less-than-stellar foes. Because of that, pro football interest really wasn't that high. Walker was aware of Etchevarry because he ranked highly in national collegiate passing stats but allegedly drafted him because of a publicity photo he saw. In it, a smiling and helmet-less Etchevarry was rearing back, the ball tucked neatly behind his head, to throw a pass. The legend, supported by both Walker and Etchevarry in later years, is that Walker thought Etchevarry's photo form was so sublime he drafted him solely because of that qualification.

Whatever the case, it turned out perfect for all concerned. Etchevarry really could throw and eventually became one of the greatest quarterbacks in Canadian football history, the linchpin of Walker's offensive juggernauts in Montreal.

Eventually, but not in Walker's first year.

Etchevarry was still getting a feel for the Canadian game and didn't have much help offensively aside from O'Quinn, who was on his way to becoming an excellent player. That combination was still maturing, and the rest of the squad lacked even the very potential for offensive firepower. The top backs were holdover Virgil Wagner, a "Canadianized" American who'd been Montreal's top back in the 1949 Grey Cup run, Jim "the Jet" Ostendarp, a former New York Giant, and former Alabama All-American Ed "Suitcase" Salem.[25] The team's line, led by holdover Herbie Trawick, the first black player in the Canadian Football League (CFL) and the first that Walker coached as a head man, was good, but depth was lacking. Voyles, the Hamilton coach and Walker's old collegiate rival (Voyles coached at William & Mary), said at midseason that Montreal had the best first team among the Big Four. "But after that . . ."

---

25 The "Suitcase" appellation was a familiar sports nickname of the time and usually denoted a well-traveled player in any sport. How Salem acquired it is unclear, however. The former Crimson Tide star played one season with the NFL's Washington Redskins and one season in Montreal. He later started a chain of famous drive-in diners (Ed Salem's) in Birmingham.

Voyles's assessment ended with the second-team verdict unspoken but crystal clear. He wouldn't make any hay by stating the facts because the Als' second team, like most of the second teams in the league, was an all-Canadian bunch. With more and better Americans filling rosters across the league, the sorry play of most of the Canadian players was beginning to stand out. Montreal, where the local colleges had even less of a football tradition than they did further west, was particularly hamstrung, since local boys, who could supplement their meager football salaries with full-time jobs, were most likely to fill the Canadian roster spots. Walker's first team finished 2–10 and in last place in the Big Four.

Although no miracles had been expected, that was a disappointment. Walker told them it would take time, and when the season was over he surprised his bosses by asking for a raise for both himself and his erstwhile assistant Jimmy Dunn, a New Englander who didn't get high marks for coaching knowledge but who was very loyal. Montreal's ownership balked at first, supported to some extent by the Montreal press corps, which had clashed with Walker over postgame locker room access (they were used to having it, and Walker was neither used to, nor inclined to, give it). Whether Montreal's ruling triumvirate thought Walker was performing poorly, or whether they were just negotiating, they did offer the post to Vic Obeck, the McGill College coach who had served as Montreal's part-time line coach in 1952. Obeck turned the offer down (or maybe it wasn't an official offer—newspaper accounts from that day are not conclusive), and the Als eventually resigned Walker and Dunn for another year—with the raises Walker had sought. Everyone held their breath, hoping for better stuff in 1953.

The big problem in Walker's debut season was personnel, but there were other problems as well. Walker needed some time to figure out the Canadian game, and the Alouettes needed some time to figure out Walker.

Players, Canadian and American alike, say it was clear that Walker knew more football than anybody they'd ever been around. But some things were lost in translation. There were some communication problems.

For starters, Walker's accent was difficult for the Canadians and his penchant for throwing in French phrases (or at least what he thought were French phrases) didn't help. Fellow Alabamian Forrest "Fob" James, an Auburn University star who played one CFL season for Walker in the late 1950s (and who later was elected governor of Alabama), said this sort of bilingual mangling was common among American gridders (and, indeed, Americans in general) and quite unpopular:

> *I pulled into a gas station in Montreal once, and got out saying, as was standard at the time, "Check the tires, clean the windshield, fill her up," and so on, using as many of my French words as I could, but certainly not speaking entirely in French. "Buddy," the station attendant said to me—he was clearly ticked off—"you're either going to have to speak English or French. It can't be both." I suspect Peahead had some similar problems. And he was really speaking three languages: French, English, and Alabama.*[26]

Tough accent, mangled translations—and then there was Walker's dry sense of humor. It was nearly impenetrable to many of Walker's players when he coached in America. Add the cultural barrier and the result was a lot of puzzled looks.[27]

For instance, one gloomy fall evening at practice, seldom-used reserve guard Des Findlay, a modestly talented Canadian reserve, broke his leg during a scrimmage. Walker, as was his wont, trucked no delay with practice over a mere injury and moved the scrimmage further up field while the trainer tended to Findlay. But between Findlay's moans and the arrival of an ambulance, flashing lights and all, on the field, the incident became too much of a distraction. Fed up, Walker called the discombobulated squad together for a pep talk of sorts. It was a long season, he said. There was going to be some bad luck along the way. Bad times will have to be dealt with. When the times got bad, a real football player would just buck up and tough it out. All that was true enough, said Walker. It was the reality of football and of life. But this night, he

---

26 Fob James, interview with author.
27 Some players recall deciphering both the words, and the meaning, of Walker's speeches at some later date.

wanted to make clear, was not one of those times. Motioning over his shoulder to where the wounded Alouette was being lifted into the ambulance, Walker said, "Injuries are tough . . . a broken leg is a bad thing. But gottdamn boys, it's *only Findlay*."

Defensive lineman Gerry Hogan said the Canadian players all looked at each other, thinking, "What the hell? Is this another slap on us Canadians?"

"But," said Hogan, "the more we got to thinking about it, the funnier it got. *'Goddamn! It's only Findlay.'* Years later, the highlight of our team reunions was when Findlay would show up so we could all say, well, you know . . . that Walker . . . you had to know how to take him."[28]

An equally baffling display came after an especially ugly performance against Ottawa. Walker called the team together and announced that they were going to begin the day's practice with a new drill. He called out fullback Jacques Belec, halfbacks Chuck Hunsinger and Bill Bewley, and a few other players and instructed them to form a circle and begin hopping up and down while moving to their right. Then he ordered them to hop to their left. Then he told them to jump in the air. Then he told them to hold hands while they did it.

"This went on for some time," said Hogan. "It was kind of strange but we weren't that surprised. This was when isometrics and that kind of crap was first being introduced and so coaches were always trying this new stuff. We thought it was some of that."

Finally, after the players had gotten the idea of what Walker wanted and were doing it on their own, Walker turned to the rest of the squad and said, "Look at those assholes, running and jumping like a bunch of Maypole dancers, celebrating what a shitty game they played on Saturday."[29]

In his book *Legends of Autumn: The Glory Years of Canadian Football*, Denny Boyd portrays the aforementioned tale—which team members call the "ring-around-the-rosey story"—as another example of Walker's dislike for Canadian players.[30] But

---

28 Gerry Hogan, interview with author.
29 Ibid.
30 D. Boyd, *Legends of Autumn, The Glory Years of Canadian Football*. 1997. Vancouver: Greystone Books.

even their account notes that some Americans were included in what was apparently intended as humiliation. And Belec, a Canadian fullback on Walker's early Montreal teams, said he took no special exception to the incident.

"I mean, he let everybody have it on a pretty equal basis," said Belec. "And to be honest, we had played a shitty game, just like he said."[31]

Belec and several other players agree that the incident occurred in the middle of one of the curious, Saturday-Monday doubleheaders that Big Four teams played on holiday weekends. When Montreal played Ottawa again the next day, said Belec, "We played a helluva lot better."

Whether accompanied by active demonstrations or not, Walker's sarcastic bites did leave a mark. Players remembered the point that he made, and his keen—or at least unique—understanding of psychology. When receiver Joey Pal made a sensational diving catch at practice one day, Walker walked up to him as he was dusting himself off and said, "Nice one, Pal. I'll bet if you had dropped it you would have hurt your back." (Then, as now, it was not uncommon to see a player suddenly develop an injury after botching a play.)

On another occasion, the Alouettes' punt returners were having a hard time fielding punts on an especially bright day at Molson Stadium. Walker began laying into them on the sidelines when one of the players protested, "But coach. I've been putting my hand up to block the sun like you said and everything. It's just too bright." The blood rushed to Walker's head, then receded. In a relatively calm voice he said, "Well, hell boy. What do you want me to do? Call down a gottdamn e-clipse?"[32]

Said Jacques Belec:

---

[31] Jacque Belec, interview with the author.
[32] The story was told by several of Walker's Montreal players and by one player from Walker's Wake Forest days. The identity of the players depends upon who is doing the telling. Alouette Doug McNichol remembered the episode as more of a rant against players wearing lamp black under the eyes. McNichol's version of the critical line: "Got all the black shit under their eyes and still can't catch a punt," said Walker. "Hell, what do they want me to do, call down a gottdamn e-clipse?"

He'd let you have it, often in a very sarcastic way, to make a point. But overall he had a nice personality, one that adults appreciated. He was the boss, no doubt, but he had a way of getting along with the guys that went over well. And after awhile we figured out that he was funny. He laughed at his own jokes, too. He enjoyed them. I thought he was a great guy.[33]

Montreal players were just as eager to escape Peahead's verbal lash as had been Walker's Wake Forest charges. But it was hard to avoid. Walker was very observant and his needle was always at the ready. Hogan knew he was in trouble when his father drove over to Montreal to be present when Hogan signed his third contract with the Als. It was not really a big deal—Hogan was just a reserve guard. But the senior Hogan, a proud papa, came anyway. He sat down with Walker and Gerry, exchanged pleasantries, and then launched into a lengthy speech, extolling his son's many virtues both on and off the field. As the younger Hogan recalled:

My old man was telling Peahead about all these honors I'd received as a schoolboy and all, and of course Peahead was just as nice: "Yes sir, Mr. Hogan. He is a fine boy, a fine football player, mighty fine," and so on. Then the next day at practice, of course, the first time a first-string lineman messed up, there was Peahead. "Hell, let's get Hogan in here. He was all-neighborhood six times and is a great humanitarian." You just didn't want to give him any reason to get on you.[34]

But reasons always presented themselves, even for some of the Als' biggest names. Ex-New York Giant tackle Tex Coulter, probably the highest-paid Alouette until Etchevarry signed a new contract in 1955, was taking it on the chin one day in practice, getting chewed out for all kinds of dumb stuff, when reserve Herb Capozzi, for reasons still unknown, interrupted to offer an observation of his own. That set Walker off. He began laying into Capozzi, his favorite Montreal whipping boy. Walker went over

---

[33] Jacques Belec, interview with author.
[34] Hogan, interview with author.

Capozzi's many faults in a tirade that lasted several minutes, and Coulter, the original target, was beginning to feel a little relief until Walker finally reached his summation.

"Yes, that was sure enough dumb Capozzi," Walker said. "Very dumb, about as dumb as what Tex did."[35]

Capozzi, a modest talent who later went on to be a CFL general manager and a member of Canada's parliament, was essentially the Nub Smith of Canada (until Smith himself joined Walker briefly in 1953). Like Smith, Capozzi brought on much of the razzing himself, albeit inadvertently. Trying to get Walker's attention early on in his Alouette career, Capozzi volunteered for every special team assignment possible. He wound up working his way onto almost every team—as a backup. One day, when the team was going over its special teams lineups the day before a game (it's a standard organizational maneuver for football teams; coaches call, squad by squad, for the first and second teams for all situations to line up), Capozzi kept popping up again and again. Injuries that kept a few starters sidelined that day made Capozzi even more ubiquitous than normal. Finally, Walker had had enough.

"Cuh-pozzi, you kept runnin' back and forth out here like a mailman," Walker said. "Are you trying to annoy me, boy?"

Capozzi stammered that he was just doing what he was supposed to. "You see, Coach, I'm just doing my jobs. When Coulter goes back to punt [the big tackle briefly served as the Als' punter], I play right tackle on the first string, and then I also play left tackle on the second string. And I'm on the kickoff team and . . . "

Walker cut Capozzi off with a wave of his hand. "Cuh-pozzi," he said, shaking his head, "what *ever* would we do without you?"[36]

On another occasion, Capozzi tried to give newcomer Alex Webster, an American backfielder who was a key player for Walker in 1953–1954, a special welcome to the squad. On Webster's first day at practice, with the players walking through assignments

---

35 *Montreal Star*, Nov. 13, 1957.
36 Various interviews with authors. Capozzi, however, recounts a version of the tale himself in a first-person article written for the Toronto-based *Star Weekly* magazine on April 15, 1967. In some players' versions, Walker's punch line is, "Cuh-pozzi, what the hell would I do if you just up and died?"

while dressed out only in shorts and T-shirts, Capozzi came flying in at full speed and hit Webster with his forearm while Webster was mimicking a block. Said Webster:

> *I got up and was ready to fight him and was cussing him, but they held me back. I went back to the huddle and told Etcheverry to run the same goddamn play, but he said he couldn't do it. He had a list to go by. . . . Well, a few minutes later Peahead sticks his nose in huddle and says, "Sam, let's run the play that big boy here [Webster] was wanting us to run." So we ran that same play, only this time I stepped out about two and a half steps and hid behind the tackle. And here comes Capozzi again and I fired out and just cold-cocked him. Knocked him on his ass. Peahead blew his whistle and came over and said, real casual like, "I guess that'll teach you to fuck with the Americans, huh Cah-pozzi?"*[37]

Capozzi did not learn quickly. A year or so later, he was entertaining his teammates in the clubhouse, standing on a chair imitating Walker's drawl and phraseology. The laughter stopped when the coach walked in, but Capozzi, in the middle of a riff, didn't see or hear Walker come in. He continued his unflattering portrayal while the subject listened in. Capozzi finally noticed the silence and turned around to find Walker staring at him.

"Well, Capozzi," Walker said, "I hope your next team thinks you are as funny as this one does."

In the lengthy magazine retrospective long after his playing career actually did end, Capozzi called Walker "as crusty as a piece of French bread," and noted that Walker didn't carry out his implied threat the day he caught Capozzi mimicking him. "I supposed the look of sheer terror on my face was good enough," wrote Capozzi.[38]

Walker's humor, which he apparently wielded with more vigor and regularity in Montreal than he did at Wake Forest, did not end or begin with Capozzi. Once the players had figured out that he was joking, humor, laced with invective, was the expected response from their grizzled, but beloved, coach. Belec and others

---

37 Alex Webster, interview with author.
38 *Star Weekly,* April 16, 1967.

mentioned the Als' weekly film studies as an oft-entertaining event during which Walker would stop the film not only to point out failures of execution but other oddities he found humorous.

During Walker's first season, lineman Juan "Jelly Belly" Sheridan[39] intercepted a screen pass and was running for a probable touchdown when he tripped over the remnants of the pitcher's mound at Dorlomier Park. (The Royals, Montreal's fabled triple-A baseball team, shared the stadium with the Alouettes.) Sheridan's awkward fall, which included a pronounced bounce on his famed belly, his arms and legs akimbo, was comical. Hogan said Walker not only stopped that one when the team first reviewed it but would also sometimes stop other films and go fish that film back out so he could show it to new players. "I can remember him saying, 'Damn, I ought to sell that to Walt Disney or somebody,'" said Hogan.[40]

Defensive end Doug McNichol recalled how well Walker's droll timing mixed with his love of old-school, hard-nosed, hard-hitting football. When Coulter whiffed on a block during a kickoff return drill—the defending player just ran right past the hulking tackle—Walker issued a stream of cuss words that ended with the eternal coaching command, "Run it again." The second time, said McNichol, Big Tex got it right. As the speeding defender started past Coulter, the gigantic Al reared back and punched him in the face with a big roundhouse right.

"Yeaaaah Tex," Walker nodded, "That's better."[41]

Naturally, Walker unleashed his nicknaming genius on the Alouettes just as he had at Wake Forest and Elon. Sheridan was "Jelly Belly," or just "Jelly," for short; any of several Canadian players with Polish-sounding last names was "Pollack;" and any Canadian in general was likely to be addressed as "you big Canuck."

Walker got the idea that one of his players was Portuguese—several players remembered the story but none could recall the player's name—and started calling the player "Geese," and later, "Goose." Guard Marty Martinello was "Spaghetti," even

---

39 The nickname came from Walker of course. Its origin is obvious.
40 Hogan, interview with author.
41 Doug McNichol, interview with author.

though he had only a very faint Italian heritage. Another player with an Italian-sounding name who passed through an Als' camp once—Hogan thinks the player may have been named Polizanno—drew Walker's ire for a series of long-forgotten mistakes. "Polizanno—that's I-talian, isn't it?" said Walker. "Yessir," said Polizanno. "Well, Polizanno, you ain't much of a football player. Why don't you get yourself a cart and go sell some vegetables or something."

"Of course, they'd crucify him for a line like that today," said Hogan. "But back then . . . "[42]

Walker's humor, at times both dry and crude, was mixed, as noted, with creative cussing and fit pitching. Johnny Majors, the future University of Tennessee and Pitt coach and briefly a Montreal halfback under Walker, recalled a verbal blistering from Walker when he dropped a short pass that would have produced an Alouette first down. . . . And also remembers praise—albeit praised laced with sarcasm—when he threw his 160-pound frame into Walker's ubiquitous Tuesday afternoon blocking drills. "I'd be blocking this monsters like Doug McNichol and hell, at Tennessee I was a single-wing tailback. I didn't block anybody. But I'd tried and he'd say, 'Goddamn it, that's the way. Go get 'em, midget. Go get 'em!'"[43]

Walker had matured a bit by the time he got to Canada and realized he was coaching men—not boys. So his style was somewhat different than in his college days. Most of his Montreal players interviewed liked him, especially in retrospect. He was still a tough guy and a fairly strict disciplinarian. Like many coaches before and since, he insisted upon punctuality—even super-punctuality. If the bus to practice was scheduled to leave the team's headquarters at 4 PM, it would often leave at five minutes before. When defensive lineman Sheridan, the jelly-bellied one, just missed the departure one day, he dashed around the block and caught up to the Alouette express just as it was turning onto a busy boulevard. Sheridan danced out in front of the bus, waving his arms. Walker saw him and grumbled to the bus driver, "Run his ass over."

---

[42] Hogan, interview with author.
[43] Johnny Majors, interview with author.

"We didn't run him over," said Doug McNichol, "but we didn't stop for him either."[44]

Hard shell aside, Walker is remembered as a player's coach. He was loyal to his boys when it came to salary negotiations (which Walker didn't handle directly outside of the initial contract offers to Americans) and appreciated (by most) for his sense of humor and for a certain directness that made his verbal lacerations easier to take.

Two players who played for both Walker and NFL legend Vince Lombardi voluntarily contrasted the two men's style of handling people, with Peahead getting the nod in the human relations category from both. Joel Wells, Walker's star halfback/defensive back and later a role player for the Giants when Lombardi was an assistant coach there, said, "Walker would make his point and that was it. Lombardi would be on you forever, although the next day he might have his arm around you and all. There was none of that with Peahead, which I liked. He said what he wanted to say and went on."[45]

Said Alex Webster, who played for Walker before signing as a free agent with New York:

> *I think his real strength was handling people. He got a lot out of them. He didn't lecture you. It wasn't like Lombardi, but he did have those sentences, those one-liners. He made his point and you remembered. Lombardi would be all over you for the rest of the day: "Why'd you miss that block? What were you thinking? Don't you understand this play? What were you thinking? What's the matter with you?" He'd criticize every single aspect of it. With Peahead, he said his piece and moved on. You knew you'd screwed up. And you either figured out how to fix it or he found somebody else.*[46]

Although Walker's alleged disdain for homegrown Canadian talent would eventually be part of his downfall in Montreal, many Canadian players said it was a bum rap. Potential tension over the binational issue was defused by Walker's pragmatism. He wanted

---

44 McNichol, interview with author.
45 Joel Wells, interview with author.
46 Webster, interview with author.

to win and didn't like playing Canadian players because, by and large, they weren't as good as his Americans. But when he had a Canadian who could play he'd play them. Doug McNichol, wingback Joey Pal, and halfback/kicker Bill Bewley, all Canadians, were Montreal stars under Walker. And he got good service out of modest talents like Hogan, Belec, Mike Kovac, and Martinello, the last of which, notably, was an All-CFL selection later in his career with Toronto. "I'd have to say the credit for that goes to the training I got from Coach Walker," Martinello said. "He really knew his football and if you were willing to learn, he'd teach you."[47]

Canadian Kovac said as best he could tell, Walker played the best guys.

"You always had an opportunity," said Kovac. "There was a real tryout, and some of these All-Americans from the states, they didn't do so well and he didn't play them. I don't know what else you could ask for. He was tough, but we all thought he was very fair."[48]

Added McNichol: "That [anti-Canadian] stuff was completely overblown. If you couldn't play, you didn't. If you could, you did. Now, he didn't like to take the first team out. But the reason for that is that they were better players. As far as who played, I thought he handled that all right."[49]

Walker's humor-tinged, rock-ribbed style was generally well received in Canada. He was not inspiring in the manner of the football cliché—the most famous halftime speech during Walker's Montreal tenure was probably delivered by team captain Red O'Quinn—but he did seem to command unusual loyalty, respect, and even affection. When Walker's team upset Carl Voyle's Hamilton club in 1952, Voyles credited the victory to the players' affection for their new coach. "They won it for Walker," Voyles said. "You could tell how they felt."[50]

***

---

47 Marty Martinello, interview with author.
48 Mike Kovac, interview with author.
49 McNichol, interview with author.
50 *Montreal Star*, Oct. 27, 1952.

Montreal's decision to bring back Walker for a second season—with a raise—was plagued with uncertainty, but all the doubts were soon dispelled. In his second season, Walker began to shine as both a CFL tactician and as an assimilator of talent. This latter skill was aided in no small degree by the new ownership's willingness to spend. Walker pried mammoth tackle DeWitt "Tex" Coulter away from the NFL's New York Giants with a "five-figure" offer—in other words $10,000—and lured former Florida running back Chuck Hunsinger away from the Bears. On the recommendation of Etchevarry, he signed center Tom Hugo, a rugged Hawaiian who'd played collegiately with Etchevarry at the University of Denver. He also picked up Ed Bradley, the hard-nosed Wake Forest end, after he was released by the Chicago Bears, and he acquired defensive lineman Doug McNichol, probably the best Canadian player Walker ever coached, in the college draft.

All of these players were on hand at the start of the season and, along with a year's experience under Walker for holdovers like Etchevarry, O'Quinn, Wagner, and Ray Poole, the Als were a much better team. But it was the midseason signing of former NC State fullback Alex Webster that really ignited the Montreal offense. After Webster arrived, the 1953 Als began offering hints of the offensive power that would be Walker's Canadian trademark.

Webster's late-September signing—because of weather concerns the Canadian season began in early August—is illustrative of the casual "scouting" then in effect and of Walker's still considerable persuasive powers. Webster, a New Jersey native, was drafted by the Washington Redskins after finishing his career at NC State but was cut late in the team's preseason camp. Married and moping around back home in Newark, Webster bumped into Paul Barkin, sports editor of the *Newark Star-Ledger*. Barkin asked what he was doing, heard Webster's tale of woe, and asked him if he'd mind if he made a contact or two on his behalf. As was apparently the case with every other sportswriter on the East Coast at the time, Barkin was friends with Walker. He sent him a telegram with news that Webster was available. Walker remembered the hard-charging Wolfpack runner from his coaching days at Wake Forest and was on the phone immediately:

The next morning my mother woke me up at 8:30. She said there's some crazy man on the phone who won't hang up until he talks to you. It was Peahead and he had my mom very upset. He was telling her to get my lazy ass out of bed and all and that it was a matter of life and death and so on. Anyway, I got on the phone and he said, "Webster, this is Douglas Clyde "Peahead" Walker, and I want your ass on a plane this morning and be up here in Montreal by 2:30 PM. Tonight is the deadline for imports and we need you. I've already got you booked on a flight out of LaGuardia. I'll see you when you get here. Now get moving." It sounded like a pretty good opportunity and he had everything lined up except, well, the plane ticket wasn't paid for. Peahead forgot to tell me that. I had to go to the butcher shop next door, owned by a friend, and borrow the money.[51]

Walker's cut-rate courtship of Webster continued when the player made it to Montreal. The Als got him a nice room—at the local YMCA—and left him instructions on which trolley to take to the team's practice field at the Westmount Grounds.[52] The desperate Webster made it, however, and along with Hunsinger finally gave the Montreal ground game enough punch to buy the uncannily accurate Etchevarry some time in the pocket. Webster's immediate impact affected other players in a different way. As Webster rose to prominence, Walker cut Nub Smith, the former Deacon prodigy who Walker had brought in to spice up the Montreal attack. Smith, out of football and school for more than a year (he'd spent some time in the Army), was (as usual) out of shape when he arrived in Montreal. He was soon injured, and when the running game took off with Webster in tow Walker had no choice but to let him go, his need for effective players trumping any residual loyalty.

---

51 In another version of the story, reproduced in some biographical features about Webster after he gained fame as a New York Giant's player and later coach, Webster reportedly made the contact himself. Just before he died, however, Webster himself made a point of crediting Barkin. Source: Alex Webster, interview with author.

52 The professional game did not have quite as many perks it does today.

Montreal was already competitive, but the Als began making real waves after Webster signed on. They beat Ottawa 37–21 in early October, their first win over the Roughriders since 1950, and appeared headed for the Big Four crown when a rash of injuries knocked them off course. In a pivotal game in Hamilton against the first-place Tiger-Cats, Hugo, McNichol, Etchevarry, and Jim Miller were all knocked out of the game with injuries, and the Als had already started the day without the services of linemen Coulter and Ray Cicia (another ex-Deacon). Montreal blew an 18–1 lead[53] in that game but returned home the next week to beat the Tiger-Cats 31–18 and force a tie for first with Hamilton and a playoff series for the East Division championship.[54] Webster's ninety-yard kickoff return for a touchdown helped power the clutch victory.

On paper, the Als were too beat up to match up against the Tiger-Cats. But Walker and company weren't giving up. Emotion might carry the day. It was Montreal's first playoff game in several years and was against Hamilton, a team Walker came to detest early on. In the lead up to various Hamilton games, players recall Walker telling stories about Voyles having an affair while he was at Duke (just how that was supposed to affect the players isn't clear, and why Walker of all people would level such a charge is even less so); making disparaging remarks about former Wake Forest player Bill Gregus, who was briefly a starter in the Tiger-Cat backfield; and just generally running down the industrial town just west of Buffalo. Much of Walker's ire may have stemmed from frustration at not being able to beat Hamilton. The coach laid at least some of the blame for that on the fact that a large number of the Alouettes' Canadian players were from Hamilton or the Hamilton area. In Walker's mind, that meant "distractions" every time Hamilton was on the schedule—or at least every time Montreal played at the Cats'

---

53 Canadian scoring allows single points for field goal attempts that miss the uprights but that cross the goal and are downed in the end zone. The defending team can attempt to return the ball out of the end zone to avoid the point.

54 Canadian and Big Four playoff rules changed regularly, but it was common for the playoffs to be decided by multiple games. Sometimes a best-of-three series was used, as was the case in 1953. In other years, teams played a two-game series in which the total scored in both games was the deciding factor.

lair. Doug McNichol remembers Walker grousing as the team got off the bus in Hamilton one Friday afternoon before a Saturday game. "Well," he said, "I guess all you guys are gonna go home and pump the handle and all and you won't be worth a shit for the game."[55]

High-toned inspirational messages aside, Walker had built a Montreal-Hamilton rivalry. He'd also developed strong morale and a real fighting spirit in the 1953 team. The "Limping Larks,"[56] as Montreal sportswriters took to calling the injury-riddled team, wouldn't give up, even with several starters out and a half-dozen others playing through one or more injuries. In the series opener against Hamilton, Hunsinger had to be carted off on a stretcher at one point in the first half but limped back on the field a few minutes later to block an extra point. In the waning moments of Hamilton's clinching victory in game two, a helmet-less O'Quinn charged in from the sidelines to tackle a Hamilton runner headed toward the end zone. A melee followed. Neither it nor O'Quinn's outlaw tackle changed the game's outcome (or prevented Hamilton from going on to win the series and the Grey Cup), but it did confirm Walker's place as a coach and a quiet-but-effective motivator.

With a much-improved 8–6 mark (8–8 including the playoff losses), December contract negotiations with the Alouettes went considerably faster than the year before. Less than a week after Hamilton knocked the Als out of a Grey Cup berth, Walker and Dunn were both locked up for another season. Momentum continued as Coulter re-upped for another campaign and Hugo, a "find" who Walker had managed to sign for just $250 a game, was inked to a new deal at higher pay. Walker also announced plans for a "grand Southern tour" in which he would visit the football factories in the region he called home and see what kind of prospects they had to offer for the coming season. This was essentially Walker's player procurement strategy for the rest of his Montreal tenure and a circumstance that led, quite naturally, to his later career as Southeastern scout for the New York (football) Giants.

---

55 McNichol, interview with author.
56 "Larks" was sports writing shorthand for Alouettes. "Alouette" is the French word for lark, a type of bird.

It also put him far from Canada in the wintertime.

It was about this time that Walker began a program of "importing" summer coaching help as he began preparations for the season's end. The plan sounded good in theory, and it's possible that it did add some actual practical benefits. What it mostly consisted of in fact, however, was inviting Clemson's Frank Howard, Georgia's Wally Butts, and others[57] to Montreal for a couple of weeks of coaching and carousing. Or maybe it was the other way around. Said Buddy Frick, a former University of South Carolina player that Walker lured away from the Redskins and to Montreal:

> *I do remember him bringing in Frank Howard, Wally Butts, maybe some others. I can't remember everyone that was there, but they were all just about alike. All of them were kind of rotund and they all used a lot of four-letter words. . . . I mean a lot. You also had to take care and watch out for the tobacco juice. It was flying right and left. They were just old-school coaches; Peahead was old school. Today I think coaches do it more with feel-good positive stuff. That wasn't the way those guys did it. They were in your face all the time: "Why didn't you catch that g-d pass?" and all. That was an interesting week when the other coaches were here. They really did get involved with practices. They suited up and came out and yelled at you just like Peahead.*[58]

Canadian Jacques Belec said that while football was definitely in the coaching compadres' blood; it was clear to most of the players that something else was in it too.

"I think his favorite time was the start of the season," said Belec. "He had his coaching friends—and drinking friends—who came up. That guy from Clemson [Frank Howard] came up several years. He helped coach a little, but I think he was mostly here just

---

57 Bill Hudson, an Alouette from Clemson, said he thinks Bear Bryant, a long-time Walker friend, was in the group one year while he was there. Source: Hudson, interview with author.
58 Buddy Frick, interview with author.

to have a good time, talk a little football, drink a little whiskey—or maybe more than a little."[59]

Joel Wells, a former Clemson player who played for Walker near the end of his Alouette reign, says when one of the "guest coaches" would stick their head into the huddle and say something, "the alcohol fumes would just about knock you over."[60] Hogan says he remembers Howard, his breath smelling distinctly of Kentucky bourbon, strutting around practice one day in an orange sweatshirt and orange hat with a big C on it and Peahead calling the team together to introduce the new coach to them.

"Gentlemen, we are fortunate to have with us this week one of the great men of the South, one of the great coaches in all American collegiate football, Mr. Frank Howard of Clemson."

"Why thank you, Peahead. I'm delighted to be here. You know, I've been walking around this morning, observing, and Coach, you've got some damn fine players here, damn fine. I would be very surprised—very surprised—if you don't win the goddamn Blue Cup this year."

As players snickered, an exasperated Walker said, "Gottdamn it, Frank, it's the *Grey* Cup."[61]

The 1954 season was Walker's finest hour in Canada, but his biggest contribution occurred before practice even started. It happened on Walker's annual "tour of the South" recruiting trip in the spring. Walker proved to be as able a recruiter of professionals as he had been of college men, and he mined his familiar Southern stomping grounds to pick up plenty of good American players. But he never did better than when he veered north and west in the spring of 1954 to sign Kansas receiver/defensive back Hal Patterson.

Patterson was no secret. The 6'4", 190-pounder was a superb athlete who starred in both basketball and football for the Jayhawks and also lettered in baseball. His natural abilities allowed him to play two sports at high levels, and professional scouts from both football and basketball were sniffing around. But his two-sport status also worked against him. Scouts labeled him

---

[59] Belec, interview with author.
[60] Wells, interview with author.
[61] Hogan, interview with author.

as raw in part because he didn't have as much time to hone his game in either sport because of the time spent in the other. Many evaluators also thought him a "tweener," caught between sports with not exactly the right skills to be a pro in either.

Peahead Walker thought otherwise. And when better offers failed to materialize—after much talk, Patterson wasn't selected in the fledgling NBA draft and wasn't taken until the fourteenth round of the NFL draft, when he was picked by a team (Philadelphia) that wanted to use him exclusively as a defensive back—the Montreal coach swooped in for the kill. Patterson thought Walker kind of odd but liked what he had to say. He'd be a receiver first in Montreal, not a cornerback.

"Defense just wasn't my game," said Patterson. "I liked it and all, but I thought the Canadian game, with the extra man and the big wide field, would be better for me. Then, when Peahead came to see me, he seemed to know all that and seemed to have things lined up. He had a good, highly accurate quarterback in place [Etchevarry], and some other targets. And they paid just as good or better [than the NFL]. So it seemed like the right thing for me, and it was."[62]

Indeed, it proved to be brilliant move. Patterson was an absolute phenom who wowed friends and foes alike. Soon after joining the Als, he was on his way to becoming one of the CFL's all-time greats. Johnny Majors, the future coach, saw Patterson at work during his rookie (and only) season under Walker in Montreal. "He could do anything and everything . . . about the best I've ever seen," said Majors. "He changed the whole game."[63] Fob James, another teammate, called Patterson "the most graceful, most agile athlete I've ever seen."[64]

Patterson's alleged rawness disappeared when he got to Canada. He was a complete mismatch for most CFL defenses right from the start, giving Walker a devastating weapon around which to build a jet-propelled offense. The old coach was more than happy to turn Etchevarry and company loose on an unsuspecting Big Four.

---

62 Hal Patterson, interview with author.
63 Majors, interview with author.
64 James, interview with author.

The Als averaged more than twenty-five points a game in 1954, threw almost thirty passes a contest (a veritable barrage for that era), and piled up the yards from scrimmage. Going for a first down on third down (the final down in Canadian ball) became a regular Als' stratagem, so confident was Walker in the ability of his offense to move the ball and score when necessary.

It was an exciting style that won games and, just as importantly, entertained the fans. Walker understood that he was now coaching a for-profit professional team. A big part of his success would be determined by how many fans he could put in the seats at the Alouettes' new home field, Molson Stadium at McGill University. That was no simple task. There was plenty of athletic entertainment competition in Montreal. The Canadian hockey team was a dominant force in the fledgling National Hockey League—there were lower-level hockey leagues everywhere. And the baseball Royals, just removed from the days of Jackie Robinson, were very popular. It took shrewd promotion and an exciting product for the Als to keep up. Management took care of the "promotions." The Als hired some of the first dancing girls in football, a group of scantily clad (for the era) "majorettes" who complemented the Alouette marching band; infused team press conferences with liquor (Montreal-based Seagram's was a team sponsor), always a good way to tackle the press; and even paid bribes to sportswriters to produce more Alouette copy.[65] Walker was certainly comfortable with the dancing girls and the liquor. After establishing himself in Canada, one of his regular gifts to pressmen on his Southern speaking tours was a bottle of Seagram's trademark Crown Royal whiskey, and he always appreciated the charms of the fairer sex.

Walker helped matters along off the field as well. He became a press darling in Canada, just as he'd been at Wake, thanks to his funny stories (often served up as a banquet speaker) and offbeat quips. Ironically, he was also known for the brevity of his postgame

---

65 Denny Boyd, author of *Legends of Autumn* and a member of the Canadian press at the time, noted the payola because of the uproar created when Montreal owner Ted Workman ended it in 1960. Key Montreal writers not only lost extra income but also occasionally saw their taxes audited on the basis of unreported payola from seasons past when the payola news broke.

remarks. When *Montreal Gazette* writer Vern DeGeer saw a one-thousand-word story, ostensibly written by Walker, in the *Vancouver Sun* prior to the 1955 Grey Cup game, he nearly fainted away. "Sheer Balderdash," DeGeer wrote in response. "He hasn't spoken [that many] words since he got here four years ago!"[66]

If Walker was taciturn at times, his teams spoke volumes. With Etchevarry—now nicknamed "The Rifle" by Montreal's crack public relations department, a replacement for his college *nom de marketing*, "Singling Sam"—firing passes all over the place, the Als were flashy and fun to watch.

"The big offensive game was Walker's preferred style," said Marty Martinello, "but he was clear as to why that was the case. He wanted to entertain the fans."[67]

And entertained they were. By the start of the 1956 season, Molson Stadium, which seated something less than 25,000, was all but sold out for the season before the first game was played. A standing-room crowd regularly surrounded the sidelines three or four deep for Alouette home games in the mid-1950s. Sometimes they impinged on the play.

"If you ran out of bounds, you ran into the fans," said Fob James. "Those Montreal fans were as enthusiastic as any. They didn't really believe the other team had a right to be there, and they were on them right from the start."[68]

Although ownership contended publicly that it made no profit unless it reached the Grey Cup game, the people pouring through the turnstiles allowed the Als to spend freely on new talent. It all fit together nicely. An exciting team produced more money, which led to better players and still more excitement. The old college coach had this pro thing figured out.

***

Montreal roared out of the Big Four gate in 1954, winning nine of its first ten, culminating in a 46–11 pasting of the defending Grey Cup champs from Hamilton at a sold-out Molson Stadium.

---

[66] *Montreal Gazette*, Nov. 26, 1955.
[67] Martinello, interview with author.
[68] James, interview with author.

Montreal sportswriter Vern DeGeer wrote that the explosion was like a "four-pronged tornado" hitting the stadium.[69] Patterson was the biggest wind, returning a kickoff 95 yards for a score and snagging a 105-yard touchdown pass from Etchevarry.[70] Etchevarry connected on 26 of 29 passes for the day for a record 589 yards.

Coming down off that high, Montreal lost to an inferior Toronto team the next week. But with Patterson back in high gear, Montreal pounded the Argos 41–13 in a rematch the week after that. The Als looked unbeatable and might have been had Patterson not broken his right ankle while making a tackle (like most of Walker's pro stars, he was a two-way performer) in the second Toronto game. That ended Patterson's season and put both a literal and a figurative limp in what had been an Alouette strut to the championship. They scraped out a 19–15 victory over Hamilton their next game out, rallying for two late touchdowns in a contest that featured tailback Chuck Hunsinger slugging an Argonaut player and drawing the mandatory $30 fine from the league. "The game couldn't have been more entertaining," opined Walker afterward.[71] He always did like backs who could pack a punch.

Walker rested his stars the last week of the season, allowing last-place Ottawa to win a game it had no business winning. Fans and local pressmen noticed Walker's unusual calmness during the game. The normally fidgety coach actually sat down and watched the whole contest.

Even with the giveaway, Montreal entered the two-game playoff series against Hamilton with an 11–3 record. The Als won both games in the rematch of 1953, but the scoring was down.

---

69 *Montreal Gazette*, Nov. 5, 1954

70 The Canadian field is 110 yards long, making a 105-yard pass—and even longer ones—possible. Two years later, Patterson and Etchevarry connected on a 109-yarder, a feat that seems likely to remain a CFL record for some time. "The ball seemed to hang in the air forever," said Patterson of the 109-yard pass. "I guess they'll have trouble breaking that [record]." Source: Patterson, interview with author."

71 *Montreal Star*, Nov. 17, 1954.

Even with Etchevarry hitting Webster for a 102-yard pass play, Montreal netted just 38 points in the 2 games.

That wasn't the kind of production Walker was used to when he had Patterson as a threat. But the Alouettes' firepower seemed good enough to most heading into the Grey Cup against the Edmonton Eskimos, a team that had never won a championship in the thirty-four-year history of the CFL, and which had made its way through the West Division playoffs in less-than-impressive fashion. Pop Ivy's Eskimos, running a version of the University of Oklahoma's split-T offense, had started slowly but closed by winning seven of their last eight games to clinch first place in the West. Edmonton scratched out a title series win against Winnipeg but scored only twenty-five points in the three-game series. The victory upped the closing streak to nine wins in eleven games, but the eight-point-a-game average in the championship series didn't bode well for a matchup with the high-scoring Als. In the Eskimo's favor was the fact that they'd played the final game of their playoff series on November 13. Montreal's finale against Hamilton was on November 22.

The eastern Canadian press figured Montreal would rout the westerners in the Grey Cup. The Big Four had dominated the Grey Cup matchups, both lately and in general, and Walker's offensive steamroller just looked like too much for the pedestrian bunch of Eskimos who were dubbed a "$2 team in a $200,000 event" by a Toronto newspaper columnist on the eve of the game.[72] The comment was based on the alleged economic impact of the game, which was held in Toronto in 1954 (the site rotated)—and on the standard-issue smugness of big-city Canadians looking down their nose at their prairieland kinfolk. The 5:1 odds set by bookmakers, favoring Montreal, was cut from similar cloth. That both were based on less-than-detailed knowledge of the combatants is a foregone conclusion. The eastern press of the day would have been almost ignorant of the capabilities of the western teams and was smitten with the Alouettes' avalanche of statistical achievement.

---

72 *Toronto Star*, Nov. 26, 1954.

Peahead Walker was not amused. On the eve of the game, he chastised the eastern columnists for their "lyrical outbursts"[73] and said that the contest looked pretty even to him.

He was right, as it turned out. The 1954 Grey Cup was a wire-to-wire thriller and one of the most famous games in Canadian football history. Before a crowd of almost 28,000 at Varsity Stadium, Walker's well-oiled offense performed as advertised. Etchevarry connected on 23 of 33 passes for 398 yards, with O'Quinn hauling in 14 of them for 316 yards himself. Webster, Hunsinger, and company ran for 300 more, giving Montreal a whopping 698-yard day. Edmonton's split-T found had some bite as well, especially in the first quarter, when Montreal's big line struggled to get a feel for Edmonton's speed. The Eskimos ran for 266 yards and passed for 170. Not bad, but several hundred yards short of Montreal's production. Only some plucky play by the Eskimos—and some slop from the Als—kept it close.

As the game headed down to the wire it was Montreal's cup to win. The Als recovered an Eskimo fumble at the Edmonton forty-one with four minutes left. The Als had several options for bringing home the championship. Etchevarry, perhaps in consultation with Walker, decided to go for the kill instead of attempting to sit on the ball. It worked at first. Etchevarry hit O'Quinn for twenty yards to the Edmonton twenty-one to start the drive, and then Hunsinger ran eleven yards for another first down at the Eskimo eleven. Barely three minutes remained now and the Als were within easy striking distance. A touchdown would sew things up nicely, but a field goal would do the trick, too, putting Montreal ahead by two scores. Even a missed placement from short distance would likely add one point under Canadian rules, forcing Edmonton to score a touchdown (five points at that time) and kick the point after just to tie.

Walker didn't send kicker Ray Poole into the game, however, electing to let Etchevarry and company try to score a "major" (the Canadian term for a touchdown), or at least burn a little more clock while moving even closer for a kick. It seemed like sound strategy,

---

73 *Montreal Star*, Nov. 26, 1954.

even for a team that had already lost four fumbles and had two passes intercepted. But in the next few seconds it all went awry.

From the eleven, Etchevarry pitched out to Hunsinger swinging around his left end. As he looped backward to gain some depth and clear his interference, Edmonton end Rollin Prather crashed through the play-side blocking and closed on the Alouette back. Fearing being thrown for a big loss, Hunsinger untucked the ball and uncorked a feeble sidearm lateral. The ball bounced sideways and then maybe forward. The exact direction remains the subject of debate but the eventual resting place of the pigskin is not. It landed right in the hands of Jackie Parker, an Edmonton rookie from Mississippi State and a spectacularly elusive runner who had already earned the nickname "Ol' Spaghetti Legs."[74] Though battered—Parker's spaghetti had been strained in two different places during the game—the Eskimo star was feeling no pain as he scooped up the bouncing ball near the Edmonton twenty and headed toward the goal line some ninety yards away.[75] Hunsinger was down, having been tackled by Prather after his lateral and all the blockers were either on the ground or ahead of the play. The only Alouette between Parker and the goal was Etchevarry, who set out in pursuit of Parker. It was a good race—early in his career, Etchevarry was fairly fleet afoot—but Parker was faster, even on his aching legs, and began pulling away near the Montreal thirty. He scored untouched.

That tied things up. Edmonton lineman Rob Dean booted the conversion, aided by a sure pass from center Eagle Keys, who hobbled onto the field on a broken leg to make the critical snap. Edmonton led 26–25. Montreal had two more possessions and one more good chance when Etchevarry drove the Als to midfield and then hit O'Quinn with an eighteen-yard strike to the Edmonton thirty-seven. Looking for more, O'Quinn tried to fight away from tacklers and lost the ball. Edmonton recovered Montreal's sixth lost fumble of the game.

---

74 *Edmonton Sun*, Nov. 8, 2006.
75 Parker's fabled run is always credited as a ninety-yarder, but still photos of the play clearly show him picking up the ball inside the twenty. The official yardage should thus probably be more.

That ended the contest and started a lengthy conversation: Did the Als play it right? Did the officials get it right? And, most importantly, just what was Hunsinger thinking? As to the strategy, only modest hindsight was applied. It was noted that the Montreal could have kicked a field goal after reaching the ten and all but salted the game away. But that wasn't the way football was played then and it didn't seem like the percentage play in most books, field goal kicking being far less of a sure thing then than now. Etchevarry, responsible for the play call but not the overall kick-or-go decision, said in an interview years afterward that the conservative choice never really crossed his mind. "Maybe I should have tried for a field goal or a single point (achieved by kicking the ball into or out of the end zone)," said Etchevarry, "but all I knew was that we had a great team that year. I didn't get any signal from the bench to kick and I didn't expect one. I think everybody in the park knew we were going for another touchdown."[76]

As to the multiple controversies surrounding the Hunsinger/Parker play, there's never been a simple answer. Hap Shouldice, a veteran CFL official who eventually was elected to the league's Hall of Fame, was the head arbiter for the contest. He said afterward that Hunsinger's bobble was definitely a fumble. The game was televised—the first Grey Cup on the tube—but the footage, available from only the midfield angle, does not render any clear verdict. Still photos suggest Hunsinger's bobble/pass almost certainly went forward, but the question remains as to whether it was a pass or a fumble. Notably, professional and college officials still struggle with that call.

As for Hunsinger's thinking . . . well . . .

Hunsinger, understandably despondent, said he was trying to throw a pass and then abruptly cut off interviews. "There's no use trying to talk about it," he said.[77] Had the play been ruled a pass, Montreal's worst outcome would have been a fifteen-yard penalty, assessed because Hunsinger's nearest (and really, his only) passing target, guard Ray Cicia, was an ineligible receiver. That would have been a blow but wouldn't have resulted in an Edmonton touchdown. Participants and eyewitnesses offered many

---

76 Legends of Autumn.
77 *Montreal Gazette*, Nov. 29, 1954.

opinions, but the prevailing belief was simply that Hunsinger panicked. That makes the most sense, although it must be noted that the end-of-play lateral was still a big part of football at this time. Hunsinger had already lost one fumble in the game on a similar play in the first half, while Edmonton had made some hay on lateral plays (that apparently were practiced and called) on kickoff returns.

Whatever the case, Hunsinger's teammates were dejected during the postmortems. His coach was brief and acerbic.

"I suppose it was an impulse," Walker said of Hunsinger's play.

Later, after more thought and with a new wave of reporters on hand, he added, "I guess he had a brain cramp."[78]

The "greatest goat play" in Canadian football history[79] was, for all intents, the end of Chuck Hunsinger's career.

It was a sad and strange ending to a flashy career. As a collegian, Hunsinger's star had shown so brilliantly that Birmingham sportswriter Zipp Newman penned a song about him.[80] After leaving Florida, Hunsinger enjoyed three solid NFL seasons with the Bears and two very good ones with Walker in Montreal. But the Illinois native was completely undone by his Grey Cup gaffe. He drove home with his wife and children the night after the game—the trip had been prearranged so that Hunsinger could help his father-in-law with his business—and wallowed around in self-doubt and depression for some time.

A 310-foot-long consolation telegram, inspired by a Montreal radio station and bearing the signatures of 21,947 Alouette fans, arrived at the Hunsinger home a few weeks later.

That cheered Hunsinger a bit, and he was invited back to the Montreal camp in 1955 where he made the team. But the comeback didn't last. Never a sure-handed player, Hunsinger bobbled and wobbled through the opening half of the season and

---

78 Various Canadian newspapers reported the same words.
79 *Montreal Gazette*, Nov. 29, 1954.
80 "The Hunsinger Song" was not a smash hit, but sheet music was produced. The essence and feel of the work can be gleaned from the snappy chorus: "No player is torrider; Than this lad from Florida; Hunsinger the Humdinger; You ought to see him go!"

then . . . was cut. Peahead Walker wasn't a heartless coach, but when a player suffered a brain cramp and it just wouldn't go away . . . well, there was only one thing to do.

Championship or no, the Alouettes still got a tickertape parade three days after the Grey Cup, and a few weeks after that the Als' new management—Ted Workman had purchased the majority ownership but had kept Leo Dandurand and other front office folks in place—rewarded the team's coach with his first multi-year contract. Workman gave Peahead Walker a three-year deal and a raise to $15,000 per season.[81]

Walker's delight with that last turn of events is not recorded, but he was clearly happy with the prospects for the 1955 season. The record setters from 1954 were all back, save for Webster, whose slick work for the Alouettes had caught the eye of NFL scouts. He signed with the Giants, one of the few NFL teams that could consistently top Canadian dollars when real bidding wars broke out. That was a blow, but Walker softened it by signing Pat Abruzzi, a bowling ball of a running back (5'8", 200 pounds) who stunned the college football world while playing at tiny Rhode Island University. Walker lured him away from the NFL's Baltimore Colts with a $500 signing bonus and a better opportunity for playing time. The Als had a vacancy. Baltimore, which had drafted a more highly touted fullback, Heisman Trophy winner Alan "the Horse" Ameche of Wisconsin, ahead of Abruzzi, probably did not.

Abruzzi proved to be a perfect match. Running behind the Als' massive offensive line, the little Rhode Islander was almost invisible until he popped through a hole. In his first season, he ran for 1,248 yards and scored a league-record 19 touchdowns. Given that boost, plus a healthy Patterson, Etchevarry and Montreal's offense heated up even more than they had the year before. The Als averaged 31.8 points a game and scored less than 30 on just 3 occasions (all losses). Etchevarry passed for more than 350 yards per game, O'Quinn grabbed 75 passes, wingback Joey Pal caught 43 passes . . . and finished third on the team in that department.

---

[81] The Associated Press reported the figure for the raise as a "prediction." It also reported that the contract length was two years. Montreal newspapers reported it as a three-year deal. Based on subsequent events, the latter number seems more accurate.

"They are the greatest offensive football team Canada has ever seen," wrote Vern DeGeer, the Montreal sportswriter. DeGeer was noted for his flowery prose, but it seemed justified in this case.[82]

Management of Canada's most lucrative franchise—for all its other flaws Walker's aerial circus was doing its job at the gate—was generous in doling out cash to support Walker's offensive habit. When rookie running back J. C. Caroline was cut in a surprise midseason move by the Toronto franchise, Montreal scooped him up despite having to swallow the remainder of his $14,000 per year contract. That was the same amount Etchevarry was making, giving Montreal by far the priciest backfield in the league.

But would dollars translate into a Grey Cup title? First they had to translate into a Grey Cup berth, and that almost didn't happen. In the division title game, surprising Toronto, which upset runner-up Hamilton in the championship play-in game, scored twenty-four straight points in the second quarter to take a 24–9 halftime lead against a Montreal team that had beaten them four times during the regular season by an average of twenty-two points a game. The Als were stunned. Geared to stop the passing of Toronto's Tom Dublinski, Etchevarry's statistical equal during the regular season, they were instead run over by an out-of-nowhere Argonaut ground game.

The second half was a different story, however. The Als came out like birds possessed, piled on seventeen quick points, and surged into the lead. Dublinski led Toronto on a drive that put the Argos ahead again, but Etchevarry led the Als back. A seventeen-yard scoring pass to Pal capped a drive that made it 32–30 Montreal with six minutes left to play. Dubinski set the Argos in motion again, but under pressure from Montreal's defensive front, he tossed up a soft pass that Alouette rookie Johnny Williams intercepted at midfield. Gathering the ball in, the speedy back from Southern Cal raced fifty yards for a touchdown and a 38–30 lead. Toronto would score again, but it would be too late. The dramatic halftime reversal had saved the day.

---

82 *Montreal Gazette,* Oct. 17, 1955.

Everyone assumed it was Walker who had caused it—the assumption being, of course, that the tough and profane old coach had blistered his charges during intermission with some fiery invective. Walker did have a hand in the turnaround, fine-tuning Montreal's defense and ordering Etchevarry to pound away on the ground with Abruzzi and Caroline instead of relying on the pass, but the inspirational oratory came from a different Wake Forest alum. It was O'Quinn who burned the Alouettes with his words. Red's inspiring message? Get going boys, or you'll be the next Hunsinger.

A paraphrase of the speech in the next day's *Montreal Gazette* quoted the former Deacon's climatic phrase thus: "If we blow this one, boys, we'll all be poor Chuck Hunsingers. And remember, Chuck was a fine player. Now, let's go!"[83]

The stirring, come-from-behind victory set up a Grey Cup rematch with Edmonton. Revenge offered Montreal a significant motive, but a careful Walker was taking no chances. He sent Dunn and special scout Joe Zaleski to watch Edmonton in the playoffs and then set up his Grey Cup headquarters in Whalley, a distant suburb of Vancouver, site of the 1955 game. Walker was striving to spare his squad from distractions and attempting to provide space for come clandestine practice work. What special tactics did he have in mind for Edmonton and its fearsome split T? Walker wasn't saying. His pre-Cup sessions with the press were like interviews with a Soviet press agent. Nothing of substance could be either confirmed or denied. At one point, a frustrated pressman sarcastically asked Walker if his team would wear cleats during the contest.

"Yes," Walker replied, "and no."[84]

Walker and company were on edge, fully amped for the coming showdown, but Edmonton had its psychological house in order too. After polishing off Winnipeg in the West Division Finals three days before, the Eskimos listened to the Montreal-Toronto game on the radio, pulling hard for an Alouette win. Said

---

83 *Montreal Gazette*, Nov. 21, 1955.
84 *Legends of Autumn*.

Edmonton fullback Normie Kwong, "We want to prove that [the 1954 championship] was no fluke."[85]

What with Montreal's statistical superiority in the 1954 game, the controversy surrounding the Hunsinger play and all, the flukishness of Edmonton's 1954 victory was a much-discussed theme heading into the 1955 game.

It wasn't mentioned much in the aftermath.

Pop Ivy's Eskimos battered Walker's Als, literally in some cases. Pal went out with a knee injury in the second quarter, the result of a collision with Parker. Caroline and lineman Johnny Blaicher also went down too, and Patterson was knocked out of the entire third quarter with a concussion (though afterward he couldn't recall missing any plays). Those loses hurt Montreal, but the Edmonton offense hurt it even more. With Parker running the show from quarterback now—he moved over from halfback after a midseason injury—Ivy's split T ran roughshod. Edmonton piled up 446 rushing yards. Etchevarry answered with another record-setting day in the air—508 yards on 30 of 39 passing. But the Als stumbled in scoring territory and wound up on the losing end of a 34–19 count. They didn't score at all after halftime, and observers among the record 40,000 or so at Empire Stadium thought that if the game had continued for another quarter or so the score would have been even worse.

Even though it lacked the gut-wrenching aspects of the Parker-Hunsinger affair, Walker's second Grey Cup disappointment landed harder than the first. He had all the pieces in place, but it still wasn't good enough. What was a coach to do?

Enjoy himself, enjoy the off-season.

For beginners, he coached the East in the CFL All-Star game, an easy gig that earned Walker a fat $1,000 bonus. Then he began planning for 1956, secure in his place—he was in the midst of a three-year contract and leading a powerful and proven team—and comfortable with what lay ahead. Players and friends believe it may have been one of the happiest times of his life. For nightlife mavens like Peahead and Flonnie Walker, the Montreal of the 1950s was a great place to be. Its nightclub scene, fueled by Afro-

---

85 *Montreal Gazette*, Nov. 21, 1955.

American talents who were still not warmly welcomed in much of the United States, meant there was something to do, lots to do, every night. Said Johnny Majors:

> *Montreal was a hopping place then. There were top acts from all over the world there, clubs that stayed open all night and those French Canadian girls. . . . I never really picked up French. I knew "comment ca va?" And some girls at school who I really wasn't trying to get anywhere with, taught me "voulez-vous couchez," which, I think, means do you want to go to bed with me. It was great for me. Those were interesting times. A young man could have a great time there . . . an old man too I guess. Peahead always seemed pretty happy to me. I remember when I first got up there he took me and another guy out to eat at some fancy restaurant. We sat down and he said, "Johnny, you ever eat any snails?' I said, "No sir." He said, "Well, we're going to get you some tonight and see how you like 'em." He thought that was pretty funny and all and seemed to just have a big time. I did try the snail and I liked 'em. Still eat 'em today."*[86]

Jacques Belec, who kept up with Walker regularly even after leaving the Als, said, "He did seem to have a great time there, a beautiful time, really. I know he enjoyed it. He liked the nightlife, he had a nice reputation, and he was paid okay. And hell, he was a football man and they let him coach football pretty much any way he wanted for most of the time he was there. It didn't take much more than that to make him happy."[87]

Walker did enjoy considerable freedom as coach. His assistants—basically just Jimmy Dunn until the very end of his career—were pliable, and ownership didn't create too many hassles. Near the end of the 1955 season, for example, Walker spent four days on a two-gig speaking tour in North Florida (Jacksonville and Gainesville), leaving preparation for the regular-season finale to Dunn. Similarly, when the season was over, he left on his regular spring and early summer recruiting tour, which gave him ample opportunity for speaking and socializing. Not a bad life.

---

86 Majors, interview with author.
87 Belec, interview with author.

Walker may have been living the high life, but the Montreal franchise was in something of a quandary entering the 1956 season. The team was clearly the class of the East, but just as clearly, the class of the East wasn't good enough to win the Grey Cup. Some upgrades to get over the hump seemed in order, but any big signings were precluded by the salaries paid to returning stars like Etchevarry (a whopping $14,000 or more per year), Patterson, Tex Coulter, O'Quinn, Abruzzi, and Pal—and to the newly signed coach who now had a five-figure deal. Walker did try one coup, trading for massive tackle Billy Shipp from Toronto, where he'd argued (and maybe physically fought with—details of a film room incident weren't fully reported) Coach Bill Sawicki near season's end in 1955. The massive Mississippian arrived in Montreal a few weeks into the 1956 season (he was on Toronto's injured list at the time) and offered an imposing tackle tandem when paired with the equally bulky Coulter. The Als also brought in 280-pound Ray Baillie from Calgary to provide still more size and depth. The rest of the line and receiving corps were intact, and Abruzzi was back at fullback. J. C. Caroline was gone, however, along with Belec, Hunsinger, and the others who filled in at halfback during the 1955 season. In their place Walker brought in NFL journeyman (and future award-winning CFL coach) George Brancato and American rookies Bob Pascal of Duke and Fob James of Auburn. James, probably not the best back on a good Auburn team, was Walker's primary target. He gave the future governor a $3,000 signing bonus and a $12,000 salary for a year's play—among the highest on the team. James recalled the frustration felt by teammate Joe Childress, a first-round pick in the NFL draft, who received a slightly smaller bonus and salary to play in America. "And because of the currency situation at the time, I really got about five percent more than that," said James. "So it was quite a deal."[88]

None of the new acquisitions were sensational, but during the regular season it didn't manner. Etchevarry was brilliant again, completing better than 60 percent of his passes while throwing for 32 touchdowns and more than 4,700 yards (better than 330 yards

---

88 James, interview with author.

per game). O'Quinn and Pal were solid receivers. "Prince Hal" Patterson was extraordinary. In the finest season of a brilliant career, he hauled in eighty-eight passes to lead to the league while averaging almost twenty-two yards per catch, an astonishing figure for so high a volume. With opposing defenses scrambling to get their arms around the Montreal passing game, Abruzzi ran wild again, breaking his own single-season touchdown record (he scored twenty in 1956) and once again leading the league in rushing.

With all that firepower at its disposal, Montreal ran roughshod over the opposition—including Edmonton. The teams squared off in a preseason matchup in August—such East-West exhibitions were standard affairs—and Montreal pummeled the Eskimos 33–0. Strange results are standard procedure in professional preseason games, with one team placing more emphasis on a game's outcome than the other, but Edmonton players at the time thought Walker pushed that envelope in the preseason tilt, taking revenge there for past Grey Cup indignities.

In the two-game East Finals series, Montreal faced the Hamilton squad that it so thoroughly dominated during the season, save for an after-it-was-all-over blowout loss at season's end, in which Walker rested his starters. Hamilton was much sharper in the playoffs than it had been during the season, however. The Tiger-Cats used familiarity to breed a better defensive game plan. Flipping the standard idea against the Als, Hamilton focused on Abruzzi and Patterson and forced Etchevarry to turn to O'Quinn (eleven catches) and James (eighty-eight yards rushing). A fluky play—the Als occasionally benefitted from some of those too—clinched the victory in the fourth quarter. Joey Pal fumbled a Hamilton punt, but teammate Jack Dwyer, a rookie from Loyola Marymount, scooped up the loose ball and ran thirty yards to the Hamilton thirty-four. Etchevarry led the Als in from there, providing them with a nine-point cushion heading into game two (the series was decided on total points). The extra points weren't needed but were comforting all the same, as Montreal rallied to beat the Tiger-Cats 48–41 in a wild game at a raucous Molson Stadium. Hamilton officials put a $10,000 a bounty on the Als' head—the players would collect it if they knocked Montreal out of the Grey Cup—and were incensed when several controversial calls didn't go their way. They briefly considered protesting, but cooler heads prevailed. Some calls may not have been very helpful to the Tiger-Cat hopes, but in the end Hamilton had only itself to blame. Leading 41–34 late in the second half—and down just two points in the series—Hamilton surrendered an awful touchdown. Tiger-Cat defenders surrounded Abruzzi near the Hamilton fourteen-yard line and were surprised when he lateraled to guard Herb Trawick, who had missed his block and was standing, all alone, nearby. The ponderous Trawick gathered Abruzzi's toss and lumbered into the end zone to tie the game. Hamilton never recovered.

That set up a third straight match with Edmonton, and on the eve of the game the Als were certainly hopeful. "This is what we wanted, what we've been playing for," said Walker.[89]

Unfazed by past results, or understanding that there were simply more Montreal bettors in the country, Canadian bookies once again installed the Als as favorites. But some observers thought something was different in the air. Hal Pawson of the *Edmonton Journal* noted that western teams have always "been able to rely on eastern disdain as a weapon, but for the first time since the Edmonton Eskimos launched Canada's East-West Grey Cup football classic 35 years ago, the East is confused and uncertain."[90] Some football men thought (as usual) that the Easterners had too much scoring power, but others, looking at the lean and hard Eskies, many of whom had been lured north from Bud Wilkinson's great Oklahoma football teams, thought it might be a rout.

And it was. It was all even at 20–20 midway through the third quarter when Edmonton went on a tear. The Eskimos ripped huge holes in the Montreal line for Kwong, Parker and "alternate"

---

89 *Montreal Gazette*, Nov. 19, 1956.
90 *Edmonton Journal*, Nov. 21, 1956.

fullback Johnny Bright[91] and hounded Etchevarry into one his worst days ever. He passed for less than three hundred yards, connected on less than fifty percent of his passes, and threw four interceptions. Montreal turned the ball over seven times in all (Fob James alone lost three fumbles) and just generally fell apart as Edmonton's second-half onslaught gained steam. Eskimo players took particular glee in the failure of the big Montreal line against a smaller—but far more mobile—bunch of Eskimos. Edmonton tackle Roger Nelson said it was "the easiest line play of the year. . . . That Shipp . . . he went down like the Titanic."[92]

Montreal end Doug McNichol said the Edmonton offense—it was quite similar to a modern-day option attack—was difficult to defend. But he thought then and later that Montreal could have done it if Walker had been willing to make some changes:

We played the 5–4 defense and that's all we ever played," said McNichol. "If we had changed, maybe gone to a 4–3 which was coming in to favor at that time, I think we'd have won some Grey Cups. But we didn't and Edmonton knew exactly what to do. It was tough. In the 5–4, if the got by the end [McNichol's post] there was no one to help. If we had gone to the 4–3, there would have been a linebacker or a safety out there and I don't think they'd have run like they did. But it was a different offense, kind of an option. The

---

91 Bright, a collegiate star at Drake, is remembered for his (obviously) pivotal role in the notorious "Johnny Bright Incident" during a 1951 game between Drake and Oklahoma A&M. The first prominent African American to play on A&M's home field in Stillwater, Bright's jaw was broken on a vicious—and extremely late—second-quarter hit by A&M's Wilbanks Smith. The elbow smash, Smith's third late hit on Bright in the game, didn't immediately drive Bright from the contest. A few plays later, broken jaw and all, he completed a sixty-one-yard touchdown pass. But he was finished after that. The play on which Smith smashed into Bright's face was captured by sequential photographs that showed Smith pounding Bright long after the play. The racial aspect of the play shocked citizens around the country and probably helped speed up the integration of college football.

92 *Legends of Autumn*, p. 66.

quarterback might fake off tackle and pitch it, or he might keep it. It was a very good offense, damn good. We couldn't do much with it.[93]

Just to make sure there were no more "fluke" comments, Edmonton quarterback Don Getty, the first Canadian quarter to win a Grey Cup game, tossed a seventeen-yard touchdown pass to Jackie Parker on the game's last play, the finishing touch on a 50-27 thrashing.

Well, almost the finishing touch. An extra point try remained, but Edmonton never got the chance to pile on one more. Fans flooding the field to celebrate stole the game ball. Officials couldn't restore order—and couldn't find the ball . . . or any other ball. All eighteen pigskins that had been prepped for the game had been kicked into the stands or stolen in the postgame melee by the rampaging fans. So the game ended right there.

Peahead Walker was despondent. "We played a terrible game," he said. "One of our worst of the year."[94]

He was a no-show at the annual post-Grey Cup banquet that night. Called upon to say a few words, there was an awkward silence as Cup officials realized one of the most prolific banquet speakers in the world was missing from the show.

It shouldn't have been a surprise. Walker knew how to deliver a good line. He also knew when nothing needed to be said at all.

Walker's Canadian career spiraled downward for there. After the 1956 season, he dabbled with a possible move within the CFL. Rumors had him in Hamilton, Toronto, and possible even out west.

In early December, Walker told Montreal sportswriters that he would never consider leaving a team after coming up short in three straight Grey Cups.[95] That didn't jibe exactly with the grist in the rumor mill, but it meshed with the eventual reality. He stayed, which made owner Ted Workman and the front office happy. Shortly after Walker put an end to the new job rumors, Montreal

---

93 McNichol, interview with author.
94 *Ottawa Citizen*, Nov. 26, 1956.
95 *Montreal Star*, Dec. 11, 1956.

General Managed Leo Dandurand said, "Doug [meaning Peahead] is our man."[96]

But their man was running out of men.

Coulter and Trawick both retired after the 1956 season, punching big holes in the Alouette line. The team's core was still more or less intact, but it was aged far beyond its actual years. And Walker's magic touch for finding new players was fading. The halfback slot was particularly troublesome. James left to become an Army engineer, first step on the road to governor; and Pascal went into private business, first step on the road to making millions selling propane. Walker went out recruiting again and replaced them with Joel Wells, the Clemson star, and Tennessee's Majors, who'd finished second to Paul Hornung in the 1956 Heisman Trophy voting. Wells, who followed Frank Howard's advice and spurned the NFL to play for Walker, turned out to be a solid player. He was especially good on defense. Majors, however, was a bust.

"His problem," said teammate Buddy Frick, "was that he couldn't do anything real well. His strength was—and this was typical of the old single-wing tailback—that he could run and punt and pass and kick, you know, do all those things a little bit. But they already had somebody in Montreal who could do each of those better than him. Then he got beat up a little and couldn't play and that was that."[97]

Said Majors, "I was a realist about pro football. I wanted to play but I was smart enough to realize I wasn't that good, wasn't that big, and it was nothing I could count on. So I just did the best I could and enjoyed the time I spent there. Staying out all night, getting up late, shooting some pool, and then going to practice . . . there were worse ways to spend a year. And I got paid $10,000 to do it, which was pretty good at the time."

Majors said that when Walker finally cut him late in the season, he let him down easy.

"He just called me and said, 'Johnny, you know you probably ought to just go down to UT and start coaching. I think you'd be real good at that.' He wasn't really cutting me, just pointing me in that direction. Well, more than pointing. He'd

---

96 *Montreal Gazette*, Dec. 14, 1956.
97 Frick, interview with author.

already made a call and had me a job lined up as a student assistant."[98]

Walker's ability to interact with players in a mature, straightforward way was appreciated by most of his Montreal charges. It did not necessarily mesh with his image as a tough and crude old bird or as a joke-cracking banquet raconteur, but it was an essential part of his personality say the men who played for him in Canada (and in college as well). Webster and Etchevarry, both of whom went on to become professional coaches, lauded Walker's ability to handle young men. Canadian players Marty Martinello and Mike Kovac, both of whom blossomed later in their careers, said Walker's coaching turned them into good players. Kovac said his relationship with Walker was quite close. "We did have some long talks in private when I was having some contract problems," Kovac said. "He wasn't a guy that you just went up and started chatting with any old time. But if you needed to, you could."

Jacques Belec, like Johnny Majors, said that when his career came to a more or less involuntary end, Walker handled matters professionally and with surprising insight:

> *I'd hurt my shoulder several times. I played in the Grey Cup with a dislocated shoulder in fact—had it all taped up. My last two years [Belec's career begin in 1954; he retired during the 1956 season], I was worried about the shoulder and so I kind of backed off. I wanted to be able to do things after football, you know, play golf and squash, do other things. I had a good surgeon who fixed it up, but I didn't want to hurt it again. Peahead noticed that and then one day he said to me, "Well, Jock, I guess it's about over for you. You're worried about getting hurt. . . . It's been fun hasn't it?"*[99]

***

Walker's Als started the 1957 season 5–2, good enough for first place in the Big Four. But it was an illusion. Montreal won several

---

[98] Majors, interview with author.

[99] Belec, interview with author. Later, with some help from Walker, Belec got a part-time job in sports broadcasting and is credited with creating French phrases for football positions and other football lingo still in use by CFL broadcasters today.

close, low-scoring games early on to stay in the title race but was clearly a different team from the offensive juggernauts of the past. The revamped line struggled to create running space or to protect Etchevarry, and the receiving just wasn't as sharp; even when he had time to hit the target, it wasn't a sure thing. Consequently, offensive production plummeted. Etchevarry threw just fourteen touchdown passes against twenty-two interceptions, Abruzzi's rushing totals fell again, and Montreal's per game scoring average dropped by almost three touchdowns a game to 20.7. The Als got banged up late—as did most of teams in the Big Four—and dropped six of their last seven. They closed with back-to-back losses to last-place Toronto 40–27 and 27–0. That left Montreal at 6–8 and in third place. An upset victory over Ottawa in the East semifinals helped cheer things up a bit, but Hamilton, now under legendary coach Jim Trimble, erased any good feelings by winning the two-game championship series 56–11, including 39–1 in game two.[100]

The team extended Walker's contract following the 1957 season and admitted that it was time to rebuild, which offered Walker some unusual cover. And the Als were a little better in 1958. Etchevarry was a little sharper, Wells took over from Abruzzi as the main ball carrier, and NC State's Dick Hunter replaced Majors in the backfield. But Patterson, who shouldered an even bigger load in 1957 as the offense fell apart, was injured throughout the 1958 season and suffered through his worst pro season. Instead of losing back-to-back games to Toronto to end the season, the Als won two straight over the Argos to finish 7–6–1. But, in a semifinal rematch with Ottawa, Montreal lost to the Roughriders and their Canadian quarterback Russ Jackson. "They were fired up," said Walker, "and we weren't."[101]

The slight improvement in 1958 was appreciated, but as the 1959 season began, Ted Workman made it clear that the one-year

---

100 Trimble, known as "Jungle Jim" for his wild statements and occasionally wild actions—he twice assaulted Montreal sportswriter Ian McDonald—coached more than twelve seasons in Canada and the NFL, including a stop in Montreal in the mid-1960s. Later he was part of a company that created and introduced the "slingshot" goal posts—a single post supporting the crossbar and two uprights—to both professional and college football.
101 *Montreal Gazette*, Nov. 13, 1958.

rebuilding "era" was over. Following a meeting with Walker and his coaching staff, Workman announced that the Als were moving to a "produce-or-else system." Enough had been done over the past two years, Workman believed, for the Als to return to the Grey Cup, although it should be noted that Grey Cup performance was not necessarily the bottom line. Montreal sports columnist Red Fisher, a sort of Workman mouthpiece (apparently the bribes really did work), wrote in late summer of 1959 that Grey Cups "are not that important as long as a football team can produce exciting football. As long they're exciting they're worthwhile to watch."[102] Whether Fisher's tale was an exact recitation of the party line or not, it did drive home an important point: the Als were a business and one that had succeeded famously under Walker's tutelage. Anyone pondering a change in the Montreal coaching office had best keep in mind that whatever else he did, Walker fielded teams that packed 'em in. But given the tools Walker at Walker's disposal, the Als should be able to pack Molson Stadium and win the Grey Cup, too—or so Workman thought. With his okay, Montreal had increased the size of the staff, adding coaches and scouts. Walker got his second full-time assistant in 1958 when Harvey Johnson, who played for Walker's old friends Carl Voyles at William & Mary, joined the staff. Johnson stayed in that post for a year before becoming the team's chief scout. His coaching position was taken by Pat Preston, Walker's former "orphan star" at Wake Forest.[103] Montreal was, by Workman's account, spending far more than its competitors on "development," a category that included not only scouting but also expensive contracts for imports, etc. Workman said near the end of the 1959 season that Montreal's "development" outlay was $200,000 more than that its next nearest rival. That might have been rhetorical justification for Montreal's postseason moves in 1959 when Workman cleaned house, but it might have been the truth.

And there were other, "internal" problems afoot as well.

---

102 *Montreal Star*, Aug. 28, 1959.
103 The list of Alouette assistants does not include the preseason "help" afforded by Howard, Butts, and, occasionally, Canadian coaches such as Jack Hennemeir or Vic Obeck.

Grey Cup winners, contenders, or otherwise, Walker's Als were, throughout his time in Montreal, a decidedly all-American bunch. He drove his imports hard—most of his Americans played both ways all the way—while leaving most of his Canadians in the garage. That this continued to happen while Montreal sank behind Hamilton, which had by far the best Canadian players in the East, grated on Alouette leaders. Early in his career as Montreal's main owner, Workman professed his commitment to the development of more and better Canadian players, especially from Quebec. "I wanted to make the Montreal Alouettes a great Canadian football club," Workman said.[104]

Workman and the front office had made their wishes known to Walker several times, but before the 1959 season they presented him with a detailed operational plan. Every player that dressed (twenty-eight was the max that could dress at that time) must be used in the game, and no player should play more than forty (of sixty) minutes. These rules would have forced Walker to play Canadians more than he did, but he seems to have considered them more as guidelines, if he considered them at all.

Canadian and Americans who played for Walker thought the import controversy was overblown, although there's a mix of opinions as to whether it might have been handled better.

Canadian lineman Mike Kovacs said, "There certainly wasn't any of this 'Yank, you're here to steal my job' thing, which is kind of how it was portrayed in the press and outside of the team. And I guess you can attribute a lot of that to Coach Walker, who was a tough guy, but a fair one. You always had the opportunity. There was a real tryout I thought, and some of these All-Americans from the states, they didn't do so well and he didn't play them. It was pretty simple."[105]

American Buddy Frick, who played on some of the Montreal teams near the end of Walker's career, said, "I think he was willing to play more Canadians. And he always seemed fair about it to me. He played Doug McNichol, who was very good, and huge, and he played some others [Canadians], but he wanted to win and he

---

[104] Legends of Autumn.
[105] Mike Kovacs, interview with author.

thought you needed the best guys on the field to do that. I don't think he really cared where they came from."[106]

Ex-players disagreed on the quality of the Canadian players at that time. Alex Webster, the former coach, thought the key to Canadian football at the time was the Canadians themselves and that teams with good Canadians prospered.

Frick, on the other hands, thought the Canadians were second rate. "I always thought a CFL team would have lost to an NFL team 50–0, and the Canadians would have been the main reason for that. Generally, they just weren't as good at that time. They were still coming around."[107]

Early in his career, Walker worked with McGill coach Vic Obeck and local high school coaches to stage clinics that would improve the knowledge of both coaches and players. Later, he let Belec "borrow" some Alouettes to tape a weekly segment on football terminology and tactics for his show on French-Canadian TV, which was designed, in part, to stir interest in football in Quebec.

"He was always very supportive of developing football here," said Belec.[108]

What he did not support was putting an inferior team on the field, and in Walker's mind, that generally meant playing his eight to twelve imports (the number varied during his career) ahead of the Canadians. As far as that goes, Walker just wasn't big on substitutions. His best teams at Wake Forest had enough good players that he managed to establish a rotation at some positions, such as end and tackle (and, oddly enough, quarterback/tailback), but a lingering verdict on all his college teams was that he had a good first team but not much after that.

That mentality may have carried over to Canada. Certainly Walker's reputation did.

Gerry Hogan said when his brother-in-law met NFL coaching legend Don Shula at a celebrity golf tournament in the

---

106 Frick, interview with author.
107 Ibid. Frick's notion of CFL vs. NFL matchups was roughly on target. Eight exhibition contests between the CFL and American pro leagues were staged from 1950 to 1961 and the NFL/AFL won seven of them. The only CFL victory was by Hamilton over the then-fledgling Buffalo Bills of the AFL in 1961
108 Belec, interview with author.

1980s, they discussed Hogan's playing career. When Shula learned that Hogan had played for Walker, he first reaction was, "Did he ever get to play?"

"He was joking," said Hogan, "but it was obvious [Walker] had a reputation in the coaching fraternity for not playing very many people. And it was deserved. I don't think it was Canadian-Import. He just played all his regulars too much. The Americans he brought in, he just wore them out."[109]

Wells recalled trying to call timeouts just to catch his breath:

> *My first game I was playing running back and cornerback and the other guys [the other team] were passing it just about every down, so as a corner I was running like crazy and I was just about pooped in the middle of the second quarter. So I said, "Hell, let's call timeout." But some of my teammates said, "You can't. It's against the rules." You could put subs in, but you couldn't call timeouts, not for anything unless a player actually was declared injured. It was tough. I went up there at 197, 198 pounds that first year and finished under 180.*[110]

Walker's huge linemen suffered even more. Perennial Big Four All-Star Tex Coulter, a near three-hundred-pounder, was a force in every game—until he wore out. Walker understood this but thought a worn-out Coulter was better than the alternative, so he never subbed for him. But Coulter and his backup, the aforementioned Canadian Gerry Hogan, worked on some special signals. "He [Coulter] would let me know when he needed a break," said Hogan. "Peahead was so wrapped up in the game he didn't notice."[111]

Hogan and Coulter's self-substitution scheme went on for several games. Then one game Peahead turned around and saw Tex on the bench. It was no great feat. Coulter was hard to miss. "Tex, what the hell are you doing here?" he said. "We've only got eleven on the field!"

---

109 Hogan, interview with author.
110 Wells, interview with author.
111 Hogan, interview with author.

"No Coach," said Coulter, "Hogan's in for me."

"Hogan?!" said Walker. Then, after a pause, "That's what I mean. We only got eleven men on the field!"[112]

If there was any intra-team animosity between homegrown players and imports, it was over salary. The Canadians were paid half what the Americans were—or less. Consequently, nearly all of them worked a full-time job in addition to playing. Obtaining a job, or the career prospects in a particular city, were often more important to Canadian players than the actual salary. Belec, drafted by both an eastern team (Montreal) and a western team (Winnipeg) told the leaders of both organizations that he was interested in a job in the financial services industry. Winnipeg found him a position with a company there, and Montreal lined up a post with the Montreal office of Ontario-based London Life, which agreed to assign Belec to Montreal for two to three years. "After that, I'd have to go where they needed me," he said. "But it was a pretty good deal. I did have to drive straight from work to practice and that could be a pretty long day, but I was in good shape after football was over. And I understand about the Americans. That's what they had to pay them to get them there."[113]

Belec and Doug McNichol, who had an "office job" in Hamilton, had it better than most of their Canadian teammates. Most worked in industrial jobs—at the Molson plant for example—or toiled at some other menial job. Herbie Trawick, a "Canadianized" American[114] who broke the CFL color barrier several years before Walker arrived, worked as a doorman at a fancy Montreal restaurant. It was not his preferred job, but it was the best he could do. Racism, though tempered with greater opportunity and a spot on a CFL roster, still existed in postwar Canada.

---

112 Belec, interview with author.
113 Ibid.
114 That is, he counted as a Canada player and not an import because of his ancestry. He was born in the United States and was an American citizen, but one side of his family was from Canada. Other Americans, like former Wake Forest star Ray Cicia, became "Canadian" after marrying a Canadian girl. The rule on that was the player must marry a Canadian citizen and live in Canada for three years.

Johnny Majors, an American who enjoyed the sweet life of an import who was paid for practice for two or three hours each afternoon and play a game on one (and occasionally) two days a week, said he sometimes wondered what the Canadian players thought about the system.

"I'm sure they thought we [the Americans] were a bunch of rich goof offs or something," said Majors. "Here they are dragging in from work and we're all jumping around, hyper and ready to go because just got up at one o'clock."[115]

Both Canadians and Americans could ask for raises, and at least one of each did following the 1958 season. Their fates suggest the direction of the franchise under a more assertive Workman. Canadian fullback Wally Lencz, the hard-nosed son of a Montreal butcher, asked for a raise and got it. Dick Hunter, a back from NC State, also wanted more.

He played his next season in Ottawa.

Although Workman had proclaimed the rebuilding process over, the 1959 season was marked by the sort of frantic activity that marks a team in transition. Walker added former Wake Forest and Chicago Bear great Pat Preston to his coaching staff, ostensibly to drill the offensive linemen in the art of pass blocking. He also brought in more than forty new players for preseason tryouts, including five "pre-Canadianized" Americans—American collegiate players with Canadian ancestry who turned up through a specialized scouting search—and more than thirty new potential imports. As the preseason drills headed toward live scrimmages, players in both groups were dropping like flies. Two of the "pre-Cans" couldn't agree to a contract and quit. Another, Boston College star Cliff Poirer, signed then quit after phoning to tell the club that Canadian football was "tougher than he thought."[116] Neither of the other two Canadianized players ever made an impact. On the American side, a robust group of thirty-seven imports was whittled to twenty-five in less than two weeks of practice. The defections—several of the Americans slunk away in the dead of night without informing Walker or team management—became the big preseason story in Montreal, especially when one of them was

---

115 Majors, interview with author.
116 *Montreal Star*, July 9, 1959.

LSU fullback John Brodnax, the most highly touted new import on the roster. "Red" Brodnax, co-star on LSU's national championship team of 1958 ("The Chinese Bandit" team), had been penciled in as the replacement for the fading Pat Abruzzi, who'd been traded to Calgary in March. Brodnax's surprise departure left Montreal with a gaping hole at a critical position. Workman would have liked to have seen Wally Lencz fill it, but skill-wise that was wishful thinking. Wells stepped in at fullback part time, but most of the load was taken on by former Kansas State All-American Veryl Switzer, who came to Montreal from Calgary in the Abruzzi deal following a couple of seasons with the Green Bay Packers and two years in the Army. Other newcomers included end Ron Siminksi from Furman, wing back Bill Glosson from Texas Southern, and halfback Jim Colclough from Boston College.

The new group was probably a little better defensively—at least part of the reason for trading Abruzzi was because he wasn't much of a defensive presence—but it lacked the trademark offensive punch of Walker's best teams. Indeed, the Als tumbled all the way to the bottom of the Big Four in offense, averaging just 14.1 points per game, or less than half the average of the 1956 team. Injuries and shifting personnel played a big role. Switzer ran hard but wasn't a breakaway threat. Patterson hurt his knee again, this time in September, and was seldom heard from again. O'Quinn, feted on "Red O'Quinn Day" at Molson Stadium, turned in a workman-like year with a league-leading fifty-three catches, but he was no longer able to break the long play with frequency, especially not with Patterson out. Defensive end Ted Elsby was lost of the year with a dislocated shoulder. Wells was hurt and knocked out of three games. Placekicker Bill Bewley missed a third of the games. On and on the painful litany went. Some new players were signed, like halfback George Dixon, who was cut by the Packers at the start of the NFL season, and Hawaiian lineman Gilbert Ane, cut by the Bears. But as the losses piled up, Walker mostly had to make do with what he had. By the end of the sad season he was forced to extreme measures, like throwing rookie Wes Gideon of Trinity University into the fray as a defensive back. Gideon had worked solely as a quarterback on the Import Reserve up until that point.

And yet, with all that happened before it was over, the season did not look like a lost cause when it began. A month into the campaign, Montreal upset Hamilton to forge a tie for first place at 4–1. The team appeared stout defensively—a new look for Walker in Canada—and was winning with big plays like Billy Hudson's punt block for a score against the Tiger-Cats. It was the rest of the Big Four that was in turmoil as the end of September neared. But from that peak the Als went straight downhill. Montreal lost six straight before stopping moribund Toronto in a very un-Als-like 4–3 score. Bewley, back from an ankle injury, booted a twenty-yard field goal with three minutes left to secure the victory. Except for the outcome, the contest was emblematic of the Als' season. They played hard defense but were bumblers on offense.

Walker got the blame, of course. The one-time offensive genius was criticized for playing his top players too much and for eschewing the new, "modern" method of game management in which a coach on the sidelines, perhaps with help from an assistant in the press box, called all the plays. Walker still let Etchevarry call the game—still believed that the players understood better, or at least as well as he, what was going on during a game. Walker still enjoyed teaching his players the game and not just their assignments. Alex Webster, later coach of the NFL's Giants, said Etchevarry was a great leader who meshed well with Walker and understood what he wanted in a game. Walker enjoyed that kind of teaching and made the players teach each other the game. Majors remembered Walker ordering someone to teach a reserve halfback named Simpson to catch the ball one day in practice after Simpson had missed a string of passes. Players also recalled Walker's willingness to listen to their suggestions. Belec said he let players adjust blocking assignments if they saw better ways to run plays. He also recalled a game in which halfback J. C. Caroline was injured but wouldn't tell Walker and stayed in the game, running at half speed:

Etcheverry called a play for him and he went nowhere of course. I said, "Sam what the hell are you doing you SOB! Don't give him the ball." Sam said, "Well, we need someone at that position who can run." I said, "Well, tell Peahead." "You tell him," he said—and so I

> did. I went over to the sidelines at the next break. Peahead had already heard me and Etcheverry, so he knew something was up. I said, "Coach, give us a goddamn halfback who can run." He didn't say anything about it. He just put someone else in. . . . Thinking about it, if he had a weakness, that may have been it. He didn't really control the game the way he might have, didn't let us benefit from all he knew and he knew a lot. Sam called the plays. He was pretty good at running a game, but not perfect. I gave him hell sometimes for the calls he made. I know Peahead heard that, too, but I think he really wanted us to work it out amongst ourselves. Not every other coach would have done that. Some are so tied up in what they've done, or the fact that they didn't see it. Not Peahead. If you were trying to win, he'd listen. He didn't have a lot of crap about him.[117]

McNichol, who liked Walker a lot, said that the coach's inflexibility during games was his singular weakness. As noted, McNichol's opinion is that Walker's unwillingness to change his defense probably cost him a Grey Cup.

"He was very good at preparation," said McNichol. "We always knew what the other team was going to do. His biggest fault was he didn't make adjustments during a game. I think that was a problem. He just didn't want to do it, or wouldn't do it. I don't know which."[118]

As the offense declined in 1959, Walker was actually criticized for passing too much—or letting Etchevarry call too many passes—but the Als were in a catch-22 by then. Because the quality of the running backs and linemen had declined, the team wasn't able to run like it had before. Etchevarry's still-accurate arm—he completed fifty-six percent of his passes in 1959—remained the Als' most potent weapon, even if it wasn't as potent as it had been. That was the boat the Als were in as the season drifted away. With just five victories by late October, the Als were on the cusp of making the playoffs. But there was little chance of anything good happening after that. Rumors were flying. It seemed obvious to all of Montreal's sporting press that Walker's time was

---

117 Belec, interview with author.
118 McNichol, interview with author.

done. The team was floundering, Walker and the owner didn't see eye to eye on a number of issues, and an edict had been issued.[119]

In late October, Walker and Flonnie attended the Ladies Quarterback Club's monthly meeting in Montreal. At the end of the event, as Montreal General Manager Gorman Kennedy looked on, the president of the ladies group presented Walker with a gift—a travel bag. "Well," said a beaming Walker, "this is going to come in mighty handy." The crowd roared.[120]

Walker and company managed to pull out a closing victory over Hamilton, which pulled most of its starters, to gain the last playoff berth, but that didn't prove to be much of a triumph. Ottawa embarrassed the Als in the semifinals 43–0. Montreal fans in Ottawa serenaded Walker after the game with "Goodnight Ladies" and other farewell tunes, and *Star* columnist Hal Atkins noted that ever since rumors of Walker's demise began swirling, his popularity had skyrocketed. Several readers had written Atkins, suggesting that Montreal management hold a referendum among season ticket holders to see if they really wanted to let Walker go. "Maybe a lot of those folks who were quick to judge did a little solid analyzing and found Ol' Peahead has not done too badly and in looking at what's happened in the [Toronto] Argo camp since 1954 [the Argos had finished last five straight years], it's probably better having the devil you know than the devil you don't know."[121]

Whether public sentiment was building behind Walker or not is impossible to say, but the straight-laced Workman wanted nothing to do with a devil, be it a known one or otherwise. Two days after the season-ending debacle, Walker was fired.

Workman's official statement was tortured and confusing, in part because the team offered Walker an unspecified

---

119 Aside from play calling, overpaying for imports and the Canadian-import imbroglio, Workman was also on the way to becoming a religious/morality zealot who, after Walker left, attempted to start a new movement known as "moral rearmament," a kind of condition of employment with the Alouettes. Players were asked to sign statements giving up an assortment of vices—nearly all of which were part of Walker's life. The veteran players rebelled against the idea and Walker almost certainly would have too. To what extent there was friction between Walker and Workman over this issue is not clear.

120 *Montreal Star*, Oct. 27, 1959.

121 *Montreal Star*, Nov. 7, 1959.

noncoaching job and in part because that's the way Workman's mind worked.

Walker, as was his wont, cut through the crap. Translating the proceedings and Workman's monologue for Vern DeGeer of the *Montreal Gazette*, he said, succinctly, "I've been fired."

In an interview some time after the actual firing, Workman said the main conflict with Walker was not about some vague complaint about the coach's ability to achieve progress but was simply the culmination of their disagreement over the use of Canadian players.

Perhaps. But the housecleaning at the end of 1959—GM Gorman Kennedy was also let go—and the speed with which the emptied posts were filled suggested there were other motives as well. It seems likely that Workman had already hired his new coach, Florida State's Perry Moss, before he announced Walker's firing. The *Toronto Star* reported as much, and Moss's hiring was announced the same week Walker was fired, quick work in the days before the Internet, cell phones, and easy air connections between Florida and Montreal.

Moss was Walker's opposite in just about every way. He was a young man, just thirty-four, a "boy wonder" coach who the year before had been hired as both coach and athletic director at Florida State, a school on the way to becoming a national football power but at that time of Moss' election not yet there. Moss' only FSU team went 4–6, and he was hanged in effigy twice during the season—unusual treatment during the first-season honeymoon period. That didn't dissuade Workman, who liked Moss's youth and ramrod discipline, which the Als' owner may have mistaken for high moral bearing. And Moss was a handsome, well-spoken man, not given to funny, off-color stories or, say players there during his tenure, much humor at all.

***

The mark Doug Walker left on Montreal's sporting world was considerable. In eight seasons, he compiled a 64–52–1 record, led the Alouettes to three Grey Cups, and nearly put them in two others. More importantly—and this was more obvious at the time than it is in hindsight—he created a sensation.

"In many ways, Peahead made football in Montreal," said Gerry Hogan. "For those three years [1954–1956] we [the Alouettes] were about as popular as the Canadiens. The town was really excited. The team went into a long bad period after that and for a long time when people talked about the great years of the Alouettes, that's what they were talking about."[122]

Walker's Alouettes sold out, or all but sold out, Molson Stadium for six straight seasons. Montreal was the CFL's best draw during that period, bringing in crowds that dwarfed the audiences at many other league sites. Although the owners, especially Workman, were profligate spenders, it was a successful franchise while Walker was there.

Indeed, one of the best judgments on Walker's Montreal legacy is the fate of the football team after he left. Instead of a strict disciplinarian, Moss turned out to be an officious puppeteer who was hated by Etcheverry, Patterson, and O'Quinn, the team's veteran nucleus. Years later, Patterson recalled that Moss "treated us like children. Peahead was strict and tough, but he knew what he was doing. Moss just thought he knew."[123]

Moss's Montreal teams never won more than five games in a season and never made the playoffs, much less the Grey Cup. Workman's impetuous decision to trade "the rebellious" Patterson along with Etchevarry a week after the end of the 1960 season denuded the team's already declining team pool more quickly than otherwise might have happened. But it was soon apparent that Moss was in over his head. He struggled with the Canadian game but more importantly in dealing with people and assessing talent. In 1961, with Etcheverry gone (he wound up jumping to the NFL's Chicago Cardinals rather than report to Hamilton), Moss brought twelve quarterbacks to camp and kept six of them on the team. The opening day starter, Nelson Yarborough, was cut five games into the season.

After Moss was fired, he wound up coaching a semipro team in West Virginia and then was hired to coach Marshall University. He went 0–9–1 in his only season at Marshall and was dismissed

---

122 Hogan, interview with author.
123 Patterson, interview with author.

after the NCAA uncovered recruiting violations committed by his staff. Perhaps he was not the moral crusader Workman had envisioned after all.[124]

The Als suffered through a lost decade after Walker's dismissal. Under Moss and his immediate successors, the team floundered. The club finally returned to the Grey Cup—and won—in 1969 with Sam Etcheverry coaching the team and Red O'Quinn (who had turned down an offer to become an assistant coach in 1959 after Walker's firing) serving as general manager.

La Tête du Pois would have been proud. Two of his guys got together and worked it out without him.

That was just the way he liked it.

---

[124] Moss eventually achieved some football success as a coach in the Arena Football League in the 1990s.

CHAPTER 10

THE END OF A GOOD STORY

There is no record as to exactly which night it was that Peahead Walker first finished off his dinner plate and walked to the podium to begin his address. But whenever the first time was, it was certainly not Walker's last. His career as a featured speaker on the athletic banquet circuit rivaled his coaching career for both longevity and success. He was already an accomplished keynoter by the middle of his Wake Forest College coaching tenure, and from that point on he didn't let up until his health failed him in the last year or so of his life.

Walker spoke at sports banquets of all sizes and shapes across the eastern United States. Written accounts of his engagements place him in such diverse locales as Richmond and Norfolk, VA; Mt. Carmel, PA; Burlington and Gastonia, NC; Cheraw, SC; and Newark, NJ. He was a regular at the "Touchdown" or "Quarterback" clubs in Jacksonville, and Gainesville, FL, and at various service clubs in his adopted, late-life home of Charlotte, NC. Walker spoke so frequently at the famed Atlanta Touchdown Club that in 1969 the club gave him an engraved silver tray recognizing his service. Walker was so moved by the surprise honor that he "couldn't even gasp out a single joke," wrote Charlie Roberts, a Walker confidant and *Atlanta Constitution* reporter who attended the event.

""It's just been wonderful coming here all these years," said Walker.[1]

Club members lauded Walker for his near-perfect attendance, meaning, apparently, that he drove (or took a train) to Atlanta for the club's in-season meetings on a regular basis (the club was founded in 1938, just after he arrived at Wake Forest).

---

1 *Atlanta Constitution*, Jan. 19, 1969.

While at Wake Forest (and possibly while at Elon, though it's not clear how much speaking he was doing while coaching there) he spoke mostly to generate publicity for his school and football teams, perhaps receiving some small honorarium or expense money. After leaving coaching in late 1959, the pace of his speaking engagements may or may not have picked up, but his requirement to get paid for talking almost surely did. It was a significant part of his "retirement" income and he was disinclined to give that up, although he likely would have done it for free if he could. He clearly enjoyed being in front of a crowd.

***

Folks who heard Walker at the podium recall a you-had-to-be-there-to-understand-it sort of charisma. What so many found captivating was a combination of Walker's comedic timing, his somewhat comical appearance, and, as former player Ken Bridges noted, the rumble of his gravelly, Deep South drawl.

Bridges was no particular fan of Walker, but allowed that his old coach was a whiz on the rubber chicken trail nonetheless.

"The banquet circuit loved him," said Bridges. "The man could tell a joke and the raspy voice of his, it just made it that much funnier."[2]

Said former Alabama Governor Fob James, who played for Walker in Montreal, "He was one of the funniest men I've ever known or heard. He really could have been a standup comic."[3]

Walker's drawl was a nice touch, but many observers thought both it and Walker's podium persona—he played the backwoods hick—were highly calculated. Former Florida State coach Bobby Bowden, who was from Walker's hometown of Birmingham, met Peahead while Bowden was beginning his coaching career in the late 1950s (Bowden coached at Howard, one of Walker's several alma maters,) and Peahead was in town for a speech. Bowden thought Walker laid things on a little thick, and he would probably know. During his long coaching career, the folksy Bowden was a noted master of the technique himself.

---

[2] Ken Bridges, interview with author.
[3] Fob James, interview with author.

"He was country, or maybe I should say Southern, and he wanted to be country, so he tried to be country," said Bowden. "I don't think he was that country, not at all. He was very confident, very poised. He'd come up and speak to anybody. But out in front of the crowd, he sounded like a real hick, which was exactly what he intended I believe."[4]

Walker did not have a lot of hobbies, but he reveled in social contact. He liked big meals or a night spent with good friends and a good bottle of whiskey around a table, or both—best of all—a good meal followed by a bottle. The main course at most such gatherings was certainly sports—the vast majority of Walker's friends seem to have been coaches or sportswriters—but it was served up with a generous helping of humor. Strange and humorous occurrences, exaggerated events, and preposterous tales were exchanged and, at least in Walker's case, salted away for future use. Indeed, many of the stories told about Walker originated in someone else's life. But if they fit his persona, then Walker or some other storyteller—his old pal Herman Hickman is given considerable credit for spreading the Peahead legend up and down the East coast—would change a fact or two and make Walker the butt/protagonist of the piece. Other Walker stories became so well known—a part of the Peahead canon as it were—that explaining or correcting them eventually generated stories of their own. For example, the quintessential story about Walker's tough-guy gruffness—his on-the-field order to a team doctor to "make [an injured player who wasn't breathing] breathe"—eventually took on a life of its own.[5] Some people remembered the incident at Wake Forest while others remembered it . . . in Montreal. The version related by Hickman during his banquet monologues placed the exasperated Walker at a high school early in his career. At late-life banquet gigs, Walker attempted to set the record straight, though not as to factual particulars such as which player, team, or year. No, Walker wanted everyone to know that he wasn't the cold-hearted coach portrayed in the story. It's true that the player wasn't breathing, he said; and it's true that, in frustration, he told the doctor to "make" the player

---

4 Bobby Bowden, interview with author.
5 See Chapter 7 and the Introduction for more.

breathe. "But I never actually ordered the *player himself* to breathe," Walker said. "That would be just be wrong."[6]

Most of Walker's stories were drawn from his experiences as an athlete and coach. That's not to say that all of them were true but merely to acknowledge that they contained the seed of a truthful idea that sprouted into a full-fledged tale.

Many stories were told in the abstract, the identity of the participant being of no particular importance, or the lack of particulars affording easy transference to a new person at any given telling. One well-worn saga involved a minor league baseball umpire sent to call a key game between a pair of heated, small-town rivals. The ump knew he was going to be in for a long day, but things went even worse than expected. The game was a nail biter all the way. Every call seemed critical. Naturally, the visiting team rallied late to take a one-run lead in the top of the ninth. Just as naturally, the homestanders loaded the bases with two outs in the bottom of the frame. The batter was cautious and the count eventually mounted to three-and-two. Something had to happen on the next pitch and, as umpiring fate would have it, the next pitch was a borderline doozy—a fastball near the outside corner of the plate, right at the batter's chest, one of the toughest calls an ump can face. As the spheroid thudded into the catcher's mitt, it was obvious to both sides that it was going to be a very near thing. A hush fell over the park and everyone looked to the umpire for a sign. An ever-so-pregnant pause came and went. More time passed. Finally, the beleaguered ump stuck both arms out and cried, "Tie ball! Throw another one!"[7]

Similarly, the following story was told both by and about Walker, regarding a seldom-used player on one of his Wake Forest football teams. The player—Wake Forest storyteller supreme Doc Murphrey always claimed it was him, but in other tellings other names were used—wasn't much of a footballer but was very

---

6 *Washington Star*, Sept. 19, 1968.
7 *Raleigh News & Observer*, Sept., 13, 1948 and various interviews.

popular.[8] In fact, that was the key to the story—the player's perennial position on the Deacon bench. At regular intervals during the games, his campus chums would break into a "we want (Murphrey, or whoever)" chant. This went on for several games, maybe even several years. Finally, near the end of Murphrey's senior season, with Wake comfortably ahead in one of its games, the chant again rolled out of the stands. "We want Mur-phrey, we want Mur-phrey." Walker heard this, smiled, walked over to the Deacon bench and said, "Mur-phrey (or whoever), your friends are calling for you."

"Yessir," said Murphrey hopefully.

"Waaaall," drawled Walker, "then why doncha go up there in the stands and join them?"[9]

The tale mirrors another, which has a slightly more plausible ring, in which Walker purportedly gave in to the "Rudy urge."[10] Supposedly in the early 1940s, Walker ran off an unpromising young center who had come to "play for free,"—that is, be a walk-on—only to find himself asking the young man to return as practice fodder after injuries (and perhaps war-time exodus) thinned the Deacon roster. Near the end of the year, Wake faced VMI in a game in Winston-Salem.[11] The young man asked Walker if he could make the trip. Walker told him that there was no room on the bus but that if he could make his own way to the game he could dress out and sit on the bench. The young man made it to Winston and to the game. But some teammates didn't

---

8 Murphrey, a decent high school football player, had a career at Wake Forest that fit the tale. A diminutive tailback on teams featuring all-time greats at the position like Nick Sacrinty and Red Cochran, Murhprey seldom played. He remained a loyal Deacon, however, and followed in Walker's footsteps as a banquet hall entertainer. For years, he was a regularly occurring phenomenon at Wake Forest football games, where, clad in a Peahead-like sports coat of an immodest hue and his trademark straw hat, he'd take a turn with the megaphone (and later microphone) on the cheerleading podium in an effort to get the Deacon faithful fired up.
9 Doc Murphrey, audio recording.
10 The reference is to Rudy Ruettiger, a walk-on at Notre Dame in the 1970s whose dream to play college football for the Irish was finally realized during the final two plays of the final game of his senior season. The moment, and Ruettiger's quest, was immortalized in the eponymous 1993 film.
11 Wake and VMI did play in Winston-Salem in November 1942.

think that was enough. They begged Walker to put him in, and, late in the game with Wake ahead by four touchdowns, Walker's soft spot bubbled to the surface. He put the young, untested man into the game, at his normal center position. On the first play from scrimmage, the erstwhile gridder snapped the ball over the tailback's head. A livid Walker had to be restrained from running onto the field and dragging he young man to the sidelines with his bare hands. "Get that sonofabitch out of there before he beats us," screamed Walker. "What is he, a gottdamn VMI spy or something?"[12]

On the stump, Walker dredged up old saws, like the coach who sorted his players by sending them all running pell mell through a forest (the backs dodged trees, the linemen ran into them) to describe his coaching friends and foes. But he also came up with some new lines, many produced on the spur of the moment. Asked how he thought of pal/nemesis Frank Howard's 1958 Clemson team would do in the Sugar Bowl against LSU's famous "Chinese Bandits,"[13] Walker told reporters (and later, banquet audiences) that, "I'm not worried about any Chinese bandits because they [Clemson] have a Mongolian Idiot for a coach."[14]

Another celebrated banquet exchange involving Walker and Howard (they performed as a duo, a regular act if you will, at a number of events) involved trading insults around the name of Christine Jorgensen, the first publicly known recipient of gender reassignment surgery. Jorgensen created a sensation upon her

---

12 *Chapel Hill Weekly*, July 22, 1970 and various interviews.
13 The 1958 LSU team featured all-American halfback Billy Cannon but was probably best known for a ferocious second-string defense that coach Paul Dietzel rotated into the game en masse. Playing with reckless abandon, the "Bandits" didn't give up a touchdown all season and became huge fan favorites and a lasting part of LSU football lore. The name came from a remark Dietzel made to reporters, comparing the swarming play of the second stringers to Chinese bandits, which made more sense then than now because the term was popularly known through the "Terry and the Pirates" cartoon strip. Terry, a sort of Indiana Joneseque adventurer, regularly fought Chinese bandits.
14 Perkins, V., *Howard: The Clemson Legend*. 1990. Brentwood, TN: Howard Books.

outing in late 1952,[15] and it was still a hot topic when Walker and Howard got together one night before an all-male crowd of Rotarians, or football fans, or whatever group it was on this particular occasion.

Howard, speaking first, told the audience that it was his duty to announce that Walker had just completed the "Jorgensen treatment" himself. Walker responded to Howard's coarse insult with a coarser reply: because of Howard's betrayal of Walker's "secret," Howard shouldn't expect to avail himself of Walker's newly acquired, Jorgensenesque charms.

Walker's words were coarser and more direct. But the main memory of the evening for eyewitnesses like former Tennessee Coach Johnny Majors, was the sharpness of Walker's wit.

"He was quick," said Majors. "He could come up with stuff on the fly. Guys like Howard—he was pretty typical of what you'd hear from coaches at these dinners—had prepared stuff. But Peahead could think on his feet. I don't think he ever had any notes. He just talked and one story would lead to another."[16]

Besides his off-the-cuff skills, Walker also had a sizeable repertoire of self-deprecating stories. He apparently understood, like most good speakers, how such tales subtly softened his position, bringing him down to earth—and to his listeners. It's also quite probable that Walker made himself the subject of some of the stories because he was a good "fit."

Heck, some might even have been true.

Some, like a story about a naive Walker ordering apple pie a la mode at a fancy restaurant and then telling the waiter "to put some ice cream on top of it, too" are clearly "borrowed" material. The same story was told about "dumb jocks" before and after Walker. Others, like a brief vignette involving Walker and a game film session sound more authentic. In the film story, Walker is watching footage of a Wake Forest game during the offseason in the company of a visiting coach. Suddenly he spots one of his players loafing through an assignment. Walker starts cussing the boy and telling his companion all he'd do to punish and correct the offender

---

[15] The concept and practice was known as early as the 1920s, but the early test cases kept a low profile.
[16] Johnny Majors, interview with author.

when practice starts again when he suddenly stops. "Damn," says Walker. "I believe that boy has graduated."

There was a library of outrageous stories about how Walker got some less-than-brilliant footballer into, or through, school. They always drew a laugh because they fit a popular perception and because there was some factual basis: at both Wake and Elon, Walker didn't always field a scholar-filled lineup.

Specific players were often named in the stories—sensibilities on such matters were a bit different at the time—with legendary Deacon academic casualties Nub Smith and Bill Gregus being among the most common targets. Most of the tales carried a standard formula: an unqualified player was given a one-question, do-or-die test that usually consisted of an absurdly simple question. If he got it right, he was admitted/allowed to stay in school. If he missed it he was denied/kicked out. Sometimes the academicians in the stories are stooges of the athletic powers. In others their role is essentially that of incredulous bystander.

One such tale had Walker visiting a Wake Forest dean, pleading for him to give Smith one last chance to stay in school. "Dean, whatta you say we break it all down to one question," says Walker. "It can be math or English, you choose." The skeptical-but-pliable dean agreed and on the appointed day, Smith and Walker showed up at his office.

"What'll it be, dean?" Walker asked.

"I've chosen math," said the dean. "Here's your question. What is seven plus six?"

Walker's eyes lit up. He couldn't believe his good fortune (or perhaps recognized the dean's complicity) in asking a question involving numbers common to the football field. "Nub!" he said. "Just think about football and how much you get for a touchdown and an extra point and all. Then think about what would happen if you got two!"

Smith nodded, pondered the question for awhile and finally said, "fourteen?"

The dean's shoulders slumped. Walker stomped the floor. "Aw, hell, dean," said Walker. "He's only two off. Ain't that close enough?"

Walker's mind was quick and . . . adult-oriented. Repartee like the exchange about Christine Jorgensen was common. The all-male audiences of the day—service clubs were rarely mixed gender at that time and touchdown/quarterback clubs were still less likely to produce a gender mix—chortled at the bawdy jokes and innuendo.

While good for audiences, this was bad for posterity. Newspapers couldn't print some tales, and, as a result, some Walker stories exist only as rumor. One that dealt with peculiarities surrounding the circumcision of Choo Choo Justice—he apparently was quite shifty, even as a babe—is often referenced but never told. Famed sports columnist Furman Bisher, of the *Charlotte News* and *Atlanta Journal*, once wrote that it was the best banquet story he'd ever heard but did not record its content.

Walker's abilities as a humorist were manifest in the written word as well as the spoken. His fanciful vision of a future Rose Bowl (see chapter 5) is well-written and clever given the inside audience for which it was intended. He was also prone to written practical jokes, like the solicitation letter he sent his friend Herman Hickman from one "Flash Jones" of McKeesport, PA, a two-hundred-pound halfback of unusual abilities. "I have admired you [Hickman] for a long time," wrote the Flash, "so I would like to come to your wonderful university and play football under your expert tutelage." Flash, the letter noted, had scored twenty-six touchdowns the previous year, made all his extra points (save one that was completely on target before it was blocked), and could run a 9.8 hundred-yard dash (a near world record at that time). "Of course," wrote the talented and truthful prospect, "I can probably do no better than ten-flat in full football equipment." Jones was also a superb student and an excellent baseball player. And his brother "Killer," a rising junior, wanted to follow him to school but couldn't come on the proposed recruiting trip because "he sometimes [got] a little mean when we [left] him out of the cage and cut out his raw-meat diet."[17]

Of wider distribution and interest were two letters Walker wrote to newspapers in the late 1950s. The first was an open letter

---

17 *The Herman Hickman Reader*, p. 10.

to Frank Howard warning him to be on his best behavior during an upcoming football goodwill trip to France. Among other things, Walker advised Howard to "try not to be chewin' tobacco" when he kisses a lady on the hand; "buy some coats that match your pants," and that if/when he belched while dining with royalty to say, 'Excuse me your highness,' not 'Dawg but them taters wuz good.'" Walker closed by writing that "I thought the age of miracles had come when they started talking of a man on the moon. That isn't near as ridiculous as turning [Howard] loose in Paris."

Walker called Howard to read him the letter and to get his permission to send it off. In his autobiography, Howard said he was fine with the contents but was worried when Walker told him that if it did get printed, Howard would have to come up with a reply. "I told him he'd better not get it published then 'because I can't come up with an answer as clever as your letter.'"[18]

No problem, said Walker. He'd write Howard's answer, too. In fact, he already had.

In the "response," Frank Howard's "ghost writer" took Walker to task for offering etiquette and fashion advice: "You, the Maxwell Bodenheim of the coaching business offering advice?"[19] Walker's ability to insult himself is quite remarkable, displaying, as it does, not only a sense of humility but a certain honesty about difficult subjects as well. Howard/Walker writes that "when the Baptists kicked you out at Wake Forest for being a heathen, Herman Hickman felt sorry for you and hired you as an assistant at Yale. . . . " Then he writes that a wealthy Yale alumni paid for Walker's first year's pay in Montreal and that the "history department at Yale calls the two most socially significant movements in modern history . . . the chasing of Pancho Villa into Mexico and the running of you into the north woods of Canada." Finally, he [i.e., Walker himself] nicked Walker about his age and his looks, noting that the mug shot that accompanied the first letter in some papers "must have been made years ago. . . . The

---

18 *Howard: The Clemson Legend.*
19 The reference to Bodenheim is obscure but would have been better known at the time. An American poet from Mississippi, Bodenheim and his "wife" lived on the streets of New York in the 1950s before their sensational double murder in 1954.

last time I saw you I remember an old, haggard, wrinkled face—a map of disaster from what the Edmonton coach hopes to do to you in the Canadian League every year."

Tromping on the tragedies of his own coaching career does not seem to have phased Walker—nor did wishing himself a gruesome death, which was the conclusion to the letter "Howard" had penned. "I hope you freeze to death in Canada next fall—or that the French population in Montreal burns you at the stake—like Jo Ann of Ark—when you lose the Grey Cup again."[20] Ouch, the friends of Peahead Walker might have thought. Those who knew Peahead actually penned his own attack, might have been even more amazed. But as usual Walker got the last laugh The final impression left with readers is that of Howard as academic buffoon. The tragic misspelling of Joan of Arc in the last line is credited to Howard's account since he is the listed author.

***

Walker's ouster in Montreal did not send him directly into the banquet circuit bread line. Although he turned sixty-one shortly after he was canned, he still had something left in the tank. And he had contacts. Calls were made and options weighed. By the end of February, Walker had signed on with the New York Giants of the NFL as their chief scout for the Southeast, or, as it was indelicately and unofficially put, the "white South."

Walker's boss in New York was Jim Lee Howell, a former coach whose double first name gives away his Deep South origin.[21] He was an Arkansas native to be exact. Walker knew Howell to some degree before coming to New York, and there is some evidence he knew him quite well. Howell grew up just a few hours away from Walker's pal Paul "Bear" Bryant in central Arkansas and starred at the state university in the early 1930s. After college, he starred with the Giants for ten years (he was a 6'5" end) and then was hired as a coach at nearby Wagner College. When the Giants fired pro bowl

---

20 *Howard: The Clemson Legend.*
21 Howell was still the Giants' coach in 1960 and was only indirectly Walker's supervisor that year. From the end of the 1960 season on, after Howell retired from coaching, he was in charge of all the Giants' scouts, Walker included.

fullback Steve Owens as coach in 1953, they offered the position to Howell, who led the team to three NFL title games between 1954 and 1960. Howell was the losing coach in the famed 1958 overtime game with Baltimore and is probably better known for hiring future Hall of Famers Vince Lombardi and Tom Landry as his assistants than for his own coaching work. But he was a solid, hard-nosed coach himself and a well-respected football personnel man during his twenty-one years in that position.

Howell was likely familiar with Walker when the Giants brought him on board. If not, there were others in the Giants' fold who were. Alex Webster, Walker's old Montreal halfback, was a Giants' mainstay at that time and remembers being asked for a review of his old coach (he offered a positive one).[22]

Walker's scouting post was not unique, but it wasn't all that common either. In the 1950s, NFL teams were just coming out of the Depression and the lean years of the war, and not every franchise had a big scouting department—or even a scouting department at all. Some clubs made draft picks based on newspaper clippings. The penny-pinching Pittsburgh Steelers paid a local hobbyist—he was a mortician by trade—to collect press releases and statistical information for them prior to the draft. That was, for years, the extent of the club's scouting, the effects of which were regularly reflected in the league standings.

The Giants, one of the league's most successful and lucrative franchises, were different. They were scouting innovators, if only because they actually performed the chore on a regular basis. The work in those days was based on the baseball model. Film of prospects in action was hard to obtain and not much trusted, and national television broadcasts of collegiate games were just coming into vogue. Consequently, a man on the scene who could see prospects in person and pick up the inside dope was very much in demand. Walker's job, then, was to talk to coaching friends in the region, figure out where the prospects were, and then go see them play. Pooling the reports of Walker and other scouts—his old Canadian Football League (CFL) nemesis, Pop Ivy, joined Howell's scouting team a few years into Walker's tenure—the

---

22. Alex Webster, interview with author.

Giants decided which players they wanted to draft or otherwise offer contracts.

And then Walker had to help sign them.

Throughout Walker's scouting days, NFL teams faced intense competition for the outgoing crop of collegians. Teams from the CFL continued to battle for players in the early 1960s, and then an all-out bidding war broke out with the brand new American Football League (AFL). While the competition for big-name players like Billy Joe Cannon, Gayle Sayers, and Joe Namath dominated the news of the AFL-NFL signing wars, teams had to compete for players up and down the line. Every player was up for grabs, which is where scouts came in. The draft would be held, and then the scouts would be sent their marching orders. One season, the Giants fired off a telegram to Walker instructing him to go sign several Southern players as soon as possible. Rough monetary details were included. Walker's legendary telegraphic response, filed a day later, read, "Got one, wounded two others. Peahead."[23]

Aided by Walker's scouting work, the Giants continued to field strong teams into the mid-1960s but then began to fade near decade's end. Walker's signature signee was Auburn star Tucker Fredrickson, the number one overall pick in the 1965 draft and a Pro Bowler as a rookie.[24] It's difficult to argue that Fredrickson, whose career was hampered by injuries, was better than 1965 Rookie of the Year Gayle Sayers, one of the NFL's all-time great players, but the Giants weren't sure they could sign Sayers, who was drafted by the AFL's Kansas City Chiefs. Fredrickson, with Walker on the case, was a surer thing.

The Giants had an ongoing Southern flavor throughout the 1960s. A number of solid players were drafted and signed on Walker's recommendation, including Joel Wells, who Walker recruited from Montreal. There was also some busts. Walker was

---

23 Ray Walsh, interview with author.
24 Walker and the Giants, perhaps taking advantage of the fact that Fredrickson didn't have an agent, signed him to a three-year, no-cut contract that included a $30,000 bonus. Alabama's Joe Namath, who came out one year later, signed with the AFL's New York Jets for a $400,000 bonus. "I guess I should have had an agent," Fredrickson said in an interview years after the fact. Source: Giants.com.

vociferous in recommending and then helping the team sign Mississippi quarterback Glynn Griffing, one of the stars of the Rebels' unbeaten 1962 team and 1963 Sugar Bowl winner. But after one season as an understudy to aging star Y.A. Tittle, the Giants gave up on Griffing. The new coaching staff either found Walker's assessment to be in error or harbored ill feelings over Griffing's decision (even though it was approved by head coach Allie Sherman) to miss practice the week before he 1963 NFL Championship game to get married. As it turned out, starter Tittle injured his knee early in the game and probably shouldn't have played the rest of the way. But after a brief, unavoidable appearance by Griffing, Tittle returned, hobbling his way to five interceptions, including a game ender in the end zone that preserved Chicago's 14–10 victory. Griffing did not return—not in that game nor any other. He was released during the offseason and decided to give up football for what turned out to be a very successful career in business (insurance to be exact). Ironically, Griffing was the subject of an NBC documentary entitled "The Making of a Pro" that was aired in December 1963 two weeks prior to the NFL title game. Peahead Walker, the man who signed Griffing, received significant air time in the hour-long show, commenting on both Griffing's potential and the importance of the quarterback in the professional system.

Walker seemed to lead a carefree and happy existence during his scouting days. Alex Webster recalled seeing him around the Giants' training camp, laughing and cutting up with other team officials. Ray Walsh, who worked in the Giants' front office as kind of a "semi-intern" in the 1960s, said Walker was an infrequent visitor to the team's nerve center but made quite an impression when he did show up.

"He and a Jim Lee [Howell] must have been close friends," said Walsh. "They'd close the door and laugh and laugh. You could hear them all over the office. . . . And Peahead! What a dapper guy. You couldn't forget him. He wore these immaculate suits, some white and some dark, but always with a vest. And a big stick pin. I remember once he even had a jewel-handled walking stick. And he was the last person, well, the only person really, who I ever saw in real life wearing spats. I mean, I saw them in the movies, but he was the only one in real life."[25]

Walker's outlandish dress was nothing new, of course. Since his Wake Forest days, and possibly before, he'd been a notable dresser, if not necessarily a dapper one.[26] At Wake Forest, Walker was mostly a "zoot suiter" who wore dark shirts, odd combinations of sportscoats, baggy pants, and outrageous ties. His ties were so famous, in fact, that fans and even strangers mailed new ones to him throughout his career. Former player Pride Ratterree found a group of ties bearing the images of scantily clad women during a trip to Philadelphia, bought up a bunch, and shipped them to his former coach who called and said, "Ratterree, you trying to get me lynched?"[27] In Montreal and thereafter, Walker adopted a more conservative big-city look. Folks who knew him in Canada don't recall seeing him in anything other than a dark suit and a white shirt. Photos from the 1960s confirm this idea and also suggest Walker had given up the exotic neckwear. His post-Wake Forest neckwear is duller than an off-tackle play. But the style and cut of the suits, and the outlandish extras noted in New York, do suggest that Walker was doing okay financially.

Glynn Griffing, the aforementioned quarterback from Ole Miss, recalled that when Walker came to "court" him, he was well dressed and a "real gentleman.

"He took me and my girlfriend out to dinner and was just the nicest, most laidback person you can imagine," said Griffing. "It really made an impression, in part, I guess, because he was coming from the Giants, from New York. I was expecting someone

---

25 Walsh, interview with author.
26 There's no evidence that Walker's career as a sartorial sensation had begun to bloom before he reached Deaconland. Team photos from his Elon tenure show Walker either in a uniform (baseball), standard-issue coaching gear (football), or a rather plain-looking suit (basketball). Of course, the photos are black and white, so the suit could be bright blue or something, but that doesn't seem to be the case. And it does appear to be the same suit from 1931 to 1933, which would fit with Walker's, and the school's, fiscal fortunes during that time. There's also no mention of Walker's unusual haberdashing while at Elon. It was mentioned frequently later in his career, so he either came to the idea later in life or just couldn't afford it until then.
27 Pride Ratterree, interview with author.

different, you know, one of those fast talkers. He wasn't like that at all, but he did sell us on New York. I remember he said, 'Why would you want to play anywhere else?'"[28]

***

Walker's career with the Giants lasted nearly ten years. He also continued some baseball scouting work with the New York Yankees into the 1960s. The frequency and intensity of that work is impossible to gauge. It was almost certainly a part-time, "bird dog" assignment.[29]

The Walkers set up shop in Charlotte not long after leaving Montreal. Although the growing city wasn't home to Peahead Walker or his beloved Flonnie, the move made sense. The couple was quite at home in North Carolina, and Charlotte was already a transportation hub, especially for travel in the Southeast. They found a nice apartment overlooking Myers Park Country Club. Walker made the town his base for his scouting work and banquet appearances and he connected with old players and old friends. Former Deacon star Dave Harris, now a successful high school football coach and administrator in Charlotte, got a call from Peahead every month or so. "Watcha doing for lunch today, Dave?" he said. Harris, if available, would collect his former coach and take him out for a meal. The Ranch House, a landmark restaurant on Charlotte's west side, was a favorite destination. "He just liked to get a good meal, a big steak usually, and to talk awhile," said Harris. "He was in demand as a speaker all the time—I got him for a couple of things—but he just overall seemed very happy, very content."[30]

That happiness was short-lived. Walker's health was failing. Years of hard work and hard living—a long association with both tobacco and alcohol and too much good food were the culprits—began to wear on Walker as he approached seventy. His circulation

---

28 Glynn Griffing, interview with author.
29 The term comes from hunting, where a good bird dog will point a hunter toward his prey. Bird dog scouts locate potential prospects, who are then checked out in some detail by full-time scouts.
30 Dave Harris, interview with author.

was poor; various organs and systems were failing. On some days it was a struggle just to breathe, even if he ordered a doctor to make him do it.

In the spring of 1970 Walker suffered a stroke. He was hospitalized but recovered enough to return home to his apartment. Flonnie called friends—mostly Walker's old players—to tell them Peahead was dying. Could they come and visit? Many could and did.

Dewey Hobbs, now a Baptist minister in Marion, NC, got the call and came as soon as he could. Walker was struggling. He'd had all the heart surgery he could stand. He labored to take each breath. He spent most of the visit lying down.

Still, it was a remarkable two hours, Hobbs recalled. The two men talked about old times and games played years ago, but mostly they talked about family, loyalty, and the meaning of it all. It felt to Hobbs like a conversation with a man who wanted to come to terms with his maker—maybe even to make a confession. It was a surprise coming from a man who few would have accorded much religious interest, but there it was. Had Hobbs and others misunderstood or underestimated "The Head" all these years? Recalls Hobbs:

> *(Walker) said at one point, "Dewey, I want to know about any pains in life you've had." I told him about our six-year-old son who was diagnosed with a brain tumor. They did the surgery, but miraculously, there was no tumor. It was still difficult. We spent a month at [Charlotte's] Mercy Hospital while I was pastor in Wingate [a nearby town]. . . . Tears came to his eyes when I told him that. "It's made you a better man and pastor," he said. "That's the difference between you and [John] Gibson [another Walker player turned pastor]. He's never had that kind of pain." I had a few tears, too. I had more closeness with him than I realized, and I understood what it all had meant to him, the relationships*

and all. He cared and he kept up with his players; he knew what they'd done."[31]

Above Walker's bed was a series of pennants (in some ways it looked like a young boy's room Dave Harris recalled)—one for each stop in his career. They were arranged in chronological order from bottom to top. There was an Atlantic Christian banner on the bottom, followed by Elon, Wake Forest, and, yes, Yale. Then there was a pennant from Montreal and one from the Giants. Adjacent was a wall covered with dozens of photos of the men who had played for Walker, as well as his coaching friends. Hobbs said Walker pointed at one ex-Deacon player who had done well in business after his playing days. Walker's lips curled in disgust, an expression Hobbs had seen many times on the Wake Forest practice field. "How come he's never done anything for Wake Forest?" Walker asked. Hobbs had no answer but that was fine. None was expected. After some silence, Walker looked at Hobbs and said, "I know what you've done. You been preaching, never made any money really. But you were class agent for ten years. That's good. You gave back. You tried."

"I realized how he felt," said Hobbs. "If you played on scholarship, you were forever in debt to the school, to Wake Forest. In spite of what happened to him with President Tribble and all, he was still loyal. If you made money, you were in debt to Wake Forest."[32]

More players came to visit. Pat Preston led a big group—Herb Cline, Pat Geer, and Harry Clark were among the others present—who sat around with the coach and told stories for hours. Walker, Preston later recalled, seemed to enjoy it.[33]

The bitter end soon arrived. Charlotte sportswriter Bob Quincy, probably relying on conversations with Flonnie, wrote that Walker, "weak and heartbroken," struggled out of his bed and collapsed on the floor of his apartment. He begged Flonnie to leave him be this time—he'd already been in the hospital three times in the past year—and let him die in his own home.

---

31 Dewey Hobbs, interview with author.
32 Ibid.
33 *Chapel Hill Weekly*, July 22, 1970.

She couldn't do it. Walker suffered a series of convulsions as his brain chemistry went haywire. Then he lapsed into a coma. She called the ambulance and he was taken to the hospital to begin what Flonnie called his "living death." Shortly after Walker was hospitalized for the last time, his old pal Jim Weaver passed away in Greensboro. In a poignant letter to Kate Dunn Weaver, Flonnie Walker recalled the "close friendship and a togetherness in teaching of honor and pride for the life we lived and gave to our men. . . ."

Flonnie went on to tell her old friend that she was "hoping to just keep from completely breaking down under the strain of the living death that continues with Petie. . . . He was wholly unconscious before he was taken back [to the hospital] for the fourth and final time. . . . He will not regain consciousness. He is, as they say, terminal—from hour to hour, day to day. His heart remains the only living thing."[34]

On July 16 that too expired and the world was suddenly just a little less colorful. Peahead Walker was dead.

***

His funeral, three days later, was a grand affair. Hundreds—some estimates put the crowd at a thousand or more—overflowed Christ Episcopal Church, a large and tony house of worship a few blocks from the Walkers' Charlotte home. The pall bearers were a who's who of college coaching, albeit with a decidedly Southern flavor. Frank Howard and Bear Bryant were among them, of course, as were Wally Butts of Georgia and Bud Wilkinson of Oklahoma fame. It might have been the first time that

---

[34] Flonnie Walker letter to Kate Dunn Weaver. Personnel correspondence of Jim Weaver. Wake Forest University archives.

Butts and Bryant were in the same place at the same time since their famous libel trial in 1963.[35]

D.C. Walker III said Bryant singled him out for special attention among Peahead's many relatives at the funeral. Bryant "timed" the twelve-year-old running several distances, lined him up in a stance, and "just basically did a little recruiting on me. I guess he knew I was special to Peahead, and, I'd guess he thought it wasn't a terrible idea to be nice to me, just in case I grew up to be any good at football." Later, Bryant told Walker's grandson that Peahead was the best friend he'd ever had.[36]

The front of the church was covered with flowers. A large, football-shaped arrangement was paid for by a group of Walker's players at Wake. Its inscription read, "From the boys you made into men."[37] Bryant was among those who spoke. It was a sad time, he said, but added that there was no real cause to morn a life like Peahead Walker's.

"He did a bit of everything in his time," said Bryant. "Now, death is not to be taken lightly, but some people are lucky to get more out of life than others. Peahead was one of those."[38]

Walker was buried at Charlotte's Elmwood Cemetery, alongside several Confederate soldiers, two governors, and one movie star.[39] Afterward, as workers resodded the grave site, a number of friends and acquaintances braved the summer heat to stand around and tell stories. Charlotte sportswriter Bob Quincy opined that Peahead would have liked the conversation, seeing as how it was mostly funny stories and praise for him.

After it was all over, the family and a few others adjourned to a local establishment that served both food and strong drink—attendees recall the emphasis was on the latter—for a party that lasted well past dusk.

---

35 A *Saturday Evening Post* story accused Butts and Bryant of conspiring to fix the 1962 Georgia-Alabama game. Butts was Georgia's athletic director at the time, having been forced out of the coaching position two years before, sued, and eventually won a $460,000 settlement. But his reputation was ruined, as was his friendship with Byrant.
36 D.C. Walker III, interview with author.
37 *Chapel Hill Weekly*, July 22, 1970.
38 *Charlotte Observer*, July 22, 1970.
39 The latter is Randolph Scott, the Western movie icon and Charlotte native.

Mickey Walker said that when they pulled into the parking lot of what was obviously a bar, his wife was incredulous. "She said, 'What in the world are you doing?'" Walker recalled. "I told her that there was no disrespect intended. Far from it. It was just what we do and it's what *he* would have wanted us to do."

"A couple hours later," Walker said, "my wife came up to me and said, 'This is the best and funniest funeral I've ever been to.'"[40]

Her husband just nodded.

It couldn't have ended any other way.

---

40 Walker III, interview with author.

INDEX

Abernethy, L.F., 100
Abruzzi, Pat, 397, 416
Allen, Boyd, 315
Amick, T.C., 88
Anderson, Heartley "Hunk", 132, 162
Anderson, John, 115
Andrews, J.W., 98
Ane, Gilbert, 416
Appenzeller, Herb, 9, 115, 194, 220, 231, 232, 236, 243, 263, 268, 272, 277, 292
Arakas, Jimmy, 24
Auffarth, Bob, 269, 321
Baltisaris, George, 282
Barbour, Elmer, 207, 214, 223, 238
Barclay, John, 72
Barkin, Paul, 382
Barkouskie, Ray, 348
Barney, J.W., 134
Barnhill, Robert, 235
Barrier, Smith, 300, 359
Bartos, Herb, 196, 203, 245
Bauer, Moe, 330
Beal, Walter, 55
Beaty, Mary D., 184
Beaudouin, Harry, 149
Belec, Jacques, 373, 375, 386, 401, 408
Berry, Ed, 33, 36, 38
Bershak, Andy, 255
Bessemer, Henry, 26
Bewley, Bill, 373, 381, 416
Bistroff, Joe, 65

Black, Joe, 102
Blackerby, Carroll, 310, 313, 336
Blaicher, Johnny, 400
Blalock, Joe, 182
Blanchard, Felix, 236
Bock, Garnett, 84
Bodenheim, Maxwell, 432
Bowden, Bobby, 14, 15, 424
Bowlby, Bob, 328
Boyd, Denny, 373, 389, 400
Boyd, Dick, 180
Boykin, Roma, 74
Boylin, Jack, 73, 98
Bradley, Ed, 283, 295, 297, 310, 382
Bradley, Hal, 124, 127, 128, 132
Brancato, George, 402
Brembs, Dutch, 247
Brewer, Jennie, 141, 336, 345
Bridges, Ken, 155, 272, 279, 322, 331
Briggs, Charles, 95
Briggs, Howard, 91, 125
Briggs, Mike, 60, 125
Bright, Johnny, 405
Brinkley, Rock, 24, 222, 223, 238, 240, 244, 269, 276, 280
Brogden, Jeff, 213, 301
Broyles, Frank, 317
Bruno, John, 230, 238
Bryant, Paul, 156, 181, 196, 205, 231, 286

Bunn, Jimmie, 115
Bunting, Dick, 338
Burtner, George, 208
Butler, Butch, 241
Butts, Wally, 174, 222, 242, 386, 441
Byrd, Curly, 250
Byrd, Irvin, 165
Caddell, Hugh, 105
Caddell, Paul, 90
Cameron, Eddie, 206, 264, 313
Camp, Jim, 256, 297
Camp, Walter, 305, 359
Campbell, Orville, 294
Cannon, Billy Joe, 428
Capozzi, Herb, 375
Capps, Burnie, 207, 282
Carlton, D.J., 35, 129
Caroline, J.C., 398
Carr, Claude, 34, 362
Carroll, Charlie, 92
Carson, Bud, 339
Caruso, Joe, 132
Charles, Ezzard, 357
Cheek, Paul, 60, 124
Cicia, Ray, 309, 315, 321, 395, 414
Clair, Frank, 368
Clark, George, 229, 238, 295, 301
Clark, Harry, 298, 440
Clark, Walter, 159
Clayton, Joe, 91
Cline, Herb, 191, 440
Coble, Roy, 333
Cochran, Red, 196, 199, 276, 279, 286, 298, 307, 427
Colclough, Jim, 416

Cone, Fred, 343
Cook, Joseph, 78
Copley, Jim, 203, 216
Corboy, Frank, 81
Cornogg, Ulysses, 255, 279
Counselman, J.S., 34
Crabtree, Clem, 168
Creed, Tommy, 245
Croom, Clay, 255, 276
Crowe, Clem, 368
Currie, Bill, 323
Curtis, Tony, 369
Dandurand, Leo, 397, 407
Daniels, Daronce, 85
Davis, Andy, 309
Davis, Dickie, 9, 23, 149, 176, 227, 265, 271, 273, 279, 312, 320, 323, 327, 330, 332, 336, 339, 342
Davis, Glenn, 236, 237
DeGeer, Vern, 390, 391, 398, 420
DeRogatis, Al, 285
Dillon, Charles C., 39
DiTomo, Anthony, 256, 276
Dixon, George, 416
Doak, Robert, 99
Dofflemeyer, Kenzie, 94
Donahue, Tom, 24, 25, 267, 346
Donovan, Art, 277
Dowda, Harry, 276, 277, 283
Dublinski, Tom, 398
Duchess, John, 323
Duke, Benjamin, 109
Duncan, Jim, 255, 315, 326
Duncavage, Joe, 167, 169, 203
Dunn, Jimmy, 371, 401
Eagles, T.R., 36

Earnshaw, George, 55
Edwards, Jimmie, 125
Edwards, Marshall, 160, 165, 167
Effird, H.T., 94
Eisenhower, Dwight D., 262
Elsby, Ted, 416
Enright, Rex, 243, 253
Ensley, Enoch, 25
Etcheverry, Sam, 9, 377, 417, 422
Farress, Rick, 220
Faurot, Don, 307
Faust, David, 93, 103
Feathers, Beattie, 228, 313, 347
Fetzer, Tom, 222, 281, 299, 301
Filchock, Frankie, 369
Findlay, Des, 372
Finnance, Bill, 174, 335, 338
Fisher, Red, 410
Fletcher, Gus, 63
Foldberg, Hank, 236
Folger, Fred, 301
Foreman, Dick, 236, 245
Fowler, Vernon, 91
Fredrickson, Tucker, 435
Frick, Buddy, 386, 407, 411, 412
Fuller, Andrew, 124
Fuller, Dave, 156, 159
Fulmer, Rose, 272
Fuson, Herschel, 236, 237
Fysal, Ellis, 116, 117, 129, 143, 147
Gagliordi, Mike, 256
Gantt, Bob, 207
Gaona, Bob, 24, 335
Gardner, O. Max, 104

Garrison, Buck, 234, 289
Geer, Pat, 167, 440
George, Biff, 15, 268
George, Bill, 2, 5, 6, 178, 264, 267, 268, 271, 298, 321, 331, 349
Gerrity, Hank, 85
Getty, Don, 406
Gibson, John, 269
Gideon, Wes, 416
Givler, Carl, 167, 203
Glosson, Bill, 416
Godfriaux, Henry, 187
Goldberg, Marshall, 217
Graham, Frank Porter, 113
Graham, Otto, 205
Grandy, Malcolm, 292
Grant, Bud, 368
Grant, Fred, 218, 221
Greason, Murray, 2, 10, 85, 139, 147, 203
Greer, Lamar, 154
Gregus, Bill, 298, 308, 309, 321, 323
Griffing, Glynn, 436, 437
Grove, Lefty, 56
Groves, Henry, 185, 189
Gwinn, Terry, 24
Haddock, Jesse, 345
Haggard, Carl, 24, 174, 256, 275, 287, 299
Hair, Raymond, 333
Halliday, Jack, 326
Hanula, Bernie, 256, 282, 298, 309
Hardy, Robert, 79
Harper, W.A., 83, 107
Harrington, Milton, 63
Harris, Buck, 174

Harris, Dave, 211, 213, 226, 228, 238, 239, 244, 270, 289, 438
Harris, Ed, 284
Harris, Mary Arden, 211, 228, 340
Hauselt, Jimmy, 118, 132, 133, 136
Hawkins, Erskine, 27
Hayes, Billy, 339
Hayman, Lew, 368
Hearn, Charles, 58, 60
Heisman, John, 34, 43
Hendricks, J.A., 37
Hendrickson, Horace, 92
Herbert, Dick, 205
Hickman, Herman, 49, 50, 267, 284, 350, 360, 364, 425, 431, 432
Hill, Dan, 252
Hobbs, Cliff, 219
Hobbs, Dewey, 9, 173, 193, 212, 217, 225, 232, 240, 269, 278, 281, 286, 297, 342, 439
Hobbs, John, 244
Hoey, Ed, 255, 277, 302, 309, 315
Hogan, Gerry, 57, 373, 412, 413, 421
Hoke, E.R., 104
Holt, Robert L., 109
Hooks, Gene, 16, 61, 177, 330, 340
Howard, Frank, 10, 188, 205, 219, 240, 261, 343, 386, 387, 407, 428, 432, 441
Howell, Jim Lee, 433
Howell, Mildred, 181

Hubert, Pooley, 219
Hugo, Tom, 382
Hunsinger, Chuck, 382, 391, 396, 399
Hunter, Dick, 409, 415
Ivy, Frank, 368
Jackson, Levi, 361
Jackson, Russ, 409
James, Forrest, 372
Jamieson, Bob, 115
Jay, William M., 81
Jett, John, 160, 188, 255
Jobe, Tal, 125
Johnson, E.C., 152
Johnson, Harvey, 410
Johnson, Ryland, 126
Jones, Buck, 207, 262
Jones, Pee Wee, 247, 314
Jones, Red, 93
Jorgensen, Christine, 428, 431
Kapriva, Frank, 167
Karpus, Ed, 315, 325, 326
Kazmaier, Dick, 360
Kellogg, Bobby, 255, 281
Kelly, Dick, 193. 243
Kelly, George, 282
Kennedy, Frank, 343
Kennedy, Gorman, 419, 420
Keys, Eagle, 368, 394
Kiphuth, Bob, 363
Kirkland, Gordon, 122, 133
Kissell, Ed, 321, 327, 337, 339, 342
Kissell, John, 264
Kitchin, Thurman, 333, 341
Kitchin, Walt, 281
Kline, Jim, 309
Knotts, Ernie, 230
Koch, Joe, 336

Kovac, Mike, 381, 408, 411
Kuchinski, Joe, 165
Kwong, Normie, 400
Lail, Bud, 308, 311
Landry, Tom, 434
Lanning, Tom, 91
Latham, Walter, 124
Layden, Elmer, 252, 300
Layton, Melvin, 23
Lencz, Wally, 415, 416
Leonetti, Bob, 264, 265, 277, 298, 302
Lindley, Ike, 124
Lindsey, Rupert, 42
Listopad, Ed, 326
Locke, William, 98
Loftus, Charley, 363
Lombardi, Vince, 380, 434
Long, Patty Beal, 90
Longwell, J.B., 31
Lowe, W.E., 87
Lund, Bob, 238, 282
Mabry, Buck, 229
Majors, Johnny, 23, 178, 379, 388, 401, 408, 415, 429
Makar, Joe, 218
Maness, William, 112, 136, 189
Mann, Ted, 197
Marion, F.J., 133
Marshall, R.C., 44
Marshall, Ray, 122
Martinello, Marty, 378, 381, 390, 408
Mastrobattisto, Al, 132
Matthews, Ray, 343
McAfee, George, 158, 180, 193, 307
McAteer, J.L., 32

McCrary, Rube, 327
McEver, Gene, 223
McFadden, Banks, 182
McKissack, Dick, 326
McLean, William Jerry, 72
McMillan, John D., 243
McMillin, Alvin, 101
McNichol, Doug, 374, 378, 379, 381, 382, 385, 405, 411, 414
McWilliams, Ted, 236
Medlecot, Dick, 329
Medlin, Charles, 240
Mewborn, Horace, 60
Milam, John, 325
Miller, Bill, 327, 334, 344
Miller, Jim, 384
Milner, Orvis, 282
Mitchell, Charley, 283
Molloy, Ed, 365
Mooney, Ed, 348
Moran, W.C., 136
Morris, Dal, 147
Morse, Tom, 328
Moss, Perry, 420
Mullins, Willard, 363
Murphrey, Willis, 176, 261
Namath, Joe, 262, 435
Neal, Ralph, 120, 129
Neely, Jess, 46, 182, 188, 263
Nelson, Roger, 405
Nemetz, Al, 236
Newman, Dan Long, 89, 90
Newman, Danny, 121
Newman, John Urquhart, 90
Newman, Zipp, 396
Newsome, Webb, 114, 120, 125, 132
Newton, Doc, 132, 162

Neyland, Robert, 156, 235, 281
Norman, Jordan, 121
O'Quinn, John, 279
O'Rourke, Jim, 348
Ognovich, Nick, 222, 299
Owens, George, 222
Owens, Steve, 434
Paletta, Leon, 24
Palmer, Arnold, 179
Palmer, Tom, 23, 276, 321
Pambiachi, Gene, 309
Parker, Jackie, 394, 406
Pascal, Bob, 402
Paschal, George W., 293
Pate, Rupert, 159
Patrick, Neale, 20
Patterson, Hal, 387, 403
Pawson, Hal, 404
Pearson, Lindell, 152, 154
Pendergast, John, 159, 161, 165
Perry, Johnny, 198, 203, 206, 207, 233
Perry, Russ, 207, 218, 219, 221, 224, 291
Phelan, Jimmy, 368
Pittman, John, 160
Poirer, Cliff, 415
Polanski, John, 167, 171, 180, 188
Pollaci, Lou, 302
Poole, Barney, 236
Poole, Ray, 382, 393
Poteat, Hubert, 254
Powell, Jim, 282
Powell, Ken, 293
Powers, Allen, 159, 164, 184
Prather, Rollin, 394

Preston, Pat, 153, 154, 187, 194, 199, 207, 216, 255, 267, 272, 307, 355, 410, 415, 440
Price, Katherine E., 271
Proctor, J.B., 282
Pruitt, J.V., 167, 186, 187, 189, 190
Putnam, Jim, 66
Quincy, Bob, 295, 312, 440, 442
Rabenhorst, Harry, 44
Radman, George, 170
Rast, Holt, 317
Ratterree, Pride, 24, 175, 177, 194, 195, 214, 234, 238, 241, 246, 265, 272, 277, 289, 291, 437
Rheinhard, Glen, 24
Rice, Grantland, 153, 363
Ringgold, Johnny, 158
Roberson, Charles, 318
Roberts, Charlie, 114, 423
Robertson, Dave, 57
Robinson, Jackie, 389
Rodgers, Ed, 147
Rogers, Tom, 169, 196, 254, 255, 355
Roye, Paul, 123, 125, 127
Rubino, Tony, 209
Ruffa, Tony, 189
Ruth, Babe, 50
Sacrinty, Nick, 219, 222, 223, 228, 239, 241, 244, 247, 276, 282, 298, 307, 427
Sacrinty, Otis, 207, 216, 234, 235, 238, 239, 246, 280, 283, 298
Salem, Ed, 370

Sawicki, Bill, 402
Sayers, Gayle, 435
Scarton, Francis, 321, 325, 326, 334, 338, 341, 346, 348
Schlitter, Don, 136
Senogle, Terry, 268
Sharkey, Ed, 230
Shaughnessy, Clark, 217, 305
Shelburne, J.M., 39
Shelton, Amos, 137
Shepherd, Dave, 91
Sheridan, Juan, 378
Sherman, William Tecumseh, 17
Shipp, Billy, 402
Shirley, Jim, 345
Shouldice, Hap, 395
Shula, Don, 412
Simmons, I.F., 32
Sims, Earl, 90, 94
Slater, Walt, 283
Smathers, Bob, 223, 225, 246
Smith, Bill, 22
Smith, Howard, 125, 128
Smith, L.E., 87, 111, 117, 128, 132, 155, 169
Smith, Red, 91, 363
Smith, Roland, 105
Snavely, Carl, 240, 251, 275, 293, 339
Sniscak, George, 23, 328, 329
Songin, Butch, 277
Souchak, Mike, 314, 346
Soufas, Harry, 323, 356
Spencer, Frank, 75

Spencer, Larry, 260, 332, 334, 339
Spinney, Art, 277
Sprock, Mike, 314
Stagg, Amos Alonzo, 224
Stallings, Jack, 120
Starford, Bill, 213, 221
Staton, Jim, 321, 325, 338, 344, 369
Stautner, Ernie, 277
Stengel, Casey, 74
Stevens, John, 213
Stevenson, Mary, 86
Stokes, Durwood T., 80
Strayhorn, Ralph, 206
Streit, Bill, 36, 39
Studer, Gordon, 296, 298
Stutts, Bobby, 176, 318
Sulzby, James, 36
Sutherland, Jock, 172, 261
Switzer, Veryl, 416
Szafaryn, Lee, 293
Tatum, Jim, 68, 167, 205, 346
Teague, Eddie, 208
Thorpe, Jim, 63, 100
Tipton, Eric, 164
Travaligne, Dick, 321
Trawick, Herb, 370, 404, 407, 414
Trexler, Bru, 182
Tribble, Harold, 341, 350, 353, 354, 355, 440
Tuck, Hal, 60
Tuck, Lawrence, 125
Turner, J.T., 121
Tushak, Dick, 218
Utley, Phil, 200, 196, 203
Van Cleave, A.R., 81
Van Dorn, Mamie, 369

Villa, Pancho, 432
Voyles, Carl, 368
Wade, Jake, 141, 148, 186
Wade, Wallace, 46, 96, 140, 149, 152, 157, 164, 167, 172, 209, 251, 275, 284, 295, 313, 346
Waggoner, James, 80, 82, 127, 130
Waggoner, Paul, 78, 86, 93
Wagner, Virgil, 370
Waivers, Paul, 159, 161
Walker, Archie, 120, 145, 308
Walker, Carolyne, 195, 232, 336
Walker, Doak, 324, 355
Walker, Erskine, 181
Walker, Howard, 28
Walker, Kate, 28
Walker, Lester, 28
Walker, Mickey, 22, 196, 262, 307, 308, 443
Walker, Miriam, 17, 21, 25, 29
Walker, Walter Hill, 72, 232
Walker, Zachary T., 78
Wall, Dwight, 70
Walser, Rudy, 132, 137
Walsh, Adam, 286
Walsh, Ray, 435, 436
Warner, Glenn, 100, 172, 291
Warren, Bob, 147
Warren, Casper C., 354
Waters, N.B., 124, 125
Watts, Flonnie Horenthal, 22, 145, 335
Weathers, Virgil, 64
Weaver, James H., 138, 140, 147, 167, 184, 196, 203, 227, 303, 322, 329, 342, 352, 357, 441
Webb, Bill, 236
Webster, Alex, 376, 377, 380, 382, 383, 412, 417, 434, 436
Weiner, Art, 293
Wells, Don, 224
Wells, Joel, 380, 387, 407, 435
Wickham, Otto, 32
Wilkie, Gordon, 115
Wilkinson, Bud, 404, 441
Williams, Charles B., 44
Williams, Johnny, 398
Williams, Pete, 95, 106, 120, 122, 123
Williams, Ted, 205
Williams, Tommy, 125
Willoughby, Avalee, 32, 33, 36
Wilson, Edwin O., 356
Winborne, Wally, 161
Wirtz, George, 159, 233
Wolf, Ray, 160, 188, 204, 157
Woodruff, Bob, 316
Woolbert, Eddie, 168
Wooten, Dal, 62
Workman, Ted, 389, 397, 406, 409, 410, 415, 419, 420, 422
Yost, Fielding, 34, 47, 224
Zaengle, George, 102
Zaleski, Joe, 399
Zrakas, Jimmy, 349

IMAGES

HOWARD FOOTBALL 1919 *Photos courtesy Samford University Archives*
Howard College's 1919 football team, including star quarterback Peahead Walker, middle row, third from left.

HOWARD BASEBALL 1921
D.C. "Peahead" Walker with the Howard College baseball team in the spring of 1921. Walker is in the back row, second from right, wearing the confidently impish grin and a uniform that seems to fit just a little better than everyone else's.

ELON BASKETBALL 1930-31
Walker's 1930-31 basketball team won nine and lost 12 games.

Photos courtesy of Elon University Athletics

ELON BASEBALL 1933
Coach D.C. "Peahead" Walker with the 1933 Elon College baseball team, which won the North State Conference title, Walker's fourth baseball title in six seasons at Elon. Walker, in the middle of the middle row, is in uniform, and a clean one at that.

ELON FOOTBALL 1933.
Members of Elon College's 1933 football team strike action poses in what appears to be the home plate area of the school's one-field athletic complex. Note the less-than-pristine turf conditions.

PIVOTAL CLASS
The 1939 Deacons, including the fabled "Flaming Sophs", who really got Walker's program off the ground at Wake. Among the key players pictured are big John Jett (82), Gallopin' Tony Gallovich (95), Johnny Ringgold (98), and Williamy Mayberry (50).

OLD GORE FIELD *Photos courtesy of Wake Forest Historical Museum.*
Old Gore Field at Wake Forest College, packed to the gills, for a big game during the Peahead Walker years.

"BUB" & POLANSKI
Erskine "Bub" Walker, Peahead's brother (and briefly, a Wake assistant), with John Polanski, the Deacon's great Catholic fullback, in 1939.

Courtesy Wake Forest Historical Museum.

PEAHEAD & BILL GEORGE
Peahead Walker and Bill George, All-American and NFL Hall of Famer. Presumably, this photo was taken on the west campus.

Courtesy Wake Forest Athletics.

IMAGES

DEWEY HOBBS *Photo by Tucker Mitchell.*
The Rev. Dewey Hobbs, star tackle on Walker's World War II era teams, and later a spiritual mentor of sorts. Hobbs, a Baptist preacher, found the crusty and profane Walker to be a surprisingly spiritual and honorable man as they got to know each other later in their lives.

DICKIE DAVIS *Photo by Cindy Mitchell.*
Dickie Davis and a faithful friend in the town of Wake Forest, spring 2009. Davis was a prize recruit for Walker and Wake Forest, but found Peahead tough to take at times.

PEAHEAD & NICK SACRINTY *Courtesy of Wake Forest Athletics.*
Walker with Nick Sacrinty, one of his many fine tailbacks.

PRIDE RATTEREE *Photo by Tucker Mitchell.*
Pride Ratteree, one of several Deacons from the Walker era who still had their helmet, half a century after their last game.

PEAHEAD WITH SNAVELY
Peahead Walker with UNC Coach Carl Snavely (seated) at an unidentified event.

Courtesy of Wake Forest Athletics.

PEAHEAD VS. UNC
Walker on the sidelines for the 1945 game against Carolina in Chapel Hill. A radio play-by-play man is right beside him.

Courtesy Herb Appenzeller.

PEAHEAD, WEAVER AND BOST
Walker looks over a *Saturday Evening Post* story written about him, in the company of Wake Forest publicist Tom Bost (standing) and Deacon Athletic Director Jim Weaver. The 8-page spread included many of the best-known Walker stories.

Courtesy of Wake Forest Athletics.

IMAGES

DEACON BRAINTRUST *Courtesy of Wake Forest Athletics.*
Walker and the Deacon football staff, circa 1948. Note the snappy shoes, except on coach Greason (far left).

PEAHEAD & GREASON
Walker on the sideline with his long-time sidekick, Deacon assistant Murray Greason.

Courtesy Wake Forest Historical Museum.

Photos courtesy of Carl Haggard, personal collection.

BIG RED
Red Cochran, one of Walker's all-time greats, both before and after World War II. In between, he flew a B-24 bomber.

HAGGARD & HARRIS
Wingback Carl Haggard and end Buck Harris, in the late 1940's.

THE ROCK
Richard "Rock" Brinkley, an all-conference football player for Wake just after World War II. Brinkley covered himself – sometimes quite harshly – as a sports columnist for the *Old Gold & Black*, Wake's student newspaper. Later he became a philosophy professor.

IMAGES

VICTORY AT TENNESSEE
Walker and the Deacons whoop it up after beating fourth-ranked Tennessee in Knoxville on Oct. 26, 1946.

PEADHEAD WALKER '49 DIXIE BOWL
Peahead Walker offers up some pre-game instructions at the 1949 Dixie Bowl in Birmingham.

Courtesy Wake Forest Athletics.

FABLED '48 FROSH *Courtesy Wake Forest Musem.*

Walker's recruiting powers were at their peak when he brought the "Four Horsemen" of North Carolina – the all-state high school backfield of that year -- intact, to Wake Forest. Shown here, from left to right, are: Bozo Roberson, Bobby Stutts, Dickie Davis and Nub Smith. Alas, they never quite panned out as imagined, although Davis turned out to be a fine defender and a great clutch passer.

PEAHEAD HARD AT WORK
Walker (far right) judges a beauty contest along with Miss North Carolina (center) at the state fair.

Courtesy Wake Forest Athletics.

IMAGES

P-E-A-H-E-A-D *Courtesy Wake Forest Muesum.*
The Wake Forest College band, with help from high school bands from Ahoskie and Elizabeth City, N.C., spells out 'P-E-A-H-E-A-D' before a Groves Stadium crowd on Oct. 21, 1950. The band also spelledx 'T-R-I-B-B-L-E' that day, in honor of the school's newly appointed president, but reports from the time say the Peahead spelling drew a bigger cheer. That probably didn't help the coach-president relationship, which would soon head down a bumpy path.

HALF-TON *Courtesy Yale University Archives.*
Peahead Walker pal Herman "Half-Ton" Hickman on the set of "The Herman Hickman Show," a short-lived comedy skit show produced in 1952-53.

463

LA TETE DE POIE
Peahead Walker after he went up north and became "Doug."

Courtesy Wake Forest Athletics.

MRS. PEAHEAD
"Flonie" Walker (center) at an Elon College Athletics event in the 1960s. Her name tag reads, "Mrs. Peahead Walker."

ABOUT THE AUTHOR

Tucker Mitchell is an award-winning writer who spent more than thirty years in the newspaper business as reporter, writer, columnist, editor, publisher and owner. He's a graduate of Wake Forest University, where he somehow managed to obtain a degree in History, which is sort of a long, slow form of journalism.

Tucker is married to Cindy. They have two grown children, and two grandchildren.

This is Tucker's second book. His first work, the critically unacclaimed *Hornets Never Lie*, was published in 1989. Copies are available for the asking and a small fee.

Readers are encouraged to write Tucker at:

tucker@peahead.com

Made in the USA
Columbia, SC
29 October 2021